Middle School 2-1

중간고사 완벽대비

적중100

영어 기출 문제집

중2

능률 | 김성곤

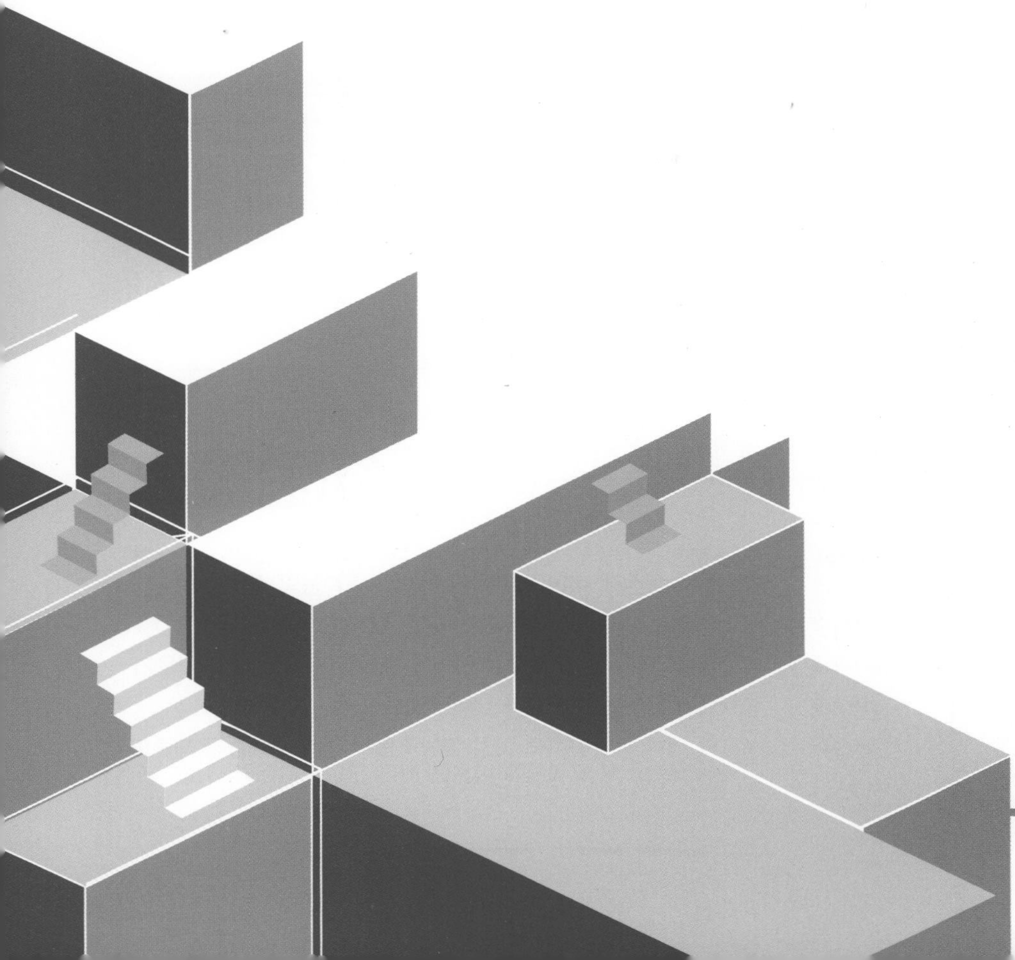

Best Collection

구성과 특징

교과서의 주요 학습 내용을 중심으로 학습 영역별 특성에 맞춰 단계별로 다양한 학습 기회를 제공하여 단원별 학습능력 평가는 물론 중간 및 기말고사 시험 등에 완벽하게 대비할 수 있도록 내용을 구성

Words & Expressions

Step1 Key Words 단원별 핵심 단어 설명 및 풀이
Key Expression 단원별 핵심 숙어 및 관용어 설명
Word Power 반대 또는 비슷한 뜻 단어 배우기
English Dictionary 영어로 배우는 영어 단어

Step2 실력평가 단원별 수시평가 대비 주관식, 객관식 문제풀이

Step3 서술형 대비 학업성취도 및 수행능력평가 대비 서술형 문제풀이

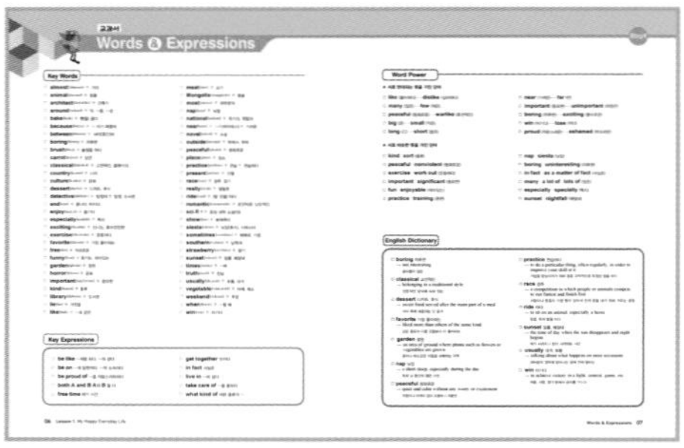

Conversation

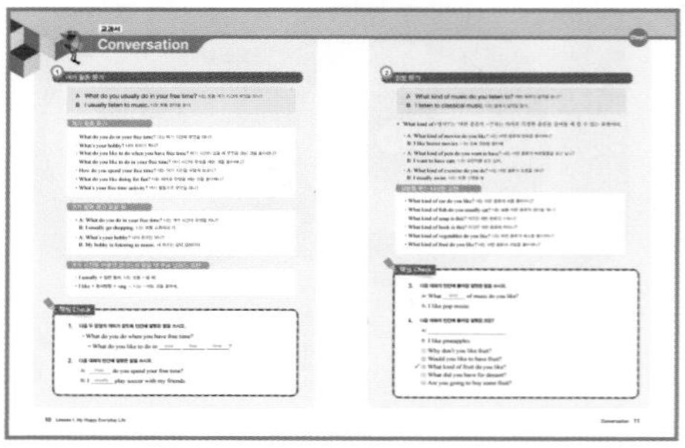

Step1 핵심 의사소통 소통에 필요한 주요 표현 방법 요약
핵심 Check 기본적인 표현 방법 및 활용능력 확인

Step2 대화문 익히기 교과서 대화문 심층 분석 및 확인

Step3 교과서 확인학습 빈칸 채우기를 통한 문장 완성 능력 확인

Step4 기본평가 시험대비 기초 학습 능력 평가

Step5 실력평가 단원별 수시평가 대비 주관식, 객관식 문제풀이

Step6 서술형 대비 학업성취도 및 수행능력평가 대비 서술형 문제풀이

Grammar

Step1 주요 문법 단원별 주요 문법 사항과 예문을 알기 쉽게 설명
핵심 Check 기본 문법사항에 대한 이해 여부 확인

Step2 기본평가 시험대비 기초 학습 능력 평가

Step3 실력평가 단원별 수시평가 대비 주관식, 객관식 문제풀이

Step4 서술형 대비 학업성취도 및 수행능력평가 대비 서술형 문제풀이

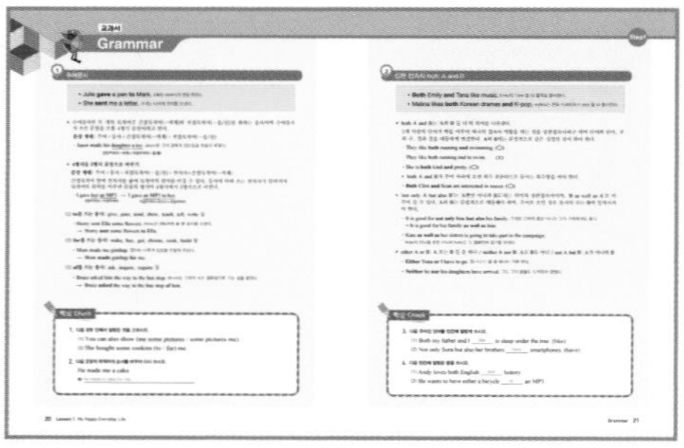

Reading

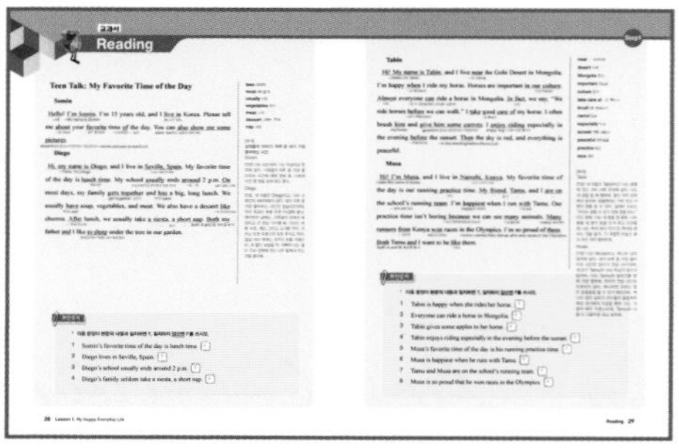

Step1 구문 분석 단원별로 제시된 문장에 대한 구문별 분석과 내용 설명
확인문제 문장에 대한 기본적인 이해와 인지능력 확인

Step2 확인학습A 빈칸 채우기를 통한 문장 완성 능력 확인

Step3 확인학습B 제시된 우리말을 영어로 완성하여 작문 능력 키우기

Step4 실력평가 단원별 수시평가 대비 주관식, 객관식 문제풀이

Step5 서술형 대비 학업성취도 및 수행능력평가 대비 서술형 문제풀이
교과서 구석구석 교과서에 나오는 기타 문장까지 완벽 학습

Composition

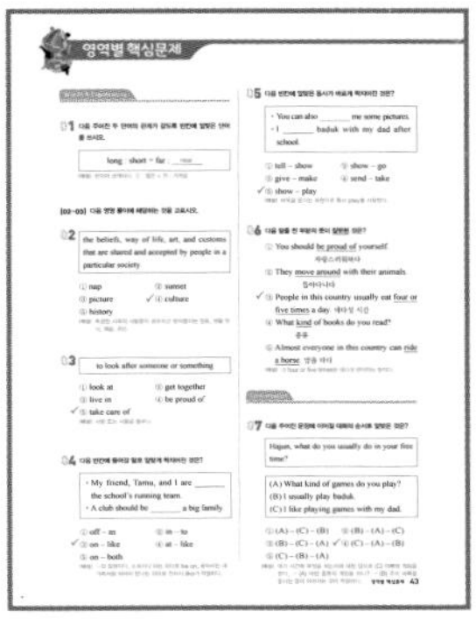

|영역별 핵심문제|

단어 및 어휘, 대화문, 문법, 독해 등 각 영역별 기출문제의 출제 유형을 분석하여 실전에 대비하고 연습할 수 있도록 문제를 배열

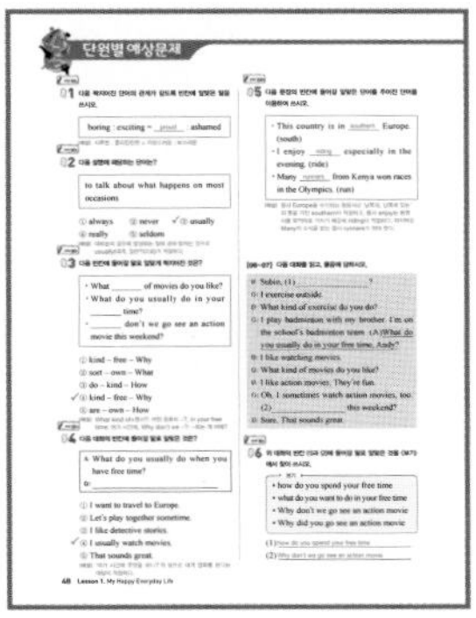

|단원별 예상문제|

기출문제를 분석한 후 새로운 시험 출제 경향을 더하여 새롭게 출제될 수 있는 문제를 포함하여 시험에 완벽하게 대비할 수 있도록 준비

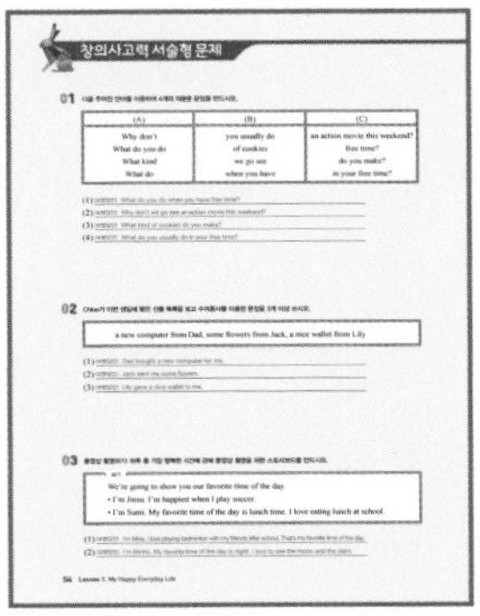

|서술형 실전 및 창의사고력 문제|

학교 시험에서 점차 늘어나는 서술형 시험에 집중 대비하고 고득점을 취득하는데 만전을 기하기 위한 학습 코너

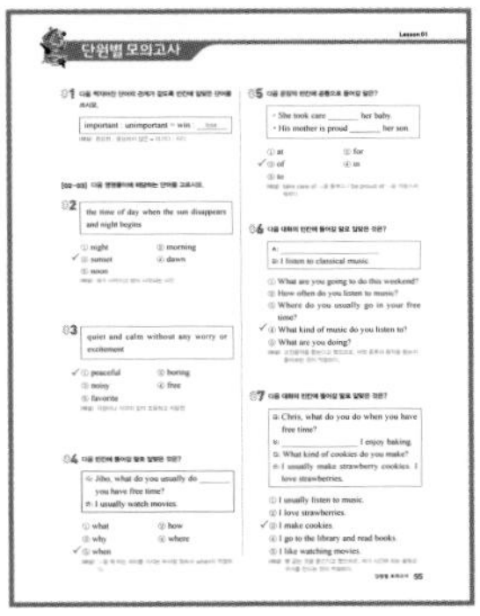

|단원별 모의고사|

영역별, 단계별 학습을 모두 마친 후 실전 연습을 위한 모의고사

INSIGHT on the textbook

교과서 파헤치기

- **단어Test1~3** 영어 단어 우리말 쓰기, 우리말을 영어 단어로 쓰기, 영영풀이에 해당하는 단어와 우리말 쓰기
- **대화문Test1~2** 대화문 빈칸 완성 및 전체 대화문 쓰기
- **본문Test1~5** 빈칸 완성, 우리말 쓰기, 문장 배열연습, 영어 작문하기 복습 등 단계별 반복 학습을 통해 교과서 지문에 대한 완벽한 습득
- **구석구석지문Test1~2** 지문 빈칸 완성 및 전문 영어로 쓰기

이책의 차례

Contents

Lesson **1**

Express Yourself

의사소통 기능

- 관심사 묻고 답하기
  A: What are you interested in?
  B: I'm interested in baseball.
- 허락 요청하고 답하기
  A: May I take a picture here?
  B: Yes, you may. / No, you may not.

언어 형식

- 동명사
  Taking selfies is part of daily life for many teens.
- 감각동사
  My pictures **look good** when I use filters.

교과서

Words & Expressions

Key Words

- □ **appropriate** [əpróupriət] 형 적절한
- □ **awesome** [ɔ́:səm] 형 멋진, 굉장한
- □ **baseball** [béisbɔ̀:l] 명 야구
- □ **borrow** [bárou] 동 빌리다 (↔ lend)
- □ **bother** [báðər] 동 괴롭히다
- □ **break** [breik] 동 (법률 · 약속 등을) 어기다
- □ **bring** [briŋ] 동 가져오다, 데려오다
- □ **carefully** [kέərfəl] 부 신중하게, 조심스럽게
- □ **carrier** [kǽriər] 명 캐리어, 운반[이동] 장치
- □ **choose** [ʧu:z] 동 고르다
- □ **clothes** [klouz] 명 옷
- □ **comment** [káment] 명 의견, 논평
- □ **copy** [kápi] 동 복사하다
- □ **dictionary** [díkʃənèri] 명 사전
- □ **display** [displéi] 동 (작품을) 전시하다, 보여주다
- □ **environment** [inváiərənmənt] 명 환경
- □ **etiquette** [étikit] 명 에티켓, 예절
- □ **exciting** [iksáitiŋ] 형 신나는, 흥미진진한
- □ **fact** [fækt] 명 사실
- □ **filter** [fíltər] 명 필터, 여과기
- □ **finally** [fáinəli] 부 마지막으로, 마침내
- □ **healthy** [hélθi] 형 건강에 좋은, 건강한
- □ **hurt** [hə:rt] 동 다치다, 해치다
- □ **impossible** [impásəbl] 형 불가능한 (↔ possible)
- □ **incorrect** [ìnkərékt] 형 틀린, 정확하지 않은 (↔ correct)
- □ **interesting** [íntərəstiŋ] 형 흥미로운, 재미있는
- □ **leave** [li:v] 동 남기다
- □ **nervous** [nə́:rvəs] 형 긴장되는, 불안해 하는
- □ **outdoors** [áutdɔ:rz] 부 야외에서, 옥외에서
- □ **part** [pɑ:rt] 명 부분
- □ **perfect** [pə́:rfikt] 형 완벽한
- □ **personal** [pə́rsənl] 형 개인의, 사적인
- □ **photography** [fətágrəfi] 명 사진술
- □ **post** [poust] 동 올리다, 게시하다
- □ **poster** [póustər] 명 포스터
- □ **prepare** [pripέər] 동 준비하다
- □ **probably** [prábəbli] 부 아마도
- □ **public** [pʌ́blik] 형 공공의
- □ **recipe** [résəpi] 명 조리법
- □ **report** [ripɔ́:rt] 명 보고서
- □ **restroom** [réstru:m] 명 화장실
- □ **result** [rizʌ́lt] 명 결과 (↔ cause)
- □ **rude** [ru:d] 형 무례한
- □ **selfie** [sélfi:] 명 셀피
- □ **share** [ʃεər] 동 공유하다
- □ **silly** [síli] 형 바보 같은, 어리석은
- □ **solve** [sɑlv] 동 해결하다
- □ **sometimes** [sʌ́mtàimz] 부 가끔
- □ **subject** [sʌ́bdʒikt] 명 과목
- □ **surprisingly** [sərpráiziŋli] 부 놀랍게도
- □ **survey** [sərvéi] 명 조사
- □ **teens** [ti:nz] 명 십대
- □ **topic** [tápik] 명 주제
- □ **understand** [ʌndərstǽnd] 동 이해하다

Key Expressions

- □ **agree with** ~에 동의하다
- □ **around the world** 세계 곳곳에, 세계적으로
- □ **be interested in** ~에 관심[흥미]이 있다
- □ **break the law** 법을 어기다
- □ **check out** 확인하다
- □ **find out** 발견하다, 찾아보다
- □ **first of all** 무엇보다도
- □ **from A to B** A에서 B로
- □ **have fun** 즐거운 시간을 보내다
- □ **in front of** ~ 앞에
- □ **just like** 꼭 ~와 같이
- □ **keep in mind** 명심하다
- □ **look at** ~을 보다
- □ **sound + 형용사** ~하게 들리다
- □ **spend 시간 -ing** ~하는 데 시간을 보내다
- □ **take a picture[photo] (of)** (~의) 사진을 찍다

Word Power

※ 서로 반대되는 뜻을 가진 단어

- □ **appropriate**(적절한) ↔ **inappropriate**(부적절한)
- □ **carefully**(신중하게) ↔ **carelessly**(부주의하게)
- □ **exciting**(신나는) ↔ **boring**(지루한)
- □ **finally**(마지막으로) ↔ **firstly**(첫 번째로)
- □ **impossible**(불가능한) ↔ **possible**(가능한)
- □ **incorrect**(틀린) ↔ **correct**(맞는)
- □ **outdoors**(야외에서) ↔ **indoors**(실내에서)
- □ **perfect**(완벽한) ↔ **imperfect**(불완전한)
- □ **public**(공공의) ↔ **private**(사적인)
- □ **rude**(무례한) ↔ **polite**(공손한)

※ 서로 비슷한 뜻을 가진 단어

- □ **bother**(괴롭히다) : **annoy**(귀찮게 하다)
- □ **comment**(의견) : **remark**(견해)
- □ **display**(전시하다) : **exhibit**(전시하다)
- □ **fact**(사실) : **truth**(진실)
- □ **finally**(마지막으로) : **lastly**(마지막으로)
- □ **hurt**(해치다) : **injure**(다치게 하다)
- □ **nervous**(불안해 하는) : **anxious**(불안해 하는)
- □ **result**(결과) : **consequence**(결과)

English Dictionary

□ **appropriate** 적절한
→ correct or suitable for a particular time, situation, or purpose
특정한 시간, 장소 또는 목적에 맞거나 적합한

□ **bring** 가져오다, 데려오다
→ to take something or someone with you to the place where you are now, or to the place you are talking about
어떤 사람이나 사물을 지금 당신이 있는 장소나 말하는 장소로 데려오거나 가져오다

□ **comment** 의견, 논평
→ an opinion that you express about someone or something
어떤 사람이나 사물에 대해 표현하는 의견

□ **etiquette** 에티켓, 예절
→ the formal rules for polite behavior in society or in a particular group
사회나 특정한 그룹 안에서 공손한 행동에 대한 공식적 규칙

□ **fact** 사실
→ a piece of information that is known to be true
진실이라고 알려진 정보

□ **healthy** 건강에 좋은
→ good for your body
몸에 좋은

□ **post** 올리다
→ to put a message or computer document on the Internet so that other people can see it
다른 사람들이 볼 수 있도록 인터넷에 메시지나 컴퓨터 서류를 올리다

□ **prepare** 준비하다
→ to make plans or arrangements for something that will happen in the future
미래에 발생할 무언가를 위해 계획하거나 준비를 하다

□ **public** 공공의
→ available for anyone to use
누구든지 사용 가능한

□ **recipe** 조리법
→ a set of instructions for cooking a particular type of food
특정한 종류의 음식을 요리하기 위한 일련의 지시 사항

□ **result** 결과
→ something that happens or exists because of something that happened before
이전에 발생한 어떤 것 때문에 발생하거나 존재하는 어떤 것

□ **rude** 무례한
→ speaking or behaving in a way that is not polite and is likely to offend or annoy people
공손하지 않거나, 사람들의 기분을 상하게 하거나, 짜증나게 하기 쉬운 방식의 말과 행동을 하는

□ **share** 공유하다
→ to have or use something with other people
다른 사람과 함께 무언가를 갖거나 사용하다

□ **solve** 해결하다
→ to find or provide a way of dealing with a problem
어떤 문제를 처리하는 방식을 발견하거나 제공하다

서답형

01 다음 짝지어진 단어의 관계가 같도록 빈칸에 알맞은 말을 쓰시오.

perfect : imperfect – possible : ________

[02~03] 다음 빈칸에 들어갈 말로 적절한 것은?

02

They're ________ the law by employing such young children.

① displaying ② leaving
③ catching ④ bringing
⑤ breaking

03

The loud noise made sleep ________.

① impossible ② appropriate
③ healthy ④ incorrect
⑤ careful

04 다음 빈칸에 공통으로 들어갈 말로 알맞은 것은?

• Do you ________ to go swimming? • He acts just ________ a child.

① alike ② similar
③ like ④ play
⑤ as

중요

05 다음 밑줄 친 부분과 의미가 가장 가까운 것을 고르시오.

The information you gave us was <u>not true</u>.

① proper ② incorrect
③ accurate ④ complete
⑤ correct

중요

06 다음 중 밑줄 친 부분의 뜻풀이가 바르지 <u>않은</u> 것은?

① It would not be <u>appropriate</u> for me to discuss that now. (적절한)
② Would it <u>bother</u> you if I put on some music? (괴롭히다)
③ Can I <u>borrow</u> your pen for a minute? (빌려주다)
④ I've got some very <u>exciting</u> news for you. (재미있는, 흥미로운)
⑤ Style and colour are a matter of <u>personal</u> taste. (개인의)

[07~08] 다음 영영풀이에 해당하는 단어를 고르시오.

중요

07

to put a message or computer document on the Internet so that other people can see it

① prepare ② post
③ download ④ publish
⑤ report

08

good for your body

① health ② healthy
③ exercise ④ wealthy
⑤ worthy

서답형

09 다음 빈칸에 들어갈 알맞은 단어를 〈보기〉에서 찾아 쓰시오. (형태 변화 가능)

보기
hurt understand display share

(1) All the exam results will be ________ on the notice board.
(2) Was anyone ________ in the accident?
(3) Tom and Bill ________ the same room.
(4) She doesn't ________ English.

01 다음 짝지어진 두 단어의 관계가 같도록 빈칸에 알맞은 말을 쓰시오. (주어진 철자가 있는 경우, 주어진 철자로 시작할 것)

(1) big : small = polite : r________

(2) stupid : smart = private : ________

(3) reason : cause = consequence : ________

02 다음 빈칸에 공통으로 들어갈 말을 쓰시오.

- We'll have to check him ________ before we employ him.
- Did you find ________ whether there are any seats left?

중요

03 다음 빈칸에 들어갈 말을 〈보기〉에서 찾아 쓰시오.

보기

carefully impossible
perfect interesting

(1) That's a(n) ________ question.

(2) You need to think very ________ about which course you want to take.

(3) You're very lucky to have ________ teeth.

(4) He was faced with a seemingly ________ task.

04 다음 주어진 우리말에 맞게 빈칸을 채우시오. (철자가 주어진 것도 있음)

(1) Paul은 발표를 해야 할 때마다 항상 긴장한다.
➡ Paul ________ gets n________ whenever he has to give a presentation.

(2) 그것은 아마도 내가 지금까지 본 영화 중 가장 최고의 영화이다.
➡ It's ________ the ________ movie I have ever seen.

중요

05 다음 우리말에 맞게 주어진 단어를 바르게 배열하시오.

(1) 몇몇의 친구를 파티에 데려와도 괜찮나요?
(to, if, it, some, bring, the, OK, is, party, I, friends, ?)
➡ ________________

(2) 이 문서를 복사하고 보내주시겠어요?
(it, send, this, out, copy, and, could, letter, you, ?)
➡ ________________

(3) 그들의 마지막 콘서트는 정말로 멋졌어.
(last, awesome, really, their, was, concert)
➡ ________________

고난이도

06 다음 영영풀이에 해당하는 말을 주어진 철자로 시작하여 쓰고, 알맞은 것을 골라 문장을 완성하시오. (형태 변화 가능)

- c________: an opinion that you express about someone or something
- e________: the formal rules for polite behaviour in society or in a particular group
- r________: something that happens or exists because of something that happened before

(1) He died as a ________ of his injures.

(2) You will be able to learn all about court ________.

(3) He made helpful ________ on my work.

교과서

Conversation

1 관심사 묻고 답하기

A What are you interested in? 너는 무엇에 관심이 있니?
B I'm interested in baseball. 나는 야구에 관심이 있어.

- 'What are you interested in?'은 '너는 무엇에 관심이 있니?'라는 의미로 상대방의 관심을 물을 때 쓰는 표현이다.
- 'I'm interested in ~.'은 '나는 ~에 관심이 있다.'의 의미로 관심을 나타내는 표현이며 in 뒤에는 명사나 동명사가 올 수 있다.
- 'Are you interested in ~?'은 '너는 ~에 관심이 있니?'의 의미로 상대방의 관심을 물어볼 때 사용하는 표현이다. 관심 여부에 대해 'Yes, I am.' 또는 'No, I'm not.'으로 대답할 수 있다.

관심 묻기

- What are you interested in? 너는 무엇에 관심이 있니?
- Which ~ are you interested in? 너는 어느 ~에 관심이 있니?

관심사 대답하기

- I'm interested in ~.
- I have an interest in ~. 나는 ~에 관심이 있다.

관심을 표현하기

- I like ~. 나는 ~을 좋아한다.
- I enjoy ~. 나는 ~을 즐겨한다.
- I love ~. 나는 ~을 아주 좋아한다.
- I'm into ~. 나는 ~에 빠져 있다.

핵심 Check

1. 다음 우리말과 일치하도록 빈칸에 알맞은 말을 쓰시오.

A: ________ are you ________ in? (너는 무엇에 관심이 있니?)
B: ________ really ________ in magic. (나는 정말 마술에 관심이 있어.)

2. 다음 주어진 단어를 이용하여 대화를 완성하시오.

(1) A: ________ ________ ________ ________ ________? (animals, interested, are, in, you)
B: No, I'm not. ________ ________ ________ ________. (in, I'm, plants, interested)

(2) A: ________ ________ ________ ________ ________ ________?
(are, in, what, subject, you, interested)
B: I'm interested in economics.

2 허락 요청하고 답하기

A May I take a picture here? 여기서 사진을 찍어도 되나요?

B Yes, you may. / No, you may not. 네, 됩니다. / 아니요, 안 됩니다.

■ 'May I+동사원형 ~?'을 사용하여 상대방에게 허락의 여부를 물을 수 있다.

허락을 요청하는 표현

- May I 동사원형 ~?
- Can I+동사원형 ~?
- Is it OK if I ~?
- I'm wondering if I ~.
- Would it be all right if I ~?
- Do you mind if I ~?

■ 'Do you mind if ~?'로 시작하는 의문문에서 mind는 '싫어하다, 꺼리다'라는 뜻이므로 Of course not. 이나 Not at all.이 '전혀 꺼리지 않는다.'는 의미로 허락의 의미를 나타낸다.

허락을 구하는 질문에 대한 대답 (mind가 쓰이지 않은 경우)

1. 허락하기
   - Yes, you may[can].
   - Sure.
   - Of course.
   - Certainly.
   - Why not?
   - No problem.
   - Sure. Go ahead.
   - Okay.
2. 거절하기
   - No, you may[can] not.
   - I'm sorry, but you can't.
   - I'm afraid you can't.
   - Not right now.
   - I'm afraid not.
   - No way!

■ 허락을 요청하는 말에 거절하는 경우에는, 보통 간단히 이유를 덧붙인다.

핵심 Check

3. 다음 우리말과 일치하도록 빈칸에 알맞은 말을 쓰시오.

(1) **A:** ________ ________ okay ________ I ________ your pen? (네 펜을 빌려도 될까?)

B: Of course. (물론이지.)

(2) **A:** May ________ turn ________ the TV? (내가 TV를 켜도 될까?)

B: I'm ________ not. I'm doing my homework. (유감이지만 안 돼. 나는 숙제를 하는 중이야.)

4. 다음 주어진 단어를 이용하여 대화를 완성하시오.

A: ________ ________ ________ ________ ________ ________ ________ ________.

(umbrella, share, I, I'm, your, if, can, wondering)

B: Sure.

Conversation 교과서 대화문 익히기

A. Listen & Talk 1 A

G: ❶Look at these club posters. ❷What are you interested in?
B: ❸I'm interested in cooking. ❹What about you?
G: I'm interested in ❺photography.

G: 동아리 포스터들을 봐. 너는 어떤 것에 관심이 있니?
B: 나는 요리에 관심이 있어. 너는 어때?
G: 나는 사진에 관심이 있어.

❶ look at: ~을 보다
❷ 'What are you interested in?'은 '너는 무엇에 관심이 있니?'라는 의미로 상대방의 관심을 물을 때 쓰는 표현이다.
❸ I'm interested in ~.'은 '나는 ~에 관심이 있다.'의 의미로 관심을 나타내는 표현이며 in 뒤에는 명사나 동명사가 올 수 있다.
❹ 'What about you?'는 상대방의 의견을 묻기 위한 표현으로, 'How about you?'로 바꾸어 쓸 수 있다.
❺ photography: 사진

Check(√) True or False

(1) They are looking at club posters. T ☐ F ☐

(2) They are all interested in cooking. T ☐ F ☐

B. Listen & Talk 1 B

B: What ❶are you going to do this weekend?
G: I'm going to go to a baseball game with my brother.
B: ❷Are you interested in baseball?
G: ❸Not really. I'm going to the baseball game ❹because my brother likes baseball.
B: You're so ❺nice! Then what are you interested in?
G: I'm more interested in soccer. I ❻want to go to a soccer game ❼ someday.

B: 이번 주말에 뭐 할 거야?
G: 나는 동생하고 야구 보러 갈 거야.
B: 너는 야구에 관심 있니?
G: 사실은 좋아하지 않아. 나는 내 동생이 좋아해서 야구 보러 가는 거야.
B: 너 정말 착하다! 그럼 너는 어떤 것에 관심 있니?
G: 나는 축구에 더 관심 있어. 언젠가 축구 경기를 보러 가고 싶어.

❶ be going to 동사원형: ~할 예정이다 this weekend: 이번 주말에
❷ 'Are you interested in ~?'은 '너는 ~에 관심이 있니?'의 의미로 상대방의 관심을 물어볼 때 사용하는 표현이다.
❸ Not really: 사실은 그렇지 않아.
❹ because는 이유를 나타내는 접속사로 because 다음에는 주어와 동사가 오며, '~이기 때문에'의 의미를 지닌다.
❺ nice: 친절한(= kind)
❻ want to 동사원형: ~하기를 원하다
❼ someday: (미래의) 언젠가

Check(√) True or False

(3) The girl's brother likes baseball. T ☐ F ☐

(4) The girl is interested in soccer. T ☐ F ☐

Listen & Talk 1 C

G: ❶What are you looking at?

B: I'm looking at TV program listings. ❷What show should I watch?

G: Well, ❸what are you interested in?

B: I'm interested in music.

G: Then ❹how about watching the *Friday Pop Music Show*?

B: I'm actually not ❺a big fan of pop music. I like to listen to rap music.

G: Then ❻why don't you watch *Hit the Beat*?

B: Good idea.

❶ look at: ~을 보다 What are you looking at?: 뭐 보고 있니?
❷ What+명사: what이 의문형용사로 쓰인 것이다. should: ~해야 한다
❸ what are you interested in?: 너는 무엇에 관심이 있니?
❹ 'how about (동)명사 ~?'는 권유하는 말로, 'what about (동)명사 ~?'로 바꾸어 말할 수 있다.
❺ big fan: 열렬한 팬
❻ Why don't you ~?는 상대방에게 권유할 때 쓰이는 표현으로 '~하는 게 어때?'라는 의미이다.

Listen & Talk 2 A

B: ❶May I bring my dog on the bus?

W: ❷Yes, you may. But you ❸should put your dog in the carrier.

❶ May I 동사원형 ~?은 허락을 요청하는 표현으로 Can I 동사원형 ~?으로 바꾸어 쓸 수 있다. bring: 데려오다
❷ May I 동사원형 ~?으로 질문했으므로, Yes, you may.나 No, you may not.으로 대답할 수 있다.
❸ should는 '~해야 한다'라는 의미의 조동사로 뒤에 동사원형을 쓴다.

Listen & Talk 2 B

G: Hi. ❶Can I go in now?

M: Sure. Let me see your ticket, please.

G: Here it is. May I ❷record the music in the concert hall?

M: ❸No, you may not.

G: Okay. May I ❹take pictures of the band?

M: No, you may not. You can ❺only take pictures in front of the concert hall. Please enjoy the concert.

G: Oh, okay. Thank you.

❶ May I go in now?와 같은 의미이다.
❷ record: 녹음하다, 녹화하다
❸ May I 동사원형 ~?의 허락을 요청하는 말에 대한 거절의 대답으로 No, you may not.이 사용되었다. 다른 표현으로 I'm afraid not.을 쓸 수 있다.
❹ take pictures of ~: ~의 사진을 찍다
❺ only: 오직, 오로지 in front of: ~ 앞에

Listen & Talk 2 C

B: Excuse me.

M: Hello. ❶What can I do for you?

B: May I ❷borrow this new science book?

M: No, you may not. Students can't take new books home.

B: Then ❸may I copy some pages from the book? I need ❹them for my science report.

M: Yes, you may. But please don't ❺share them online.

B: Okay, I ❻won't. Thank you!

❶ What can I do for you?: 무엇을 도와드릴까요? (= How can I help you?)
❷ borrow: 빌리다
❸ May I 동사원형 ~?: ~해도 될까요? copy: 복사하다 some: 조금, 약간, 일부
❹ them은 앞 문장의 some pages (from the book)를 의미한다.
❺ share: 공유하다
❻ won't = will not

Let's communicate 1

A: What are you interested in?

B: ❶I'm interested in music.

A: ❷Why don't you go to a concert hall this weekend?

B: ❸Sounds good. May I record the music there?

A: Yes, you may. / No, you may not.

❶ be interested in: ~에 관심이 있다
❷ Why don't you ~?: ~하는 게 어때? (= How about (동)명사 ~? = What about (동)명사 ~?)
❸ sound + 형용사: ~하게 들리다

Conversation 교과서 확인학습

● 다음 우리말과 일치하도록 빈칸에 알맞은 말을 쓰시오.

Listen & Talk 1 A

G: Look at these club ________. ________ are you interested in?

B: I'm interested ________ ________. What about you?

G: I'm interested ________ ________.

해석

G: 동아리 포스터들을 봐. 너는 어떤 것에 관심이 있니?

B: 나는 요리에 관심이 있어. 너는 어때?

G: 나는 사진에 관심이 있어.

Listen & Talk 1 B

B: ________ are you ________ ________ ________ this weekend?

G: ________ ________ to go to a baseball game ________ my brother.

B: ________ you interested ________ baseball?

G: Not really. I'm going to the baseball game ________ my brother likes baseball.

B: You're so nice! Then ________ ________ ________ interested in?

G: I'm ________ ________ in soccer. I want to ________ ________ a soccer game ________.

B: 이번 주말에 뭐 할 거야?

G: 나는 동생하고 야구 보러 갈 거야.

B: 너는 야구에 관심 있니?

G: 사실은 좋아하지 않아. 나는 내 동생이 좋아해서 야구 보러 가는 거야.

B: 너 정말 착하다! 그럼 너는 어떤 것에 관심 있니?

G: 나는 축구에 더 관심 있어. 언젠가 축구 경기를 보러 가고 싶어.

Listen & Talk 1 C

G: What are you looking at?

B: I'm looking at TV program listings. ________ ________ should I watch?

G: Well, ________ ________ ________ ________ ________?

B: ________ ________ ________ music.

G: Then how ________ ________ the *Friday Pop Music Show*?

B: I'm actually not ________ ________ ________ ________ pop music. I like to listen to rap music.

G: Then why ________ ________ watch *Hit the Beat*?

B: Good idea.

G: 뭐 보고 있니?

B: TV 프로그램 편성표 보고 있어. 어떤 걸 봐야 할까?

G: 음, 너 어떤 분야에 관심이 있니?

B: 나는 음악에 관심이 있어.

G: 그러면 "Friday Pop Music Show"를 보는 게 어때?

B: 사실 팝 음악을 많이 좋아하지는 않아. 나는 랩 음악 듣는 걸 좋아해.

G: 그러면 "Hit the Beat"을 보는 건 어때?

B: 좋은 생각이야.

Listen & Talk 1 D

A: ________ are you interested ________?

B: ________ interested in games and social media. What about you?

A: I'm ________ ________ music and ________ ________.

B: ________ are ________ interested in social media.

A: 너는 무엇에 관심이 있니?

B: 나는 게임과 소셜 미디어에 관심이 있어. 너는 어때?

A: 나는 음악과 소셜 미디어에 관심이 있어.

B: 우리는 둘 다 소셜 미디어에 관심이 있구나.

Listen & Talk 2 A

B: May I ________ my dog on the bus?

W: ________, ________ ________. But you should put your dog ________ ________ ________.

B: 버스에 제 개를 데리고 타도 되나요?

W: 네, 됩니다. 하지만 당신은 개를 캐리어에 넣어야 해요.

Listen & Talk 2 B

G: Hi. Can I ________ in now?

M: Sure. ________ me ________ your ticket, please.

G: Here it is. May I ________ the music in the concert hall?

M: No, you ________ ________.

G: Okay. May I ________ pictures of the band?

M: ________, ________ ________ ________. You can only take pictures ________ ________ ________ the concert hall. Please enjoy the concert.

G: Oh, okay. Thank you.

해석

G: 안녕하세요. 지금 안에 들어가도 되나요?
M: 그럼요. 티켓을 보여 주시겠어요?
G: 여기 있어요. 콘서트홀 안에서 노래를 녹음해도 되나요?
M: 아니요, 안 됩니다.
G: 알겠습니다. 밴드 사진은 찍어도 되나요?
M: 아니요, 안 됩니다. 콘서트홀 앞에서만 사진을 찍을 수 있어요. 즐거운 관람되세요.
G: 아, 알겠습니다. 감사합니다.

Listen & Talk 2 C

B: Excuse me.

W: Hello. What ________ ________ do for you?

B: May I ________ this new science book?

W: No, you ________ ________. Students can't ________ new books home.

B: Then may I ________ some pages from the book? I need them for my science report.

W: Yes, you ________. But please don't ________ them online.

B: Okay, I ________. Thank you!

B: 실례합니다.
W: 안녕하세요. 무엇을 도와드릴까요?
B: 이 새로 출시된 과학책 빌려도 될까요?
W: 아뇨, 불가능합니다. 학생들은 새로 출시된 책을 집으로 가져갈 수 없어요.
B: 그러면 책에서 몇 장 정도 복사해도 될까요? 과학 보고서 쓰는 데 필요해서요.
W: 네, 그러세요. 하지만 그걸 인터넷상에 공유하지는 마세요.
B: 네, 안 그럴게요. 감사합니다!

Let's communicate 1

A: ________ ________ you interested in?

B: ________ ________ in music.

A: ________ don't you go to a concert hall this weekend?

B: Sounds good. ________ ________ record the music there?

A: Yes, you may. / No, you may not.

A: 너는 무엇에 관심이 있니?
B: 나는 음악에 관심이 있어.
A: 이번 주말에 콘서트홀에 가는 건 어때?
B: 그거 좋겠다. 거기서 음악을 녹음해도 될까?
A: 그래, 돼. / 아니, 안 돼.

Do It Yourself A

M: Hey, Yumi. What are you ________?

G: Hello, Mr. King. I'm preparing for tomorrow's __________. It is about one of my ________.

M: That sounds fun! What ________ ________ ________ in?

G: ________ ________ ________ photography. I will talk about it tomorrow.

M: Oh, ________ ________ ________ photography, too.

G: Really? Then may I ________ you ________ ________ ________ for my presentation?

M: Sure.

M: 유미야. 뭐 하고 있니?
G: 안녕하세요, King씨. 저는 내일 발표를 준비하고 있어요. 제 관심사 중 하나에 대한 거예요.
M: 그거 재미있겠다! 너는 어떤 것에 관심이 있니?
G: 저는 사진에 관심이 있어요. 저는 그것에 대해 내일 이야기할 거예요.
M: 오, 나도 역시 사진에 관심이 있어.
G: 정말요? 그렇다면 제 발표에 대해 몇 가지 조언을 부탁해도 될까요?
M: 물론이지.

01 다음 주어진 문장과 의미하는 바가 다른 하나를 고르시오.

May I take pictures here?

① I'm wondering if I can take pictures here.
② Can I take pictures here?
③ Is it okay if I take pictures here?
④ Could you take pictures here?
⑤ Do you mind if I take pictures here?

02 다음 대화의 빈칸에 들어갈 말로 적절하지 않은 것은?

A: May I borrow this new science book?
B: ________________ Students can't take new books home.

① I'm afraid not.
② I'm sorry, but you can't.
③ Why not?
④ No, you may not.
⑤ I'm afraid you can't.

03 다음 주어진 문장 뒤에 나올 대화의 순서로 가장 적절한 것은?

What are you interested in?
(A) Sounds good. May I bring my pet there?
(B) I'm interested in soccer.
(C) Why don't you go to a soccer filed this weekend?
(D) Yes, you may.

① (B) - (A) - (C) - (D)
② (B) - (A) - (D) - (C)
③ (B) - (C) - (A) - (D)
④ (C) - (A) - (B) - (D)
⑤ (C) - (B) - (A) - (D)

[01~03] 다음 대화를 읽고, 물음에 답하시오.

G: What are you looking at?
B: I'm looking at TV program listings. What show should I watch? (①)
G: Well, what are you interested in?
B: I'm interested in ___(A)___. (②)
G: Then how about watching the *Friday Pop Music Show*? (③)
B: (④) I like to listen to rap music.
G: (⑤) Then why don't you watch *Hit the Beat?*
B: Good idea.

중요
01 위 대화의 ①~⑤ 중 주어진 문장이 들어갈 알맞은 곳은?

I'm actually not a big fan of pop music.

① ② ③ ④ ⑤

02 위 대화의 빈칸 (A)에 들어갈 말로 적절한 것은?

① science ② art
③ fashion ④ movies
⑤ music

03 위 대화의 내용과 일치하지 않는 것은?

① They are talking about what show the boy will watch.
② The boy is looking at TV program listings.
③ The *Friday Pop Music Show* is related to rap music.
④ The boy likes rap music.
⑤ The boy can listen to rap music from *Hit the Beat*.

[04~07] 다음 대화를 읽고, 물음에 답하시오.

B: Excuse me.
M: Hello. ①What can I do for you?
B: ②May I borrow this new science book?
M: ___(A)___ ③Students can't take new books home.
B: ④Then may I copy some pages from the book? I need ⓐthem for my science report.
M: Yes, you may. But please don't share ⓐ them online.
B: ⑤Okay, I will. Thank you!

04 Where are they now?

① library ② theater
③ hospital ④ classroom
⑤ concert hall

중요
05 위 대화의 빈칸 (A)에 들어갈 말로 적절한 것은?

① Yes, you may.
② No, you may not.
③ Yes, you can.
④ No problem.
⑤ Why not?

서답형
06 위 대화의 밑줄 친 ⓐthem이 공통으로 가리키는 것을 본문에서 찾아 쓰시오. (6 단어)

➡ ____________________

서답형
07 위 대화의 ①~⑤ 중 어색한 곳을 고르고 바르게 고치시오.

__________ ➡ __________

[08~09] 다음 대화를 읽고, 물음에 답하시오.

A: ①What are you interested in?
B: ②I'm interested in animals.
A: ③Why don't you go to an art museum this weekend?
B: ④Sounds good. 거기서 새들에게 먹이를 줘도 되나요?
A: ⑤No, you may not.

08 위 대화의 ①~⑤ 중 흐름상 어색한 문장을 고르시오.

① ② ③ ④ ⑤

서답형

09 위 대화의 밑줄 친 우리말을 영작하시오. (6단어)

➡ ______________________

중요

10 다음 짝지어진 대화가 어색한 것은?

① A: Is it okay if I take photos of the paintings there?
B: Sure, go ahead.
② A: Excuse me. May I sit here?
B: Of course. It's already taken.
③ A: Would it be alright if I leave early?
B: No problem.
④ A: Can I bring my pet to your house?
B: Certainly.
⑤ A: May I borrow your pen now?
B: I'm afraid not. This is the only one that I have.

[11~13] 다음 대화를 읽고, 물음에 답하시오.

M: Hey, Yumi. What are you doing?
G: Hello, Mr. King. (①) ⓐIt is about one of my interest. (②)
M: ⓑThat sounds fun! What are you interested in?
G: ⓒI'm interested in photography. (③) ⓓI will talk about it tomorrow.
M: Oh, I'm interested in photography, too.
G: Really? (④) ⓔThen may I ask you for some advice for my presentation?
M: Sure. (⑤)

11 위 대화의 ①~⑤ 중 주어진 문장이 들어갈 알맞은 곳은?

I'm preparing for tomorrow's presentation.

① ② ③ ④ ⑤

서답형

12 위 대화의 ⓐ~ⓔ 중 어색한 곳을 고르고 바르게 고치시오.

______________ ➡ ______________

서답형

13 위 대화의 내용과 일치하도록 빈칸을 완성하시오.

Both Yumi and Mr. King ________ ________ in ________. Yumi ________ give a ________ about photography ________. Yumi asks Mr. King ________ ________ for ________ ________.

[01~03] 다음 대화를 읽고, 물음에 답하시오.

B: ___(A)___ are you going to do this weekend?
G: ①I'm going to go to a baseball game with my brother.
B: (in, you, are, baseball, interested, ?)
G: ②Not really. ③I'm going to the baseball game because my brother likes baseball.
B: ④You're so nice! Then ___(B)___ are you interested in?
G: ⑤I'm less interested in soccer. I want to go to a soccer game someday.

01 위 대화의 (A)와 (B)에 알맞은 의문사를 쓰시오.

(A) ________ (B) ________

02 위 대화의 괄호 안에 주어진 단어를 알맞게 배열하시오.

➡ ____________________

중요
03 위 대화의 ①~⑤ 중 어색한 곳을 고르고 바르게 고치시오.

________ ➡ ________

[04~05] 다음 대화를 읽고, 물음에 답하시오.

B: May I bring my dog on the bus?
W: ___(A)___ But you should put your dog in the carrier.

04 다음 영영풀이에 해당하는 단어를 대화에서 찾아 쓰시오.

to take something or someone with you to the place where you are now, or to the place you are talking about

➡ ____________________

중요
05 위 대화의 흐름상 빈칸 (A)에 들어갈 말을 쓰시오. (3 단어)

➡ ____________________

06 다음 대화의 순서를 바르게 배열하시오.

(A) Then how about watching the *Friday Pop Music Show*?
(B) I'm interested in music.
(C) I'm actually not a big fan of pop music. I like to listen to rap music.
(D) What are you interested in?

➡ ____________________

중요
07 다음 대화의 ①~⑤ 중 어색한 곳을 모두 고르고 바르게 고치시오.

M: Hey, Yumi. ①What are you doing?
G: Hello, Mr. King. ②I'm preparing for tomorrow's presentation. It is about one of my interests.
M: That sounds fun! ③What are you interested in?
G: I'm interested in photography. ④I talk about it tomorrow.
M: Oh, I'm interested in photography, too.
G: Really? ⑤Then may I ask you for some advise for my presentation?
M: Sure.

➡ ____________________

교과서

Grammar

1 동명사

- **Taking** a walk in the evening is her habit. 저녁에 산책하는 것은 그녀의 습관이다.
- **Seeing** is **believing.** 보는 것이 믿는 것이다. (백문이 불여일견)

■ 동명사는 '동사원형+-ing'의 형태로 '~하는 것, ~하기'라는 의미로 문장에서 주어, 보어, 목적어 역할을 한다.

■ 동명사가 주어로 쓰이는 경우, 동사는 단수 동사를 쓴다.

■ 동명사는 주어를 보충하는 말인 주격보어로 사용될 수 있다.

■ 명사 역할을 하지만 동사의 성격을 가지므로 뒤에 보어나 목적어를 가질 수 있다.

■ 동명사는 타동사의 목적어로 쓰이며, 전치사의 목적어로도 쓰인다. 부정사는 전치사의 목적어로 쓰일 수 없음에 주의한다.

■ avoid, consider, deny, enjoy, finish, give up, keep, mind, recommend, stop, suggest 등은 동명사를 목적어로 갖는 동사이다. like, love, begin, start 등은 동명사와 부정사를 둘 다 목적어로 가질 수 있다.

- **Becoming** a scientist is difficult. [주어] 과학자가 되는 것은 어렵다.
- My hobby is **singing**. [주격 보어] 나의 취미는 노래하는 것이다.
- I like **dancing**. = I like to **dance**. [목적어] 나는 춤추는 것을 좋아한다.

동명사 vs. 현재분사

■ 동명사와 현재분사의 형태는 동일하지만 쓰임은 서로 다르다.

■ 동명사는 뒤에 보어나 목적어를 가지면서 명사의 역할을 하지만, 현재분사는 be동사와 함께 진행형을 만들거나 명사를 수식하는 형용사 역할을 한다.

- I stopped **playing** computer games. [동명사] 나는 컴퓨터 게임을 하는 것을 멈추었다.
- The boy **playing** computer games is Tom. [현재분사] 컴퓨터 게임을 하는 소년은 Tom이다.

핵심 Check

1. 다음 괄호 안에서 알맞은 것을 고르시오.

(1) (Taking / Take) selfies is part of daily life for many teens.

(2) I finished (reading / to read) the book.

2. 다음 문장에서 틀린 부분을 찾아 바르게 고쳐 쓰시오.

Make silly faces is really fun!

__________ ➡ __________

2 감각동사

- Monica **felt** happy as her husband was with her. Monica는 남편이 함께 있어서 행복했다.
- Jake **looked** worried when he heard the news. Jake는 그 소식을 듣고 걱정스러워 보였다.

■ 감각동사란 냄새 맡고, 맛보고, 느끼는 등의 감각을 표현하는 동사를 말한다. 감각동사 다음에 형용사를 쓰면 주어의 상태가 '~하게 보이다, 들리다, 냄새가 나다, 맛이 나다, 느껴지다' 등의 의미가 된다.

- look ~하게 보이다, smell ~한 냄새가 나다, sound ~하게 들리다, taste ~한 맛이 나다, feel ~하게 느끼다

■ 감각동사는 형용사를 보어로 취한다. 우리말 해석으로는 부사일 것 같지만 영어 표현에서는 부사를 쓰지 않으므로 주의해야 한다.

- Robert **looks** happy. (○) Robert는 행복해 보인다.
  Robert looks happily. (×)
- The roses **smell** good. 장미들이 좋은 냄새가 난다.
- The food **tastes** great. 그 음식은 좋은 맛이 난다.

■ 감각동사 뒤에 보어로 명사나 대명사가 올 때는 명사 앞에 like를 쓴다.

- It **felt like** a rock. 그것은 바위같이 느껴졌다.

핵심 Check

3. 다음 괄호 안에서 알맞은 것을 고르시오.

(1) I feel (nervous / nervously).

(2) Kim looked (sad / sadly).

(3) The music sounds (interesting / interestingly).

4. 다음 문장에서 틀린 부분을 찾아 바르게 고쳐 쓰시오.

But sometimes my selfies don't look me.

__________ ➡ __________

01 다음 문장에서 어법상 어색한 부분을 바르게 고쳐 쓰시오.

(1) Walk is good for your health.

______ ➡ ______

(2) Playing sports are interesting.

______ ➡ ______

(3) These cookies taste sweetly.

______ ➡ ______

(4) It looked a star.

______ ➡ ______

02 다음 빈칸에 알맞은 것은?

________ in a few years is very difficult.

① English master ② Master English
③ Mastering English ④ Mastered English
⑤ English to master

03 다음 중 어법상 어색한 문장은?

① Joel doesn't like eating pizza.
② Riding a bike is not difficult.
③ She finished writing the report.
④ Playing online games are boring.
⑤ Do you need to hand in your homework today?

04 다음 빈칸에 알맞은 것은?

The scarf felt ________.

① beautifully ② rough ③ hardly
④ softly ⑤ smoothly

01 다음 중 밑줄 친 부분의 성격이 다른 것은?

① When I was young, riding a bike in the park was fun.
② Belma finished cleaning her room.
③ My hobby is listening to music.
④ Her daughter was sleeping.
⑤ Jenny is good at dancing.

중요
02 다음 중 어법상 올바른 문장은?

① The music played by the band didn't sound sweetly.
② The soup that my mom cooked for me smelled deliciously.
③ Jane looked beautifully today.
④ The pizza tasted sweetly.
⑤ Mike felt hungry.

서답형
03 다음 괄호 안에서 알맞은 것을 고르시오.

(1) She sounded (excited / excitedly).
(2) Cinderella felt (like a princess / a princess).
(3) (Grow / Growing) beautiful flowers is her hobby.
(4) Daniel is fond of (exercise / exercising) *Teakwondo*.

04 다음 빈칸에 알맞은 것은?

Terry ________ very shy last night.

① heard ② looked
③ saw ④ found
⑤ thought

05 다음 중 어법상 어색한 문장은?

① Donald's hobby is practice drawing.
② I enjoy taking selfies.
③ She likes to listen to music.
④ Brook finished reading the book.
⑤ Jogging in the morning is good for your health.

중요
06 다음 빈칸에 들어갈 알맞은 말을 모두 고르시오.

They ________ swimming in the river last summer.

① decided ② wanted
③ enjoyed ④ practiced
⑤ agreed

서답형
07 다음 우리말과 의미가 같도록 괄호 안의 어구를 이용하여 영작하시오.

(1) TV로 올림픽 경기를 보지 않을래? (the Olympic Games, how, watch, on TV)
➡ ________________________________
(2) 그녀의 노래는 아름답게 들린다. (sound)
➡ ________________________________

08 다음 빈칸에 알맞지 않은 것은?

The boy looked ________.

① very lonely ② carefully
③ tired ④ strong
⑤ like a hero

서답형

09 다음 그림을 보고 주어진 어휘를 이용하여 빈칸에 한 단어씩 채워 문장을 완성하시오.

________ ________ is really fun. (play)

중요

10 다음 중 어법상 올바른 문장은?

① Kenneth agreed practicing to play the piano every day.
② Gloria loves singing when she has free time.
③ Erica couldn't finish to do the dishes.
④ Do you mind to come here?
⑤ Harry gave up to go to the concert on account of a bad cold.

11 다음 두 문장의 빈칸에 알맞은 말이 바르게 짝지어진 것은?

• Grace felt ________. • This bread smells ________.

① sick – nice ② sickly – nicely
③ sick – nicely ④ sickly – nice
⑤ sickness – nicely

서답형

12 다음 문장의 빈칸에 알맞은 말을 쓰시오.

The music sounds ________ an electric piano.

중요

13 다음 문장의 빈칸에 알맞은 것은?

Will you stop ________ so much noise? I am studying for the final exam.

① make ② made
③ to make ④ making
⑤ to making

14 다음 중 어법상 잘못된 것은?

① The cookies she gave to me tasted delicious.
② Her dress smelled like a rose.
③ Tony felt greatly when he won the race.
④ The girl wearing the glasses looked friendly.
⑤ Thomas looked tired after the hard work.

서답형

15 다음 빈칸에 괄호 안에 주어진 어휘를 변형하거나 다른 어휘를 추가하여 쓰시오.

(1) Why did you give up ________ the guitar? (play)
(2) ________ a lot makes me happy. (smile)
(3) Have you finished ________ your report? (write)
(4) I'm interested in ________ to Switzerland. (go)

16 다음 밑줄 친 부분 중 어법상 틀린 것은?

① June felt very ill after he finished the work.
② The crowd sounded excited with the goal in the second half.
③ The soup smells like a fish.
④ Both Victoria and her sister look lovely.
⑤ The vegetables Davis bought tasted freshly.

중요

17 다음 〈보기〉의 밑줄 친 부분과 쓰임이 같은 것은?

보기
He recommended going to a doctor instead of using home treatments.

① Being a good friend is important.
② My greatest pleasure is watching my son play center forward for his team.
③ At that time, she was doing her math homework.
④ They enjoyed singing to the guitar last night.
⑤ Kim is afraid of speaking in front of people.

18 다음 빈칸에 알맞은 말이 순서대로 짝지어진 것은?

- Strawberry juice ________ cold.
- His voice ________ upset.

① feels – sounds ② sounds – feels
③ tastes – smells ④ smells – tastes
⑤ looks – tastes

서답형

19 다음 주어진 단어를 알맞게 변형하여 빈칸을 완성하시오.

(1) Teresa practices ________ the violin every day. (play)
(2) ________ healthy food is very important. (have)
(3) My last wish is ________ her again. (see)
(4) Children are fond of ________ as high as possible. (swing)

20 다음 문장 중 어법상 옳지 않은 것은?

① The spaghetti my mom made for me last night tasted great.
② The mountain covered with trash looked terrible.
③ The cake was very cold and hard, so it felt a rock.
④ Dancing is my hobby.
⑤ My dad likes cooking dinner for us on holidays.

서답형

21 다음 문장에서 틀린 부분을 찾아 바르게 고쳐 다시 쓰시오.

(1) Solving math problems are interesting.
➡ ____________________
(2) Lisa is good at solve difficult math problems.
➡ ____________________
(3) Strawberry candy tastes sweetly.
➡ ____________________
(4) You look a totally new person in that suit.
➡ ____________________

01 다음 빈칸에 괄호 안에 주어진 어휘의 알맞은 형태를 쓰시오. (필요한 경우 단어를 추가할 것.)

(1) What does the woman suggest ________ next time? (do)

(2) ________ a good friend is important. (have)

(3) I'm fond of ________ books. (read)

(4) Thank you for ________ me to your party. (invite)

중요

02 다음 〈보기〉와 같이 두 문장을 한 문장으로 만들 때 빈칸을 알맞게 채우시오.

보기

I enjoy in-line skating. It's my hobby.

➡ In-line skating is my hobby.

(1) Isaac likes playing sports. It is fun.

➡ ________ sports is ________ for Isaac.

(2) Kelly wants to be a doctor. But it is difficult.

➡ ________ a doctor is ________ for Kelly.

(3) My pet dog likes sleeping. It makes him happy.

➡ ________ makes my pet dog ________.

(4) Abe does not eat fast food. It makes him healthy.

➡ ________ ________ fast food makes Abe ________.

(5) Buzz works hard every day. It makes him tired.

➡ ________ hard every day makes Buzz ________.

03 다음 빈칸을 괄호 안의 단어를 이용하여 적절하게 채우시오. (필요하면 어형을 바꾸시오.)

(1) Cindy cooked many Korean foods for us last night. (taste, delicious)

➡ They ________ ________.

(2) Vivian cleaned her house all day long yesterday. (feel, tire)

➡ She ________ ________.

(3) Laura got wonderful gifts on her birthday. (look, happy)

➡ She ________ ________.

(4) Tom bought some roses and gave them to Molly. (smell, nice)

➡ They ________ ________.

(5) Mike broke the window. (sound, upset)

➡ His mom ________ ________.

04 다음 그림을 보고 주어진 어휘를 이용하여 빈칸에 한 단어씩 채워 문장을 완성하시오.

The *samgyupsal* we had yesterday ________ ________.

05 자신의 경우에 맞게 다음 질문에 답하시오.

(1) What are you interested in?

➡ ______________________________

(2) What do you usually enjoy doing when you have free time?

➡ ______________________________

06 다음 그림을 보고 주어진 어휘를 이용하여 빈칸에 한 단어씩 채워 문장을 완성하시오.

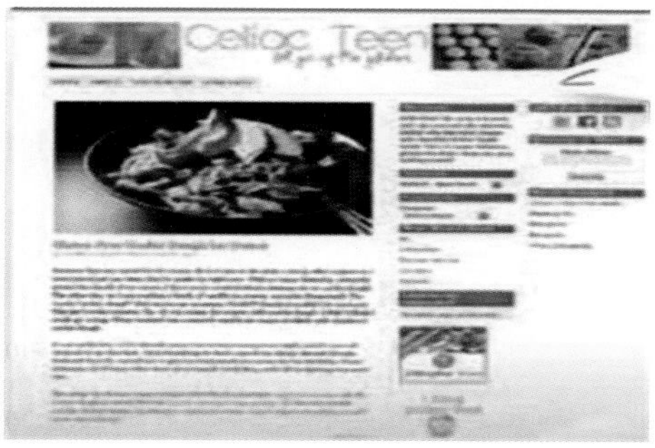

She loves ________ healthy food. She looks ________ for her recipes. (cook, famous)

07 다음 우리말과 같도록 주어진 표현을 활용하여 문장을 완성하시오.

Sarah는 좋은 의사처럼 보였다.
➡ Sarah ________ ________ ________ ________ doctor. (look, good)

중요

08 우리말에 맞게 주어진 어휘를 활용하여 문장을 완성하시오.

(1) 수영을 배우는 것은 그렇게 어렵지 않다. (learn)
➡ ________ to swim is not so difficult.

(2) 바다에서 수영하는 것은 쉽지 않다. (swim)
➡ ________ in the sea ________ ________ ________.

(3) 지석이는 바둑을 잘 둔다. (play)
➡ Jiseok is good at ________ baduk.

(4) Clark는 휴일에 식구들을 위해 요리하는 것을 좋아한다. (cook)
➡ Clark likes ________ for his family on holidays.

(5) Mary의 취미는 동물을 돌보는 것이다. (take)
➡ Mary's hobby is ________ ________ ________ animals.

고난이도

09 다음 문장에서 어색한 곳을 찾아 바르게 고쳐 전체 문장을 다시 쓰시오.

(1) Grandmother's story sounded really interestingly.
➡ ________________________________

(2) Judy didn't like the food. She said the food tasted very bitterly.
➡ ________________________________
____

(3) The meat we had at the restaurant didn't taste beef.
➡ ________________________________
____

(4) Watch action movies are exciting.
➡ ________________________________

(5) Keep early hours are good for the health.
➡ ________________________________

10 다음 괄호 안의 단어의 어형을 어법에 맞게 바꿔 빈칸에 한 단어씩 써 넣으시오.

(1) After the conversation, she sounded ________. (nerve)

(2) The flowers look ________. (beauty)

(3) I like ________ to music. ________ to music is a lot of fun. (listen)

(4) I have to avoid ________ junk food. ________ junk food is not good. (eat)

11 다음 우리말을 영작하시오. (3 단어)

요리하는 것은 재미있어 보인다.

➡ ________________________________

교과서

Reading

All About Selfies!

#Selfie Facts

Are you interested in selfies? You probably like to post selfies on
be interested in: ~에 관심[흥미]이 있다 / = posting
social media, but how much do you know about selfies? Here are some
얼마나 많이 / 동사 / 주어
interesting facts.

1. Robert Cornelius took the world's first selfie in 1839.
   take the selfie: 셀피를 찍다
2. *Selfie* became a new word in the dictionary in 2013.
   전치사 in은 공간이나 장소를 나타내는 '…에서'의 의미와 특정 연대를 나타내는 '…에'의 의미가 있다.
3. Buzz Aldrin took the first space selfie in 1966.
   우주 셀피

#*Selfie* Survey

Taking selfies is part of daily life for many teens, but do teens really
동명사구 Taking selfies가 주어로 쓰였는데, 이때 동명사구는 3인칭 단수로 취급한다.
enjoy it? To find out, we did a survey. We asked three questions to 300
부사적 용법(목적)
students from ages 14 to 16. Let's look at the results. Surprisingly, 90
from A to B: A부터 B까지 / ~을 보다
percent of the girls take selfies, but only 15 percent of the boys take
percents (X) / 단지
selfies. Also, 93 percent of these students said that they use filters.
percents (X) / 지시형용사 / 접속사

The survey also showed that the students take selfies at school the
접속사
most. Check out some of the students' comments.
확인해 보라 / s로 끝나는 복수명사는 소유격을 만들 때 어포스트로피만 붙인다.

interest 관심, 흥미
post 게시하다
social media 소셜 미디어
survey (설문) 조사
result 결과
filter 필터, 여과기
outdoors 옥외[야외]에서
comment 논평, 의견

확인문제

● 다음 문장이 본문의 내용과 일치하면 T, 일치하지 않으면 F를 쓰시오.

1 People are interested in selfies and know about selfies very much. ☐

2 In 1839, Robert Cornelius took a selfie for the first time in the world. ☐

3 Before 2013, it wasn't possible to look up the word *selfie* in the dictionary. ☐

4 In 1966, Buzz Aldrin took the world's first selfie. ☐

5 The students take selfies at home the most. ☐

Lewis, 14, England Selfies are awesome. Making silly faces is really fun!
경탄할 만한, 기막히게 좋은 / 동명사구 Making silly faces가 주어로 쓰였는데, 이때 동명사구는 3인칭 단수로 취급한다.

Minwoo, 16, Korea I enjoy taking selfies, but some students spend too much time doing it.
taking은 동사 enjoy의 목적어로 쓰인 동명사이다. / spend+시간+ ~ing: ~하는 데 시간을 쓰다

Kate, 15, Denmark My pictures look good when I use filters. But sometimes my selfies don't look like me.
look(…하게 보이다), sound(…하게 들리다), feel(…하게 느끼다) 등의 감각동사 뒤에는 형용사가 온다. / 빈도부사 sometimes는 문장 맨 앞에 써도 된다 / look like+명사: ~처럼 보이다

#Selfie Etiquette

You should follow etiquette for selfies. Ask yourself these questions before you take, post, or look at selfies.
셀피 예절 / 간접목적어 / 직접목적어 / 접속사

1. Where am I?

Choose appropriate places to take selfies. Don't take selfies in hospitals or public restrooms. It may bother other people.
부정명령문은 명령문 앞에 Don't를 쓴다. / = to take selfies in hospitals or public restrooms

2. Who can see this?

Keep in mind that anyone can see your selfies. Choose carefully when you post them.
명심하라 / your selfies

3. What kinds of comments should I leave?

Leave nice comments on other people's selfies. Don't be rude.
부정명령문은 명령문 앞에 Don't를 쓴다.

That sounds easy, doesn't it? Follow these tips and have fun with your selfies!
look(…하게 보이다), sound(…하게 들리다), feel(…하게 느끼다) 등의 감각동사 뒤에는 형용사가 온다. / 즐거운 시간을 보내다

awesome 경탄할 만한, 기막히게 좋은, 굉장한
silly 우스꽝스러운, 어리석은, 유치한
etiquette (사회 · 특정 직종 구성원 사이의) 예의, 예절
appropriate 적절한, 알맞은
public 공공의, 대중의
restroom 화장실
bother 신경 쓰이게 하다, 귀찮게 하다
leave 남기다, 떠나다
rude 무례한, 버릇없는

확인문제

● 다음 문장이 본문의 내용과 일치하면 T, 일치하지 않으면 F를 쓰시오.

1 Sometimes Kate's selfies don't look like her. ☐

2 You should choose suitable places to take selfies. ☐

3 You should carefully choose when to post selfies. ☐

4 Don't be rude when you leave comments on other people's selfies. ☐

Reading 교과서 확인학습 A

- 우리말을 참고하여 빈칸에 알맞은 말을 쓰시오.

1 All _______ Selfies!

2 #Selfie _______

3 _______ you _______ _______ selfies?

4 You probably like _______ _______ _______ on social media, but _______ _______ do you know about selfies?

5 _______ _______ some interesting facts.

6 Robert Cornelius _______ _______ _______ _______ _______ in 1839.

7 *Selfie* _______ _______ _______ _______ in the dictionary in 2013.

8 Buzz Aldrin _______ _______ _______ _______ _______ in 1966.

9 #Selfie _______

10 _______ _______ is part _______ _______ _______ for many teens, but do teens really enjoy it?

11 _______ _______ _______, we did a survey.

12 We asked three questions to 300 students _______ _______ _______ _______ _______.

13 _______ _______ _______the results.

14 Surprisingly, _______ _______ _______ _______ _______ take selfies, but only 15 percent of the boys _______ _______.

15 _______, 93 percent of these students said that _______ _______ _______.

16 The survey also showed that the students _______ _______ _______ _______ the most.

17 Check out _______ _______ _______ _______ _______.

18 Lewis, 14, England　Selfies are _______.

1 셀피에 대한 모든 것!

2 셀피와 관련된 사실들

3 당신은 셀피에 관심이 있는가?

4 당신은 아마 소셜 미디어에 셀피를 게시하기를 좋아할지도 모르지만, 셀피에 대해 얼마나 많이 알고 있는가?

5 여기 몇 가지 재미있는 사실들이 있다.

6 로버트 코닐리어스가 1839년에 전 세계 최초의 셀피를 찍었다.

7 selfie는 2013년에 사전에 신조어로 등재되었다.

8 버즈 올드린이 1966년에 최초의 우주 셀피를 찍었다.

9 셀피 설문 조사

10 셀피 찍기는 많은 십대들에게 일상생활의 한 부분인데, 십대들은 정말로 그것을 즐기고 있는가?

11 알아보기 위해 우리는 설문 조사를 했다.

12 우리는 14세에서 16세 사이의 학생 300명에게 세 가지를 질문했다.

13 그 결과를 보자.

14 놀랍게도, 소녀들의 90퍼센트가 셀피를 찍지만, 소년들의 15퍼센트만이 셀피를 찍는다.

15 또한 이 학생들의 93퍼센트는 필터를 사용한다고 대답했다.

16 설문은 또한 학생들이 학교에서 가장 많이 셀피를 찍는다는 것을 보여 주었다.

17 학생들의 의견 몇 가지를 확인해 보라.

18 루이스, 14세, 영국: 셀피는 굉장하다.

19 _______ _______ _______ is really fun!

20 Minwoo, 16, Korea I enjoy _______ _______, but some students spend too much time _______ _______.

21 Kate, 15, Denmark My pictures _______ _______ when I use filters.

22 But sometimes my selfies _______ _______ _______ _______.

23 #Selfie _______

24 You should _______ _______ _______ selfies.

25 _______ _______ these questions _______ you take, post, or look at selfies.

26 1. Where _______ _______?

27 Choose _______ _______ to take selfies.

28 _______ _______ _______ in hospitals or public restrooms.

29 It may _______ other people.

30 2. Who can _______ _______?

31 _______ _______ _______ that anyone can see your selfies.

32 _______ _______ when you post them.

33 3. _______ _______ _______ comments should I _______?

34 _______ nice _______ _______ other people's selfies.

35 Don't _______ _______. That _______ _______, _______ _______?

36 Follow these tips and _______ _______ _______ your selfies.

19 우스꽝스러운 표정을 짓는 것은 정말로 재미있다!

20 민우, 16세, 한국: 나는 셀피 찍는 것을 즐기지만 몇몇 학생들은 그것을 하는 데 너무 많은 시간을 쓴다.

21 케이트, 15세, 덴마크: 내 사진은 필터를 사용할 때 멋져 보인다.

22 하지만 가끔 나의 셀피가 나처럼 보이지 않는다.

23 셀피 예절

24 당신은 셀피 예절을 따라야 한다.

25 셀피를 찍고, 게시하거나 보기 전에 스스로 이 질문들을 물어보라.

26 1. 내가 어디에 있는가?

27 셀피를 찍기에 적합한 장소를 선택하라.

28 병원이나 공중화장실에서 셀피를 찍지 마라.

29 그것은 다른 사람들을 신경 쓰이게 할 수 있다.

30 2. 누가 이것을 볼 수 있는가?

31 누구나 당신의 셀피를 볼 수 있다는 것을 명심하라.

32 그것들을 게시할 때 신중하게 골라라.

33 3. 어떤 코멘트를 남겨야 하는가?

34 다른 사람들의 셀피에 상냥한 코멘트를 남겨라.

35 무례하게 굴지 마라. 쉬운 것처럼 들린다, 그렇지 않은가?

36 이러한 조언들을 따라서 당신의 셀피와 즐거운 시간을 보내라!

Reading 교과서 확인학습 B

• 우리말을 참고하여 본문을 영작하시오.

1 셀피에 대한 모든 것!

➡ ______________________________

2 셀피와 관련된 사실들

➡ ______________________________

3 당신은 셀피에 관심이 있는가?

➡ ______________________________

4 당신은 아마 소셜 미디어에 셀피를 게시하기를 좋아할지도 모르지만, 셀피에 대해 얼마나 많이 알고 있는가?

➡ ______________________________

5 여기 몇 가지 재미있는 사실들이 있다.

➡ ______________________________

6 로버트 코닐리어스가 1839년에 전 세계 최초의 셀피를 찍었다.

➡ ______________________________

7 *selfie*는 2013년에 사전에 신조어로 등재되었다.

➡ ______________________________

8 버즈 올드린이 1966년에 최초의 우주 셀피를 찍었다.

➡ ______________________________

9 셀피 설문 조사

➡ ______________________________

10 셀피 찍기는 많은 십대들에게 일상생활의 한 부분인데, 십대들은 정말로 그것을 즐기고 있는가?

➡ ______________________________

11 알아보기 위해 우리는 설문 조사를 했다.

➡ ______________________________

12 우리는 14세에서 16세 사이의 학생 300명에게 세 가지를 질문했다.

➡ ______________________________

13 그 결과를 보자.

➡ ______________________________

14 놀랍게도, 소녀들의 90퍼센트가 셀피를 찍지만, 소년들의 15퍼센트만이 셀피를 찍는다.

➡ ______________________________

15 또한 이 학생들의 93퍼센트는 필터를 사용한다고 대답했다.

➡ ______________________________

16 설문은 또한 학생들이 학교에서 가장 많이 셀피를 찍는다는 것을 보여 주었다.

➡ ______________________________

17 학생들의 의견 몇 가지를 확인해 보라.

➡ ______________________________

18 루이스, 14세, 영국: 셀피는 굉장하다.

➡ ______________________________

19 우스꽝스러운 표정을 짓는 것은 정말로 재미있다!

➡ ____________________

20 민우, 16세, 한국: 나는 셀피 찍는 것을 즐기지만 몇몇 학생들은 그것을 하는 데 너무 많은 시간을 쓴다.

➡ ____________________

21 케이트, 15세, 덴마크: 내 사진은 필터를 사용할 때 멋져 보인다.

➡ ____________________

22 하지만 가끔 나의 셀피가 나처럼 보이지 않는다.

➡ ____________________

23 셀피 예절

➡ ____________________

24 당신은 셀피 예절을 따라야 한다.

➡ ____________________

25 셀피를 찍고, 게시하거나 보기 전에 스스로 이 질문들을 물어보라.

➡ ____________________

26 내가 어디에 있는가?

➡ ____________________

27 셀피를 찍기에 적합한 장소를 선택하라.

➡ ____________________

28 병원이나 공중화장실에서 셀피를 찍지 마라.

➡ ____________________

29 그것은 다른 사람들을 신경 쓰이게 할 수 있다.

➡ ____________________

30 누가 이것을 볼 수 있는가?

➡ ____________________

31 누구나 당신의 셀피를 볼 수 있다는 것을 명심하라.

➡ ____________________

32 그것들을 게시할 때 신중하게 골라라.

➡ ____________________

33 어떤 코멘트를 남겨야 하는가?

➡ ____________________

34 다른 사람들의 셀피에 상냥한 코멘트를 남겨라.

➡ ____________________

35 무례하게 굴지 마라. 쉬운 것처럼 들린다, 그렇지 않은가?

➡ ____________________

36 이러한 조언들을 따라서 당신의 셀피와 즐거운 시간을 보내라.

➡ ____________________

[01~03] 다음 글을 읽고, 물음에 답하시오.

Are you (A)[interested / interesting] in selfies? You probably like to post selfies on social media, but how much do you know about selfies? Here (B)[is / are] some (C)[interested / interesting] facts.

1. Robert Cornelius took the world's first selfie in 1839.
2. *Selfie* became a new word in the dictionary in 2013.
3. Buzz Aldrin took the first space selfie in 1966.

서답형

01 괄호 (A)~(C)에서 어법상 알맞은 낱말을 골라 쓰시오.

(A)________ (B)________ (C)________

02 위 글의 제목으로 알맞은 것을 고르시오.

① Are You Interested in Selfies?
② Selfie Survey
③ Who Took the World's First Selfie?
④ Selfie Facts
⑤ Selfie Etiquette

03 위 글의 내용과 일치하지 않는 것은?

① 위 글은 셀피에 관한 몇 가지 재미있는 사실들을 소개하고 있다.
② 사람들은 소셜 미디어에 셀피를 게시하려고 셀피를 찍는다.
③ 세계 최초로 셀피를 찍은 사람은 Robert Cornelius이다.
④ selfie가 사전에 신조어로 등재된 것은 2013년이다.
⑤ 우주에서 처음 셀피를 찍은 사람은 Buzz Aldrin이다.

[04~06] 다음 글을 읽고, 물음에 답하시오.

#Selfie Survey

ⓐTaking selfies is part of daily life for many teens, but do teens really enjoy it? To find out, we did a survey. ⓑWe asked three questions to 300 students from ages 14 to 16. Let's look at the results.

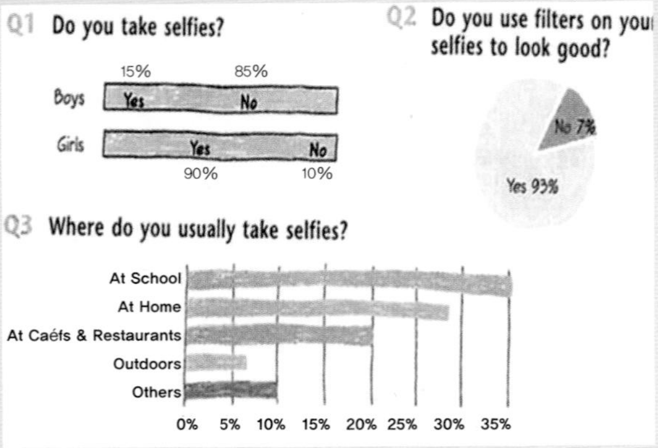

Surprisingly, 90 percent of the girls take selfies, but only 15 percent of the boys take selfies. Also, 93 percent of these students said that they use filters. The survey also showed that the students take selfies at school the most. Check out some of the students' comments.

중요

04 위 글의 밑줄 친 ⓐTaking과 문법적 쓰임이 같은 것을 고르시오.

① I was listening to music.
② They were working over there.
③ My hobby is playing baseball.
④ He was dancing on the floor.
⑤ She was eating dinner.

서답형

05 위 글의 밑줄 친 ⓑ를 우리말로 옮기시오.

➡ ____________________

____

06 위 도표의 내용과 일치하지 않는 것은?

① 소년들의 85%가 셀피를 찍지 않는다.
② 소녀들의 10%가 셀피를 찍지 않는다.
③ 7%의 학생들은 필터를 사용하지 않는다.
④ 학생들이 두 번째로 셀피를 많이 찍는 장소는 카페나 식당이다.
⑤ 카페나 식당보다 학교에서 셀피를 찍는 학생들이 15% 더 많다.

[07~09] 다음 글을 읽고, 물음에 답하시오.

#Selfie Etiquette

You should follow etiquette for selfies. Ask yourself ⓐthese questions before you take, post, or look at selfies.

1. Where am I?
   Choose appropriate places ⓑto take selfies. Don't take selfies in hospitals or public restrooms. It may bother other people.
2. Who can see this?
   Keep in mind that anyone can see your selfies. Choose carefully when you post them.
3. What kinds of comments should I leave?
   Leave nice comments on other people's selfies. Don't be rude.

서답형

07 위 글의 밑줄 친 ⓐ가 가리키는 것을 본문에서 찾아 쓰시오.

(1) ____________________
(2) ____________________
(3) ____________________

중요

08 위 글의 밑줄 친 ⓑto take와 to부정사의 용법이 같은 것을 고르시오.

① I am glad to meet you again.
② He must be smart to solve it.
③ Give me a chair to sit on.
④ It is not easy to learn English.
⑤ She grew up to be a scientist.

서답형

09 다음 문장에서 위 글의 내용과 다른 부분을 찾아서 고치시오.

Before you take, post, or look at selfies, you should keep in mind that no one can see your selfies.

__________ ➡ __________

[10~12] 다음 글을 읽고, 물음에 답하시오.

#Selfie Facts

Are you interested in selfies? You ⓐprobably like to post selfies on social media, but ⓑ셀피에 대해 얼마나 많이 알고 있니? Here are some interesting facts.

1. Robert Cornelius took the world's first selfie in 1830.
2. *Selfie* became a new word in the dictionary in 2013.
3. Buzz Aldrin took the first space selfie in 1966.

10 위 글의 밑줄 친 ⓐprobably와 바꿔 쓸 수 있는 말을 모두 고르시오.

① perhaps ② actually
③ exactly ④ maybe
⑤ completely

서답형

11 위 글의 밑줄 친 ⓑ의 우리말에 맞게 한 단어를 보충하여, 주어진 어휘를 알맞게 배열하시오.

selfies / know / much / you / about / do

➡ ______________________

서답형

12 다음 질문에 대한 알맞은 대답을 완성하시오.

Q: Who took the first space selfie?
A: It was ____________________.

[13~16] 다음 글을 읽고, 물음에 답하시오.

#Selfie Survey

Taking selfies is part of daily life for many teens, but do teens really enjoy it? ⓐTo find out, we did a survey. We asked three questions to 300 students from ages 14 to 16. Let's look at the results.

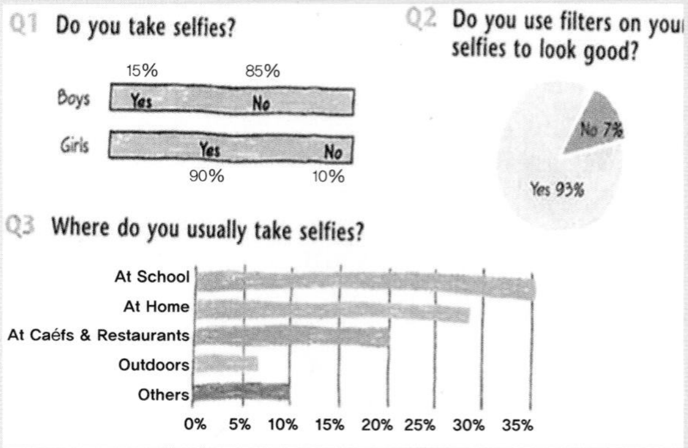

Surprisingly, 90 percent of the girls take selfies, but only 15 percent of the boys take selfies. Also, 93 percent of these students said that they use filters. The survey also showed that the students take selfies at school the most. Check out some of the students' comments.

Lewis, 14, England Selfies are ___ⓑ___. Making silly faces is really fun!

Minwoo, 16, Korea I enjoy taking selfies, but some students spend too much time doing it.

Kate, 15, Denmark My pictures look good when I use filters. But sometimes my selfies don't look like me.

13 위 도표를 보고 대답할 수 없는 질문은?

① What percent of the girls said that they take selfies?
② How many students use filters to look good?
③ What percent of the students take selfies at school?
④ Why do students like to take selfies at school?
⑤ Where do students take selfies more, at home or at cafés & restaurants?

14 위 글의 밑줄 친 ⓐTo find와 to부정사의 용법이 다른 것을 고르시오.

① I use my computer to do the work.
② I have much work to do today.
③ He stopped to listen to music.
④ This book is easy to read.
⑤ He must be foolish to do such things.

중요

15 위 글의 빈칸 ⓑ에 들어갈 알맞은 말을 고르시오.

① terrible ② awkward
③ boring ④ disappointing
⑤ awesome

서답형

16 다음 질문에 대한 알맞은 대답을 주어진 단어로 시작하여 쓰시오. (3단어)

Q: Why does Kate say that sometimes her selfies don't look like her?
A: Because ____________________.

[17~19] 다음 글을 읽고, 물음에 답하시오.

#Selfie Etiquette

You should follow etiquette for selfies. Ask yourself these questions before you take, post, or look at selfies.

1. (A)[Where is here? / Where am I?]
   Choose ⓐappropriate places to take selfies. Don't take selfies in hospitals or public restrooms. It may bother other people.
2. Who can see it?
   Keep in mind that anyone can see your selfies. Choose carefully when you post (B)[it / them].
3. What kinds of comments should I leave?
   Leave nice comments __ⓑ__ other people's selfies. Don't be rude.

That sounds (C)[easy / easily], doesn't it? Follow these tips and have fun __ⓒ__ your selfies.

서답형

17 위 글의 괄호 (A)~(C)에서 어법상 알맞은 것을 골라 쓰시오.

(A)__________ (B)__________ (C)__________

18 위 글의 밑줄 친 ⓐappropriate와 바꿔 쓸 수 있는 말을 모두 고르시오.

① popular ② proper
③ common ④ favorite
⑤ suitable

중요

19 위 글의 빈칸 ⓑ와 ⓒ에 들어갈 전치사가 바르게 짝지어진 것은?

① on – for ② in – with
③ in – from ④ for – to
⑤ on – with

[20~22] 다음 대화를 읽고, 물음에 답하시오.

Boy: Bonny, did you see the results of the selfie survey?
Bonny: No, I didn't. Are ⓐthey interesting?
Boy: Yes. (①) Not many boys take selfies. (②) Also, a lot of teens use filters on their selfies. (③) Where do students take selfies most often? (④)
Bonny: I don't know. (⑤) Maybe at a restaurant?
Boy: No. It's at school!
Bonny: Oh, you're right. My classmates also take selfies in the classroom.

서답형

20 위 대화의 밑줄 친 ⓐthey가 가리키는 것을 본문에서 찾아 쓰시오.

➡ ______________________________

21 위 대화의 흐름으로 보아, 주어진 문장이 들어가기에 가장 적절한 곳은?

Can you guess?

① ② ③ ④ ⑤

22 위 대화의 내용과 일치하지 않는 것은?

① Bonny는 셀피 설문조사의 결과를 보지 못했다.
② 소년은 설문조사의 결과가 흥미롭다고 생각한다.
③ Bonny는 학생들이 셀피를 가장 많이 찍는 장소를 알고 있다.
④ 소년은 학생들이 셀피를 가장 많이 찍는 장소가 학교라고 말했다.
⑤ Bonny의 학급 친구들도 교실에서 셀피를 찍는다.

[01~03] 다음 글을 읽고, 물음에 답하시오.

#Selfie Facts
ⓐAre you interested in selfies? You probably like to post selfies on social media, but how much do you know about selfies? ⓑ여기에 몇 가지 재미있는 사실들이 있다.

1. Robert Cornelius took the world's first selfie in 1839.
2. *Selfie* became a new word in the dictionary in 2013.
3. Buzz Aldrin took the first space selfie in 1966.

01 위 글의 밑줄 친 ⓐ를 다음과 같이 바꿔 쓸 때 빈칸에 알맞은 말을 쓰시오.

Do you have an ________ in selfies?

02 위 글의 밑줄 친 ⓑ의 우리말에 맞게 주어진 어휘를 이용하여 5단어로 영작하시오.

some

➡ ______________________

중요
03 다음 문장에서 위 글의 내용과 다른 부분을 찾아서 고치시오.

It was possible to look up *selfie* in the dictionary before 2013.

__________ ➡ __________

[04~06] 다음 글을 읽고, 물음에 답하시오.

#Selfie Etiquette
You should follow etiquette for selfies. Ask yourself these questions before you take, post, or look at selfies.

1. Where am I?
   ⓐ셀피를 찍기에 적절한 장소를 선택해라. Don't take selfies in hospitals or public restrooms. It may bother other people.
2. Who can see this?
   Keep in mind that anyone can see your selfies. Choose carefully when you post them.
3. What kinds of comments should I leave?
   Leave nice ____ⓑ____ on other people's selfies. Don't be rude.

중요
04 위 글의 밑줄 친 ⓐ의 우리말에 맞게 주어진 어휘를 이용하여 6단어로 영작하시오.

appropriate

➡ ______________________

05 다음 질문에 대한 알맞은 대답을 주어진 단어로 시작하여 쓰시오. (5 단어)

Q: Why shouldn't we take selfies in hospitals or public restrooms?
A: Because ______________________.

06 위 글의 빈칸 ⓑ에 들어갈 알맞은 말을 본문에서 찾아 쓰시오.

➡ ______________________

[07~09] 다음 글을 읽고, 물음에 답하시오.

#Selfie Facts

Are you __ⓐ__ in selfies? You probably like to __ⓑ__ selfies on social media, but how much do you know about selfies? Here are some interesting facts.

1. Robert Cornelius took the world's first selfie in 1839.
2. *Selfie* became a new word in the dictionary in 2013.
3. Buzz Aldrin took the first space selfie in 1966.

07 중요 본문의 한 단어를 변형하여 위 글의 빈칸 ⓐ에 들어갈 알맞은 말을 쓰시오.

➡ ____________________

08 다음 주어진 영영풀이를 참고하여 빈칸 ⓑ에 철자 p로 시작하는 단어를 쓰시오.

to publish something such as a message or picture on a website or using social media

➡ ____________________

09 다음 질문에 대한 알맞은 대답을 주어진 단어로 시작하여 쓰시오. (2 단어)

Q: When did Robert Cornelius take the world's first selfie? A: It was ____________________.

[10~12] 다음 글을 읽고, 물음에 답하시오.

#Selfie Survey

Taking selfies is part of daily life for many teens, but do teens really enjoy ⓐit? To find out, we did a survey. We asked three questions to 300 students from ages 14 to 16. Let's look at the results.

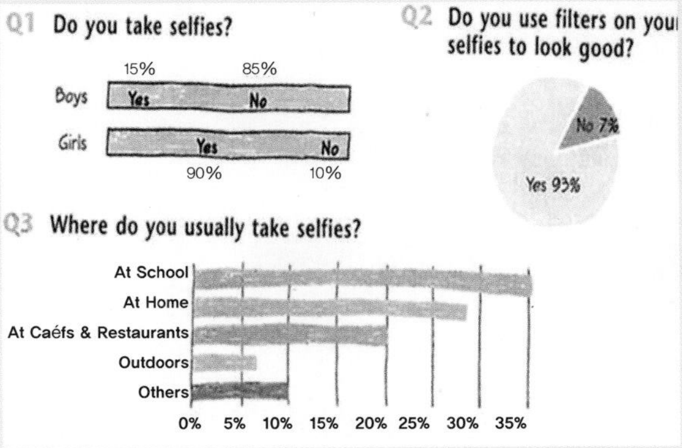

Surprisingly, 90 percent of the girls take selfies, but only 15 percent of the boys take selfies. Also, 93 percent of these students said that they use filters. The survey also showed that the students take selfies __ⓑ__ the most. Check out some of the students' comments.

10 위 글의 밑줄 친 ⓐit이 가리키는 것을 본문에서 찾아 쓰시오.

➡ ____________________

11 다음 질문에 대한 알맞은 대답을 빈칸에 쓰시오.

Q: How many students take selfies at cafés & restaurants? A: ____________ students take selfies at cafés & restaurants.

12 중요 위 글의 빈칸 ⓑ에 들어갈 알맞은 말을 쓰시오.

➡ ____________________

교과서

구석구석

Project Link

Our group is interested in dance. We made a dance. We recorded a dance video and posted it online. You can see it at www.yutu.com.

be interested in: ~에 관심[흥미]이 있다 / make의 과거형 / record: 녹음하다, 녹화하다 / recorded와 posted가 병렬구조 / = a dance video

구문해설 • post: 올리다, 게시하다

해석

우리 그룹은 춤에 관심이 있다. 우리는 춤을 만들었다. 우리는 춤 비디오를 녹화하고 그것을 온라인에 올렸다. 너는 그것을 www.yutu.com에서 볼 수 있다.

Think and Write

Be a Great Internet User!

When we use the internet, we should follow some rules. Then we can enjoy the internet more. First of all, we should follow language rules because people may not understand us. Also, we should post only true information. People may believe our incorrect information. Finally, we should not leave rude comments. We can hurt others' feelings. Keep these rules in mind. Then you will be a great internet user!

~할 때 / follow the rule: 규칙을 따르다 / 그러면 / = Above all / ~해야만 한다 / because + 주어 + 동사 / ~이 아닐지도 모른다 / = In addition / ~일지도 모른다(추측) / 마지막으로 / s로 끝난 말의 소유격: others's(X) / 지시형용사, this(X) / ~이 될 것이다

구문해설 • follow the rule: 규칙을 따르다 • first of all: 우선, 다른 무엇보다 먼저 • post: 게시하다 • incorrect: 부정확한 • rude: 무례한 • keep in mind: 명심하다

멋진 인터넷 사용자가 되어라! 우리가 인터넷을 사용할 때, 우리는 몇 가지 규칙을 따라야 한다. 그러면 우리는 인터넷을 더 즐길 수 있다. 무엇보다, 사람들이 우리를 이해하지 못할 수도 있기 때문에 우리는 언어 규칙들을 따라야 한다. 또한, 우리는 오직 사실인 정보만을 게시해야 한다. 사람들은 우리의 부정확한 정보를 믿을지도 모른다. 마지막으로, 무례한 코멘트를 남기지 말아야 한다. 우리는 다른 사람들의 감정을 다치게 할 수 있다. 이런 규칙들을 명심해라. 그러면 너는 멋진 인터넷 사용자가 될 것이다!

Culture Link

A student from the United States is interested in the environment. He created a cartoon superhero, *GoGreenMan*, and posted it online. He also helps the environment just like his character, *GoGreenMan*.

명사+콤마(,)+명사: 동격 / ~와 꼭 같이 / 동격

구문해설 • environment: 환경 • character: 캐릭터, 등장인물

미국 출신의 한 학생은 환경에 관심이 있다. 그는 GoGreenMan이라는 만화의 수퍼 영웅을 만들어 인터넷에 게시했다. 그는 또한 그의 캐릭터 GoGreenMan과 꼭 같이 환경을 돕는다.

영역별 핵심문제

Words & Expressions

01 다음 제시된 단어를 사용하여 자연스러운 문장을 만들 수 없는 것은? (형태 변화 가능)

보기
leave display understand prepare

① Various styles of suits are _______ in the shop windows.
② _______ the sauce while the pasta is cooking.
③ Danny, don't _______ Ellen while she's reading.
④ She _______ a message on his phone.
⑤ I'm sorry, I don't _______. Can you explain that again?

02 다음 우리말에 맞게 빈칸을 완성하시오.

(1) 나는 가끔 늦게까지 일을 해야 한다.
➡ I _______ have _______ work late.
(2) 바보 같은 질문을 그만해.
➡ Stop asking _______ questions.
(3) 이 근처에 공중전화가 있나요?
➡ Is _______ a _______ telephone near here?
(4) 오늘밤은 야외에서 밥을 먹기에 충분히 따뜻한 날씨이다.
➡ It's _______ enough to eat _______ tonight.

03 다음 빈칸에 들어갈 알맞은 말을 〈보기〉에서 골라 쓰시오. (형태 변화 가능)

보기
do have sound spend

(1) His ideas _______ interesting.
(2) Stacey _______ all her free time painting.
(3) We _______ a survey of parents in the village last year.
(4) The children were _______ so much fun.

04 다음 짝지어진 낱말의 관계가 나머지 넷과 다른 것은?

① display – exhibit
② exciting – boring
③ fact – truth
④ hurt – injure
⑤ nervous – anxious

05 다음 빈칸에 알맞은 말이 순서대로 바르게 나열된 것은?

- _______ beginning to end, the movie's plot is awesome.
- He could not keep _______ mind what she was saying.
- The average child spends three to four hours _______ front of the TV.

① From – in – from
② From – at – in
③ From – in – in
④ For – at – in
⑤ For – in – from

Conversation

06 다음 짝지어진 대화가 어색한 것은?

① A: May I use your cup?
B: I'm afraid not. It's broken.
② A: What sport are you interested in?
B: I like to play volleyball.
③ A: Is it okay if I clean the blackboard?
B: I'm sorry, but some students are still taking notes.
④ A: Can I borrow your notebook?
B: Of course. I'm sorry.
⑤ A: I'm afraid you can't take pictures in the concert hall.
B: I'm sorry. I didn't know that.

[07~10] 다음 대화를 읽고, 물음에 답하시오.

B: What are you ___(A)___ (go) to do this weekend?
G: I'm ___(B)___ (go) to go to a baseball game with my brother.
B: ①Are you interesting in baseball?
G: ②Not really. I'm going to the baseball game ___(C)___ my brother likes baseball.
B: ③You're so nice! ④Then what are you interested in?
G: I'm more interested in soccer. ⑤I want to go to a soccer game someday.

07 위 대화의 주어진 go를 이용해 빈칸 (A)와 (B)에 공통으로 들어갈 말을 쓰시오.

➡ ____________________

08 위 대화의 빈칸 (C)에 들어갈 알맞은 말을 고르시오.

① because ② when
③ therefore ④ though
⑤ while

09 위 대화의 밑줄 친 ①~⑤ 중에서 어색한 것을 고르고 바르게 고치시오.

____________ ➡ ____________

10 위 대화를 읽고 답할 수 없는 질문은?

① What will the girl do this weekend?
② What does the girl's brother like?
③ Does the girl like baseball?
④ What is the boy interested in?
⑤ Where does the girl want to go someday?

[11~12] 다음 대화를 읽고, 물음에 답하시오.

A: (A)너는 무엇에 관심이 있니?
B: I'm interested in games and social media. What about you?
A: I'm interested in music and social media.
B: (B)(both, in, are, media, we, social, interested)

11 위 대화의 (A)의 밑줄 친 우리말과 일치하도록 영작하시오.

➡ ____________________

12 위 대화의 (B)의 괄호 안에 있는 단어를 바르게 배열하시오.

➡ ____________________

Grammar

13 다음 괄호 안의 말을 이용하여 빈칸에 알맞게 쓰시오.

(1) Thanks for ________ me. (invite)
(2) ________ soccer is exciting. (play)

14 다음 중 어법상 올바른 것은?

① Emma cooked some Indian food and it tasted greatly.
② The girls who greet us at the gate look friendly.
③ The flowers Joyce gave to me smelled sweetly.
④ Belma sounded seriously after she heard the news.
⑤ Her dress which was made of pure silk felt smoothly.

15 다음 밑줄 친 부분의 쓰임이 다른 하나는?

① Writing a story is exciting.
② Angie loves watching movies.
③ There are some birds singing in the tree.
④ His dream job is becoming a kindergarten teacher.
⑤ She is really excited about going to Hawaii.

16 다음 우리말을 영어로 바르게 옮긴 것은?

당신의 연설을 들은 후로 저는 새로 태어난 사람 같습니다.

① I felt a new man after I listened to your speech.
② I felt a new man like after I listened to your speech.
③ I felt a new man after I like listened to your speech.
④ I felt a new man after I listened to your speech like.
⑤ I felt like a new man after I listened to your speech.

17 다음 우리말과 같은 뜻이 되도록 주어진 어구를 활용하여 문장을 완성하시오.

(1) 영화를 보는 것은 하나의 모험이다. (watch, a movie, adventure) (6 단어)
➡ ______________________

(2) 이 책을 읽는 것은 친구와 커피 한 잔 하는 것 같았다. (like, have, a coffee) (11 단어)
➡ ______________________
____

(3) 제 사생활에 대해선 그만 얘기하고 싶어요. (stop, talk, personal life) (9 단어)
➡ ______________________

(4) 원은 각이 없기 때문에 부드럽게 느껴진다. (circles, have no angles) (8 단어)
➡ ______________________

(5) 내 컴퓨터에서 이상한 소리가 나요. (sound) (4 단어)
➡ ______________________

18 다음 문장에서 어법상 잘못된 부분을 찾아 바르게 고쳐 쓰시오.

(1) All the food smells greatly.
__________ ➡ __________

(2) It neither smells nor tastes fish.
__________ ➡ __________

19 다음 중 어법상 어색한 것은?

① Amy is interested in climbing mountains.
② The strawberry cake looks delicious.
③ Jogging in the morning can keep your heart strong.
④ Stop to read that book, and go out and play.
⑤ The music the band is playing sounds good.

20 다음 문장에서 어법상 잘못된 부분을 찾아 바르게 고쳐 쓰시오.

(1) Mike denied to spend time with the bad people at that time.

_______________ ➡ _______________

(2) Break bad habits are not easy to do in a short period.

_______________ ➡ _______________

Reading

[21~23] 다음 글을 읽고, 물음에 답하시오.

#Selfie Facts

Are you interested ___ⓐ___ selfies? You probably like ⓑto post selfies ___ⓒ___ social media, but how (A)[many / much] do you know about selfies? Here are some (B)[boring / interesting] facts.

1. Robert Cornelius took the world's first selfie in 1839.
2. *Selfie* became a (C)[new / famous] word in the dictionary in 2013.
3. Buzz Aldrin took the first space selfie in 1966.

21 위 글의 빈칸 ⓐ와 ⓒ에 들어갈 전치사를 빈칸에 쓰시오.

ⓐ_______________ ⓒ_______________

22 위 글의 밑줄 친 ⓑto post와 to부정사의 용법이 같은 것을 고르시오.

① He has no friends to play with.
② He began to read the book.
③ This cell phone is easy to use.
④ I want something to write with.
⑤ I should be happy to go with you.

23 위 글의 괄호 (A)~(C)에서 문맥상 알맞은 낱말을 골라 쓰시오.

(A)__________ (B)__________ (C)__________

[24~26] 다음 글을 읽고, 물음에 답하시오.

#Selfie Survey

(A)Taking selfies is part of daily life for many teens, but do teens really enjoy it? To find out, we did a survey. We asked three questions to 300 students from ages 14 to 16. Let's look at the results.

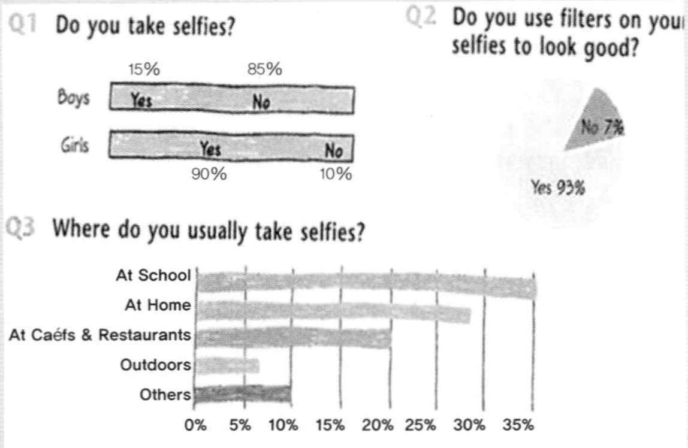

Surprisingly, ___ⓐ___ percent of the girls take selfies, but only ___ⓑ___ percent of the boys take selfies. Also, ___ⓒ___ percent of these students said that they use filters. The survey also showed that the students take selfies at school the most. Check out some of the students' comments.

Lewis, 14, England Selfies are awesome. Making silly faces is really fun!

Minwoo, 16, Korea I enjoy taking selfies, but some students spend too much time doing it.

Kate, 15, Denmark My pictures look good when I use filters. But sometimes my selfies don't look like me.

24 위 글의 밑줄 친 (A)Taking과 바꿔 쓸 수 있는 말을 쓰시오.

➡ _______________________

25 위 글의 빈칸 ⓐ~ⓒ에 들어갈 알맞은 숫자를 쓰시오.

ⓐ________ ⓑ________ ⓒ________

26 위 글의 내용과 일치하지 <u>않는</u> 것은?

① Lewis comments that selfies are amazing.
② Minwoo enjoys taking selfies.
③ Minwoo spends too much time taking selfies.
④ Kate's pictures look good when she uses filters.
⑤ Sometimes Kate's selfies don't look like her.

[27~28] 다음 글을 읽고, 물음에 답하시오.

You should follow etiquette for selfies. Ask yourself these questions before you take, post, or look at selfies.

1. Where am I?
   Choose appropriate places to take selfies. Don't take selfies in hospitals or public restrooms. It may bother other people.
2. Who can see this?
   Keep in mind that anyone can see your selfies. Choose carefully when you post them.
3. What kinds of comments should I leave?
   Leave nice comments on other people's selfies. Don't be rude.

27 위 글의 제목으로 알맞은 것을 고르시오.

① How to Ask Yourself Questions
② Selfie Etiquette
③ Selfie Facts
④ Have Fun with Your Selfies
⑤ Selfie Survey

28 위 글을 읽고 대답할 수 <u>없는</u> 질문은?

① What is the etiquette for selfies?
② When should you ask yourself the questions about etiquette for selfies?
③ Who can see your selfies?
④ Where should you post your selfies?
⑤ What kinds of comments should you leave on other people's selfies?

[29~30] 다음 글을 읽고, 물음에 답하시오.

Selfie __①__

- Robert Cornelius took the world's first selfie.
- ⓐ<u>*Selfie* became a new word in the dictionary in 2013.</u>
- Buzz Aldrin took the first space selfie.

Selfie __②__

- Do you take selfies?
- ⓑ<u>Do you use filters on your selfies looking good?</u>
- ⓒ<u>Where usually do you take selfies?</u>

Selfie __③__

- ⓓ<u>Choose appropriate places to take selfies.</u>
- Choose your selfies carefully when you post them.
- ⓔ<u>Leave nice comments on other people's selfies.</u>

29 위 글의 빈칸 ①~③에 들어갈 알맞은 말을 쓰시오.

ⓐ________ ⓑ________ ⓒ________

30 위 글의 밑줄 친 ⓐ~ⓔ 중 어법상 <u>틀린</u> 개수를 고르시오.

① 1개 ② 2개 ③ 3개 ④ 4개 ⑤ 5개

단원별 예상문제

출제율 95%

01 다음 〈보기〉와 같은 관계가 되도록 빈칸에 알맞은 말을 쓰시오.

보기

outdoors – indoors

(1) carelessly – ________

(2) correct – ________

출제율 85%

02 다음 제시된 의미에 맞는 단어를 주어진 철자로 시작하여 빈칸에 쓰고, 알맞은 것을 골라 문장을 완성하시오.

- a________: correct or suitable for a particular time, situation, or purpose
- p________: available for anyone to use
- r________: speaking or behaving in a way that is not polite and is likely to offend or annoy people

(1) ________ libraries are good for finding information.

(2) I didn't mean to be ________, but I had to leave early.

(3) I don't think jeans can be ________ for the party.

[03~04] 다음 밑줄 친 단어와 바꿔 쓸 수 있는 단어를 고르시오.

출제율 90%

03

The exam was <u>unexpectedly</u> easy.

① usually ② luckily ③ surprisingly ④ interestingly ⑤ strangely

출제율 100%

04

Charlie thinks that money will <u>deal with</u> all his problems.

① improve ② solve ③ decide ④ share ⑤ spend

출제율 90%

05 다음 중 의도하는 바가 나머지와 <u>다른</u> 하나는?

① May I eat snacks in the theater?
② Can I eat snacks in the theater?
③ Is it okay if I eat snacks in the theater?
④ Are you sure that I can eat snacks in the theater?
⑤ Do you mind my eating snacks in the theater?

출제율 90%

06 다음 주어진 문장의 뒤에 나올 대화의 순서를 알맞게 쓰시오.

What are you doing?
(A) That sounds fun! What are you interested in?
(B) Oh, I'm interested in photography, too.
(C) I'm interested in photography. I will talk about it tomorrow.
(D) Really? Then may I ask you for some advice for my presentation?
(E) I'm preparing for tomorrow's presentation. It is about one of my interests.

➡ ________________

[07~10] 다음 대화를 읽고, 물음에 답하시오.

G: Hi. (A)Can I go in now?
M: Sure. (①)
G: Here it is. (②) May I record the music in the concert hall?
M: No, you may not. (③)
G: Okay. May I take pictures of the band? (④)
M: ______(B)______ You can only take pictures in front of the concert hall. Please enjoy the concert. (⑤)
G: Oh, okay. Thank you.

출제율 85%

07 위 대화의 ①~⑤ 중 주어진 문장이 들어갈 알맞은 곳은?

Let me see your ticket, please.

① ② ③ ④ ⑤

출제율 95%

08 주어진 〈보기〉에서 (A)와 바꾸어 쓸 수 있는 것의 개수를 고르시오.

보기

May Will Should
Is it okay if Would it be all right if

① 1개 ② 2개 ③ 3개 ④ 4개 ⑤ 5개

출제율 100%

09 위 대화의 흐름상 빈칸 (B)에 들어갈 수 있는 말을 주어진 단어를 이용하여 쓰시오.

➡ ______________________________ (may)

출제율 95%

10 위 대화를 읽고 답할 수 없는 질문은?

① Where are they?
② What kind of music does the band play?
③ Is it possible to take pictures of the band?
④ Where can the girl take pictures?
⑤ Can the girl record the music in the concert hall?

[11~12] 다음 대화를 읽고, 물음에 답하시오.

B: Excuse me.
M: Hello. (①) What can I do for you?
B: May I borrow this new science book? (②)
M: No, you may not. (③)
B: Then may I copy some pages from the book? (④) I need them for my science report.
M: Yes, you may. (⑤) But please don't share them online.
B: Okay, I won't. Thank you!

출제율 95%

11 위 대화의 ①~⑤ 중 주어진 문장이 들어갈 알맞은 곳은?

Students can't take new books home.

① ② ③ ④ ⑤

출제율 85%

12 위 대화의 내용과 일치하지 않는 것을 모두 고르시오.

① 남자아이는 과학 보고서를 위해 책을 빌리는 것을 원했다.
② 남자아이는 과학 보고서에 필요한 새 책을 복사할 수 있다.
③ 남자아이는 복사한 것을 온라인에 공유해서는 안 된다.
④ 학생들은 책을 집에 가져갈 수 없다는 것이 원칙이다.
⑤ 남자아이는 과학에 관한 프레젠테이션이 내일 있다.

출제율 95%

13 다음 우리말과 같도록 빈칸에 알맞은 말을 쓰시오.

Kate는 웃을 때 사랑스럽게 보인다.
➡ Kate ________ ________ when she smiles.

출제율 95%

14 다음 중 어법상 자연스러운 문장은?

① He gave up to become a lawyer and decided to be a teacher.
② Breaking this wall looks almost impossible!
③ Practice to make eye contact with yourself in the mirror.
④ Eat strawberries is great!
⑤ Do you mind to park my car here?

출제율 90%

15 다음 문장에서 어법상 잘못된 부분을 찾아 바르게 고쳐 쓰시오.

(1) Read a story is exciting.
________ ➡ ________
(2) They are just watching each other without say a word.
________ ➡ ________
(3) I like chocolate cake because it tastes sweetly.
________ ➡ ________
(4) You always sound a broken record.
________ ➡ ________

[16~18] 다음 글을 읽고, 물음에 답하시오.

#Selfie Facts
Are you interested in selfies? You probably like to post selfies on social media, but how much do you know about selfies? Here are ⓐ some interesting facts.
1. Robert Cornelius ___ⓑ___ the world's first selfie in 1839.
2. *Selfie* became a new word in the dictionary in 2013.
3. Buzz Aldrin ___ⓒ___ the first space selfie in 1966.

출제율 95%

16 위 글의 밑줄 친 ⓐ가 가리키는 것을 우리말로 쓰시오.

(1) ________________
(2) ________________
(3) ________________

출제율 100%

17 위 글의 빈칸 ⓑ와 ⓒ에 공통으로 들어갈 알맞은 말을 고르시오.

① had ② took
③ kept ④ gave
⑤ did

출제율 90%

18 다음 문장에서 위 글의 내용과 다른 부분을 찾아서 고치시오.

There were many space selfies before 1966.

➡ ________________

[19~21] 다음 글을 읽고, 물음에 답하시오.

#Selfie Etiquette
You should follow etiquette for selfies. Ask yourself these questions before you take, post, or look at selfies.
1. Where am I?
Choose appropriate places to take selfies. Don't take selfies in hospitals or public restrooms. It may bother other people.
2. Who can see this?
Keep in mind that anyone can see your selfies. Choose carefully when you post them.
3. What kinds of comments should I leave?
Leave nice comments on other people's selfies. Don't be rude.
ⓐThat sounds easy, isn't that? Follow these tips and have fun with your selfies.

출제율 95%

19 위 글의 내용을 다음과 같이 정리하고자 한다. 빈칸 (A)와 (B)에 들어갈 알맞은 단어를 본문에서 찾아 쓰시오.

When you take selfies, there is ___(A)___ to follow. You should take, post, or look at selfies after asking yourself three ___(B)___ such as 'Where am I?', 'Who can see this?' and 'What kinds of comments should I leave?'

(A) ____________ (B) ____________

출제율 90%

20 다음 중 셀피 예절에 속하지 않는 것을 고르시오.

① 병원이나 공중 화장실에서는 셀피를 찍지 마라.
② 누구나 당신의 셀피를 볼 수 없도록 해야 한다는 것을 명심해라.
③ 셀피를 게시할 때는 신중하게 골라라.
④ 다른 사람들의 셀피에 상냥한 코멘트를 남겨라.
⑤ 무례하게 굴지 마라.

출제율 95%

21 위 글의 밑줄 친 ⓐ에서 어법상 틀린 부분을 찾아 고치시오.

____________ ➡ ____________

[22~23] 다음 글을 읽고, 물음에 답하시오.

What do you think about posting selfies?
Which do you agree with?
It is awesome and fun!
☑ It has some bad points.

Why? Some students use filters on their selfies too much. And they post the same selfies again and again. I think it's a ⓐwaste of time!

출제율 85%

22 위 글에서 셀피를 온라인상에 게시하는 행위에 대해 부정적으로 생각하는 이유 두 가지를 우리말로 쓰시오.

(1) ______________________________
(2) ______________________________
____

출제율 100%

23 위 글의 밑줄 친 ⓐwaste와 같은 의미로 쓰인 것을 고르시오.

① Don't waste your energy on them.
② We should recycle industrial waste.
③ I don't want to waste this opportunity.
④ It's a waste of money to buy it.
⑤ Waste water is pumped into the river.

서술형 실전문제

[01~03] 다음 대화를 읽고, 물음에 답하시오.

M: Hey, Yumi. What are you doing?
G: Hello, Mr. King. I'm preparing ___ⓐ___ tomorrow's presentation. It is about one ___ⓑ___ my interests.
M: That sounds fun! What are you interested ___ⓒ___?
G: I'm interested in photography. I will talk ___ⓓ___ it tomorrow.
M: Oh, I'm interested ___(A)___, too.
G: Really? Then 제 발표에 대해 몇 가지 조언을 부탁해도 될까요?(may, some, advice)
M: Sure.

01 위 대화의 빈칸 ⓐ~ⓓ에 들어갈 전치사를 〈보기〉에서 찾아 쓰시오.

보기

about of in for

ⓐ______ ⓑ______ ⓒ______ ⓓ______

02 위 대화의 빈칸 (A)에 들어갈 알맞은 어구를 본문에서 찾아 쓰시오.

➡ ____________________

03 위 대화의 밑줄 친 우리말을 주어진 단어를 이용해 영어로 옮기시오.

➡ ____________________

중요

04 다음 문장에서 어법상 잘못된 부분을 찾아 바르게 고쳐 쓰시오.

(1) Watch sports is fun.
______ ➡ ______

(2) Keep to do it until the sugar stops completely melting.
______ ➡ ______

(3) Her wish was become a friend of animals.
______ ➡ ______

(4) On arrive in Tokyo, I called him.
______ ➡ ______

(5) My pictures look nicely when I use filters.
______ ➡ ______

(6) Some say the coffee beans smell sweet chocolate.
______ ➡ ______

05 다음 우리말을 주어진 어구를 이용하여 영작하시오.

(1) 영어를 배우는 것은 재미있다. (interesting) (4 단어)
➡ ____________________

(2) 학생들은 컴퓨터 게임을 하는 데 너무 많은 시간을 보낸다. (spend, do computer games) (8 단어)
➡ ____________________

(3) 그녀는 그 소식을 듣고 얼굴이 창백해졌다. (turn, pale, at) (7 단어)
➡ ____________________

(4) 그 과일은 딸기 같은 맛이 나지 않았다. (fruit, strawberries) (6 단어)
➡ ____________________

(5) 그것들은 아주 부드럽고 따뜻하게 느껴졌다. (they, so, soft, warm) (6 단어)
➡ ____________________

중요
06 다음 주어진 대화의 내용과 일치하도록 빈칸을 알맞게 채워 대화를 요약하는 문장을 완성하시오.

> **Ella:** Your computer game is very loud. I can't study at all. I have a test tomorrow.
> **Eric:** Sorry. I will turn off my computer.

➡ Eric will stop ____________________.

[07~08] 다음 글을 읽고, 물음에 답하시오.

> Lewis, 14, England Selfies are awesome. Making silly faces is really fun!
> Minwoo, 16, Korea I enjoy taking selfies, but some students spend too much time ⓐdoing it.
> Kate, 15, Denmark ⓑ내 사진들은 필터를 사용할 때 좋아 보인다. But sometimes my selfies don't look like me.

중요
07 위 글의 밑줄 친 ⓐdoing it이 가리키는 것을 본문에서 찾아 쓰시오.

➡ ____________________

08 위 글의 밑줄 친 ⓑ의 우리말에 맞게 한 단어를 보충하여, 주어진 어휘를 알맞게 배열하시오.

> look / I / pictures / filters / use / my / when

➡ ______________________________

[09~11] 다음 글을 읽고, 물음에 답하시오.

> #Selfie Etiquette
> You should follow etiquette for selfies. Ask yourself these questions before you take, post, or look at selfies.
> 1. Where am I?
> Choose (A)[appropriate / unsuitable] places to take selfies. Don't take selfies in hospitals or public restrooms. ⓐIt may (B)[bother / encourage] other people.
> 2. Who can see this?
> Keep in mind that anyone can see your selfies. Choose carefully when you post them.
> 3. What kinds of comments should I leave?
> Leave nice comments on other people's selfies. Don't be (C)[polite / rude].
> That sounds easy, doesn't it? Follow these tips and ⓑhave fun with your selfies.

중요
09 위 글의 괄호 (A)~(C)에서 문맥상 알맞은 낱말을 골라 쓰시오.

(A)________ (B)________ (C)________

10 위 글의 밑줄 친 ⓐIt이 가리키는 것을 본문의 단어를 이용하여 쓰시오. (필요한 경우 형태를 바꾸시오.)

➡ ______________________________
____

11 위 글의 밑줄 친 ⓑhave fun과 바꿔 쓸 수 있는 말을 쓰시오.

➡ ______________________________

창의사고력 서술형 문제

01 다음 그림을 참고하여 관심사를 묻고, 갈 장소를 권유하는 대화를 완성하시오.

A: ______________________________

B: I'm interested in historical works of art.

A: ____

B: Sounds good. ______________________________ there?

A: ______________________________

02 다음 A와 B에 주어진 어휘를 한 번씩만 사용하여 〈보기〉와 같은 형식의 문장을 완성하시오.

보기

That sounds interesting.

A: feel, look, sound, smell, taste

B: nervous, happy, good, terrible, sweet

(1) ____

(2) ____

(3) ____

(4) ____

(5) ____

03 인터넷 사용 규칙과 그 규칙을 만든 이유를 바탕으로 건강한 인터넷을 만들도록 권유하는 글을 쓰시오.

Rules	Reasons
We should follow language rules.	Because people may not understand us.
We should post true information.	Because people may believe our incorrect information.
We shouldn't leave rude comments.	Because we can hurt others' feelings.

When we use the internet, we should follow some rules. Then we can enjoy the internet more. First of all, we should follow (A)________________ because people may not understand us. Also, we should post only true information. People may believe our (B)________ information. (C)________, we should not leave rude comments. We can hurt others' feelings. Keep these rules (D)________________. Then you will be a great internet user!

단원별 모의고사

01 다음 밑줄 친 단어와 바꿔 쓸 수 <u>없는</u> 단어를 고르시오.

> This school is <u>awesome</u> and I like my classmates, too.

① amazing ② terrific
③ fantastic ④ terrible
⑤ great

02 다음 짝지어진 두 단어의 관계가 <u>다른</u> 하나를 고르시오.

① rude – polite ② finally – lastly
③ bother – annoy ④ comment – remark
⑤ advice – tip

03 다음 우리말과 일치하도록 빈칸을 채우시오. (주어진 철자가 있을 경우 주어진 철자로 시작할 것)

(1) 궁중 예절에 관한 모든 것을 배울 수 있을 것이다.
➡ You ________ be ________ to learn all about court e________.

(2) 그것은 흥미로운 질문이다.
➡ That's ________ ________ ________.

(3) 나는 새 옷 쇼핑하는 것을 즐긴다.
➡ I ________ ________ for new ________.

(4) 우리가 새 카펫을 고르는 데 많은 시간이 걸렸다.
➡ It took us a ________ of time to ________ a new carpet.

04 <보기>의 어휘를 사용하여 문장을 완성하시오. (형태 변화 가능)

> 보기
> agree spend sound look

(1) The twins ________ at each other and smiled.
(2) That ________ wonderful.
(3) I'm afraid I don't ________ with that.
(4) I think you ________ too much time playing computer games.

05 다음 대화의 괄호 (A)~(C)에서 알맞은 것을 골라 쓰시오.

> **A:** What are you interested in?
> **B:** I'm interested in (A)[animals / movies / music / books].
> **A:** (B)[Which / Why / How / What] don't you go to a theater this weekend?
> **B:** Sounds good. May I (C)[take photos of the paintings / eat snacks / feed the birds / record the music] there?
> **A:** No, you may not.

(A)________ (B)________ (C)________

[06~08] 다음 대화를 읽고, 물음에 답하시오.

> **B:** Excuse me.
> **M:** Hello. ①<u>What can I do for you?</u>
> **B:** May I <u>(A)</u> this new science book?
> **M:** No, you may not. ②<u>Students can take new books home.</u>
> **B:** Then may I <u>(B)</u> some pages from the book? ③<u>I need them for my science report.</u>
> **M:** Yes, you may. ④<u>But please don't share them online.</u>
> **B:** ⑤<u>Okay, I won't.</u> Thank you!

06 위의 대화는 도서관에서 이루어지는 것이다. (A)와 (B)에 들어갈 단어를 〈보기〉에서 골라 쓰시오.

보기

advise spend borrow solve hurt copy

(A)________ (B)________

07 주어진 영영풀이에 해당하는 단어를 대화에서 찾아 쓰시오.

to have or use something with other people

➡ ____________________

08 위 대화의 밑줄 친 ①~⑤ 중 흐름상 어색한 것을 고르시오.

① ② ③ ④ ⑤

[09~10] 다음 대화를 읽고, 물음에 답하시오.

A: What are you interested in?
B: ____(A)____ What about you?
A: ____(B)____
B: 우리는 둘 다 소셜 미디어에 관심이 있어.

09 A와 B의 관심을 나타낸 그림을 보고 빈칸 (A)와 (B)에 알맞은 말을 쓰시오.

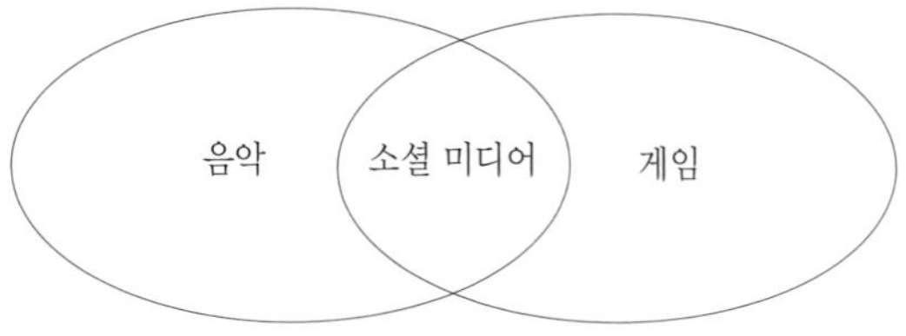

(A) ______________________________

(B) ______________________________

10 위 대화의 밑줄 친 우리말을 영작하시오.

➡ ______________________________

[11~12] 다음 대화를 읽고, 물음에 답하시오.

G: Hi. Can I go in now?
M: Sure. Let me see your ticket, please.
G: Here it is. May I record the music ____(A)____ the concert hall?
M: No, you may not.
G: Okay. 밴드의 사진을 찍어도 될까요? (pictures, of, I, the band, may, take ?)
M: No, you may not. You can only take pictures ____(B)____ front of the concert hall. Please enjoy the concert.
G: Oh, okay. Thank you.

11 위 대화의 밑줄 친 우리말에 맞게 주어진 어구를 바르게 배열하시오.

➡ ______________________________

12 위 대화의 빈칸 (A)와 (B)에 공통으로 들어갈 전치사를 쓰시오.

➡ ____________________

13 다음 중 어법상 어색한 것은?

① Did you enjoy playing soccer with your friends after school?
② Cooking is a useful hobby.
③ I'm proud of win the prize.
④ May I have dinner after I finish reading this book?
⑤ Harold didn't like to clean his room.

14 다음 빈칸에 공통으로 들어갈 수 없는 것은?

- Angelina ________ lonely.
- It ________ soft.

① is ② seems ③ feels
④ wants ⑤ looks

15 다음 〈보기〉의 밑줄 친 말과 용법이 다른 하나는?

보기
Harry enjoyed playing soccer with his friends after school.

① Some students practiced playing soccer.
② Speaking a foreign language is difficult.
③ Marianne is good at singing.
④ His dream is traveling around the world.
⑤ She saw her daughter swimming in the pool.

16 다음 그림을 참고하여 빈칸에 알맞은 말을 쓰시오.

This hotel room smells ________ ________ ________.

17 다음 문장에서 어법상 어색한 부분을 찾아 바르게 고쳐 다시 쓰시오.

(1) My pictures look beautifully when I use filters.
➡ ____________________

(2) Stop play games and be sincere.
➡ ____________________

[18~19] 다음 글을 읽고, 물음에 답하시오.

#Selfie Facts
Are you interested in selfies? You probably like ⓐto post selfies on social media, but how much do you know about selfies? Here are some interesting facts.

18 위 글의 밑줄 친 ⓐto post와 바꿔 쓸 수 있는 단어를 쓰시오.

➡ ____________________

19 위 글의 뒤에 올 내용으로 가장 알맞은 것을 고르시오.

① 소셜 미디어의 발전
② 셀피에 관한 몇 가지 재미있는 사실들
③ 셀피에 대한 사람들의 반응
④ 셀피에 많은 시간을 보내는 사람들
⑤ 소셜 미디어에 셀피를 게시하는 법

[20~22] 다음 글을 읽고, 물음에 답하시오.

#Selfie Survey
Taking selfies is part of daily life for many teens, but do teens really enjoy it? To find out, we did a survey. We asked three questions to 300 students from ages 14 to 16. Let's look at the results.

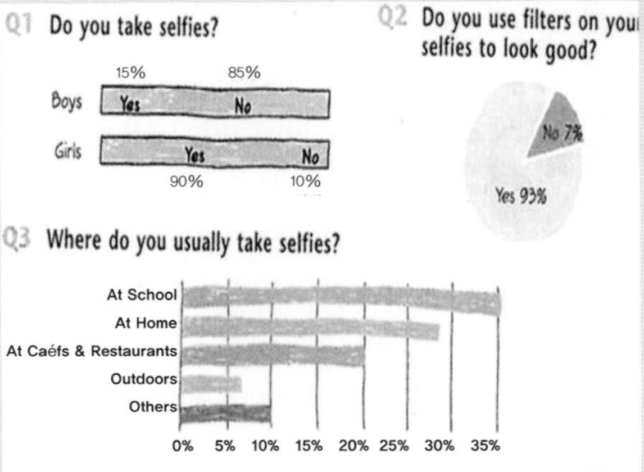

Surprisingly, 90 percent of the girls take selfies, but only 15 percent of the boys take selfies. Also, 93 percent of these students said that they use filters. The survey also showed that the students take selfies at school the most. Check out some of the students' ___ⓐ___.

Lewis, 14, England　Selfies are (A)[awful / awesome]. Making silly faces is really fun!

Minwoo, 16, Korea　I enjoy taking selfies, but some students spend too much time doing it.

Kate, 15, Denmark　My pictures look (B)[good / well] when I use filters. But sometimes my selfies don't look (C)[at / like] me.

20 위 글의 빈칸 ⓐ에 들어갈 알맞은 말을 고르시오.

① reports　② comments
③ articles　④ essays
⑤ summaries

21 위 글의 괄호 (A)~(C)에서 문맥상 알맞은 낱말을 골라 쓰시오.

(A)________ (B)________ (C)________

22 위 도표의 내용과 일치하지 <u>않는</u> 것은?

① 85 percent of the boys don't take selfies.
② 10 percent of the girls don't take selfies.
③ 7 percent of the girls don't use filters on their selfies.
④ More than one third of the students take selfies at school.
⑤ There are much more students who take selfies at home than those who do so outdoors.

[23~25] 다음 글을 읽고, 물음에 답하시오.

#Selfie Etiquette

You should follow etiquette for selfies. ⓐ <u>Ask yourself these questions after you take, post, or look at selfies.</u>

1. Where am I?
   Choose appropriate places to take selfies. Don't take selfies in hospitals or public restrooms. It may bother other people.
2. Who can see it?
   ⓑ<u>Keep in mind that anyone can see your selfies.</u> Choose carefully when you post them.
3. What kinds of comments should I leave?
   Leave nice comments on other people's selfies. Don't be rude.

That sounds easy, doesn't it? Follow these ⓒ <u>tips</u> and have fun with your selfies.

23 위 글의 밑줄 친 ⓐ에서 문맥상 낱말의 쓰임이 적절하지 <u>않은</u> 것을 찾아 알맞게 고치시오.

____________ ➡ ____________

24 위 글의 밑줄 친 ⓑ를 다음과 같이 바꿔 쓸 때 빈칸에 알맞은 말을 쓰시오.

Be sure to ________ that anyone can see your selfies.

25 위 글의 밑줄 친 ⓒ<u>tips</u>와 <u>다른</u> 의미로 쓰인 것을 고르시오.

① Give me some <u>tips</u> for buying a computer.
② He gave the waiters generous <u>tips</u>.
③ Can you tell me useful <u>tips</u> on how to save money?
④ You should take my <u>tips</u> for a race.
⑤ I want to get good <u>tips</u> on the trip.

Lesson **2**

Eat Right, Be Happy!

의사소통 기능

- 충고하기
  You'd better eat breakfast every day.
- 추천 요청하고 답하기
  A: What do you recommend?
  B: I recommend the pizza.

언어 형식

- 주격 관계대명사
  What do students **who** live in other countries eat for lunch?
  A plantain is a fruit **which** looks like a banana.
- 빈도 부사
  We **usually** eat a salad as an appetizer.

교과서

Words & Expressions

Key Words

- □ **add** [æd] 동 더하다
- □ **also** [ɔ́:lsou] 부 또한
- □ **always** [ɔ́:lweiz] 부 항상
- □ **appetizer** [ǽpitàizer] 명 식전 음식
- □ **as** [æz] 전 ~로서
- □ **balanced** [bǽlənst] 형 균형이 잡힌
- □ **bean** [bi:n] 명 콩
- □ **breakfast** [brékfəst] 명 아침 식사
- □ **British** [brítiʃ] 형 영국의
- □ **carrot** [kǽrət] 명 당근
- □ **celebrate** [séləbrèit] 동 축하하다, 기념하다
- □ **choice** [tʃɔis] 명 선택, 종류
- □ **common** [kámən] 형 흔한
- □ **contest** [kántest] 명 대회, 콘테스트
- □ **culture** [kʌltʃər] 명 문화
- □ **curry** [kə́:ri] 명 카레
- □ **delicious** [dilíʃəs] 형 맛있는
- □ **drop** [drap] 동 떨어뜨리다
- □ **Eastern** [í:stərn] 형 동양의
- □ **else** [els] 형 그 밖의, 다른
- □ **enough** [inʌf] 형 충분한
- □ **especially** [ispéʃəli] 부 특히
- □ **exercise** [éksərsàiz] 동 운동하다
- □ **fresh** [freʃ] 형 신선한
- □ **fried** [fraid] 형 튀겨진
- □ **fry** [frai] 동 튀기다
- □ **grocery** [gróusəri] 명 식료품
- □ **have** [həv] 동 먹다
- □ **health** [helθ] 명 건강
- □ **healthy** [hélθi] 형 건강에 좋은
- □ **include** [inklú:d] 동 포함하다
- □ **Indian** [índiən] 형 인도의
- □ **instead** [instéd] 부 대신에
- □ **less** [les] (양 · 정도가) 더 적은
- □ **local** [lóukəl] 형 현지의, 지역의
- □ **main dish** 주요리
- □ **meat** [mi:t] 명 고기, 육류
- □ **mixed** [mikst] 형 섞인, 복합된
- □ **more** [mɔ:r] 형 더 큰, 더 많은
- □ **noodle** [nú:dl] 명 국수
- □ **often** [ɔ́:fən] 부 종종, 자주
- □ **onion** [ʌnjən] 명 양파
- □ **order** [ɔ́:rdər] 동 주문하다
- □ **other** [ʌðər] 형 다른
- □ **paella** [paielə] 명 파엘라(쌀, 닭고기, 생선, 채소를 넣은 스페인 요리)
- □ **part** [pa:rt] 명 부분
- □ **pho** [fou] 명 포(베트남 쌀국수)
- □ **plantain** [plǽntən] 명 열대의 파초속(屬)의 일종; 그 과실(**cooking banana**)
- □ **recommend** [rékəménd] 동 추천하다
- □ **rule** [ru:l] 명 규칙
- □ **serve** [sə:rv] 동 음식물을 제공하다[권하다]
- □ **side dish** 반찬
- □ **slowly** [slóuli] 부 천천히
- □ **sometimes** [sʌmtàimz] 부 가끔, 때때로
- □ **Spanish** [spǽniʃ] 형 스페인의
- □ **special** [spéʃəl] 형 특별한
- □ **suggestion** [səgdʒéstʃən] 명 제안
- □ **sweet** [swi:t] 형 달콤한, 단
- □ **sweets** [swi:ts] 명 단 음식, 단것
- □ **tired** [taiərd] 형 피곤한
- □ **traditional** [trədíʃənl] 형 전통적인
- □ **turkey** [tə́:rki] 명 칠면조
- □ **usually** [jú:ʒuəli] 부 보통, 대개
- □ **vegetable** [védʒətəbl] 명 야채
- □ **Vietnamese** [viètnə:mí:z] 형 베트남의
- □ **Western** [wéstərn] 형 서양의

Key Expressions

- □ **a lot of** 많은
- □ **at least** 적어도, 최소한
- □ **at the end of** ~의 끝에
- □ **be ready to** 동사원형 ~할 준비가 되다
- □ **both A and B** A와 B 둘 다
- □ **check out** 확인하다, 조사하다
- □ **come from** ~에서 나오다, ~ 출신이다
- □ **come with** ~와 함께 나오다, ~이 딸려 있다
- □ **feel like** ~ ~하게 느끼다
- □ **for a long time** 오랫동안
- □ **get a cold** 감기에 걸리다
- □ **get a discount** 할인받다
- □ **had better** 동사원형 ~하는 것이 좋다[낫다]
- □ **have** ~ **in common** 공통으로 ~을 가지다
- □ **heat** ~ **up** ~을 덥히다
- □ **How about** (동)명사~? ~은 어때?
- □ **put A in B**: A를 B에 넣다
- □ **stay at** ~에 머무르다
- □ **such as** ~와 같은
- □ **take care of** ~을 돌보다
- □ **taste** 형용사 ~한 맛이 나다
- □ **thank** (**you**) **for** ~에 대해 감사하다
- □ **these days** 요즘, 최근
- □ **throw away** 버리다
- □ **try** + 음식 음식을 먹어 보다, 맛을 보다
- □ **win an award** 상을 받다

Words Power

※ 서로 반대되는 뜻을 가진 단어

- □ **add**(더하다) ↔ **subtract**(빼다)
- □ **different**(다른) ↔ **same**(같은)
- □ **fresh**(신선한) ↔ **rotten**(상한, 부패한)
- □ **less**((양 · 정도가) 더 적은) ↔ **more**(더 큰, 더 많은)
- □ **common**(흔한) ↔ **rare**(희귀한, 드문)
- □ **part**(부분) ↔ **whole**(전체)
- □ **include**(포함하다) ↔ **exclude**(배제하다)
- □ **Eastern**(동양의) ↔ **Western**(서양의)

※ 서로 비슷한 뜻을 가진 단어

- □ **celebrate**(축하하다, 기념하다) : **congratulate**(축하하다)
- □ **delicious**(맛있는) : **tasty**(맛있는)
- □ **exercise**(운동하다) : **work out**(운동하다)
- □ **enough**(충분한) : **sufficient**(충분한)

※ 요리와 관련된 동사

□ **add**(더하다) □ **bake**(굽다) □ **boil**(끓이다) □ **chop**(자르다) □ **cut**(자르다)
□ **fry**(튀기다) □ **mix**(섞다)

English Dictionary

□ **appetizer** 식전 음식
→ a small dish that you eat before a meal
식사 전에 먹는 적은 요리

□ **breakfast** 아침 식사
→ the meal you have in the morning 아침에 먹는 식사

□ **common** 흔한
→ happening often and to many people or in many places 자주 그리고 많은 사람이나 장소에서 발생하는

□ **contest** 대회, 콘테스트
→ a competition or a situation in which two or more people or groups are competing with each other
대회나 둘 또는 그 이상의 사람이나 그룹이 서로 경쟁하는 상황

□ **fried** 튀겨진
→ having been cooked in hot oil 뜨거운 기름 안에서 요리되는

□ **grocery** 식료품
→ food and other goods that are sold by a grocer or a supermarket
식료품 잡화상이나 슈퍼마켓에 의해서 팔려지는 음식이나 다른 상품들

□ **local** 현지의, 지역의
→ relating to the particular area you live in, or the area you are talking about 당신이 살고 있는 특정한 지역과 관련 있는 아니면 당신이 얘기하고 있는 장소

□ **mixed** 섞인, 복합된
→ consisting of several different types of things or people 몇몇의 다른 종류의 사물이나 사람으로 구성되어 있는

□ **noodle** 국수
→ a long thin piece of food made from a mixture of flour, water, and eggs, usually cooked in soup or boiling water
밀가루, 물, 달걀의 혼합물로 만들어진 보통 국이나 끓는 물에서 요리되는 길고 얇은 음식의 조각

□ **order** 주문하다
→ to ask for food or a drink in a restaurant, bar etc.
식당이나 술집에서 음식이나 음료를 요청하다

□ **recommend** 추천하다
→ to advise someone to do something, especially because you have special knowledge of a situation or subject 특히 당신이 그 상황이나 주제에 대한 특별한 지식을 갖고 있기 때문에 누군가에게 무엇을 하라고 조언하다

□ **serve** 음식물을 제공하다
→ to give someone food or drink, especially as part of a meal or in a restaurant, bar etc. 식당이나 술집 등에서 특히 식사의 일부분으로 누군가에게 음식이나 음료를 주다

□ **suggestion** 제안
→ an idea, plan, or possibility that someone mentions, or the act of mentioning it 누군가가 언급한 생각, 계획, 가능성이나 그것을 언급하는 행동

□ **sweets** 단 음식, 단것
→ a small piece of sweet food made of sugar or chocolate 설탕이나 초콜릿으로 만들어진 작은 조각의 단 음식

□ **tired** 피곤한
→ feeling that you want to sleep or rest
자거나 쉬기를 원하는 감정

□ **usually** 보통, 대개
→ used to talk about what happens on most occasions or in most situations
어떤 일이 대부분의 경우나 상황에서 벌어지는 것을 언급할 때 쓰이는

□ **vegetable** 야채
→ a plant that is eaten raw or cooked, such as a cabbage, a carrot, or peas 예를 들어 양배추, 당근 또는 완두콩 같은 날것으로 먹거나 요리해 먹는 식물

□ **Western** 서양의
→ in or from the west of a country or area
어떤 나라나 지역의 서쪽에서 또는 서쪽으로부터

서답형

[01~02] 다음 <보기>와 같은 관계가 되도록 주어진 빈칸에 알맞은 말을 쓰시오. (주어진 철자로 시작할 것)

01

보기

Korea - Korean

(1) tradition – ____________

(2) Vietnam – ____________

02

보기

suggest - suggestion

(1) choose – ____________

(2) arrive – ____________

서답형

03 다음 우리말에 맞게 주어진 단어를 이용해 빈칸을 완성하시오.

학교는 건강에 좋은 음식만을 제공하려고 애쓴다.

➡ The school tries to offer only ________ food. (health)

중요

04 다음 중 밑줄 친 부분의 뜻풀이가 바르지 않은 것은?

① I help the students to fry onions. (튀기다)

② I recommend this book to anyone with an interest in animation. (추천하다)

③ I chose this coat because the other ones were all too expensive. (다른)

④ Women usually live longer than men. (종종, 자주)

⑤ We had bacon and eggs for breakfast. (아침 식사)

[05~06] 다음 빈칸에 들어갈 말로 적절한 것을 고르시오.

05

Vitamin A is found in liver and green ____________.

① vegetables ② meat

③ flower ④ carrot

⑤ meal

중요

06

I will be in a speech ________ tomorrow.

① contest ② concert

③ content ④ compete

⑤ prize

07 다음 밑줄 친 부분과 의미가 가장 가까운 것을 고르시오.

Trying new foods is an exciting experience.

① Touching ② Turning

③ Tasting ④ Smelling

⑤ Chewing

서답형

08 다음 빈칸에 들어갈 알맞은 단어를 <보기>에서 찾아 쓰시오. (형태 변화 가능)

보기

slowly more often

(1) You'll have to be ________ careful next time.

(2) How ________ do you see your parents?

(3) She spoke ________, choosing her words carefully.

중요
[01~02] 다음 빈칸에 공통으로 들어갈 말을 쓰시오.

01

- Bad dreams are fairly ________ among children.
- All successful people have one thing in ________.

02

- When I ________ a cold, I often blow my nose.
- Children and seniors can ________ a discount of 3 dollars.

중요
03 다음 주어진 우리말에 맞게 빈칸을 채우시오. (철자가 주어진 것도 있음)

(1) It's Dad's birthday and we're ________ out for a meal to c________. (오늘은 아빠의 생일이야, 그래서 우리는 축하하기 위해 외식할 거야.)
(2) Have I given you ________ ________? (내가 너에게 충분한 돈을 주었니?)
(3) ________ ________ and ________ provide fiber and vitamins. (신선한 과일과 채소는 섬유질과 비타민을 제공한다.)

04 다음 짝지어진 두 단어의 관계가 같도록 빈칸에 알맞은 말을 쓰시오.

(1) high : low = rare : ________
(2) awesome : wonderful = sufficient : ________

중요
05 다음 영영풀이에 해당하는 단어를 골라 빈칸에 쓰시오.

보기: sweets celebrate contest cookies

(1) a competition or a situation in which two or more people or groups are competing with each other
➡ ____________
(2) a small piece of sweet food made of sugar or chocolate
➡ ____________

06 다음 문장의 빈칸에 알맞은 것을 〈보기〉에서 찾아 쓰시오.

보기: side dish grocery onion suggestion

(1) Can I order the potatoes as a ________ ________?
(2) Are you all happy with his ________?
(3) Chop the ________ finely.
(4) He started to work at a ________ store.

07 다음 우리말에 맞게 주어진 어구를 바르게 배열하시오.

(1) 너는 내가 케이크를 자르기를 원하니?
(me, the cake, do, to, cut, want, you ?)
➡ ______________________________
(2) 나는 항상 파리에 가기를 원해 왔다.
(wanted, Paris, I've, to, always, to, go)
➡ ______________________________

교과서

Conversation

1 충고하기

You'd better eat breakfast every day. 너는 매일 아침밥을 먹는 게 좋아.

- 'had better + 동사원형'은 '~하는 게 좋겠다'라는 의미로 상대방에게 충고나 조언을 하는 표현이다.
- 충고하는 말에 대답할 경우, 상대방의 충고에 대해 고마움을 표현하거나 자신의 생각을 덧붙여 대답할 수 있다.

충고하기

- You'd better + 동사원형. ~하는 게 좋겠다.
- (I think) you should + 동사원형 ~.
- Maybe you should + 동사원형 ~.
- Why don't you ~?

- 'I think you should + 동사원형~.'에서 think 다음에 접속사 that이 생략되어 있다. should는 도덕적 의무를 이야기할 때 사용하는 조동사로 must, have to에 비해 일상 회화 표현에서 자주 사용한다.

충고의 말에 답하기

- That's a good idea. 좋은 생각이다.
- I guess I should. 그래야 할 것 같아.
- OK, I will. Thanks. 그렇게 할게. 고마워

핵심 Check

1. 다음 우리말과 일치하도록 빈칸에 알맞은 말을 쓰시오.

A: ________ ________ stop watching TV ________ going to bed. (너는 잠자리에 들기 전에 TV를 그만 보는 게 좋겠다.)

B: Okay, ________ try. Thanks. (좋아, 노력할게. 고마워.)

2. 다음 대화의 순서를 바르게 배열하시오.

(A) Fast food is not good. You'd better eat healthy food.

(B) How often do you eat fast food?

(C) Okay, I will.

(D) Three times a week.

➡ ______________________________

2 추천 요청하고 답하기

A What do you recommend? 무엇을 추천하시겠어요?

B I recommend the pizza. 저는 피자를 추천합니다.

- recommend(추천하다)를 사용하여 추천을 요청하고 대답할 수 있다. What do you recommend?는 '무엇을 추천하시겠어요?'라는 의미로 추천을 요청하는 표현이다.

추천 요청하기

- What do you recommend?
- What would you recommend?
- What 명사 do you recommend?
- Which 명사 do you recommend?
- Do you have any recommendations?
- Can[Could] you recommend ~?

추천 요청에 답하기

- I [strongly] recommend ~.
- I'd like to recommend ~.
- I suggest ~.
- I advise ~.
- ~ is recommended.

recommend

- 주어 recommend 명사 ~.
  ex) I recommend a sandwich for lunch. (나는 점심식사로 샌드위치를 추천한다.)
- 주어 recommend (that) 주어 동사 ~.
  ex) I recommend (that) you should consult your doctor. (나는 네가 의사와 상담하기를 권고한다.)
  = It is recommended (that) you should consult your doctor.

핵심 Check

3. 다음 우리말과 일치하도록 빈칸에 알맞은 말을 쓰시오.

A: Can ________ ________ any good Chinese restaurants near here? (이 근처에 좋은 중국 음식점 있으면 추천해 주시겠어요?)

B: ________ is one next to the bank. (은행 옆에 하나 있어요.)

4. 다음 우리말과 일치하도록 빈칸에 알맞은 말을 쓰시오.

A: ________________________________ (어떤 운동을 추천하시겠어요?)

B: ________________________________ hiking. (나는 하이킹을 강력히 추천합니다.)

5. 다음 주어진 단어를 이용하여 대화를 완성하시오.

A: ________________________________ (recommend, you, book, do, what)

B: ________________________________ (this, like, book, I'd, to, recommend)

A. Listen and Talk 1 A

G: I think ❶I eat too many ❷sweets ❸these days.
B: ❹That's not good for your health. ❺You'd better eat fruit instead.

G: 나 요즘 단 걸 너무 많이 먹는 것 같아.
B: 그건 건강에 좋지 않아. 대신에 과일을 먹는 게 좋아.

❶ think와 I 사이에는 접속사 that이 생략되어 있다.
❷ sweets: 단 음식, 단것
❸ these days: 요즘, 최근
❹ That은 앞 문장의 내용인 eating too many sweets를 가리킨다. be good for: ~에 좋다 health: 건강
❺ You'd better ~. = You had better ~. : ~하는 게 좋겠다. had better 다음에는 동사원형이 나와야 한다. instead: 대신에

Check(√) True or False

(1) The girl likes to eat fruit. T ☐ F ☐

(2) The girl will eat sweets a lot. T ☐ F ☐

B. Listen and Talk 1 B

G: You ❶look very tired today. Didn't you sleep well?
B: Yes, I did. But I ❷often feel tired these days, ❸especially in the morning.
G: Do you usually eat breakfast?
B: No, I don't.
G: You'd better eat breakfast. Breakfast ❹gives you energy.
B: I didn't know that. Do you have ❺any other suggestions?
G: Well, you ❻should also exercise every day. That will help you.
B: Okay. I will.

G: 너 오늘 매우 피곤해 보인다. 잠을 잘 못 잤니?
B: 아니, 잘 잤어. 그런데, 나 요즘 자주, 특히 아침에 쉽게 피곤해져.
G: 너 아침밥을 주로 먹니?
B: 아니, 먹지 않아.
G: 아침밥을 먹는 게 좋아. 아침밥은 너한테 힘을 주거든.
B: 나 그건 몰랐어. 또 다른 제안 해 줄 것 있니?
G: 음, 너는 또한 매일 운동해야 해. 그게 도움이 될 거야.
B: 알겠어. 그럴게.

❶ look + 형용사: ~하게 보이다 tired: 피곤한
❷ 빈도부사는 일반동사의 앞에, be동사와 조동사의 뒤에 위치한다. often: 종종, 자주
❸ especially: 특히 in the morning: 아침에
❹ give는 4형식 동사로 간접목적어(~에게), 직접목적어(~을, 를)를 취한다. give you energy: 너에게 에너지를 주다
❺ any other: 어떤 다른 suggestion: 제안
❻ should + 동사원형: ~해야 한다

Check(√) True or False

(3) The boy slept well but didn't eat breakfast. T ☐ F ☐

(4) The girl knows that breakfast is important. T ☐ F ☐

Listen and Talk 1 C

G: Justin, our school cooking ❶contest is tomorrow. ❷What are you going to make?
B: I'm going to make sandwiches.
G: What do you want to put in ❸them?
B: Chicken, cheese, and eggs.
G: You'd better ❹put vegetables in your sandwiches. How about onions and carrots?
B: No, I'm not going to ❺add them. I don't like ❻those vegetables.
G: That's not a good idea. Mr. Kim said we should make ❼healthy food for the contest.
B: You're right. I should go ❽grocery shopping and buy onions and carrots.

❶ contest: 대회, 콘테스트(= competition)
❷ be going to 동사원형: ~할 것이다
❸ them은 sandwiches를 지칭한다.
❹ put A in B: A를 B에 넣다
❺ add: 더하다. them은 onions and carrots를 가리킨다.
❻ vegetables가 복수형이므로 that이 아니라 those를 사용해야 한다.
❼ healthy: 건강에 좋은
❽ grocery: 식료품

Listen and Talk 2 A

G: ❶It's my first time here. ❷What do you recommend?
M: I recommend ❸the pizza and salad.

❶ It's my first time here: 저 여기 처음 왔어요.
❷ What do you recommend?: 무엇을 추천해 주시겠어요? recommend: 추천하다
❸ pizza: 피자 salad: 샐러드

Listen and Talk 2 B

B: Good morning, Jiwoo. ❶What are you doing right now?
G: I'm ❷searching for a restaurant for my class party.
B: Wow! When is the party?
G: It's next Friday. We ❸want to go to Bella's Restaurant, but ❹it is too expensive.
B: ❺Why don't you check out Chang's Restaurant? I ❻went there once. The food and prices were good.
G: Sounds great. What do you recommend there?
B: I recommend the noodle soup.
G: ❼I think we should go there. Thank you.

❶ are doing은 현재진행형(be동사의 현재형+동사ing)으로 '~하고 있다'라는 뜻이다. What are you doing?: 너는 무엇을 하고 있니?
❷ search for: ~를 찾다
❸ want+to부정사: ~하기를 원하다 go to 장소: ~에 가다
❹ it = Bella's Restaurant
❺ Why don't you ~?: ~하는 게 어때? check out: 확인하다, 조사하다
❻ once: 한 번
❼ I think 다음에 that이 생략되어 있다. 'I think (that) 주어 should 동사원형 ~.'는 '나는 ~해야 한다고 생각한다'라는 뜻이다.

Listen and Talk 2 C

W: Hello. ❶Are you ready to order?
B: It's my first time here. What do you recommend?
W: I recommend the chicken sandwich. ❷It is the most popular item at our restaurant.
B: Well, I don't like chicken very much. ❸ Could you recommend something else?
W: How about the turkey sandwich?
B: Oh, I love turkey. I'll have that.
W: ❹Why don't you order a drink with the sandwich? You ❺can get a 500-won discount.
B: That's great. Then I'll have an orange juice, too.

❶ be ready to 동사원형: ~할 준비가 되다
❷ It은 the chicken sandwich를 가리킨다. the most popular는 popular의 최상급 형태로 '가장 인기 있는'이라는 뜻이다.
❸ Could you recommend something else? = What else do you recommend?: 다른 거 추천해 주시겠어요? -thing으로 끝나는 부정대명사(something, anything, nothing 등)는 보통의 다른 명사들과 달리 형용사가 뒤에서 수식한다.
❹ Why don't you ~?: ~하는 게 어때? (= How about (동)명사 ~?= What about (동)명사 ~?)
❺ get a discount: 할인받다

● 다음 우리말과 일치하도록 빈칸에 알맞은 말을 쓰시오.

Listen & Talk 1 A

G: ________ ________ ________ ________ too many ________ ________ ________.

B: That's not ________ ________ your ________. ________ ________ eat fruit ________.

해석

G: 나 요즘 단 걸 너무 많이 먹는 것 같아.
B: 그건 건강에 좋지 않아. 대신에 과일을 먹는 게 좋아.

Listen & Talk 1 B

G: You ________ very tired today. Didn't you sleep well?

B: Yes, I did. But I ________ ________ ________ these days, especially in the morning.

G: Do you ________ ________ breakfast?

B: No, I don't.

G: ________ ________ ________ breakfast. Breakfast ________ ________ ________.

B: I didn't know that. Do you have ________ ________ ________?

G: Well, you ________ ________ ________ every day. That will help you.

B: Okay. I will.

G: 너 오늘 매우 피곤해 보인다. 잠을 잘 못 잤니?
B: 아니, 잘 잤어. 그런데, 나 요즘 자주, 특히 아침에 쉽게 피곤해져.
G: 너 아침밥을 주로 먹니?
B: 아니, 먹지 않아.
G: 아침밥을 먹는 게 좋아. 아침밥은 너한테 힘을 주거든.
B: 나 그건 몰랐어. 또 다른 제안해 줄 것 있니?
G: 음, 너는 또한 매일 운동해야 해. 그게 도움이 될 거야.
B: 알겠어. 그럴게.

Listen & Talk 1 C

G: Justin, our school cooking ________ is tomorrow. What are you ________ ________ make?

B: I'm going to make sandwiches.

G: ________ do you want to ________ ________ ________?

B: Chicken, cheese, and eggs.

G: ________ ________ put vegetables ________ your sandwiches. How ________ onions and carrots?

B: No, ________ ________ ________ ________ add them. I don't like those vegetables.

G: That's not a good idea. Mr. Kim said ________ ________ make ________ food for the contest.

B: You're right. ________ ________ go grocery shopping and buy onions and carrots.

G: Justin, 우리 학교 요리 대회가 내일이야. 뭐 만들 거니?
B: 샌드위치 만들 거야.
G: 뭐 넣을 거니?
B: 치킨이랑 치즈랑 계란.
G: 너 샌드위치에 채소 넣는 게 좋을 거야. 양파랑 당근은 어때?
B: 싫어. 안 넣을 거야. 나 그 채소들 싫어해.
G: 그건 좋은 생각이 아니야. 김 선생님은 요리 대회에서 건강에 좋은 음식을 만들어야 한다고 했어.
B: 네 말이 맞아. 나 식료품 쇼핑 가서 양파와 당근을 사야겠다.

Listen and Talk 2 A

G: ________ my ________ ________ here. ________ do you ________?

M: ________ ________ the pizza and salad.

해석

G: 저 여기 처음 왔어요. 추천해 주시겠어요?

M: 저는 피자와 샐러드를 추천해요.

Listen and Talk 2 B

B: Good morning, Jiwoo. ________ ________ ________ ________ right now?

G: I'm ________ ________ a restaurant for my class party.

B: Wow! ________ is the party?

G: It's next Friday. We want to go to Bella's Restaurant, but it is ________ ________.

B: Why ________ ________ ________ out Chang's Restaurant? I ________ there once. The food and prices were good.

G: ________ great. ________ ________ you ________ there?

B: I ________ ________ ________ ________.

G: I ________ ________ ________ go there. Thank you.

B: 안녕, Jiwoo. 너 지금 뭐 하고 있니?

G: 학급 파티 때 갈 식당을 찾고 있어.

B: 와! 파티가 언제야?

G: 다음 주 금요일이야. 우리는 Bella 식당에 가고 싶은데, 너무 비싸.

B: Chang 식당을 찾아보는 건 어때? 나 거기 한번 간 적 있어. 음식이랑 가격 다 괜찮았어.

G: 좋을 것 같아. 거기서 어떤 것을 추천하니?

B: 나는 국수를 추천해.

G: 내 생각에 우리 거기 가야겠다. 고마워.

Listen and Talk 2 C

W: Hello. ________ ________ ________ to order?

B: It's my first time here. ________ ________ ________ ________?

W: I ________ the chicken ________. It is ________ ________ ________ item at our restaurant.

B: Well, I don't like chicken very much. Could you ________ ________ ________?

W: How ________ the turkey sandwich?

B: Oh, I love turkey. I'll have that.

W: Why ________ ________ order a drink ________ the sandwich? You can ________ a 500-won ________.

B: That's great. Then I'll have an orange juice, too.

W: 안녕하세요. 주문하시겠어요?

B: 저 여기 처음 왔어요. 추천해주시겠어요?

W: 치킨 샌드위치 추천합니다. 그게 우리 식당에서 가장 인기 있는 메뉴에요.

B: 음, 제가 치킨을 별로 안 좋아해요. 다른 거 추천해주시겠어요?

W: 칠면조 샌드위치는 어떠세요?

B: 아, 저 칠면조 좋아해요. 그걸로 주세요.

W: 음료랑 샌드위치를 같이 주문하는 게 어떠세요? 500원 할인받을 수 있어요.

B: 좋네요. 그럼 오렌지 주스도 주세요.

Do It Yourself A

G: ________ for lunch today?

B: We have four choices. Which ________ do you want?

G: Well, I want some noodles. ________ ________ ________ ________?

B: I recommend the ________ noodles.

G: That ________ ________. I will have that. What about you?

B: I don't know. I'm not hungry.

G: But for your ________, you'd ________ have some food. Why ________ ________ ________ some tomato soup?

B: All right. I ________.

G: 오늘 점심은 어떤 거야?

B: 우리에겐 네 개의 선택들이 있어. 너는 어떤 것을 원하니?

G: 글쎄, 나는 면을 원해. 너는 어떤 것을 추천하니?

B: 나는 볶음면을 추천해.

G: 그거 맛있겠다. 나는 그걸 먹을래. 너는 어때?

B: 나는 잘 모르겠어. 배가 고프지 않아.

G: 하지만, 너의 건강을 위해서는 음식을 좀 먹는 게 좋아. 토마토 수프를 먹어 보는 게 어떻겠니?

B: 그래. 그렇게 할게.

01 다음 주어진 문장과 바꾸어 쓸 수 있는 것은?

You'd better eat breakfast every day.

① What do you think about eating breakfast every day?
② Do you want to eat breakfast every day?
③ Do you eat breakfast every day?
④ Why do you eat breakfast every day?
⑤ Why don't you eat breakfast every day?

[02~03] 다음 대화의 빈칸에 알맞은 것을 고르시오.

02

G: I think I eat too many sweets these days.
B: That's not good for your health. ____________________

① You'd better eat more.
② You'd better eat fruit instead.
③ You'd better gain more weight.
④ You'd better go to school by bus.
⑤ You'd better read books.

03

G: It's my first time here. What do you recommend?
M: ____________________

① You'd better go there one more time.
② I'll make the pizza and salad.
③ She made us a delicious salad.
④ I recommend the pizza and salad.
⑤ Why don't we have the pizza and salad?

04 다음 주어진 문장의 뒤에 나올 대화의 순서를 알맞게 쓰시오.

I have a cold.

(A) I recommend green tea.
(B) What do you recommend?
(C) You'd better drink some tea.

➡ ____________________

[01~04] 다음 대화를 읽고, 물음에 답하시오.

G: You look very (A)________ today. Didn't you sleep well?
B: Yes, I did. (①) (B)________ I often feel tired these days, especially in the morning. (②)
G: Do you usually eat breakfast?
B: No, I don't. (③)
G: (④) Breakfast gives you energy.
B: I didn't know that. Do you have any other suggestions? (⑤)
G: Well, you should also exercise every day. (C)That will help you.
B: Okay. I will.

01 위 대화의 ①~⑤ 중 주어진 문장이 들어갈 알맞은 곳은?

You'd better eat breakfast.

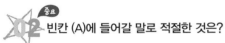

① ② ③ ④ ⑤

중요
02 빈칸 (A)에 들어갈 말로 적절한 것은?

① happy ② tired ③ angry
④ interested ⑤ excited

03 빈칸 (B)에 들어갈 말로 적절한 것은?

① So ② Because ③ And
④ Since ⑤ But

서답형
04 밑줄 친 (C)That이 가리키는 것을 본문에서 찾아 쓰시오.

➡ ____________________

[05~08] 다음 대화를 읽고, 물음에 답하시오.

G: Justin, our school cooking contest is tomorrow. (A)________________
B: I'm going to make ⓐsandwiches.
G: What do you want to put (B)__________ ⓑthem?
B: Chicken, cheese, and eggs.
G: You'd better put vegetables (C)__________ ⓒthem. How about ⓓonions and carrots?
B: No, I'm not going to add ⓔthem. I don't like those vegetables.
G: That's not a good idea. Mr. Kim said we should make healthy food for the contest.
B: You're right. I should go grocery shopping and buy onions and carrots.

05 빈칸 (A)에 들어갈 말로 적절한 것은?

① What are you doing?
② Where are you going to go?
③ What are you going to make?
④ Did you make sandwiches?
⑤ How are you going to make sandwiches?

중요
06 빈칸 (B)와 (C)에 공통으로 들어갈 말로 적절한 것은?

① in ② for ③ to
④ with ⑤ by

07 밑줄 친 ⓐ~ⓔ가 가리키는 것이 같은 것끼리 짝지어진 것을 고르시오.

① ⓐ, ⓑ, ⓒ ② ⓐ, ⓑ, ⓔ
③ ⓐ, ⓒ, ⓔ ④ ⓑ, ⓒ, ⓓ
⑤ ⓑ, ⓓ, ⓔ

서답형

08 다음 영영풀이에 해당하는 단어를 대화에서 찾아 쓰시오.

a plant that is eaten raw or cooked, such as a cabbage, a carrot, or peas

➡ ____________________

09 다음 짝지어진 대화가 어색한 것은?

① A: You'd better go to bed early.
B: OK, I will. Thanks.

② A: I think you should exercise every day.
B: That's a good idea.

③ A: What kind of pet do you recommend?
B: The dog is recommended.

④ A: Why don't you go home early and rest?
B: You'll be okay.

⑤ A: I recommend the pizza and salad.
B: Thanks for your recommendations.

서답형

10 괄호 안의 단어를 순서대로 배열하여 충고하는 말을 완성하시오.

A: I want to be taller.
B: Then _________ _________ _________ _________ _________. (milk, had, you, drink, better)
A: Thank you for your advice.

[11~14] 다음 대화를 읽고, 물음에 답하시오.

B: Good morning, Jiwoo. What are you doing (A)right now?
G: ①I'm searching for a restaurant for my class party.
B: Wow! When is the party?
G: ②It's next Friday. We want to go to Bella's Restaurant, ③but it is too expensive.
B: (B)Why don't you check out Chang's Restaurant? ④I've never been there. The food and prices were good.
G: Sounds great. What do you recommend there?
B: ⑤I recommend the noodle soup.
G: I think we should go there. Thank you.

11 위 대화의 ①~⑤중 흐름상 어색한 문장을 고르시오.

① ② ③ ④ ⑤

12 밑줄 친 (A)right과 같은 의미로 쓰인 문장을 고르시오.

① The clock in my room never told the right time.
② People have the right to determine their own future.
③ The bookstore is actually right next to my company.
④ People should always try to do the right thing and help others.
⑤ Walk straight ahead and you'll see the post office on your right.

중요

13 밑줄 친 (B)의 의도로 알맞은 것은?

① 확신 ② 변명 ③ 충고
④ 사과 ⑤ 소망

14 위 대화를 읽고 알 수 없는 내용은?

① What kind of food does the boy recommend?
② What is Jiwoo doing right now?
③ What kind of party will be held next Friday?
④ Where is Chang's Restaurant?
⑤ What does Jiwoo think about the boy's recommendations?

[01~02] 다음 주어진 문장의 뒤에 나올 대화의 순서를 알맞게 쓰시오.

01

What's for lunch today?

(A) I recommend the fried noodles.
(B) Well, I want some noodles. What do you recommend?
(C) We have four choices. Which one do you want?
(D) That sounds delicious. I will have that.

➡ ______________________________

중요 **02**

What are you going to make?

(A) Chicken, cheese, and eggs.
(B) I'm going to make sandwiches.
(C) What do you want to put in them?

➡ ______________________________

[03~05] 다음 대화를 읽고, 물음에 답하시오.

G: ①You look very tired today. Didn't you sleep well?
B: Yes, I did. ②But I often feel tired these days, especially in the morning.
G: Do you usually eat breakfast?
B: ③Yes, I do.
G: You'd better eat breakfast. ④Breakfast gives you energy.
B: ⑤I didn't know that. Do you have any other (A)<u>suggest</u>?
G: Well, (B)<u>너는 또한 매일 운동해야 해</u>. That will help you.
B: Okay. I will.

중요 **03** 위 대화의 ①~⑤ 중 흐름상 <u>어색한</u> 곳을 바르게 고치시오.

➡ ______________________________

04 밑줄 친 (A)<u>suggest</u>를 알맞은 형태로 쓰시오.

➡ ______________________________

05 밑줄 친 (B)의 우리말을 영작하시오.

➡ ______________________________

[06~08] 다음 대화를 읽고, 물음에 답하시오.

B: Good morning, Jiwoo. (A)______ are you doing right now?
G: I'm searching ⓐ_____ a restaurant ⓑ_____ my class party.
B: Wow! (B)_____ is the party?
G: It's next Friday. We want to go to Bella's Restaurant, but ⓒ<u>it</u> is too expensive.
B: (C)_______ don't you check out Chang's Restaurant? I went ⓓ<u>there</u> once. The food and prices were good.

중요 **06** 빈칸 (A)~(C)에 알맞은 의문사를 쓰시오.

➡ (A)________ (B)________ (C)________

07 빈칸 ⓐ와 ⓑ에 공통으로 들어갈 단어를 쓰시오.

➡ ______________

08 밑줄 친 ⓒ와 ⓓ가 가리키는 것을 대화에서 찾아 쓰시오.

➡ ______________________________

교과서

Grammar

1 주격 관계대명사

- He wanted to talk to friends **who** were far away. 그는 멀리 있는 친구들과 이야기하고 싶어 하였다.
- I have a dog **which** has a long tail. 나는 긴 꼬리를 가진 개를 갖고 있다.

■ 관계대명사는 접속사와 대명사의 역할을 한다. 관계대명사절은 명사를 수식해 주는 절로 관계대명사절이 꾸며 주는 말을 선행사라고 하고 관계대명사는 앞의 선행사와 같은 대상을 가리킨다. 관계대명사절이 되기 전의 문장에서 주어로 쓰였으면 주격 관계대명사로, 소유격으로 쓰였으면 소유격 관계대명사로, 목적격으로 쓰였으면 목적격 관계대명사가 된다. 주격 관계대명사는 관계대명사절에서 주어 역할을 하므로 그 다음에는 동사가 온다.

- This is the book. It(=The book) has many pictures.
  = This is the book **which**[**that**] has many pictures. (주격)
- This is the book. He bought it(=the book).
  = This is the book **which**[**that**] he bought. (목적격)
- This is the book. Its(=The book's) cover is white.
  = This is the book **whose** cover is white. (소유격)

■ 관계대명사는 선행사에 따라 다음과 같이 사용되며, 목적격 관계대명사는 생략할 수 있다.

	주격	소유격	목적격
사람	who/that	whose	whom[who]/that
동물, 사물	which/that	whose/of which	which/that

- I saw a man **who**[**that**] was wearing a black shirt. 나는 검은 셔츠를 입고 있는 남자를 보았다.

■ 관계대명사 that은 who, whom과 which 대신 사용할 수 있으며 소유격은 없다. 또한 선행사가 '사람+동물[사물]'인 경우에는 반드시 that을 써야 한다.

- There were a boy and his dog **that** lived in a small house. 작은 집에 사는 소년과 그의 개가 있었다.

핵심 Check

1. 다음 우리말에 맞게 빈칸에 알맞은 말을 쓰시오.

(1) 노래하고 있는 저 소년을 봐라.

➡ Look at that boy __________ is singing.

(2) 나는 Hemingway에 의해 쓰여진 책을 읽었다.

➡ I read the book __________ was written by Hemingway.

2 빈도부사

- He is **always** busy. 그는 항상 바쁘다.
- He **never** gets up early. 그는 절대로 일찍 일어나지 않는다.

■ **빈도부사**

빈도부사는 빈번함의 정도나 횟수를 나타내는 부사로, 주로 일반동사 앞에, be동사나 조동사 뒤에 위치한다.

■ **빈도부사의 종류**

always (항상, 언제나) 〉 usually (대개, 보통) 〉 often[frequently] (종종, 자주) 〉 sometimes (때때로, 가끔) 〉 rarely[seldom, hardly] (드물게, 거의 ~ 않는) 〉 never (결코 ~ 않는)

- Mike is **always** late for school. (Mike는 항상 학교에 늦는다.)
- I **often** play soccer with my friends after school. (나는 방과 후에 종종 친구들과 축구한다.)
- She **sometimes** watches movies on TV. (그녀는 때때로 TV에서 영화를 본다.)
- He **never** does the dishes after dinner. (그는 저녁 식사 후에 절대로 설거지를 하지 않는다.)

■ **빈도부사가 조동사 앞에 오는 경우**

조동사 used to, have to, ought to의 경우, 보통 빈도부사가 그 앞에 위치한다.

- We **always** have to be careful of others. (우리는 언제나 다른 사람들을 신경 써야 해.)

핵심 Check

2. 다음 우리말에 맞게 빈칸에 알맞은 말을 쓰시오.

(1) 그는 항상 일간 신문을 읽는다.

➡ He __________ reads a daily newspaper.

(2) 그 여자는 종종 운동을 한다.

➡ The woman __________ does exercise.

(3) 버스가 시간을 전혀 안 지켜요.

➡ The bus is __________ on time.

01 다음 빈칸에 들어갈 알맞은 것은?

He was looking for the person ________ came to meet him.

① who ② whose ③ whom
④ which ⑤ what

02 다음 문장에서 어법상 <u>어색한</u> 부분을 바르게 고쳐 쓰시오.

(1) She bought a book who looked very heavy.
_____________ ➡ _____________
(2) Richard is the man which helped me yesterday.
_____________ ➡ _____________
(3) Mary helps sometimes her mom.
_____________ ➡ _____________
4) I always will miss you.
_____________ ➡ _____________

03 다음 빈칸에 들어갈 말로 알맞은 것은?

He doesn't like computer games. So he ________ plays computer games.

① always ② usually ③ often
④ sometimes ⑤ seldom

04 다음 우리말에 맞게 괄호 안에 주어진 어구를 빈칸에 바르게 배열하시오. (필요하면 어형을 바꿀 것)

(1) 나는 꿈이 있는 사람이다. (a man, a dream, has, who)
➡ I am ______________________________.
(2) 저는 종종 산책을 합니다. (go, walk, often, a, for)
➡ I ______________________________.

01 다음 빈칸에 들어갈 알맞은 것은?

> Nara is wearing a hat ________ is too big for her.

① who ② whose
③ whom ④ which
⑤ where

02 중요 다음 밑줄 친 부분 중 어법상 바르지 않은 것은?

① Main dishes often include meat or fish.
② I always drink a glass of milk in the morning.
③ People usually can see auroras in the polar areas.
④ Bella is sometimes late for school.
⑤ I never mix business with pleasure.

03 다음 빈칸에 들어갈 수 있는 말이 다른 하나는?

① There was a king ________ name was Alexander.
② What do students ________ live in other countries eat for lunch?
③ He read the book ________ his dad bought for him.
④ Nancy heard the news ________ made her happy.
⑤ Did you meet the girl ________ wanted to talk with you?

서답형
04 다음 문장에서 never가 들어갈 곳은?

> • One ① is ② too ③ old ④ to ⑤ learn.

서답형
05 다음 괄호 안에서 알맞은 말을 고르시오.

(1) Andy (rarely goes / goes rarely) to a night club.
(2) Success (is often / often is) reached through the little thing.
(3) Mr. Kim is a doctor (who / which) lives in Seoul.
(4) There was a box (who / which) was full of books.
(5) The white dog (who / that) is playing with Jane is very cute.

06 중요 다음 중 어법상 옳은 문장은?

① A plantain is a fruit who looks like a banana.
② This is the girl which showed me the way.
③ A dog who has a long tail runs after a boy.
④ The man was the thief which stole her purse.
⑤ Is this the computer which you bought last Saturday?

서답형
07 다음 우리말에 맞게 주어진 단어를 넣어 문장을 다시 쓰시오.

> 나의 엄마는 항상 아침에 일찍 일어나신다.
> ➡ My mom gets up early in the morning. (always)

➡ ______________________________

08 다음 두 문장을 한 문장으로 바르게 바꾸면?

• The woman has long hair.
• The woman is drinking water.

① The woman has that long hair is drinking water.
② The woman who she has long hair is drinking water.
③ The woman whom has long hair is drinking water.
④ The woman who has long hair is drinking water.
⑤ The woman which has long hair is drinking water.

서답형

09 다음 주어진 단어를 이용하여 적절한 질문을 쓰시오.

A: ____________________________? (often)
B: I sometimes help him after school.

서답형

10 다음 우리말에 맞게 괄호 안의 말을 넣어 문장을 다시 쓰시오.

(1) 네가 서두르면, 너는 항상 학교에 제시간에 갈 수 있다.
• If you hurry up, you can go to school on time. (always)
➡ ____________________________

(2) 부모는 그들의 자식을 위해 자주 큰 희생을 한다.
• Parents make great sacrifices for their children. (often)
➡ ____________________________

(3) 이곳은 거의 그 문제에 대해 토론할 장소가 아니다.
• This is the place to talk about the problem. (hardly)
➡ ____________________________

중요

11 다음 밑줄 친 that의 용법이 나머지 넷과 다른 것은?

① Jiho is a boy that is always kind to others.
② Winter is the season that comes after autumn.
③ People used to believe that the earth was a flat surface.
④ The book that Mary gave me has many interesting stories.
⑤ I have a friend that lives in New York.

서답형

12 다음 문장에서 생략할 수 있는 것을 찾아 쓰시오.

(1) Seaweed is a food that we often eat.
(2) Look at the boy who is talking with a girl.
➡ (1) ____________ (2) ____________

서답형

13 다음 괄호 안에 주어진 단어들을 바르게 배열하여 문장을 완성하시오.

(1) (the nest, Americans, fly, usually) at age 18.
➡ ____________________________

(2) (hard, it, always, so, to, is) say goodbye to friends.
➡ ____________________________

(3) (will, do, anything, I, never) like this in future.
➡ ____________________________

서답형
14 다음 두 문장을 주어진 관계대명사를 이용하여 한 문장으로 연결하시오.

(1) • A baguette is a type of bread.
• The bread is popular in France. (which)
➡ ______________________

(2) • I met the woman.
• She came from England. (who)
➡ ______________________

(3) • I have a dog.
• It has brown hair. (that)
➡ ______________________

(4) • There is a house.
• Its windows are broken. (whose)
➡ ______________________

(5) • I like the book.
• Mom bought it for me. (that)
➡ ______________________

중요
15 다음 중 어법상 올바른 문장은?

① John eats sometimes junk food.
② Samantha is always kind to me.
③ My mom used to rarely take a walk after dinner.
④ When do usually you get up?
⑤ I never will trust him again.

16 다음 빈칸에 들어갈 알맞은 것은?

This is a Vietnamese restaurant _______.

① which it looks very nice
② that I like it very much
③ who sells rice noodle soup
④ that it sells rice noodle soup
⑤ that sells rice noodle soup

17 다음 빈칸에 들어갈 말로 알맞은 것은?

I like reading books a lot. So I _______ try to read books.

① always ② seldom ③ rarely
④ sometimes ⑤ never

중요
18 다음 빈칸에 들어갈 말을 순서대로 바르게 연결한 것은?

• People _________ live in Singapore come from many different cultures. • I want to visit Paris _______ has many nice museums.

① which – that ② which – which
③ who – that ④ who – who
⑤ that – who

19 다음 빈칸에 들어갈 수 없는 것은?

He _________ avoids making decisions.

① sometimes ② often
③ always ④ frequent
⑤ seldom

서답형
20 다음 문장에서 어법상 어색한 것을 바르게 고쳐 다시 쓰시오.

(1) Are you the person which dropped this?
➡ ______________________

(2) We have to break the bad habits who can cause serious problems.
➡ ______________________

(3) She uses always my phone without asking.
➡ ______________________

01 두 문장을 관계대명사를 이용하여 한 문장으로 썼을 때, 빈칸에 해당하는 문장을 쓰시오.

(1) • ________________________________
• She is wearing glasses.
→ The girl who is wearing glasses is eating rice noodle soup.

(2) • This is the smart phone.
• ________________________________
→ This is the smart phone which is made in Korea.

(3) • ________________________________
• It is really cool.
→ Emily bought a new computer that is really cool.

(4) • Degas liked to paint the ladies.
• ________________________________
→ Degas liked to paint the ladies that were dancing.

중요
02 The following table shows how often each student studied math last week. Look carefully and answer the questions in a full sentence using a frequency adverb.

Name	Amy	Ann	Don	Elle
Times	0	2~3	5~6	8

(1) How often did Amy study math last week?
(2) How often did Don study math last week?
(3) How often did Ann study math last week?

➡ (1) ________________________________
(2) ________________________________
(3) ________________________________

03 우리말과 일치하도록 괄호 안의 어구를 순서대로 배열하시오.

(1) 빨간 치마를 입고 있는 소녀가 내 딸이다. (a, my daughter, the girl, skirt, wearing, red, is, is, who)
➡ ________________________________

(2) Jenny는 바이올린을 잘 켜는 남동생이 있다. (Jenny, brother, violin, has, plays, a, well, who, the)
➡ ________________________________

(3) Cheetah는 빨리 달릴 수 있는 동물이다. (animal, cheetah, can, is, run, that, fast, a, an)
➡ ________________________________

(4) Bill은 일요일에 항상 늦게 일어난다. (Bill, Sundays, gets, late, always, on, up)
➡ ________________________________

(5) Cindy는 월말에는 종종 바쁘다. (Cindy, busy, the month, often, the end, is, at, of)
➡ ________________________________

중요
04 다음 빈칸에 알맞은 말을 쓰시오.

(1) The girl is my sister. She is reading a book.
= The girl ________ a book is my sister.
= The girl ________ ________ ________ a book is my sister.

(2) The dog is very cute. It is sleeping beside the sofa.
= The dog ________ beside the sofa is very cute.
= The dog ________ ________ ________ beside the sofa is very cute.

05 다음은 Bella의 일상생활에 관한 표이다. 표의 내용에 맞게 〈보기〉와 같이 빈도부사를 사용하여 빈칸을 채워, Bella의 일상생활을 묘사하는 문장을 3개 쓰시오.

what	always	usually	often	never
watch TV			✓	
be late				✓
send text messages	✓			
use the Internet		✓		

보기

Bella often watches TV.

➡ Bella ________________ for school.
➡ Bella ________________.
➡ Bella ________________.

06 다음 두 문장을 한 문장으로 바꿔 쓸 때, 빈칸을 어법에 맞게 채우시오.

David is my friend. I spent my vacation with him.

(1) David is my friend ______ I spent my vacation with.
(2) David is my friend ______ I spent my vacation with.
(3) David is my friend ______ ______ I spent my vacation.
(4) David is my friend ______ ______ ______ ______ ______.

중요

07 다음 우리말에 맞게 괄호 안의 어휘를 바르게 배열하시오. (필요할 경우 단어를 바꿀 것.)

너를 보려고 거의 기다릴 수 없어. (어서 보고 싶어.)
(I, you, wait, can, see, hard, to)

➡ ________________

08 Put the following words in order adding a relative pronoun to complete the sentence. (Do not use that.)

doctors, sons, has, became, two

➡ Dan ________________.

고난이도

09 다음 문장을 주어진 빈도부사를 이용하여 다시 쓰시오.

(1) On a hot day, sunlight is enough to melt chocolate. (usually)
➡ ________________
(2) He wears very clean clothes. (always)
➡ ________________
(3) I can find a parking space downtown. (never)
➡ ________________

10 다음 그림을 참고하여 빈칸에 알맞은 말을 쓰시오.

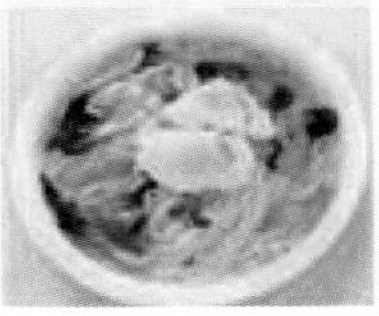

In China, noodles mean long life. On their birthday, they eat noodles ______ ______.

고난이도

11 다음 문장을 어법에 맞게 고쳐 쓰시오.

(1) It is a TV show who is always popular.
➡ ________________
(2) The painting shows a couple which are dancing.
➡ ________________
(3) I took the train that it had a restaurant.
➡ ________________
(4) I never am late for school.
➡ ________________

교과서

Reading

School Lunches Around the World

Hello, this is food reporter Minjun from Korea.
사람을 소개할 때 사용
For many students, lunch is the best part of the school day.
good의 최상급
In Korea, we often eat rice and soup for lunch.
빈도부사 often은 일반동사와 쓰일 경우 일반동사 앞에 위치한다.
We also have side dishes, such as *Bulgogi* or *Gimchi*.
반찬 = like: ~와 같은 (예를 들어)
Sometimes our school serves special dishes, such as pizza, *Bibimbap*,
빈도부사 sometimes는 문장 맨 앞에 써도 된다. = like
or pasta. What do students who live in other countries eat for lunch?
who는 선행사 students를 수식하는 주격 관계대명사이다.
Let's hear from our food reporters!

reporter 기자, 리포터
side dish 반찬, 곁들임 요리
serve (음식을) 내다, 제공하다

확인문제

- 다음 문장이 본문의 내용과 일치하면 T, 일치하지 않으면 F를 쓰시오.

1 Minjun is a reporter for a daily newspaper. ☐
2. For many students, lunch is the best part of the school day. ☐
3. In Korea, students often eat rice and soup for breakfast. ☐
4. Sometimes Minjun's school serves special dishes. ☐

Belle, France

Our school serves healthy and balanced meals.
(음식을) 내다, 제공하다
We usually eat a salad as an appetizer. Main dishes often include meat
as는 '…으로'라는 의미로 사용된 전치사이다.
or fish. We also eat fresh fruit at the end of the lunch.
~의 끝에
Oh, I can never forget about baguettes! They're great with cheese.
= baguettes
Our school also has a special rule.
We must stay at the lunch table for at least 30 minutes.
적어도

balanced 균형 잡힌
appetizer 식전 음식
rule 규칙, 규정

확인문제

- 다음 문장이 본문의 내용과 일치하면 T, 일치하지 않으면 F를 쓰시오.

1 Belle's school serves healthy and balanced meals. ☐
2 Students usually eat a salad as a main dish at Belle's school. ☐
3 Baguettes are great with cheese. ☐
4 Students must stay at the lunch table for an hour in France. ☐

Bruno, Brazil

Usually, we have beans and rice for lunch.
빈도부사 usually는 문장 맨 앞에 써도 된다.

Meat and vegetables are common in our side dishes.
common: 흔한

My favorite lunch comes with plantains. A plantain is a fruit which looks like a banana. We usually fry plantains. Our school lunches are fresh because the vegetables and fruit come from local farms.

which는 선행사 a fruit을 수식하는 주격 관계대명사이다.
look like+명사: ~처럼 보이다. 빈도부사 usually는 일반동사가 있으면 보통 일반동사 앞에 위치한다.
because + 주어 + 동사

common 흔한, 공통의
local (특정한) 지방의, 현지의

확인문제

- 다음 문장이 본문의 내용과 일치하면 T, 일치하지 않으면 F를 쓰시오.

1 Usually, Bruno's school serves beans and rice for lunch. ☐

2 Meat and vegetables are common in Bruno's main dishes. ☐

3 A plantain is a fruit which looks like a banana. ☐

4 Bruno's school lunches include fruit from other countries. ☐

Nicole, Singapore

People who live in Singapore come from many different cultures, so we have both Eastern and Western dishes at lunch.

who는 선행사 People을 수식하는 주격 관계대명사이다.
both A and B: A와 B 둘 다

Students can choose from many dishes, such as curry, noodle soup, or pasta, each day. My school won an award for healthy school food last year. Our lunches are always healthy, and they taste good, too!

such as = like: ~와 같은 (예를 들어)
won an award: 상을 받았다
빈도부사 always는 be동사와 쓰였으므로 be동사 뒤에 위치한다. 감각동사 taste 뒤에 형용사 good이 보어로 쓰였다.

Which school lunch do you want to try?
to try: 명사적 용법(목적어)

Does it have anything in common with your school lunch?
have ~ in common: ~을 공통으로 지니다.

Please leave your comments at www.chopchoplunch.com.
leave: ~을 남기다

both A and B A와 B 둘 다
Eastern 동양의, 동쪽에 위치한
Western 서양의, 서쪽에 위치한
award 상, 수상
have ~ in common ~을 공통적으로 지니다

확인문제

- 다음 문장이 본문의 내용과 일치하면 T, 일치하지 않으면 F를 쓰시오.

1 In Singapore, people come from many different cultures. ☐

2 Nicole has only Eastern dishes at lunch. ☐

3 Nicole's school won an award for healthy food this year. ☐

4 Nicole's school lunches are always healthy. ☐

5 Nicole's school lunches don't taste good. ☐

6 You may leave your comments at www.chopchoplunch.com. ☐

Reading 교과서 확인학습 A

• 우리말을 참고하여 빈칸에 알맞은 말을 쓰시오.

1 School Lunches _______ _______ _______

2 Hello, _______ _______ food reporter Minjun _______ Korea.

3 For many students, lunch is _______ _______ _______ of the school day.

4 In Korea, we _______ eat rice and soup _______ _______.

5 We also _______ _______ _______, such as *Bulgogi* or *Gimchi*.

6 Sometimes our school _______ _______ _______, such as pizza, *Bibimbap*, or pasta.

7 What do students _______ _______ _______ _______ countries eat for lunch?

8 Let's _______ _______ our food reporters!

9 Belle, _______

10 Our school serves _______ _______ _______ meals.

11 We _______ eat a salad _______ _______ _______.

12 Main dishes _______ _______ meat or fish.

13 We also eat fresh fruit _______ _______ _______ _______ _______ _______.

14 Oh, I _______ _______ _______ about baguettes!

15 They're great _______ _______.

16 Our school also _______ _______ _______ _______.

17 We must stay at the lunch table _______ _______ _______ 30 _______.

1 세계 각국의 학교 급식

2 안녕하세요. 저는 한국에서 온 음식 취재 기자 민준입니다.

3 많은 학생들에게 점심시간은 학교 일과 중 가장 좋은 부분입니다.

4 한국에서는 점심으로 자주 밥과 국을 먹습니다.

5 우리는 불고기나 김치 같은 반찬도 먹습니다.

6 때때로 우리 학교는 피자, 비빔밥 또는 파스타 같은 특식을 제공합니다.

7 다른 나라에서 사는 학생들은 점심으로 무엇을 먹을까요?

8 우리 음식 취재 기자들에게서 들어보겠습니다!

9 벨, 프랑스

10 우리 학교는 건강하고 균형 잡힌 식사를 제공합니다.

11 우리는 보통 식전 음식으로 샐러드를 먹습니다.

12 주요리는 보통 고기나 생선을 포함합니다.

13 우리는 점심의 끝에 신선한 과일도 먹습니다.

14 오, 절대 바게트를 빠뜨릴 수는 없죠!

15 바게트는 치즈와 잘 어울립니다.

16 우리 학교에는 또한 특별한 규칙이 있습니다.

17 우리는 적어도 30분간 점심 식탁에 반드시 머물러야 합니다.

18 Bruno, _______

19 Usually, we have _______ _______ _______ for lunch.

20 Meat and vegetables are _______ _______ our side dishes.

21 My favorite lunch _______ _______ _______.

22 A plantain is a fruit _______ _______ _______ a banana.

23 We _______ _______ plantains.

24 Our school lunches are fresh because the vegetables and fruit _______ _______ _______ _______.

25 Nicole, _______

26 People _______ live in Singapore come _______ _______ _______ _______, so we have _______ _______ _______ _______ _______ at lunch.

27 Students can _______ _______ many dishes, _______ _______ curry, noodle soup, or pasta, each day.

28 My school _______ _______ _______ _______ healthy school food last year.

29 Our lunches are always _______, and they _______ _______, too!

30 _______ _______ _______ do you want to try?

31 Does it _______ anything _______ _______ _______ your school lunch?

32 Please _______ your comments _______ www.chopchoplunch.com.

18 브루노, 브라질

19 보통, 우리는 점심으로 콩과 밥을 먹습니다.

20 우리의 곁들임 음식에는 고기와 채소가 흔히 나옵니다.

21 내가 가장 좋아하는 점심에는 플랜테인이 나옵니다.

22 플랜테인은 바나나처럼 생긴 과일입니다.

23 우리는 보통 플랜테인을 튀깁니다.

24 채소와 과일이 현지 농장에서 오기 때문에 우리 학교 급식은 신선합니다.

25 니콜, 싱가포르

26 싱가포르에 사는 사람들은 매우 다양한 문화권에서 오기 때문에, 우리는 점심에 동양식과 서양식을 모두 먹습니다.

27 학생들은 매일 카레, 국수 또는 파스타와 같이 많은 요리 중에서 선택할 수 있습니다.

28 우리 학교는 작년에 건강한 학교 음식 상을 받았습니다.

29 우리의 점심은 항상 건강에 좋고, 맛 또한 좋습니다!

30 여러분은 어떤 학교 급식을 먹어 보고 싶나요?

31 그것이 여러분의 학교 급식과 공통되는 것이 있습니까?

32 여러분의 의견을 www.chopchoplunch.com에 남겨 주세요.

Reading 교과서 확인학습 B

- 우리말을 참고하여 본문을 영작하시오.

1 세계 각국의 학교 급식
➡ ______________________________

2 안녕하세요, 저는 한국에서 온 음식 취재 기자 민준입니다.
➡ ______________________________

3 많은 학생들에게 점심시간은 학교 일과 중 가장 좋은 부분입니다.
➡ ______________________________

4 한국에서는 점심으로 자주 밥과 국을 먹습니다.
➡ ______________________________

5 우리는 불고기나 김치 같은 반찬도 먹습니다.
➡ ______________________________

6 때때로 우리 학교는 피자, 비빔밥 또는 파스타 같은 특식을 제공합니다.
➡ ______________________________

7 다른 나라에서 사는 학생들은 점심으로 무엇을 먹을까요?
➡ ______________________________

8 우리 음식 취재 기자들에게서 들어보겠습니다!
➡ ______________________________

9 벨, 프랑스
➡ ______________________________

10 우리 학교는 건강하고 균형 잡힌 식사를 제공합니다.
➡ ______________________________

11 우리는 보통 식전 음식으로 샐러드를 먹습니다.
➡ ______________________________

12 주요리는 보통 고기나 생선을 포함합니다.
➡ ______________________________

13 우리는 점심의 끝에 신선한 과일도 먹습니다.
➡ ______________________________

14 오, 절대 바게트를 빠뜨릴 수는 없죠!
➡ ______________________________

15 바게트는 치즈와 잘 어울립니다.
➡ ______________________________

16 우리 학교에는 또한 특별한 규칙이 있습니다.
➡ ______________________________

17 우리는 적어도 30분간 점심 식탁에 반드시 머물러야 합니다.
➡ ______________________________

18 브루노, 브라질

➡ ______________________________

19 보통, 우리는 점심으로 콩과 밥을 먹습니다.

➡ ______________________________

20 우리의 곁들임 음식에는 고기와 채소가 흔히 나옵니다.

➡ ______________________________

21 내가 가장 좋아하는 점심에는 플랜테인이 나옵니다.

➡ ______________________________

22 플랜테인은 바나나처럼 생긴 과일입니다.

➡ ______________________________

23 우리는 보통 플랜테인을 튀깁니다.

➡ ______________________________

24 채소와 과일이 현지 농장에서 오기 때문에 우리 학교 급식은 신선합니다.

➡ ______________________________

25 니콜, 싱가포르

➡ ______________________________

26 싱가포르에 사는 사람들은 매우 다양한 문화권에서 오기 때문에, 우리는 점심에 동양식과 서양식을 모두 먹습니다.

➡ ______________________________

27 학생들은 매일 카레, 국수 또는 파스타와 같이 많은 요리 중에서 선택할 수 있습니다.

➡ ______________________________

28 우리 학교는 작년에 건강한 학교 음식 상을 받았습니다.

➡ ______________________________

29 우리의 점심은 항상 건강에 좋고, 맛 또한 좋습니다!

➡ ______________________________

30 여러분은 어떤 학교 급식을 먹어 보고 싶나요?

➡ ______________________________

31 그것이 여러분의 학교 급식과 공통되는 것이 있습니까?

➡ ______________________________

32 여러분의 의견을 www.chopchoplunch.com에 남겨 주세요.

➡ ______________________________

[01~03] 다음 글을 읽고, 물음에 답하시오.

Hello, this is food reporter Minjun from Korea. For many students, lunch is the best part of the school day. In Korea, we often eat rice and soup for lunch. We also have side dishes, such as *Bulgogi* or *Gimchi*. Sometimes our school serves special dishes, such as pizza, *Bibimbap*, or pasta. What do students ___ⓐ___ live in other countries eat for lunch? Let's hear from our food reporters!

01 중요 위 글의 빈칸 ⓐ에 들어갈 알맞은 말을 모두 고르시오.

① which ② who
③ whom ④ that
⑤ what

02 위 글의 제목으로 알맞은 것을 고르시오.

① Food Reporters Around the World
② School Lunch in Korea
③ The Best Part of the Day
④ Famous Side Dishes of Korea
⑤ Wow! Pizza, Today's Special Dish

03 위 글의 내용과 일치하지 않는 것은?

① 민준이는 한국에서 온 음식 취재 기자이다.
② 많은 학생들에게 점심시간은 학교 일과 중 가장 좋은 부분이다.
③ 한국에서는 점심으로 자주 밥과 국을 먹는다.
④ 한국에서는 급식에 불고기나 김치 같은 반찬도 먹는다.
⑤ 민준이네 학교는 피자와 파스타 같은 특식을 항상 제공해 준다.

[04~06] 다음 글을 읽고, 물음에 답하시오.

Bruno, Brazil
Usually, we have beans and rice for lunch. Meat and vegetables are common in our side dishes. My favorite lunch comes ___ⓐ___ plantains. A plantain is a fruit which looks ⓑlike a banana. We usually fry plantains. Our school lunches are fresh because the vegetables and fruit come ___ⓒ___ local farms.

04 위 글의 빈칸 ⓐ와 ⓒ에 들어갈 전치사가 바르게 짝지어진 것은?

① with – from ② in – for
③ on – from ④ for – at
⑤ with – for

05 중요 위 글의 밑줄 친 ⓑlike와 같은 의미로 쓰인 것을 고르시오.

① Does she like her new house?
② Which dress do you like best?
③ How did you like the movie?
④ I hope you like it, too!
⑤ You sound like a professor.

서답형
06 다음 질문에 대한 알맞은 대답을 영어로 쓰시오. (6 단어)

Q: What do the students usually have for lunch at Bruno's school?
A: ______________________________

[07~08] 다음 글을 읽고, 물음에 답하시오.

Belle, France
Our school serves healthy and balanced meals. We usually eat a salad as an appetizer.

(①) Main dishes often include meat or fish. (②) We also eat fresh fruit at the end of the lunch. (③) Oh, I can never forget about baguettes! (④) Our school also has ⓐa special rule. (⑤) We must stay at the lunch table for at least 30 minutes.

07 위 글의 흐름으로 보아, 주어진 문장이 들어가기에 가장 적절한 곳은?

They're great with cheese.

① ② ③ ④ ⑤

서답형
08 위 글의 밑줄 친 ⓐ가 가리키는 내용을 우리말로 쓰시오.

➡ ______________________

[09~11] 다음 글을 읽고, 물음에 답하시오.

Nicole, Singapore
People who live in Singapore come from many different ___ⓐ___, so we have both Eastern and Western dishes at lunch. Students can choose from many dishes, ⓑ such as curry, noodle soup, or pasta, each day. My school won an award for healthy school food last year. Our lunches are always healthy, and they taste good, too!

중요
09 위 글의 빈칸 ⓐ에 들어갈 알맞은 말을 고르시오.

① opinions ② purposes
③ concerns ④ cultures
⑤ beliefs

서답형
10 니콜의 학교 급식의 특징 두 가지를 우리말로 쓰시오.

➡ 1. ______________________
2. ______________________

서답형
11 위 글의 밑줄 친 ⓑ와 바꿔 쓸 수 있는 한 단어를 쓰시오.

➡ ______________

12 주어진 글 다음에 이어질 글의 순서로 가장 적절한 것은?

Hello, this is food reporter Minjun from Korea.

(A) We also have side dishes, such as *Bulgogi* or *Gimchi*. Sometimes our school serves special dishes, such as pizza, *Bibimbap*, or pasta.
(B) What do students who live in other countries eat for lunch? Let's hear from our food reporters!
(C) For many students, lunch is the best part of the school day. In Korea, we often eat rice and soup for lunch.

① (A) – (C) – (B) ② (B) – (A) – (C)
③ (B) – (C) – (A) ④ (C) – (A) – (B)
⑤ (C) – (B) – (A)

[13~14] 다음 글을 읽고, 물음에 답하시오.

Hello, this is food reporter Minjun from Korea. For many students, lunch is the best part of the school day. In Korea, we often eat rice and soup for lunch. We also have side ⓐdishes, such as *Bulgogi* or *Gimchi*.

Sometimes our school serves special dishes, such as pizza, *Bibimbap*, or pasta. What do students who live in other countries eat for lunch? Let's hear from our food reporters!

중요

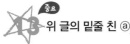

13 위 글의 밑줄 친 ⓐdishes와 같은 의미로 쓰인 것을 고르시오.

① I'll do the dishes.
② Can you dish out the potatoes?
③ How do I eat these dishes?
④ He broke the dishes by mistake.
⑤ The dirty dishes were still in the sink.

14 한국의 급식 반찬에 해당하는 것을 모두 고르시오.

① *Bulgogi* ② *Bibimbap*
③ soup ④ *Gimchi*
⑤ pasta

[15~16] 다음 글을 읽고, 물음에 답하시오.

Belle, France

Our school serves healthy and (A) [balancing / balanced] meals. We usually eat a salad as an appetizer. Main dishes often (B) [include / exclude] meat or fish. We also eat fresh fruit at the end of the lunch. Oh, I can never forget about baguettes! ⓐThey're great with cheese. Our school also has a special rule. We must stay at the lunch table for (C)[at last / at least] 30 minutes.

서답형

15 위 글의 괄호 (A)~(C)에서 문맥이나 어법상 알맞은 낱말을 골라 쓰시오.

➡ (A)________ (B)________ (C)________

서답형

16 위 글의 밑줄 친 ⓐThey가 가리키는 것을 본문에서 찾아 쓰시오.

➡ ____________________

[17~19] 다음 글을 읽고, 물음에 답하시오.

Bruno, Brazil

Usually, we have beans and rice for lunch. Meat and vegetables are common in our side dishes. My favorite lunch comes with plantains. A plantain is a fruit ⓐwhich looks like a banana. We usually fry plantains. Our school lunches are fresh because the vegetables and fruit come from local farms.

17 위 글의 밑줄 친 ⓐwhich와 문법적 쓰임이 다른 것을 고르시오.

① This is the book which I like most.
② I don't know which car goes faster.
③ Look at the bird which is in the cage.
④ Give me the pen which you have.
⑤ This is the backpack which I chose.

서답형

18 다음 빈칸 (A)와 (B)에 알맞은 단어를 넣어 Bruno의 학교 급식을 정리하시오.

• main dishes: (A)______________
• common side dishes: (B)______________

서답형

19 다음 빈칸 (A)와 (B)에 알맞은 단어를 넣어 플랜테인에 대한 소개를 완성하시오.

A plantain is a fruit which looks like (A)________ ________. People usually (B)________ plantains in Brazil.

[20~23] 다음 글을 읽고, 물음에 답하시오.

Which school lunch do you want ⓐto try? Does ⓑit have anything ⓒ공통적으로 ___ⓓ___ your school lunch? Please leave your comments ___ⓔ___ www.chopchoplunch.com.

20 위 글의 밑줄 친 ⓐto try와 to부정사의 용법이 다른 것을 모두 고르시오.

① He decided to try it.
② Show me something easier to try.
③ It is good to try this new coffee.
④ Her plan was to try the project.
⑤ He went there to try surfing.

서답형
21 위 글의 밑줄 친 ⓑ가 가리키는 것을 우리말로 쓰시오.

➡ ______________________

서답형
22 위 글의 밑줄 친 ⓒ의 우리말을 두 단어로 쓰시오.

➡ ______________

중요
23 위 글의 빈칸 ⓓ와 ⓔ에 들어갈 전치사가 바르게 짝지어진 것은?

① with – from
② at – by
③ for – to
④ with – at
⑤ for – at

[24~26] 다음 글을 읽고, 물음에 답하시오.

This is a Vietnamese restaurant __ⓐ__ sells rice noodle soup. The man __ⓑ__ works at the restaurant is serving food. The woman who has long hair is drinking water. ⓒ안경을 끼고 있는 소녀는 쌀국수를 먹고 있다. ⓓAll of them look so happily!

서답형
24 위 글의 빈칸 ⓐ와 ⓑ에 공통으로 알맞은 말을 쓰시오.

➡ ______________

서답형
25 위 글의 밑줄 친 ⓒ의 우리말에 맞게 be동사를 보충하여, 주어진 어구를 알맞게 배열하시오.

glasses / eating / who / rice noodle soup / is wearing / the girl

➡ ______________________
____

서답형
26 위 글의 밑줄 친 ⓓ에서 어법상 틀린 부분을 찾아 고치시오.

➡ ______________

[27~28] 다음 대화를 읽고, 물음에 답하시오.

A: Which country's school lunch do you want to try?
B: I want to try a school lunch from France. I love baguettes and cheese. Also, they must stay at the lunch table for at least 30 minutes. That's an interesting rule.
C: I'm interested in trying a school lunch from Singapore. ⓐChoosing both Eastern and Western dishes for lunch sounds fun. How about you?
A: I think Korean school lunches are the best. I love *Gimchi* so much!

서답형
27 위 대화를 읽고 A, B, C가 어느 나라 학교 급식을 먹고 싶어 하는지와 그 이유를 각각 우리말로 쓰시오.

➡ A: ______________________
B: ______________________
____
C: ______________________
____

28 위 대화의 밑줄 친 ⓐChoosing과 문법적 쓰임이 같은 것을 고르시오.

① I know the girl singing a song.
② He enjoys reading books.
③ I saw him entering the room.
④ They are learning English now.
⑤ Take good care of the crying baby.

[01~03] 다음 글을 읽고, 물음에 답하시오.

Hello, this is food reporter Minjun from Korea. For many students, lunch is the best part of the school day. In Korea, we often eat rice and soup for lunch. We also have side dishes, __ⓐ__ *Bulgogi* or *Gimchi*. Sometimes our school serves special dishes, __ⓑ__ pizza, *Bibimbap*, or pasta. ⓒWhat do students who lives in other countries eat for lunch? Let's hear from our food reporters!

01 다음 질문에 대한 알맞은 대답을 빈칸에 쓰시오.

Q: In Korea, what do students often eat for lunch?
A: They often eat ________ ________ ________ for lunch.

02 위 글의 빈칸 ⓐ와 ⓑ에 공통으로 들어갈 알맞은 말을 쓰시오.

➡ ____________

중요 **03** 위 글의 밑줄 친 ⓒ에서 어법상 틀린 부분을 찾아 고치시오.

__________ ➡ __________

[04~06] 다음 글을 읽고, 물음에 답하시오.

Belle, France
Our school serves healthy and balanced meals. We usually eat a salad as an appetizer. Main dishes often include meat or fish. ⓐWe also eat fresh fruit at the end of the lunch. Oh, I can never forget about baguettes! They're great with cheese. Our school also has a special rule. ⓑWe must stay at the lunch table during at least 30 minutes.

04 위 글의 밑줄 친 ⓐ를 다음과 같이 바꿔 쓰려고 한다. 주어진 영영풀이를 참고하여 아래 빈칸에 철자 d로 시작하는 단어를 쓰시오.

something sweet, such as fruit or a pudding, which you eat at the end of a meal

➡ We also eat fresh fruit as a ________ at the end of the lunch.

중요 **05** 위 글의 밑줄 친 ⓑ에서 어법상 어색한 부분을 찾아 고치시오.

__________ ➡ __________

06 다음 질문에 대한 알맞은 대답을 주어진 어구로 시작하여 쓰시오. (11 단어)

Q: What is the special rule of Belle's school?
A: The students ____________________
____________________________.

[07~09] 다음 글을 읽고, 물음에 답하시오.

Bruno, Brazil
Usually, we have beans and rice for lunch. Meat and vegetables are common in our side dishes. My favorite lunch comes with plantains. A plantain is a fruit which looks (A)[at / like] a banana. We usually (B)[fly / fry] plantains. Our school lunches are fresh because the vegetables and fruit come from (C)[global / local] farms.

07 위 글의 괄호 (A)~(C)에서 문맥상 알맞은 낱말을 골라 쓰시오.

➡ (A)________ (B)________ (C)________

08 중요 본문의 내용과 일치하도록 다음 빈칸 (A)와 (B)에 알맞은 단어를 쓰시오.

> At Bruno's school, (A)__________ and (B)__________ are common in their side dishes.

09 다음 문장에서 위 글의 내용과 다른 부분을 찾아서 고치시오.

> Bruno's favorite lunch comes with fried potatoes.

__________ ➡ __________

[10~12] 다음 글을 읽고, 물음에 답하시오.

> Nicole, Singapore
> People who live in Singapore come from many different cultures, so we have both Eastern and Western dishes at lunch. Students can choose from many dishes, such as curry, noodle soup, or pasta, each day. My school ⓐwon an award for healthy school food last year. Our lunches are always healthy, and they taste good, too!

10 다음 질문에 대한 알맞은 대답을 주어진 단어로 시작하여 쓰시오. (10 단어)

> Q: Why do the students have both Eastern and Western dishes at lunch at Nicole's school?
> A: Because __________________________
> __________________________.

11 본문의 내용과 일치하도록 다음 빈칸에 공통으로 들어갈 알맞은 단어를 쓰시오.

> Nicole's school lunches are ________ for the health, and they also taste ________!

➡ __________

12 위 글의 밑줄 친 ⓐ를 다음과 같이 바꿔 쓸 때 빈칸에 알맞은 말을 쓰시오.

> won a __________

[13~15] 다음 글을 읽고, 물음에 답하시오.

> ___ⓐ___ of My Favorite Restaurant
> My favorite restaurant is Antonio's Restaurant. It is a Spanish restaurant. It is near my home. Mixed paella is the most popular dish at this restaurant. ⓑAll of the food is really fresh and delicious, and the prices are high. I recommend this restaurant!
> My Rating ★★★★☆

13 위 글의 빈칸 ⓐ에 철자 R로 시작하는 알맞은 말을 쓰시오.

➡ __________

14 중요 위 글의 밑줄 친 ⓑ에서 흐름상 어색한 부분을 찾아 고치시오.

__________ ➡ __________

15 본문의 내용과 일치하도록 다음 빈칸 (A)와 (B)에 알맞은 단어를 쓰시오.

> The writer recommends Antonio's Restaurant because of its really (A)__________ and (B)__________ food.

교과서

구석구석

Project Link

Let's Make *Gimchi* Fried Rice!
Let's 동사원형: ~하자 fried: 튀긴

1. Cut the *Gimchi*, onions and carrots.
cut: 자르다 3개 이상 나열할 때 A, B, and C 형식으로 쓴다.
2. Put the oil in a pan, and heat it up.
put A in B: A를 B에 넣다 heat ~ up: ~을 덥히다
3. Add the *Gimchi*, and fry it for one minute.
for + 수사가 붙은 기간: ~ 동안
4. Add and fry the rice and vegetables.
5. Fry an egg, and add it on top.
= an egg 맨 위에

구문해설 • fry: 튀기다 • carrot: 당근 • add: 첨가하다

해석

김치 볶음밥을 만들자!
1. 김치, 양파 그리고 당근을 자르세요.
2. 후라이팬에 오일을 넣고, 가열하세요.
3. 김치를 넣고, 잠시 동안 볶아주세요.
4. 밥과 야채를 넣고 볶으세요.
5. 계란을 부치고 맨 위에 놓으세요.

Think and Write

Review of My Favorite Restaurant

My favorite restaurant is Antonio's Restaurant.

It is a Spanish restaurant. It is near my home.
=Antonio's Restaurant =Antonio's Restaurant
Mixed paella is the most popular dish at this restaurant.
popular의 최상급
All of the food is really fresh and delicious, and the prices are low. I
price가 비싸거나 싼 것을 표현할 때는 보통 high나 low를 사용한다.
recommend this restaurant!

My Rating ★★★★☆

구문해설 • favorite: 매우 좋아하는 • Spanish: 스페인의 • paella: 파엘라(쌀, 닭고기, 생선, 채소를 넣은 스페인 요리) • recommend: 추천하다

내가 가장 좋아하는 음식점 방문 후기
내가 가장 좋아하는 음식점은 Antonio's Restaurant이야. 그곳은 스페인 음식점이야. 그곳은 나의 집에서 가까워. 이 음식점에서 가장 인기 있는 음식은 혼합 파엘라야. 모든 음식이 정말 신선하고 맛있으며 가격도 싸. 나는 이 음식점을 추천해.
나의 평가 ★★★★☆

Culture Link

In China, people eat noodles on their birthday. Chinese people don't want to
on+특정한 날
break the noodles to live a long life.
부사적 용법(목적)
Doro wat is a chicken curry from Ethiopia. There are a lot of vegetables in it.
=many
People eat this dish for New Year's dinner.
요리
Bánh xu xê is a traditional Vietnamese cake. People eat this cake at weddings.
tradition+-al (형용사 어미)
Eating the cake means the husbands and wife will have a happy life together.
In the United States, people eat turkey to celebrate Thanksgiving. They give
부사적 용법(목적)
thanks for the food and their health.

구문해설 • a lot of: 많은(= many) • dish: 음식, 요리 • traditional: 전통적인 • celebrate: 축하하다 • give thanks for: ~에 대해 감사하다

중국에서 사람들은 그들의 생일에 국수를 먹는다. 중국 사람들은 장수하려고 국수를 자르려 하지 않는다.
Doro wat은 에티오피아의 치킨 카레 요리이다. 그 안에 많은 야채가 들어 있다. 사람들은 이 요리를 새해 만찬으로 먹는다.
Bánh xu xê는 전통적인 베트남 케이크이다. 사람들은 이 케이크를 결혼식에서 먹는다. 이 케이크를 먹는 것은 남편과 아내가 함께 행복한 삶을 살 것을 의미한다.
미국에서 사람들은 추수감사절을 기념하기 위해 칠면조 요리를 먹는다. 그들은 음식과 그들의 건강에 대해 감사한다.

영역별 핵심문제

Words & Expressions

01 다음 밑줄 친 부분의 우리말 뜻으로 알맞지 않은 것은?

① If you wash your hair too often, it can get too dry. (종종, 자주)
② Eating sweets is bad for your teeth. (달콤한)
③ Smoking can seriously damage your health. (건강)
④ Art books are expensive to produce, especially, if they contain color illustrations. (특히)
⑤ Cut the orange in half. (자르다)

02 다음 빈칸에 알맞은 단어를 고르시오.

> *Gimchi* is one of the ________ Korean foods.

① fast ② modern ③ free
④ traditional ⑤ fried

03 다음 제시된 단어를 사용하여 자연스러운 문장을 만들 수 없는 것은?

> 보기
> contest appetizer choice culture

① You have a ________ – you can stay here on your own or you can come with us.
② In our ________, it is rude to ask someone how much they earn.
③ Sara had to leave her job due to ill ________.
④ The finals of the ________ were held in the United States.
⑤ Crackers are also excellent as a(n) ________.

04 다음 대화의 밑줄 친 have와 같은 의미로 쓰인 문장을 고르시오.

> A: I'm not hungry.
> B: But for your health, you'd better have some food.

① He had to go to Germany.
② You have beautiful eyes.
③ We had our money stolen.
④ Will you have some more cake?
⑤ Do you have any brothers and sisters?

05 다음 빈칸에 공통으로 들어갈 단어를 고르시오.

> • All of them ________ from wealthy, upper class families.
> • You should install the software that ________ with the drive.

① came ② went ③ lived
④ checked ⑤ got

Conversation

[06~07] 우리말과 일치하도록 빈칸에 알맞은 말을 쓰시오.

06

> A: I want to be taller.
> B: Then ________________. (우유를 마시는 게 좋아.)
> A: Thank you ________________. (너의 충고 고마워.)

07

> G: ________________. (저 여기 처음 왔어요.) What do you recommend?
> M: ________________ and salad. (저는 피자와 샐러드를 추천해요.)

08 다음 대화의 ①~⑤ 중 어색한 곳을 모두 바르게 고치시오.

A: ①I eat too much snacks.
B: ②You'd better eating ③more healthy food.
A: ④What do you recommend?
B: ⑤I recommend chicken salad.

➡ ______ ➡ ______
______ ➡ ______

[09~12] 다음 대화를 읽고, 물음에 답하시오.

G: You look very tired today. Didn't you sleep well?
B: Yes, I did. (①) But I often feel tired these days, especially in the morning.
G: (A)Do you eat breakfast? (②)
B: No, I don't.
G: You'd better (B)________(eat) breakfast. Breakfast (C)______(give) you energy. (③)
B: I didn't know that. (④)
G: Well, you (D)________ also exercise every day. That will help you. (⑤)
B: Okay. I will.

09 위 대화의 ①~⑤ 중 주어진 문장이 들어갈 알맞은 곳은?

Do you have any other suggestions?

① ② ③ ④ ⑤

10 밑줄 친 (A)에 '보통, 대개'의 의미를 지닌 부사를 넣어 질문을 만드시오.

➡ ______________________________

11 주어진 단어를 이용해 빈칸 (B)와 (C)를 완성하시오.

➡ (B) ____________ (C) ____________

12 위 대화의 빈칸 (D)에 알맞은 말을 고르시오.

① might ② will ③ should
④ could ⑤ have

[13~15] 다음 대화를 읽고, 물음에 답하시오.

W: Hello. Are you ready (A)______ order?
B: ①It's my first time here. ②What do you recommend?
W: ③I recommend the chicken sandwich. ④It is the more popular item at our restaurant.
B: Well, I don't like chicken very much. ⑤Could you recommend something else?
W: How (B)______ the turkey sandwich?
B: Oh, I love turkey. I'll have that.
W: Why don't you order a drink (C)______ the sandwich? You can get a 500-won discount.
B: That's great. Then I'll have an orange juice, too.

13 위 대화의 ①~⑤ 중 어법상 어색한 것을 고르시오.

① ② ③ ④ ⑤

14 빈칸 (A)~(C)에 알맞은 것을 〈보기〉에서 골라 쓰시오.

보기
for about in with to

➡ (A)________ (B)________ (C)________

15 위 대화의 내용과 일치하지 않는 것은?

① The boy visits the restaurant for the first time.
② When the boy orders a drink with the sandwich, the price will be discounted.
③ The woman works for the restaurant.
④ The turkey sandwich is the most popular at the restaurant.
⑤ The boy doesn't like chicken.

Grammar

16 다음 주어진 문장의 밑줄 친 부분과 같은 역할을 하는 것을 <u>두 개</u> 고르시오.

> Eddie is a boy <u>who</u> often goes to the movies.

① Ken loves the lady <u>who</u> he worked with.
② The woman <u>who</u> is talking on the phone is my mother.
③ The girl <u>who</u> I met yesterday is my sister.
④ <u>Who</u> are you going to travel Europe with?
⑤ A scientist is someone <u>who</u> studies science.

17 다음 밑줄 친 부분의 쓰임이 <u>어색한</u> 것은?

① I <u>often</u> play computer games at home.
② His room is <u>always</u> in order.
③ Esther <u>never</u> will fail to earn popularity.
④ We <u>usually</u> eat a salad as an appetizer.
⑤ Kyle <u>sometimes</u> takes a walk to the park.

18 다음 밑줄 친 부분이 어법상 <u>어색한</u> 것은?

① It's a special phone <u>which</u> works well in the water.
② Monica lives in a house <u>which</u> has a beautiful garden.
③ Cathy is worried about the baby <u>that</u> is sick in bed.
④ *Taekwondo* is a very exciting exercise <u>who</u> started in Korea.
⑤ Where is the book <u>that</u> I gave you yesterday?

19 다음 중 어법상 올바른 것은?

① He seldom changed the opinion he had formed.
② I play sometimes sports.
③ We fry usually plantains.
④ I will do that again never.
⑤ I have a few free afternoons often a week.

20 다음 그림을 참고하고 괄호 안에 주어진 어휘를 이용하여 빈칸에 알맞은 말을 쓰시오.

Chang's Restaurant　Jin's Restaurant　Bella's Restaurant

(1) Jiwoo will go to Chang's Restaurant ____________________. (noodles)
(2) Jiwoo will go to Jin's Restaurant ____________________. (sushi)
(3) Jiwoo will go to Bella's Restaurant ____________________. (pizza)

21 다음 괄호 안에서 어법상 올바른 것을 고르시오.

(1) Our lunches (are always / always are) healthy, and they taste good, too.
(2) I (knew rarely / rarely knew) that Mike liked Ann.
(3) We (should always / always should) do something to solve problems.

22 다음 중 어법상 옳은 것은?

① She will miss always him.
② My mom watches usually TV after dinner.
③ I wake often up late on weekends.
④ You take never care of your brother.
⑤ I sometimes hang out with my friends after work.

23 주어진 어구를 이용하여 다음 우리말을 영작하시오. (관계대명사 that 사용 금지)

(1) 나는 버스에 휴대폰을 놓고 내린 소녀를 찾고 있는 중이다. (her cell phone, on the bus, look for, leave)
➡ ______________________

(2) 코끼리는 코가 긴 동물이다. (an animal, a long nose, have)
➡ ______________________

(3) 많은 책이 있는 그 상자는 아주 무겁다. (many, very, the box, have)
➡ ______________________

(4) 아빠는 항상 매우 조심해서 운전하신다. (Dad, carefully, drive his car)
➡ ______________________

(5) 너는 아기를 혼자 두어서는 절대로 안 된다. (never, alone, a baby, leave, should)
➡ ______________________

Reading

[24~26] 다음 글을 읽고, 물음에 답하시오.

Hello, this is food reporter Minjun ___ⓐ___ Korea. (①) ___ⓑ___ many students, lunch is the best part of the school day. (②) In Korea, we often eat rice and soup ___ⓑ___ lunch. (③) We also have side dishes, such as *Bulgogi* or *Gimchi*. (④) Sometimes our school serves special dishes, such as pizza, *Bibimbap*, or pasta. (⑤) Let's hear ___ⓐ___ our food reporters!

24 위 글의 흐름으로 보아, 주어진 문장이 들어가기에 가장 적절한 곳은?

What do students who live in other countries eat for lunch?

① ② ③ ④ ⑤

25 위 글의 빈칸 ⓐ와 ⓑ에 각각 공통으로 들어갈 전치사가 바르게 짝지어진 것은? (대·소문자 무시)

① from – to
② in – by
③ in – from
④ from – for
⑤ on – for

26 위 글을 읽고 대답할 수 없는 질문은?

① Where is Minjun from?
② Why is lunch the best part of the school day for many students?
③ What do students often eat as main dishes for lunch in Korea?
④ What side dishes do students have in Korea?
⑤ What does Minjun's school serve as special dishes?

[27~28] 다음 글을 읽고, 물음에 답하시오.

Belle, France
Our school serves healthy and balanced meals. We usually eat a salad ⓐas an appetizer. Main dishes often include meat or fish. We also eat fresh fruit at the end of the lunch. Oh, I can never forget about baguettes! They're great with cheese. Our school also has a special rule. We must stay at the lunch table for at least 30 minutes.

27 위 글의 밑줄 친 ⓐas와 같은 의미로 쓰인 것을 고르시오.

① Do as you like.
② This box will serve as a table.
③ As she was tired, she soon fell asleep.
④ He runs as fast as you.
⑤ As I entered the room, he was crying.

28 벨의 학교 급식에서 볼 수 <u>없는</u> 음식을 고르시오.

① a salad ② meat or fish
③ fresh fruit ④ curry
⑤ baguettes

29 주어진 글 다음에 이어질 글의 순서로 가장 적절한 것은?

Usually, we have beans and rice for lunch.

(A) A plantain is a fruit which looks like a banana. We usually fry plantains.
(B) Meat and vegetables are common in our side dishes. My favorite lunch comes with plantains.
(C) Our school lunches are fresh because the vegetables and fruit come from local farms.

① (A) – (C) – (B) ② (B) – (A) – (C)
③ (B) – (C) – (A) ④ (C) – (A) – (B)
⑤ (C) – (B) – (A)

[30~31] 다음 글을 읽고, 물음에 답하시오.

Bruno, Brazil
Usually, we have beans and rice for lunch. Meat and vegetables are common in our side dishes. My favorite lunch comes with plantains. A plantain is a fruit ___ⓐ___ looks like a banana. We usually fry plantains. Our school lunches are fresh because the vegetables and fruit come from local farms.

30 위 글의 내용과 일치하지 <u>않는</u> 것은?

① 브루노는 보통 점심으로 콩과 밥을 먹는다.
② 브루노가 좋아하는 점심에는 플랜테인이 나온다.
③ 플랜테인은 기름에 튀긴 바나나이다.
④ 브루노의 학교 급식 재료인 채소와 과일은 현지 농장에서 온다.
⑤ 브루노의 학교 급식은 신선하다.

31 위 글의 빈칸 ⓐ에 알맞은 말을 <u>모두</u> 고르시오.

① that ② who
③ what ④ which
⑤ whom

[32~33] 다음 글을 읽고, 물음에 답하시오.

Nicole, Singapore
People ⓐ<u>that</u> live in Singapore come from many different cultures, so we have ⓑ<u>both</u> Eastern and Western dishes at lunch. Students can choose from many dishes, such as curry, noodle soup, or pasta, ⓒ<u>each days</u>. My school ⓓ<u>won</u> an award for healthy school food last year. Our lunches are always healthy, and Ⓐ<u>they</u> taste good, ⓔ<u>either</u>!

32 위 글의 밑줄 친 ⓐ~ⓔ 중 어법상 <u>틀린</u> 개수를 고르시오.

① 1개 ② 2개 ③ 3개 ④ 4개 ⑤ 5개

33 위 글의 밑줄 친 Ⓐ<u>they</u>가 가리키는 것을 본문에서 찾아 쓰시오.

➡ ____________________

단원별 예상문제

[01~02] 다음 대화를 읽고, 물음에 답하시오.

G: I think I eat too many sweets these days.
B: That's good for your health. 대신에 과일을 먹는 게 좋아.

출제율 90%

01 위 대화에서 흐름상 어색한 부분을 찾아 고치시오.

__________ ➡ __________

출제율 85%

02 위 대화의 밑줄 친 우리말을 영작하시오.

➡ __________

[03~04] 다음 빈칸에 공통으로 알맞은 단어를 쓰시오.

출제율 100%

03

- Get _______ earlier, and you will become healthy.
- Most toasters take a few minutes to heat the bread _______.

➡ __________

출제율 90%

04

- He'll stay in bed for _______ least half a month.
- This happens _______ the end of summer.

➡ __________

[05~06] 다음 빈칸에 가장 알맞은 단어를 고르시오.

출제율 90%

05

A: I'm going to the Spanish restaurant. What do you recommend there?
B: I recommend the _______. It is delicious.

① sushi ② *bulgogi* ③ curry
④ paella ⑤ fish and chips

출제율 90%

06

A: My new home is too far from school.
B: You'd better take public _______.
A: What do you recommend?
B: I recommend the bus.

① accommodation ② traffic
③ transform ④ transportation
⑤ equipment

출제율 100%

07 다음 <보기>와 같은 관계가 되도록 주어진 빈칸에 알맞은 말을 쓰시오. (주어진 철자로 시작할 것)

보기
Eastern — Western

(1) rotten – f_______ (2) same – d_______
(3) rare – c_______ (4) exclude – i_______

출제율 90%

08 대화 내용의 흐름상 어색한 부분을 고르시오.

A: ①My mom's birthday is coming, but ②I have enough money.
B: ③You'd better make a gift yourself.
A: ④What do you recommend?
B: ⑤I recommend chocolate.

① ② ③ ④ ⑤

출제율 95%

09 다음 대화의 빈칸에 알맞은 것은?

A: I usually have a pain in my stomach after lunch.
B: __________

① Then you should make lunch.
② I've been eating for an hour.
③ Then you'd better eat slowly.
④ Thanks for your advice.
⑤ I should go grocery shopping.

[10~12] 다음 대화를 읽고, 물음에 답하시오.

G: Justin, our school cooking contest is tomorrow. ⓐWhat are you going to make?
B: ⓑI'm going to make sandwiches.
G: What do you want to (A)__________?
B: Chicken, cheese, and eggs. (①)
G: ⓒYou'd better put vegetables in your sandwiches. How about onions and carrots? (②)
B: No, I'm not going to add them. ⓓI like those vegetables. (③)
G: ⓔThat's not a good idea. Mr. Kim said we should make healthy food for the contest. (④)
B: You're right. (⑤)

출제율 85%

10 위 대화의 ①~⑤ 중 주어진 문장이 들어갈 알맞은 곳은?

I should go grocery shopping and buy onions and carrots.

① ② ③ ④ ⑤

출제율 95%

11 위 대화의 빈칸 (A)에 들어갈 말로 적절한 것은?

① put them in ② put it in
③ put in them ④ put in it
⑤ put it in them

출제율 90%

12 위 대화의 ⓐ~ⓔ 중 흐름상 어색한 것을 고르시오.

① ⓐ ② ⓑ ③ ⓒ ④ ⓓ ⑤ ⓔ

출제율 90%

13 다음 빈칸에 들어갈 알맞은 말을 모두 고르시오.

Joel is a person __________ sometimes listens to classical music.

① who ② whose ③ whom
④ that ⑤ which

출제율 95%

14 다음 중 어법상 옳은 문장은?

① Terry eats never anything after 7 p.m.
② She drinks usually a cup of coffee after breakfast.
③ Does your mom go often for a walk?
④ I always am nice to him.
⑤ I sometimes play baduk with Jack.

출제율 90%

15 괄호 안에 주어진 어구를 사용해 다음을 영작하시오. (that 사용 금지)

(1) 나는 주머니가 많은 조끼를 사고 싶다. (a vest, pocket, want, have, 10 단어)
➡ ____________________
(2) 나는 버스에서 음악을 듣고 있던 Eva를 만났다. (on the bus, 11 단어)
➡ ____________________
(3) 그녀는 100 단어를 말할 수 있는 앵무새를 가지고 있다. (a parrot, words, have, speak, 9 단어)
➡ ____________________
(4) 수학 문제는 내게 항상 어렵다. (math problems, for me, difficult, 7 단어)
➡ ____________________

16 주어진 어휘를 알맞은 곳에 넣어 문장을 다시 쓰시오.

(1) Dad goes to work by bike. (usually)

➡ ____________________

(2) Dorothy is busy every day. (always)

➡ ____________________

(3) I can forget about baguettes. (never)

➡ ____________________

[17~19] 다음 글을 읽고, 물음에 답하시오.

Hello, (A)[it / this] is food reporter Minjun from Korea. For many students, lunch is the best part of the school day. In Korea, we often eat rice and soup for lunch. We also have side dishes, such as *Bulgogi* or *Gimchi*. Sometimes our school serves special dishes, such as pizza, *Bibimbap*, or pasta. (B)[What / How] do students ⓐwho live in other countries (C)[eat / to eat] for lunch? Let's hear from our food reporters!

출제율 90%

17 위 글의 괄호 (A)~(C)에서 어법상 알맞은 낱말을 골라 쓰시오.

➡ (A)________ (B)________ (C)________

출제율 100%

18 위 글의 밑줄 친 ⓐwho와 문법적 쓰임이 같은 것을 고르시오.

① I wonder who wrote that letter.
② Who ever told you that?
③ The man who called you is my dad.
④ Nobody knew who he was.
⑤ Who is the captain?

출제율 95%

19 본문의 내용과 일치하도록 다음 빈칸 (A)와 (B)에 알맞은 단어를 쓰시오.

> Minjun introduces the school (A)________ of Korea, (B)________ ________ main dishes, side dishes, and special dishes.

출제율 90%

20 주어진 글 다음에 이어질 글의 순서로 가장 적절한 것은?

> Our school serves healthy and balanced meals.

(A) They're great with cheese. Our school also has a special rule. We must stay at the lunch table for at least 30 minutes.
(B) We also eat fresh fruit at the end of the lunch. Oh, I can never forget about baguettes!
(C) We usually eat a salad as an appetizer. Main dishes often include meat or fish.

① (A) – (C) – (B)   ② (B) – (A) – (C)
③ (B) – (C) – (A)   ④ (C) – (A) – (B)
⑤ (C) – (B) – (A)

[21~22] 다음 글을 읽고, 물음에 답하시오.

Belle, France
Our school serves healthy and balanced meals. We usually eat a salad as an ___ⓐ___. Main dishes often include meat or fish. We also eat fresh fruit at the end of the lunch. Oh, I can never forget about baguettes! They're great ___ⓑ___ cheese. Our school also has a special rule. We must stay at the lunch table ___ⓒ___ at least 30 minutes.

출제율 95%

21 주어진 영영풀이를 참고하여 빈칸 ⓐ에 철자 a로 시작하는 단어를 쓰시오.

> the first course of a meal which includes a small amount of food

➡ ____________________

출제율 100%

22 위 글의 빈칸 ⓑ와 ⓒ에 들어갈 전치사가 바르게 짝지어진 것은?

① for – from
② with – by
③ with – for
④ to – for
⑤ on – in

[23~24] 다음 글을 읽고, 물음에 답하시오.

> Bruno, Brazil
> Usually, we have beans and rice for lunch. Meat and vegetables are common in our side dishes. My favorite lunch comes with plantains. A plantain is a fruit which looks like a banana. We usually fry plantains. Our school lunches are fresh because the vegetables and fruit come from local farms.

출제율 85%

23 위 글을 읽고 알 수 없는 것을 고르시오.

① What do the students have for lunch at Bruno's school?
② What is common in their side dishes at Bruno's school?
③ What does Bruno's favorite lunch come with?
④ What is a plantain?
⑤ Why do they usually fry plantains?

출제율 95%

24 다음 질문에 대한 알맞은 대답을 주어진 단어로 시작하여 쓰시오. (8 단어)

Q: Why are Bruno's school lunches fresh?
A: Because ________________
________________.

[25~27] 다음 글을 읽고, 물음에 답하시오.

> Nicole, Singapore
> ⓐPeople which live in Singapore come from many different cultures, so we have both ___ⓑ___ and ___ⓒ___ dishes at lunch. Students can choose from many dishes, such as curry, noodle soup, or pasta, each day. My school won an award for healthy school food last year. Our lunches are always healthy, and they taste good, too!

출제율 90%

25 위 글의 밑줄 친 ⓐ에서 어법상 틀린 부분을 찾아 고치시오.

________________ ➡ ________________

출제율 90%

26 위 글의 빈칸 ⓑ와 ⓒ에 East와 West를 각각 알맞은 형태로 쓰시오.

➡ ⓑ________________, ⓒ ________________

출제율 95%

27 위 글의 내용과 일치하지 않는 것은?

① 싱가포르에 사는 사람들은 매우 다양한 문화권에서 왔다.
② 니콜의 학교는 점심에 동양식과 서양식을 모두 먹는다.
③ 학생들은 매일 카레, 국수, 또는 파스타와 같은 많은 요리 중에 선택할 수 있다.
④ 니콜의 학교는 올해 건강한 학교 급식상을 받았다.
⑤ 니콜의 학교 급식은 항상 건강에 좋고 맛 또한 좋다.

서술형 실전문제

[01~03] 다음 대화를 읽고, 물음에 답하시오.

G: You look very tired today. Didn't you sleep well?
B: ①No, I didn't. But I often feel tired these days, especially in the morning.
G: ②Do you usually eat breakfast?
B: No, I don't.
G: ③You'd better eat breakfast. Breakfast gives you energy.
B: I didn't know that. ④Do you have any other suggestions?
G: Well, you should also exercise every day. ⑤That will help you.
B: Okay. I will.

01 중요 위 대화의 밑줄 친 ①~⑤ 중 흐름상 어색한 부분을 골라 바르게 고치시오.

__________ ➡ __________

02 주어진 영영풀이에 해당하는 단어를 위 대화에서 찾아 쓰시오.

the meal you have in the morning

➡ __________

03 중요 위 대화의 내용에 맞게 빈칸을 채우시오.

The boy ________ ________ ________ these days, especially in the morning. The girl thinks ________ ________ ________ eat breakfast and ________ ________ ________ ________.

04 다음 두 문장을 관계대명사를 이용하여 한 문장으로 연결하시오.

(1) • I think Minhee is a girl.
• She is always kind.
➡ ______________________________
____

(2) • Teresa is singing on the stage.
• She has a beautiful voice.
➡ ______________________________
____

(3) • Cloe lives in a house.
• It has a nice swimming pool.
➡ ______________________________
____

(4) • I like the dog.
• It belongs to Kelly.
➡ ______________________________

(5) • There were a man and his horse.
• They were crossing the river.
➡ ______________________________
____

05 중요 다음 문장에서 잘못된 부분을 바르게 고쳐 문장을 다시 쓰시오

(1) The man which works at this restaurant is serving food.
➡ ______________________________
____

(2) These are the poems who was written by Robert Frost.
➡ ______________________________
____

(3) The girl is very pretty whom wears a white dress.
➡ ______________________________
____

[06~08] 다음 글을 읽고, 물음에 답하시오.

Hello, this is food reporter Minjun from Korea. For many students, lunch is the best part of the school day. In Korea, we often eat rice and soup for lunch. ⓐ우리는 또한 불고기나 김치 같은 반찬도 먹습니다. Sometimes our school serves special dishes, such as pizza, *Bibimbap*, or pasta. ⓑWhat do students who live in another countries eat for lunch? Let's hear from our food reporters!

06 다음 질문에 대한 알맞은 대답을 쓰시오. (1 단어)

Q: For many students, what is the best part of the school day?
A: ________.

07 위 글의 밑줄 친 ⓐ의 우리말에 맞게 한 단어를 보충하여, 주어진 어구를 알맞게 배열하시오.

Gimchi / side dishes / or / such as / *Bulgogi* / have / we

➡ ________________________________
____

중요
08 위 글의 밑줄 친 ⓑ에서 어법상 틀린 부분을 찾아 고치시오.

____________ ➡ ____________

[09~11] 다음 글을 읽고, 물음에 답하시오.

Belle, France
Our school serves healthy and balanced meals. We usually eat a salad as an appetizer. Main dishes often include meat or fish. We also eat fresh fruit at the end of the lunch. Oh, I can never forget about baguettes! They're great with cheese. Our school also has a special rule. We must stay at the lunch table for at least 30 minutes.

09 본문의 내용과 일치하도록 다음 빈칸 (A)와 (B)에 알맞은 단어를 쓰시오.

The (A)________ ________ at Belle's school is that students must stay at the lunch table (B)________ ________ ________ ________ ________.

중요
10 다음 빈칸 (A)~(C)에 알맞은 단어를 넣어 벨의 학교 급식을 정리하시오.

- appetizer: (A)____________
- main dishes: (B)____________
- dessert: (C)____________

11 다음 빈칸에 알맞은 단어를 넣어 바게트를 맛있게 먹는 방법을 완성하시오.

Baguettes taste great ________ ________.

창의사고력 서술형 문제

01 다음 대화의 빈칸에 주어진 단어를 이용하여 알맞은 충고의 말을 쓰시오.

A: I had a fight with my best friend. What should I do?
B: ____ (had)
A: Do you have any other suggestions?
B: ____ (should, think)

02 관계대명사를 이용하여 자신이 갖고 있는 것을 설명하는 문장을 쓰시오.

(1) I have ____.
(2) I have ____.
(3) I have ____.
(4) I have ____.

03 다음 정보를 바탕으로 음식점 방문 후기를 작성하시오.

1. What is the name of the restaurant?	Antonio's Restaurant
2. What kind of restaurant is it?	a Spanish restaurant
3. Where is it?	near my home
4. What is the most popular dish there?	mixed paella
5. How is the food?	fresh and delicious
6. How are the prices?	low

Review of My Favorite Restaurant
My favorite restaurant is Antonio's Restaurant. It is a (A)______ restaurant. It is near my home. (B)________ ________ is the most popular dish at this restaurant. All of the food is really (C) ______ and ______, and the prices are (D)______. I recommend this restaurant!

My Rating ★★★★☆

단원별 모의고사

[01~02] 다음 빈칸에 공통으로 알맞은 단어를 쓰시오.

01

- He lived ________ Busan seven years ago.
- They put some coins ________ the piggy bank.

➡ ____________________

02

- He continued working ________ a long time.
- That's not good ________ your health.
- Thanks ________ your advice.

➡ ____________________

03 다음 제시된 의미에 맞는 단어를 주어진 철자로 시작하여 빈칸에 쓰고, 알맞은 것을 골라 문장을 완성하시오.

- l________: relating to the particular area you live in, or the area you are talking about
- r________: to advise someone to do something, especially because you have special knowledge of a situation or subject
- m________: consisting of several different types of things or people

(1) Wine ________ with vinegar was good.
(2) We visited the ________ markets and saw beautiful earrings.
(3) What do you ________ for the woman?

04 〈보기〉의 어휘를 사용하여 문장을 완성하시오. (형태 변화 가능)

보기: take such check these taste

(1) Let's ________ out the new restaurant down the street.
(2) Foods ________ as fish, mushrooms, and milk have vitamin D.
(3) Don't worry about me. I can ________ care of myself.
(4) The milk I drank for lunch ________ sweet.

05 다음 대화에서 어법상 어색한 부분을 모두 찾아 고치시오. (3개)

A: I get often colds these days.
B: Then you'd better drink a lot water and washed your hands often.
A: Thank you for your advice.

➡ (1) ____________________
(2) ____________________
(3) ____________________

06 다음 밑줄 친 문장과 같은 의미가 되도록 주어진 단어를 이용해 영작하시오.

A: I'm going to the British restaurant. What do you recommend there?
B: I recommend the fish and chips. It is delicious.

➡ (1) ____________________ (which)
(2) ____________________ (recommendations)

[07~09] 다음 대화를 읽고, 물음에 답하시오.

B: Good morning, Jiwoo. (A)________
G: ①I'm searching for a restaurant for my class party.
B: Wow! (B)________
G: ②It's next Friday. ③We want to go to Bella's Restaurant, ④but it is too expensive.
B: (C)________ I went there once. ⑤The food and prices was good.
G: Sounds great. (D)________
B: I recommend the noodle soup.
G: (E)(we, I. go, think, there, should). Thank you.

07 (A)~(D)에 들어갈 말을 〈보기〉에서 골라 쓰시오.

보기
- Why don't you check out Chang's Restaurant?
- Do you have any other recommendations?
- What do you recommend there?
- When is the party?
- What do you want to do?
- What are you doing right now?

➡ (A) ________
(B) ________
(C) ________
(D) ________

08 위의 대화의 ①~⑤ 중 어법상 어색한 것을 고르시오.

① ② ③ ④ ⑤

09 괄호 (E) 안에 주어진 단어들을 바르게 배열하여 문장을 완성하시오.

➡ ________

[10~14] 다음 대화를 읽고, 물음에 답하시오.

W: Hello. Are you ready to order?
B: It's my first time here. (①) What do you recommend?
W: (②) It is the most popular item at our restaurant.
B: Well, I don't like chicken very much. (③) (A)(else, something, could, recommend, you)?
W: (④) How about the turkey sandwich?
B: Oh, I love turkey. I'll have that.
W: (⑤) Why don't you order a drink with the sandwich? You can (B)________ a 500-won discount.
B: That's great. Then I'll have an orange juice, too.

10 위 대화의 ①~⑤ 중 주어진 문장이 들어갈 알맞은 곳은?

I recommend the chicken sandwich.

① ② ③ ④ ⑤

11 Where are they now?

① hospital ② school ③ home
④ bakery ⑤ restaurant

12 주어진 영영풀이에 해당하는 단어를 대화에서 찾아 쓰시오.

to ask for food or a drink in a restaurant, bar, etc.

➡ ________

13 위 대화의 괄호 (A) 안에 주어진 단어들을 바르게 배열하여 문장을 완성하시오.

➡ ________

14 위 대화의 빈칸 (B)에 알맞은 단어를 고르시오.

① do ② take ③ give
④ get ⑤ allow

15 다음 밑줄 친 that과 바꿔 쓸 수 있는 것은?

> I want to visit the Netherlands that is famous for its windmill.

① what ② who
③ whose ④ whom
⑤ which

16 다음 중 밑줄 친 부분이 어색한 것은?

① She has a cat that has blue eyes.
② A computer is a thing which is usually on our teacher's desk.
③ One never is too old to learn.
④ I often use the Internet.
⑤ Buzz Aldrin was the astronaut who took the first space selfie.

17 다음 중 밑줄 친 that의 쓰임이 다른 것을 고르시오.(2개)

① That the earth is round is common knowledge today.
② Here is a fish that I caught this morning.
③ It's possible that he has not received the letter.
④ He is the greatest novelist that has ever lived.
⑤ She warned me that I should be more careful.

18 괄호 안의 어휘를 이용하여 우리말에 맞게 알맞은 빈도부사를 써서 영어로 옮기시오.

(1) 엄마는 아침에 대개 7시에 일어나신다. (mom, get up)
(2) Abigail은 항상 친절하고 자주 미소 짓는다. (smile, frequently, kind)
(3) Richard는 드물게 그 강으로 수영하러 갔었다. (seldom, go swimming)

➡ (1) ______________________
(2) ______________________
(3) ______________________

19 다음 문장에서 어법상 어색한 것을 찾아 고치시오.

(1) Pasta is a dish who is never popular for lunch.
(2) Look at the boy which he is dancing on the street.
(3) He helps never me.

➡ ______________________
____
____

[20~22] 다음 글을 읽고, 물음에 답하시오.

> Hello, this is food reporter Minjun from Korea. For many students, lunch is the best part of the school day. ①In Korea, we often eat rice and soup for lunch. ②We also have side dishes, such as *Bulgogi* or *Gimchi*. ③ There are many delicious side dishes in the world. ④Sometimes our school ___ⓐ___ special dishes, such as pizza, *Bibimbap*, or pasta. ⑤ What do students who live in other countries eat for lunch? Let's hear from our food reporters!

20 위 글의 ①~⑤ 중에서 전체 흐름과 관계 없는 문장은?

① ② ③ ④ ⑤

21 위 글의 빈칸 ⓐ에 들어갈 알맞은 말을 고르시오.

① keeps ② holds ③ builds
④ serves ⑤ carries

22 위 글의 뒤에 나올 내용으로 가장 알맞은 것을 고르시오.

① 민준이네 학교의 특별한 점심
② 점심에 대한 다른 나라 음식 취재 기자들의 보고
③ 점심시간에 가능한 여가활동에 대한 다른 나라 리포터들의 소개
④ 건강에 좋은 점심을 만드는 방법 소개
⑤ 동양과 서양의 점심 문화의 차이점 소개

[23~25] 다음 글을 읽고, 물음에 답하시오.

Bruno, Brazil
Usually, we have beans and rice for lunch. (①) Meat and vegetables are common in our side dishes. (②) A plantain is a fruit which looks like a banana. (③) We usually fry plantains. (④) ⓐ<u>Our school lunches are fresh because of the vegetables and fruit come from local farms.</u> (⑤)

23 위 글의 흐름으로 보아, 주어진 문장이 들어가기에 가장 적절한 곳은?

My favorite lunch comes with plantains.

① ② ③ ④ ⑤

24 위 글의 밑줄 친 ⓐ에서 어법상 틀린 부분을 찾아 고치시오.

__________ ➡ __________

25 다음 빈칸에 알맞은 단어를 넣어 plantain의 요리법에 대한 소개를 완성하시오.

People in Brazil usually ________ plantains.

[26~27] 다음 글을 읽고, 물음에 답하시오.

Nicole, Singapore
People who live in Singapore come from many different cultures, so we have ⓐ<u>both Eastern and Western dishes</u> at lunch. Students can choose __ⓑ__ many dishes, such as curry, noodle soup, or pasta, each day. My school won an award __ⓒ__ healthy school food last year. Our lunches are always healthy, and they taste good, too!

26 위 글의 밑줄 친 ⓐ에 해당하는 음식을 본문에서 찾아 쓰시오.

➡ ____________________

27 위 글의 빈칸 ⓑ와 ⓒ에 들어갈 전치사가 바르게 짝지어진 것은?

① from – for ② in – by
③ for – from ④ from – to
⑤ on – for

Lesson 3

Understand the World

의사소통 기능

- 경험 묻고 답하기
  A: Have you ever been to Brazil?
  B: Yes, I have. / No, I haven't.
- 의미 묻고 답하기
  A: What does that mean in Korea?
  B: It means good luck.

언어 형식

- 현재완료
  For a long time, Koreans **have thought** that fish are good guards.
- so ... that 구문
  It's **so** old **that** I can't really tell, but is it a fish?
  I'm enjoying this trip **so** much **that** I want to stay longer.

교과서

Words & Expressions

Key Words

- □ **arrive** [əráiv] ㊍ 도착하다
- □ **bat** [bæt] ㊔ 박쥐
- □ **beach** [biʧ] ㊔ 해변, 바닷가
- □ **bow** [bau] ㊍ (인사를 위해) 머리를 숙이다, 절하다
- □ **calendar** [kǽlənder] ㊔ 달력
- □ **Chinese** [ʧainí:z] ㊕ 중국의 ㊔ 중국어
- □ **clothes** [klouz] ㊔ 옷, 의복
- □ **colored** [kʌlərd] ㊕ 채색된, 색깔이 있는
- □ **crow** [krou] ㊍ (닭이) 울다 ㊔ 까마귀
- □ **darkness** [dɑ́:rknis] ㊔ 어둠, 암흑
- □ **evil** [í:vəl] ㊕ 사악한, 악마의
- □ **experience** [ikspíəriəns] ㊔ 경험 ㊍ 경험하다
- □ **face** [feis] ㊍ ~을 향하다
- □ **festival** [féstəvəl] ㊔ 축제
- □ **full moon** 보름달
- □ **gift shop** 선물 가게
- □ **good luck** 행운
- □ **greet** [gri:t] ㊍ 맞이하다, 환영하다
- □ **guard** [ga:rd] ㊔ 보초, 경비병
- □ **guest** [gest] ㊔ 손님
- □ **half moon** 반달
- □ **Indian** [índiən] ㊕ 인도의, 인도 사람의
- □ **international** [ìntərnǽʃənəl] ㊕ 국제적인, 세계적인
- □ **last** [læst] ㊍ 계속되다, 지속되다
- □ **last year** 작년에
- □ **lock** [lak] ㊔ 자물쇠 ㊍ 잠그다
- □ **luck** [lʌk] ㊔ 운
- □ **musical** [mjú:zikəl] ㊔ 뮤지컬
- □ **mean** [mi:n] ㊍ 의미하다
- □ **palm** [pa:m] ㊔ 손바닥, 야자나무
- □ **pay** [pei] ㊍ 지불하다
- □ **peace** [pi:s] ㊔ 평화, 화해
- □ **pillow** [pílou] ㊔ 베개
- □ **powder** [páudər] ㊔ 가루, 분말
- □ **protect** [prətékt] ㊍ 보호하다
- □ **remind** [rimáind] ㊍ 생각나게 하다, 상기시키다
- □ **represent** [rèprizént] ㊍ 나타내다, 상징하다
- □ **rooster** [rú:stər] ㊔ 수탉
- □ **rude** [ru:d] ㊕ 무례한
- □ **scary** [skέəri] ㊕ 무서운, 두려운, 겁나는
- □ **separation** [sèpəréiʃən] ㊔ 분리, 이별
- □ **shake** [artwərk] ㊍ 흔들다, 흔들리다
- □ **sister school** 자매 학교
- □ **spirit** [spírit] ㊔ 영혼, 정신
- □ **symbol** [símbəl] ㊔ 상징(물), 기호
- □ **tell** [tel] ㊍ 말하다, (정확히) 알다
- □ **toward** [tɔ:rd] ㉑ ~쪽으로
- □ **traditional** [trədíʃənl] ㊕ 전통의, 전통적인
- □ **try** [trai] ㊍ 한번 해 보다
- □ **umbrella** [ʌmbrélə] ㊔ 우산
- □ **valuable** [vǽljuəbl] ㊕ 값비싼, 귀중한, 가치 있는
- □ **victory** [víktəri] ㊔ 승리, 성공
- □ **Vietnamese** [viètnə:mí:z] ㊕ 베트남의 ㊔ 베트남어

Key Expressions

- □ **be afraid of** ~을 두려워하다
- □ **be full of** ~으로 가득 차다
- □ **blow one's nose** 코를 풀다
- □ **go away** 사라지다, 떠나가다
- □ **have been to** 장소 ~에 가 본 적이 있다
- □ **listen to** ~을 듣다
- □ **point at** ~을 가리키다
- □ **remind A of B** A에게 B를 생각나게 하다
- □ **so** 형용사/부사 **that** 주어 동사 너무 ~해서 …하다
- □ **take off** (옷 등을) 벗다
- □ **talk about** ~에 대해 이야기하다
- □ **watch over** ~을 주시하다, 지키다

Word Power

※ 서로 비슷한 뜻을 가진 단어

- □ **evil**(사악한, 악마의) – **wicked**(못된, 사악한)
- □ **greet**(맞이하다, 환영하다) – **welcome**(환영하다)
- □ **international**(국제적인, 세계적인) – **global**(세계적인)
- □ **last**(계속되다, 지속되다) – **continue**(계속하다, 지속하다)
- □ **remind**(생각나게 하다, 상기시키다) – **recall**(기억해 내다, 상기하다)
- □ **represent**(나타내다, 상징하다) – **symbolize**(상징하다)
- □ **go away** – **disappear**: 사라지다, 떠나가다
- □ **rude**(무례한) – **impolite** (버릇없는, 무례한)
- □ **separation**(분리, 이별) – **division** (분할)
- □ **spirit**(영혼, 정신) – **soul**(정신, 마음)
- □ **symbol**(상징(물), 기호) – **sign**(기호, 부호)
- □ **traditional**(전통의, 전통적인) – **conventional**(전통적인)
- □ **try**(한번 해 보다) – **attempt**(시도하다)
- □ **victory**(승리, 성공) – **success**(성공, 성과)
- □ **afraid**(두려워하는) – **frightened**(두려워하는)
- □ **watch over** – **guard**: ~을 주시하다, 지키다

English Dictionary

□ **bow** (인사를 위해) 머리를 숙이다, 절하다
→ to lower your head or bend your body
머리를 낮추거나 몸을 구부리다

□ **crow** (닭이) 울다
→ to make the loud sound that a rooster makes 수탉이 내는 큰 소리를 만들다

□ **darkness** 어둠, 암흑
→ no light 빛이 없음

□ **evil** 사악한, 악마의
→ morally bad or wicked
도덕적으로 나쁘거나 사악한

□ **face** ~을 향하다
→ to have the front part toward something 앞 부분을 어떤 것 쪽으로 향하게 하다

□ **greet** 맞이하다, 환영하다
→ to say hello or welcome
안녕이라고 말하거나 환영하다

□ **last** 계속되다, 지속되다
→ to keep happening for a certain amount of time 일정의 시간 동안 계속 발생하다

□ **palm** 손바닥
→ the inside part of the hand between the wrist and the fingers 손목과 손가락 사이의 손 안쪽 부분

□ **pillow** 베개
→ a soft thing to put your head on while you sleep
자는 동안에 머리를 놓는 부드러운 것

□ **protect** 보호하다
→ to keep something or someone safe from danger
위험으로부터 사람이나 사물을 안전하게 지키다

□ **remind** 생각나게 하다, 상기시키다
→ to make someone remember something 누군가에게 무엇인가를 기억나게 만들다

□ **represent** 나타내다, 상징하다
→ to stand for something else 다른 무엇인가를 상징하다

□ **rooster** 수탉
→ a male chicken 수컷 닭

□ **scary** 무서운, 두려운, 겁나는
→ making people feel afraid, frightening 사람들을 두려워하고 겁나게 만드는

□ **separation** 분리, 이별
→ the act of moving two things or people apart
두 개의 사물이나 사람을 떨어지도록 움직이는 행위

□ **symbol** 상징(물), 기호
→ an object that represents something
무엇인가를 나타내는 물체

□ **traditional** 전통의, 전통적인
→ being part of something that people have done for a long time 오랜 시간 동안 사람들이 해 왔던 어떤 것의 일부인

□ **valuable** 값비싼, 귀중한, 가치 있는
→ very important or expensive 매우 중요하거나 비싼

□ **victory** 승리, 성공
→ success in defeating an opponent
상대방을 물리치는 데 있어서의 성공

01 다음 빈칸에 들어갈 말로 적절한 것은?

> In some cases, hiccups can ________ for days or even weeks!

① cause ② bring
③ invite ④ produce
⑤ last

[02~03] 다음 밑줄 친 부분과 의미가 가장 가까운 것은?

02

> All of us need to go out to meet and greet them.

① welcome ② face
③ mean ④ try
⑤ say

03 중요

> The olive wreath stands for peace and it is still sometimes used today!

① shows ② represents
③ suggests ④ stays
⑤ makes use of

04 다음 중 밑줄 친 부분의 뜻풀이가 바르지 않은 것은?

① I don't understand what you mean. (의미하다)
② A full moon is 9 times brighter than a half moon. (반달)
③ He tried praying, but that didn't ease his mind. (노력하다)
④ Meditation is helpful in training your body and spirit. (영혼, 정신)
⑤ I have to apologize to you for being rude. (무례한)

05 중요 다음 빈칸에 공통으로 들어갈 말로 알맞은 것은?

> • Be sure to ________ the door before you leave.
> • He observed the thief open the ________ of the door.

① lock ② turn
③ fix ④ pull
⑤ rock

서답형

06 다음 빈칸에 들어갈 알맞은 단어를 <보기>에서 찾아 쓰시오. (형태 변화 가능)

> 보기
> traditional scary international

(1) She told me some ________ stories.
(2) Export law became a key factor in ________ trade.
(3) She is wearing ________ Korean clothes.

서답형

07 다음 우리말과 일치하도록 괄호 안의 어구를 바르게 배열하시오.

(1) 토니는 어둠 속으로 사라졌다. (the darkness, in, got, Tony, lost)
➡ ____________________
(2) 그 소녀들은 베개 싸움을 하고 있다. (having, fight, the girls, a pillow, are)
➡ ____________________

08 다음 영영풀이에 해당하는 것은?

> in the direction of something

① against ② directly ③ far
④ toward ⑤ within

중요
01 다음 〈보기〉와 같은 관계가 주어진 빈칸에 알맞은 말을 쓰시오. (주어진 철자로 시작할 것)

보기
good – nice

(1) impolite ➡ r__________
(2) attempt ➡ t__________
(3) wicked ➡ e__________
(4) success ➡ v__________

02 다음 빈칸에 알맞은 단어를 〈보기〉에서 골라 쓰시오.

보기
arrive celebrate experience mean

(1) Staying curious allows me to continuously __________ the excitement of learning something new.
(2) That doesn't __________ that I'm lazy.
(3) What time does the next train __________?
(4) They __________ Christmas and New Year's Day together.

중요
03 다음 주어진 우리말에 맞게 빈칸을 채우시오.

(1) 그 방은 해변을 향해 있나요?
➡ Does the room __________ the beach?
(2) 2년간의 이별 후에 그 부부는 다시 만날 수 있었다.
➡ After two years of __________, the couple was __________ to meet again.

04 다음 우리말에 맞게 주어진 단어를 이용해 빈칸을 완성하시오.

그는 항아리를 색깔이 있는 물로 채웠습니다.

➡ He filled a jar with __________ water. (color)

중요
05 다음 〈보기〉에서 빈칸에 공통으로 들어갈 단어를 골라 쓰시오.

보기
in about at from of

(1) • I usually stay ________ home on Sundays.
• It is rude to point ________ a person.
(2) • I am afraid ________ dogs when they bark.
• Lemons remind people ________ things that are fresh and clean.

06 다음 우리말에 맞게 주어진 단어를 바르게 배열하시오.

(1) 그녀는 다정한 미소로 우리를 맞았다.
(with, a, greeted, smile, kind, she, us)
➡ ______________________________
(2) 그 회의는 세 시간 동안 계속되었다.
(three, the, meeting, hours, lasted)
➡ ______________________________
(3) 나는 그 동전을 그녀의 손바닥에 놓았다. (the, coin, I, her, put, palm, in)
➡ ______________________________
(4) 붉은 깃발은 위험을 나타낸다.
(a, danger, flag, represents, red)
➡ ______________________________

교과서

Conversation

1 의미 묻고 답하기

A What does that mean in Korea? 한국에서는 그게 어떤 의미니?
B It means good luck. 행운을 뜻해.

- 'What does that mean?'은 상대방의 말의 의도나 의미를 잘 이해하지 못할 때, 그 의도나 의미를 물어보는 표현이다. 대답할 때는 'It means ~.'로 의미를 설명해 준다.

의미를 묻는 표현

- What does that mean (in Korea)? (한국에서는) 그게 어떤 의미니?
- What is that exactly? 그것이 정확히 뭐니?
- I'd like to know what that means. 그것이 무슨 의미인지 알고 싶어.
- Could[Would/Will] you explain what that means? 그것이 무슨 의미인지 설명해 줄 수 있어?

- Could[Can/Would/Will] you ~?'로 시작하는 의문문은 질문을 할 때도 쓰지만, 요청이나 부탁을 하는 경우에도 사용한다. 요청이나 부탁을 받았을 경우 꼭 Yes나 No로 대답할 필요는 없다.

ex) A: Would you tell me what this sign means? (이 표지판이 무슨 의미인지 말해 줄래?)
B: It means "no smoking." ('금연'이라는 뜻이야.)

핵심 Check

1. 주어진 문장에 이어질 대화의 순서를 바르게 배열하시오.

I don't understand what this means.
(A) Yes. What does that mean?
(B) It means "very important person."
(C) Are you talking about VIP?
➡ ______________________

2. 다음 우리말과 일치하도록 빈칸에 알맞은 말을 쓰시오.

A: Could you ________ ________ the sign ________? (그 표지판이 무슨 의미인지 설명해 줄 수 있니?)
B: It means "no parking." ('주차 금지'라는 의미야.)

3. 주어진 단어를 배열하여 대화를 완성하시오.

A: It's about English sayings. Do you know the saying, "Look before you leap."?
B: No. ______________________ (that, what, to, I'd, means, like, know)
A: Sure. ______________________ before you do something. (you, it, think, carefully, means, should)

2 경험 묻고 답하기

A Have you ever been to Brazil? 너는 브라질 가 봤니?

B Yes, I have. / No, I haven't. 응. 가 봤어. / 아니, 못 가 봤어.

- 상대방의 경험에 대해 물어볼 때는, 현재완료 시제를 사용하여 'Have you 과거분사 ~?'라고 묻는다. 경험을 묻는 말에 긍정으로 대답할 경우에는 'Yes, I have.'로, 부정으로 대답할 때는 'No, I haven't.'로 대답한다.
- 완료 시제를 사용할 때는 ago, yesterday, when 등과 같이 명백한 과거를 나타내는 말과 같이 사용되지 않는다. ex) When have you met him? (×) When did you meet him? (○)
- 경험을 나타내는 현재완료와 잘 사용하는 표현은 never(결코 ~ 않는), ever(어느 때고, 한 번이라도), once(한 번), twice(두 번), three times(세 번), before(전에) 등이 있다.

  ex) I have met him three times. (나는 그를 세 번 만난 적이 있다.)
- 'have been to 장소'는 '~에 가 본 경험이 있다'의 의미이고, 'have gone to 장소'는 '~에 갔다(그래서 지금 없다)'는 의미이다. ex) Have you gone to New York? (×)

경험을 묻는 표현

- Have you ever 과거분사 ~? (~해 본 적 있니?)
- Is this your first time -ing ~? (~해 보는 것이 처음이니?)
- Do you have any experience of –ing ~? (~해 본 경험이 있니?)

경험을 묻는 질문에 대답하는 표현

- I have never 과거분사. (한 번도 ~해 본 적이 없어.)
- I have a lot of experience. (나는 경험이 풍부해.)

핵심 Check

4. 다음 우리말과 일치하도록 빈칸에 알맞은 말을 쓰시오.

A: ______________________________ the movie *Aquaman*? (너는 영화 아쿠아맨을 본 적 있니?)

B: Yes, I ________. ________ you? (응, 봤어. 너는 봤니?)

5. 대화의 순서를 바르게 배열하시오.

(A) That sounds like fun.

(B) No, I haven't.

(C) I'm going to Japan with my friends this winter.

(D) Have you been there before?

➡ ______________________________

6. 주어진 단어를 배열하여 대화를 완성하시오.

A: ______________________________ (before, had, have, *gimchi*, you)

B: Yes, I have.

Conversation 교과서 대화문 익히기

A. Listen and Talk 1 A

G: ❶Have you ever been to Brazil?
B: No, I haven't. ❷Have you?
G: Yes, I have. I went there ❸last year. ❹There was a big samba festival.
B: That sounds interesting. I ❺hope to go there someday.

G: 너는 브라질 가 봤니?
B: 아니, 못 가 봤어. 너는 가 봤니?
G: 응, 가 봤어. 작년에 거기 갔었어. 큰 삼바 축제가 있었어.
B: 재미있게 들린다. 나도 언젠가 거기 가고 싶어.

❶ 'Have you ever p.p ~?'는 경험을 묻는 표현이다. 특히 'Have you ever been to 장소?'는 '~에 가 본 적 있니?'라는 뜻으로 어떤 곳에 가 본 경험에 대해 말할 때 사용하는 표현이다. 응답은 'Yes, I have.'또는 'No, I haven't.'로 하면 된다.
❷ Have you 뒤에 'ever been to Brazil'이 생략되어 있다.
❸ last year(작년)는 과거의 특정 시점이므로 과거형 동사를 사용해야 한다.
❹ There+be동사의 과거형(was, were): ~가 있었다 festival: 축제
❺ hope는 to부정사를 목적어로 받는다.

Check(√) True or False

(1) The boy has never been to Brazil. T ☐ F ☐
(2) There was a samba festival in Brazil last year. T ☐ F ☐

B. Listen and Talk 1 B

W: ❶Welcome to the International Games Festival. ❷You can play many different traditional games here.
B: Wow! ❸It looks exciting! Which game should I play first?
W: Let's see. ❹Have you ever played *gorodki*?
B: No, I haven't. What is it?
W: It's a traditional game ❺from Russia.
B: How do I play it?
W: Put five sticks on the ground. Then ❻throw a bat at them.
B: That ❼sounds fun. I'll try that first.

W: 국제 게임 축제에 오신 걸 환영합니다. 당신은 여기서 많은 종류의 전통 게임을 할 수 있습니다.
B: 와! 재미있을 것 같아요! 어떤 게임 먼저 해야 하나요?
W: 한번 봅시다. 고로드키 게임 해 본 적 있나요?
B: 아니요. 그게 무엇인가요?
W: 러시아의 전통 게임이에요.
B: 어떻게 하나요?
W: 바닥에 다섯 개의 막대기를 놓으세요. 그리고 그것들을 향해 배트를 던지세요.
B: 재미있겠네요. 그거 먼저 할게요.

❶ welcome to ~: ~에 오신 걸 환영합니다
❷ can+동사원형: ~할 수 있다 traditional: 전통적인
❸ look + 형용사: ~하게 보이다 exciting: 흥미로운
❹ Have you ever p.p ~?: ~한 적 있니?
❺ from: (출처 · 기원) ~출신의[에서 온]
❻ throw: ~을 던지다 at: (방향) ~으로
❼ sound+형용사: ~하게 들리다

Check(√) True or False

(3) *Gorodki* is from France. T ☐ F ☐
(4) The boy is in the International Games Festival. T ☐ F ☐

Listen and Talk 1 C

B: There is a Holi festival in Busan ❶this year.
G: A Holi festival? What is ❷that?
B: It's a traditional Indian festival. ❸People throw colored powder and water at each other.
G: That sounds exciting. ❹Have you ever been to a Holi festival?
B: No, I haven't. But my Indian friend told me a lot about it.
G: When is the festival?
B: ❺It's on the last full moon of the Hindu calendar. This year, it's ❻on March 21.
G: I'd like to go. ❼Should I bring anything?
B: No, but you should wear white clothes. Then the colored powder on your clothes will look more beautiful.
G: Okay. Thank you for the information.

❶ this year: 올해
❷ that은 'a Holi festival'을 의미한다.
❸ colored: 채색된, 색깔이 있는 at each other: 서로에게
❹ Have you ever been to 장소?: ~에 가 본 적 있니? festival: 축제
❺ Holi 축제가 언제인지에 대한 설명을 하고 있다 the last full moon: 마지막 보름달(이 뜨는 날)
❻ 날짜 앞에는 전치사 on을 사용한다.
❼ should+동사원형: ~해야 한다 Should I bring ~?: ~을 가져가야 하니?

Listen and Talk 2 A

G: Jinwoo, my Korean friend, ❶gave me *Yeot* as a gift. ❷What does that mean in Korea?
B: ❸It means good luck on a test.

❶ give는 4형식 동사로 간접목적어(~에게)와 직접목적어(~을[를]) 두 개를 받을 수 있다. as: ~으로
❷ What does that mean?: 그게 어떤 의미니? in Korea: 한국에서
❸ It은 Yeot을 의미한다. 주어 mean ~: 주어는 ~을 의미한다 good luck: 행운

Listen and Talk 2 B

B: Ling's birthday is ❶this Wednesday, ❷isn't it?
G: Yes. ❸I'm going to buy a book for her. What about you?
B: Well, ❹I'm thinking about buying her an umbrella. I found a cute ❺one in a gift shop.
G: Oh, that's not a good gift for Chinese people. It means ❻something bad.
B: Really? What does an umbrella mean in China?
G: It means ❼separation. The words for *separation* and *umbrella* sound the same in Chinese.
B: I see. Then how about chocolate?
G: That's a good idea.

❶ this 요일: 이번 주 ~요일
❷ 부가의문문으로 말하는 이가 듣는 이에게 말한 내용을 확인하거나 동의를 구할 때 쓰며 '동사+주어(인칭대명사)'의 형태로 쓰인다. 앞 문장에 쓰인 동사가 be동사나 조동사이면 그대로, 일반동사이면 do동사로 쓰며, 앞 문장이 긍정이면 부정, 앞 문장이 부정이면 긍정으로 쓴다.
❸ be going to 동사원형: ~할 것이다, ~할 예정이다
❹ think about: ~에 대해 생각하다 about은 전치사이므로 뒤에 명사나 동명사가 올 수 있다. buy는 4형식 동사로 '~에게 …를 사 주다'의 의미로 사용되었다.
❺ one = umbrella
❻ -thing으로 끝나는 부정대명사(something, anything, nothing 등)는 보통의 다른 명사들과 달리 형용사가 뒤에서 수식한다.
❼ separation: 분리, 이별

Listen and Talk 2 C

G: ❶What a nice picture! Are these your friends?
B: Yes. We ❷took this picture at the beach. ❸ We had a lot of fun.
G: Oh, ❹look at that boy. That's really ❺rude.
B: Which boy?
G: The boy ❻who is making the V sign. ❼His palm is facing toward himself.
B: What's wrong with that?
G: It has a bad meaning in England. But showing your palm and making a V sign is okay.
B: What does that mean?
G: It means victory or peace.

❶ 'What+a+형용사+명사!'(감탄문) What a nice picture!: 이 사진 정말 멋지다!
❷ take a picture: 사진을 찍다
❸ have fun: 재미있다, 즐거운 시간을 보내다
❹ look at: ~을 보다
❺ rude: 무례한
❻ who는 주격 관계대명사로 who is making the V sign은 앞의 the boy를 수식하고 있다.
❼ palm: 손바닥 face: ~을 향하다 toward: ~쪽으로

• 다음 우리말과 일치하도록 빈칸에 알맞은 말을 쓰시오.

Listen and Talk 1 A

G: ________ ________ ever ________ to Brazil?

B: No, I ________. ________ you?

G: Yes, I ________. I went there ________ ________. There ________ a big samba festival.

B: That ________ interesting. I hope ________ ________ there ________.

해석

G: 너는 브라질 가 봤니?
B: 아니, 못 가 봤어. 너는 가 봤니?
G: 응. 가 봤어. 작년에 거기 갔었어. 큰 삼바 축제가 있었어.
B: 재미있게 들린다. 나도 언젠가 거기 가고 싶어.

Listen and Talk 1 B

W: Welcome ________ the International Games ________. You can play ________ ________ ________ ________ here.

B: Wow! It ________ exciting! ________ game ________ I play first?

W: Let's see. ________ ________ ________ played *gorodki*?

B: ________, ________ ________. What is it?

W: It's a traditional game ________ Russia.

B: ________ do I play it?

W: Put five sticks ________ the ground. Then ________ a bat ________ them.

B: That ________ ________. I'll try that first.

W: 국제 게임 축제에 오신 걸 환영합니다. 당신은 여기서 많은 종류의 전통게임을 할 수 있습니다.
B: 와! 재미있을 것 같아요! 어떤 게임 먼저 해야 하나요?
W: 어디 봅시다. 고로드키 게임 해 본 적 있나요?
B: 아니요. 그게 무엇인가요?
W: 러시아의 전통 게임이에요.
B: 어떻게 하나요?
W: 바닥에 다섯 개의 막대기를 놓으세요. 그리고 그것들을 향해 배트를 던지세요.
B: 재미있겠네요. 그거 먼저 할게요.

Listen and Talk 1 C

B: ________ ________ a Holi festival ________ Busan ________ year.

G: A Holi festival? What is that?

B: It's ________ ________ ________ ________. People throw ________ ________ and water at ________ other.

G: That ________ ________. ________ ________ ________ to a Holi festival?

B: No, I haven't. But my Indian friend ________ ________ a lot about it.

G: ________ is the festival?

B: It's ________ the last full moon of the Hindu calendar. This year, it's ________ March 21.

G: I'd ________ to go. ________ I bring anything?

B: No, but you should wear white ________. Then ________ ________ ________ on your ________ will look more beautiful.

G: Okay. Thank you ________ the information.

B: 올해에는 부산에서 Holi Festival이 있어.
G: Holi Festival? 그게 뭐야?
B: 인도의 전통 축제야. 사람들은 서로에게 색 파우더와 물을 던지지.
G: 재미있겠다. Holi festival에 가 본 적 있니?
B: 아니, 없어. 근데 인도 친구가 그것에 대해 많이 이야기해 줬어.
G: 축제가 언제야?
B: 힌두교 달력으로 마지막 보름달이 뜨는 날이야. 올해는 3월 21일이네.
G: 가고 싶다. 나 뭐 가져가야 하니?
B: 아니, 하지만 하얀 옷을 입어야 돼. 그러면 네 옷에 묻은 색 파우더가 더 예쁘게 보일 거야.
G: 알겠어. 정보 알려줘서 고마워.

Listen and Talk 2 A

G: Jinwoo, my Korean friend, ________ ________ *Yeot* as a gift. ________ ________ ________ ________ ________ ________?
B: It ________ good luck on a test.

Listen and Talk 2 B

B: Ling's birthday is ________ Wednesday, ________ ________?
G: Yes. I'm going to buy a book for her. What about you?
B: Well, I'm thinking ________ ________ her an umbrella. I found a cute ________ in a gift shop.
G: Oh, that's not a good gift for Chinese people. It means ________ ________.
B: Really? ________ ________ an umbrella ________ ________ ________?
G: It ________ ________. The words for ________ and *umbrella* sound the same in Chinese.
B: I see. Then how ________ chocolate?
G: That's a good idea.

Listen and Talk 2 C

G: ________ ________ nice picture! ________ these your friends?
B: Yes. We ________ this picture at the beach. We had a lot of fun.
G: Oh, ________ ________ that boy. That's really ________.
B: Which boy?
G: The boy ________ ________ ________ the V sign. His ________ ________ ________ ________ himself.
B: What's wrong with that?
G: It has a bad ________ ________ England. But showing your palm and making a V sign is okay.
B: ________ ________ ________ ________?
G: It means ________ ________ ________.

Do It Yourself

G: Hello, Santiago! What ________ you here today?
B: *Bienvenido*, Cathy. I came ________ see the Spanish festival.
G: Me, too. But what did you just say?
B: *Bienvenido*! It ________ "welcome" in Spanish. Look at those dancers. Their dance moves are so great.
G: Yes, they are.
B: ________ ________ ________ ________ ________ a Spanish festival before?
G: No, ________ ________. Santiago, can you see the big letters on the stage? ________ ________ that mean?
B: Oh, gracias. That ________ "thank you."

해석

G: 내 한국인 친구인 진우가 선물로 엿을 줬어. 한국에서는 이게 어떤 의미니?
B: 시험 잘 보라는 뜻이야.

B: Ling의 생일이 이번 수요일이야, 그렇지 않니?
G: 응. 나는 그녀에게 책을 사 줄 거야. 너는?
B: 음, 나는 우산을 사려고 생각하고 있어. 선물 가게에서 귀여운 걸 찾았거든.
G: 어, 그건 중국 사람들에게 좋은 선물이 아니야. 뭔가 나쁜 걸 뜻하거든.
B: 진짜? 중국에서 우산이 뭘 의미하는데?
G: 이별을 뜻해. 중국에서는 이별을 뜻하는 단어와 우산을 뜻하는 단어의 발음이 같거든.
B: 알겠어. 그러면 초콜릿 어때?
G: 좋은 생각이야.

G: 이 사진 정말 멋지다! 네 친구들이니?
B: 응. 우리는 해변에서 이 사진을 찍었어. 정말 재미있었어.
G: 어, 저 남자애 봐. 정말 무례하다.
B: 누구?
G: V사인을 하고 있는 애. 손바닥이 자기 쪽을 향하고 있어.
B: 그게 뭐 잘못됐어?
G: 영국에서는 나쁜 뜻을 갖고 있어. 하지만 손바닥을 보여 주면서 V사인을 만드는 건 괜찮아.
B: 그건 무슨 뜻인데?
G: 승리나 평화를 뜻해.

G: 안녕, Santiago! 오늘 여기 어쩐 일이야?
B: Bienvenido, Cathy. 나는 스페인 축제를 보러 왔어.
G: 나도. 그런데 방금 뭐라고 말했니?
B: Bienvenido! 스페인어로 "환영합니다."라는 뜻이야. 저 무용수들을 봐. 그들의 춤 움직임은 정말 멋지다.
G: 응, 그렇네.
B: 전에 스페인 축제에 가 본 적 있니?
G: 아니, 가 본 적 없어. Santiago, 무대에 있는 큰 글씨들 볼 수 있니? 무슨 뜻이야?
B: 아, gracias. 저건 "감사합니다."라는 뜻이야.

[01~02] 다음 대화의 빈칸에 알맞은 것으로 짝지어진 것은?

01

G: _________ you ever been to Brazil?
B: Yes, I _________.

① Have/have ② Can/can ③ Did /did ④ Are/am ⑤ Do/do

02

A: What does that _________ in Korea?
B: It _________s good luck.

① make ② mean ③ stay ④ find ⑤ keep

03 다음 대화의 밑줄 친 부분의 의도로 알맞은 것은?

A: Have you ever listened to Spanish music?
B: Yes, I have.

① Asking about memories
② Giving advice
③ Asking about experiences
④ Requesting
⑤ Asking about the meanings

04 다음 대화의 순서를 바르게 배열한 것은?

(A) No, I haven't. What is it?
(B) It's a traditional game from Russia.
(C) Have you ever played *gorodki*?

① (A) - (C) - (B)
② (B) - (A) - (C)
③ (B) - (C) - (A)
④ (C) - (A) - (B)
⑤ (C) - (B) - (A)

05 다음 대화에서 어법상 어색한 것을 고르시오.

G: ①Have you ever gone to a Holi festival?
B: ②No, I haven't. ③But my Indian friend told me a lot about it.
G: ④When is the festival?
B: ⑤It's on the last full moon of the Hindu calendar. This year, it's on March 21.

① ② ③ ④ ⑤

01 빈칸 (A)와 (B)에 알맞은 말을 고르시오.

> G: Jinwoo, my Korean friend, (A) ______ *Yeot* as a gift. (B)_______ does that mean in Korea?
> B: It means good luck on a test.

	(A)	(B)
①	gave	How
②	gave me	How
③	gave me	What
④	gave to me	How
⑤	gave to me	What

중요
02 주어진 문장에 이어질 대화의 순서로 가장 적절한 것은?

> Have you ever been to Brazil?

> (A) Yes, I have. I went there last year. There was a big samba festival.
> (B) No, I haven't. Have you?
> (C) That sounds interesting. I hope to go there someday.

① (A) - (C) - (B)
② (B) - (A) - (C)
③ (B) - (C) - (A)
④ (C) - (A) - (B)
⑤ (C) - (B) - (A)

[03~06] 다음 대화를 읽고, 물음에 답하시오.

> B: ⓐLing's birthday is this Wednesday, isn't it? (①)
> G: Yes. ⓑI'm going to buy a book for her. (②)
> B: Well, ⓒI'm thinking about buying her an umbrella. I found a cute one in a gift shop. (③)
> G: Oh, that's not a good gift for Chinese people. ⓓIt means bad something. (④)
> B: Really? (an, mean, in, what, umbrella, China, does, ?)
> G: It means separation. ⓔThe words for *separation* and *umbrella* sounds the same in Chinese. (⑤)
> B: I see. Then how about chocolate?
> G: That's a good idea.

03 위 대화의 ①~⑤ 중 주어진 문장이 들어갈 알맞은 곳은?

> What about you?

① ② ③ ④ ⑤

서답형
04 위 대화의 괄호 안에 주어진 단어들을 바르게 배열하여 문장을 완성하시오.

➡ ________________________________

중요
05 위 대화의 밑줄 친 ⓐ~ⓔ 중 어법상 틀린 개수를 고르시오.

① 1개 ② 2개 ③ 3개 ④ 4개 ⑤ 5개

06 위 대화를 읽고 답할 수 없는 질문을 모두 고르시오.

① What is the girl going to buy for Ling?
② What does a book mean in China?
③ When is Ling's birthday?
④ Where is the boy going to go to buy chocolate?
⑤ Is an umbrella a good present for Chinese people?

[07~08] 다음 대화를 읽고, 물음에 답하시오.

B: There is a Holi festival in Busan this year.
G: A Holi festival? (A)________________
B: It's a traditional Indian festival. People throw colored powder and water at each other.
G: That sounds exciting. (B)______________
B: No, I haven't. But my Indian friend told me a lot about it.
G: (C)_________________
B: It's on the last full moon of the Hindu calendar. This year, it's on March 21.
G: I'd like to go. (D)__________________
B: No, but you should wear white clothes. Then the colored powder on your clothes will look more beautiful.
G: Okay. Thank you for the information.

서답형

07 위 대화의 빈칸 (A)~(D)에 들어갈 말을 〈보기〉에서 골라 쓰시오.

보기
- Have you ever been to a Holi festival?
- What is Holi?
- What is that?
- When is the festival?
- Should I bring anything?
- Should I bring white clothes?
- What should I bring?

➡ (A) ______________________
(B) ______________________
(C) ______________________
(D) ______________________

08 위 대화의 내용과 일치하지 않는 것을 고르시오.

① A Holi festival will be held on March 21.
② At a Holi festival, people throw colored powder and water at each other.
③ The boy has an Indian friend.
④ At a Holi festival, people should wear colored clothes.
⑤ The boy has not been to a Holi festival.

[09~12] 다음 대화를 읽고, 물음에 답하시오.

W: Welcome to the International Games Festival. (①) You can play many different traditional games here.
B: Wow! ⓐIt looks (A)_____(excite)! Which game should I play first? (②)
W: Let's see. (③)
B: No, I haven't. What is ⓑit? (④)
W: ⓒIt's a traditional game from Russia. (⑤)
B: How do I play ⓓit?
W: Put five sticks on the ground. Then throw a bat at them.
B: That sounds fun. I'll try ⓔthat first.

09 위 대화의 ①~⑤ 중 주어진 문장이 들어갈 알맞은 곳은?

Have you ever played *gorodki*?

① ② ③ ④ ⑤

서답형

10 위 대화의 빈칸 (A)에 주어진 단어를 이용하여 빈칸을 완성하시오.

➡ ______________________

중요

11 위 대화의 밑줄 친 ⓐ~ⓔ 중에서 가리키는 대상이 다른 하나는?

① ⓐ ② ⓑ ③ ⓒ ④ ⓓ ⑤ ⓔ

서답형

12 위 대화의 내용에 맞게 빈칸을 완성하시오.

Gorodki is ________ ________ ________ ________ Russia. The way to ________ *gorodki* is ________ ________ ________ on the ground and ________ ________ ________ at them.

[01~04] 다음 대화를 읽고, 물음에 답하시오.

G: ①What a nice picture! Are these your friends?
B: Yes. ②We took this picture at the beach. We had a lot of fun.
G: Oh, look at that boy. That's really rude.
B: Which boy?
G: ③The boy which is making the V sign. (A) ____________
B: ④What's wrong with that?
G: It has a bad (B)__________(mean) in England. But showing your palm and making a V sign is okay.
B: ⑤What does that mean?
G: (C)It means victory or peace.

01 그림을 참고하고, 주어진 단어를 이용하여 빈칸 (A)에 알맞은 말을 쓰시오.

➡ ________________________________
(toward, himself, palm, face)

02 주어진 단어를 이용하여 빈칸 (B)를 채우시오.

➡ __________

03 중요 ①~⑤ 중 어법상 어색한 부분을 찾아 고치시오.

__________ ➡ __________

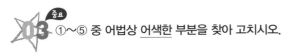

04 밑줄 친 (C)It이 가리키는 것을 본문에서 찾아 쓰시오.

➡ ________________________________

[05~07] 다음 대화를 읽고, 물음에 답하시오.

A: (A)________ do you see in this picture?
B: The girl is ⓐ______________________.
A: (B)__________ does ⓑ__________ mean in India?
B: 불운을 뜻해.

05 중요 빈칸 (A)와 (B)에 공통으로 들어갈 단어를 쓰시오.

➡ __________

06 그림을 참고하고, 주어진 단어를 이용해 빈칸 ⓐ와 ⓑ에 공통으로 들어갈 말을 쓰시오. (7단어) (cut, on, hair, get)

➡ ________________________________

07 밑줄 친 우리말을 영작하시오.

➡ ________________________________

08 중요 다음 대화의 밑줄 친 우리말을 영작하시오.

G: 너는 브라질에 가 봤니?
B: No, I haven't.

➡ ________________________________

교과서

Grammar

1 현재완료

- For a long time, Koreans **have thought** that fish are good guards.
  오랜 세월 동안, 한국인들은 물고기가 훌륭한 파수꾼이라고 생각해 왔다.
- **Have** you ever **visited** Paris before? 너는 전에 파리에 가 본 적이 있니?

■ 현재완료는 'have[has] + 과거분사'의 형태로 과거의 일이 현재까지 영향을 주는 동작 · 상태의 의미를 나타낸다.

■ 부정형은 'have[has] not + 과거분사'이며, 의문형은 'Have[Has] + 주어 + 과거분사 ~?'로 나타낸다.

- I **haven't completed** the work yet. 나는 일이 아직 안 끝났다.
- How long **have** you **lived** together? 당신들은 얼마 동안 함께 살았습니까?

■ 현재완료는 '완료(지금[막] …했다), 경험(…해 본 적이 있다), 계속((지금까지) …해 왔다), 결과(…해서 (그 결과) 지금 ~하다)'의 네 가지 용법으로 쓰인다.

완료 용법은 보통 'just, already, yet'과 같은 부사와 함께 쓰이며, 경험 용법은 'ever, never, once, before' 등과 같은 부사와 함께 쓰인다.

계속 용법은 보통 'for+기간 명사'나 'since+시간 명사'와 함께 쓰이며 결과 용법은 과거에 발생한 사건이 현재 미치고 있는 결과를 포함한다.

- They **have** already **finished** their lunch. 〈완료〉 그들은 이미 점심식사를 끝마쳤다.
- I **have** never **been** here before. 〈경험〉 저는 이곳이 처음입니다.
- He **has been** missing since last month. 〈계속〉 그는 지난달부터 실종되었다.
- She **has lost** her purse. 〈결과〉 그녀는 지갑을 잃어버렸다. (그 결과 (지갑이) 지금 없다.)

*have[has] been to vs. have[has] gone to

have[has] been to는 '~에 가 본적이 있다'는 경험을 나타내고, have[has] gone to는 '~에 가고 없다'는 결과를 나타낸다. 그러므로 have[has] gone to는 3인칭만 주어로 쓸 수 있다.

■ 현재완료는 과거의 일이 현재까지 영향을 주는 동작 · 상태를 나타내므로 과거를 나타내는 어구와 함께 쓸 수 없다.

- We **ate** lunch an hour ago. (○)
- We have eaten lunch an hour ago. (×)

핵심 Check

1. 주어진 동사를 어법에 맞게 쓰시오.

(1) They __________ __________ to Seoul. So you cannot meet them now. (go)

(2) I __________ never __________ Seoul. (visit)

(3) __________ you ever __________ *The Little Prince*? (read)

2 결과를 나타내는 so ... that 구문

- It's **so** old **that** I can't really tell, but is it a fish?
  그것은 매우 오래되어서 정말 알 수가 없는데, 그건 물고기인가요?
- This book was **so** sad **that** I cried. 이 책이 매우 슬퍼서 나는 울었어.

■ 'so+형용사[부사]+that+주어+동사'의 형태로 '매우 …해서 ~하다'라는 의미이며 원인과 그에 따른 결과를 서술할 때 쓰인다.

■ so 뒤의 형용사나 부사는 원인을 나타내며, 접속사 that 뒤에 나오는 내용은 그에 따른 결과를 나타낸다.

- I was **so** tired **that** I couldn't exercise. 나는 너무 피곤해서 운동할 수 없었다.
- He was **so** happy **that** he danced. 그는 너무 기뻐 춤을 추었다.

■ 'so … that' 구문에서 that 앞에 형용사나 부사 대신 명사가 오면 so 대신 such를 쓴다.

- He was **such** a good runner **that** I couldn't catch him. 그가 너무 빨리 달려 나는 그를 따라잡을 수가 없었다.

■ 'so+형용사[부사]+that+주어+can ~'는 '형용사[부사]+enough+to 동사원형'으로 바꿔 쓸 수 있으며, 'so+형용사[부사]+that+주어+can't ~'는 'too+형용사[부사]+to 동사원형'으로 바꿔 쓸 수 있다.

- She is **so** kind **that** she can help her friends.
  = She is kind **enough to** help her friends.
- He was **so** sick **that** he couldn't go out.
  = He was **too** sick **to** go out.

핵심 Check

2. 다음 우리말에 맞게 빈칸에 알맞은 말을 쓰시오.

(1) 나는 오늘 너무 바빠서 갈 수가 없어.

➡ I'm __________ __________ __________ I can't go today.

(2) 그의 모자는 너무 커서 그것은 그의 눈을 가렸다.

➡ His hat was __________ __________ __________ it covered his eyes.

01 다음 문장에서 어법상 어색한 부분을 바르게 고쳐 쓰시오.

(1) I have visit there many times.

______________ ➡ ______________

(2) She has finished the work yesterday.

______________ ➡ ______________

(3) Do you have cleaned your room?

______________ ➡ ______________

(4) I'm so busy what I can't go out today.

______________ ➡ ______________

(5) The room was very dirty that it smelled bad.

______________ ➡ ______________

(6) Sam has lived with his pet dog for 2015.

______________ ➡ ______________

(7) The man have lived with them for a long time.

______________ ➡ ______________

02 다음 중 어법상 어색한 것은?

① I've never heard that before.
② Have you finished your homework?
③ Joel has work for 6 hours straight.
④ The bus has just arrived.
⑤ Linda has lost her smartphone.

03 다음 대화의 빈칸에 들어갈 말로 알맞은 것은?

M: How was your trip to Vietnam?
W: It was great!
M: Did you visit Danang?
W: Yes, of course. The place was ____________ beautiful that I stayed a few more days.

① so ② such ③ very
④ too ⑤ enough

01 다음 빈칸에 알맞은 말이 순서대로 바르게 짝지어진 것은?

> • ________ you ever visited Tibet?
> • I have never ________ to Rome.

① Were – gone
② Were – been
③ Have – gone
④ Have – been
⑤ Did – being

중요 **02** 다음 문장의 밑줄 친 부분 중에서 어법상 잘못된 곳을 고르시오.

> Amy was ①too ②sick yesterday ③that she ④couldn't take part ⑤in the meeting.

03 다음 질문에 대한 응답으로 알맞은 것은?

> Has Chris ever visited Seoul?

① Yes, he is.
② Yes, he does.
③ No, he isn't.
④ No, he doesn't.
⑤ No, he hasn't.

04 다음 빈칸에 알맞은 말이 바르게 짝지어진 것은?

> Steve was ________ hungry ________ he ate all the food on the table.

① as – as
② such – as
③ so – that
④ too – to
⑤ enough – to

서답형 **05** 다음 괄호 안에서 알맞은 말을 고르시오.

(1) I have (visited / visit) Phuket, Thailand.
(2) She (have / has) gone to Jeju.
(3) You can't meet her now. She has (been / gone) to China.
(4) Ann has been to Paris (before / ago).
(5) He (doesn't have / hasn't) read *The Little Prince*.

중요 **06** 다음 중 어법상 바르지 않은 것은?

① Dad's explanation was too clear that we could understand it easily.
② They have lived there since 2010.
③ The math problems were so easy that we could solve them.
④ Evan has just finished his homework.
⑤ Emma felt so sick that she couldn't even breathe.

07 다음 우리말을 영어로 바르게 옮긴 것은?

> 나는 전에 스페인 음식을 먹어본 적이 없다.

① I didn't eat Spanish food ago.
② I don't eat Spanish food before.
③ I have never eat Spanish food before.
④ I don't have eaten Spanish food before.
⑤ I have never eaten Spanish food before.

서답형

08 다음 괄호 안에서 알맞은 말을 고르시오.

(1) Jack was (so / such) witty that he became popular among us.

(2) *Mona Lisa* is so wonderful (that / what) people love it.

(3) It gave him (so / such) a shock that his face turned white.

(4) The boxes were so heavy that I (wouldn't / couldn't) carry them.

중요

09 다음 빈칸에 알맞은 말이 순서대로 짝지어진 것은?

- Ben has lived in Jeonju _______ 5 years.
- Ben has lived in Jeonju _______ 2005.

① after – for
② for – after
③ since – for
④ for – since
⑤ as – for

10 다음 두 문장을 한 문장으로 바르게 연결한 것은?

- Amanda studied very hard.
- So she got an A⁺.

① Amanda studied very hard that she got an A⁺.
② Amanda studied so hard that she got an A⁺.
③ Amanda studied hard so that she got an A⁺.
④ Amanda studied hard enough that she got an A⁺.
⑤ Amanda studied too hard that she could get an A⁺.

중요

11 다음 중 밑줄 친 부분의 용법이 다른 하나는?

① I have already eaten dinner.
② Have you ever played golf before?
③ Harry has not written his report yet.
④ The train has just left the platform.
⑤ Emily has just finished her homework.

서답형

12 다음 문장을 주어진 어휘를 이용하여 같은 의미가 되도록 바꿔 쓰시오.

(1) Julia got so angry that she couldn't speak. (too)

➡ ______________________________

(2) Sean is so rich that he can buy the expensive car. (enough)

➡ ______________________________

(3) The panda is so cute that I can't take my eyes off him. (to)

➡ ______________________________

(4) The house was so nice that Melanie wanted to live there. (to)

➡ ______________________________

13 다음 두 문장을 한 문장으로 바르게 바꾼 것은?

- Paulinya went to Russia.
- And she still stays there.

① Paulinya went to Russia.
② Paulinya has been to Russia.
③ Paulinya hasn't gone to Russia.
④ Paulinya has gone to Russia.
⑤ Paulinya hasn't come back yet.

14 다음 우리말을 영어로 바르게 옮긴 것은?

차가 너무 막혀서 나는 학교에 늦었다.

① Traffic was too heavy that I was late for school.
② Traffic was very heavy that I was late for school.
③ Traffic was enough heavy that I was late for school.
④ Traffic was so heavy that I was late for school.
⑤ Traffic was heavy too that I was late for school.

서답형
15 다음 문장에서 어법상 어색한 것을 고쳐 다시 쓰시오.

(1) Suyeon has just arrived at Busan Station an hour ago.
➡ ______________________
____

(2) Ron and his sisters have been to England. They are there now.
➡ ______________________

(3) Grace was too fat that she wore the beautiful dress.
➡ ______________________
➡ ______________________

(4) The drama was very boring that I turned off the TV.
➡ ______________________

(5) He has lived in Busan for 2010.
➡ ______________________

서답형
16 다음 글의 밑줄 친 ⓐ, ⓑ를 알맞은 형태로 바꿔 쓰시오.

Ian ⓐhas visited Vietnam last week. But I have never ⓑgone there.

➡ ⓐ __________ ⓑ __________

서답형
17 다음 우리말을 영작했을 때 어색한 것을 찾아 고치시오.

(1) 나는 지난 월요일 이후로 그를 보지 못했다.
→ I have not seen him for last Monday.
(2) Cathy는 전에 부산에 가 본 적이 있다.
→ Cathy has gone to Busan before.
(3) 영화가 너무 지루해 나는 잠이 들어 버렸다.
→ The movie was too boring that I fell asleep.
(4) Eric은 너무 가난해서 그 차를 살 수 없었다.
→ Eric was poor enough that he couldn't buy the car.
(5) 그녀는 어제 시계를 지하철 역에서 잃어버렸다.
→ She has lost her watch at the subway station yesterday.

➡ ______________________
____

중요
18 다음 빈칸에 공통으로 들어갈 단어는?

• Joe ran too fast for his brother _____ catch him. • The girl was clever enough _____ solve the problem by herself.

① so ② to ③ of
④ as ⑤ for

Grammar 서술형 시험대비

중요 **01** 주어진 두 문장을 한 문장으로 바꿔 쓰시오.

(1) • Laura began to live in Chicago in 1998.
• She still lives there.
➡ ______________________

(2) • Dan lost his cell phone.
• So he doesn't have it now.
➡ ______________________

02 다음 문장을 so ~ that ... 구문으로 바꾸어 쓰시오.

(1) Kate is too young to drive a car.
➡ ______________________

(2) Stefanie is wise enough to give advice to her friends.
➡ ______________________

03 괄호 안에 주어진 어구를 이용하여 다음 우리말을 영어로 옮기시오.

(1) James는 그가 어릴 때부터 축구를 해 왔다. (soccer, since, a child)
➡ ______________________

(2) 비가 너무 많이 와서 우리는 밖에 나갈 수 없다. (rain, heavily, that, go outside)
➡ ______________________

(3) Charlie는 6개월 동안 한국어를 공부해 오고 있다. (has, study)
➡ ______________________

04 다음 문장을 어법에 맞게 고쳐 쓰시오.

(1) Mr. Brown has lived in New York for 2015.
➡ ______________________

(2) We have gone to Sydney.
➡ ______________________

(3) Elle hasn't taken a walk yesterday.
➡ ______________________

(4) My long padding coat is enough warm for me to endure the winter.
➡ ______________________

(5) Lylian was very afraid that she couldn't open her eyes.
➡ ______________________

중요 **05** 괄호 안의 단어를 사용하여 주어진 문장을 같은 의미가 되도록 다시 쓰시오.

(1) Mike was so sick that he couldn't go to work yesterday. (too)
➡ ______________________

(2) The *samgyetang* was too hot for Amy to eat. (so, can)
➡ ______________________

(3) His essay was so nice that his teacher was satisfied. (enough)
➡ ______________________

(4) Tom ran fast enough to catch the last bus. (so, can)
➡ ______________________

고 난이도

06 우리말과 일치하도록 괄호 안의 단어를 바르게 배열하여 문장을 완성하시오.

(1) 그의 이웃집의 파티가 너무 시끄러워서 그는 잠을 전혀 잘 수 없었다. (he, his, party, neighbor's, sleep, was, couldn't, noisy, that, all, so, at)

➡ ______________________________

____

(2) Rose는 아직 도서실에 도착하지 않았다. (Rose, library, the, arrived, not, has, yet, at)

➡ ______________________________

(3) 그 남자는 너무 친절해서 즉시 나를 도와주었다. (man, he, me, helped, kind, right, was, so, the, that, away)

➡ ______________________________

(4) 나는 Paris에 한 번 다녀왔다. (I, Paris, been, once, have, to)

➡ ______________________________

(5) Andrew는 그의 스마트폰을 기차에 놓고 내렸다. (Andrew, the, smartphone, train, left, his, has, in)

➡ ______________________________

07 Bella가 경험한 일과 경험하지 않은 일에 관한 표를 보고, 〈보기〉와 같이 문장을 완성하시오.

What	Yes/No
learn to play the piano	Yes
drive a car	No
visit Angkor Wat	Yes
taste Vietnamese food	No
practice yoga	Yes

보기

Bella has learned to play the piano before.

➡ (1) ______________________________

(2) ______________________________

(3) ______________________________

(4) ______________________________

고 난이도

08 다음 두 문장을 〈보기〉와 같이 'so ... that ~' 구문을 사용하여 한 문장으로 연결하시오.

보기

I was very sick. I had to stay in bed all day.

→ I was so sick that I had to stay in bed all day.

(1) • The flowers are very beautiful.

• Many people come to see them.

➡ ______________________________

____

(2) • The house was very expensive.

• We decided not to buy it.

➡ ______________________________

____

(3) • This dish is too spicy.

• I need to drink a lot of milk.

➡ ______________________________

____

(4) • The movie was really sad.

• I cried a lot.

➡ ______________________________

(5) • You are truly smart.

• You always get A's.

➡ ______________________________

09 두 문장의 의미가 같도록 빈칸에 알맞은 말을 쓰시오.

Stephanie went to Australia, so she isn't here now.

= Stephanie __________ __________ to Australia.

교과서

Reading

Traditional Korean Symbols

Peter is visiting Korea to meet a friend, Mina, from a sister school.
to meet은 목적을 나타내는 부사적 용법의 to부정사이다.
Peter is going to stay at her grandfather's house for a week. When he
~할 예정이다
arrives, Mina shows him the guest room.
= Mina shows the guest room to him. (3형식)

Mina: Peter, you will stay here. This guest room is full of traditional
~으로 가득 차다
Korean things. Look at this pillow.
~을 보다

Peter: What are these things?
지시형용사

Mina: They're bats.

Peter: Bats on my pillow? That's scary!
내 베개 위에 박쥐가 있는 것

Mina: Not really. In Korea, bats are symbols of luck and a long life.
그렇지 않아.

Peter: That's surprising. In many Western countries, bats remind
앞 문장의 내용을 가리킨다. remind ... of ~는 '…에게 ~을 상기시키다'라는 의미이다.
people of darkness and scary things.

Mina shows Peter her grandfather's room. Peter and Mina's
= Mina shows her grandfather's room to Peter. (3형식)
grandfather meet and greet each other.

Grandfather: Hi, Peter! Have you ever seen this kind of lock before?
현재완료 시제로 경험 용법

Peter: No, I haven't. It's so old that I can't really tell, but is it a fish?
don't(×) so ... that ~ can't 구문으로 '너무 …해서 ~할 수 없다'라는 의미이다.

Grandfather: Yes. For a long time, Koreans have thought that fish are
have thought는 현재완료 시제로, 여기서는 과거의 일이 현재까지 계속됨을 나타낸다.
good guards. Fish don't close their eyes, even when they sleep.
its(×)

Peter: That's interesting.
앞 문장의 내용을 가리킨다.

Grandfather: We think fish can watch over valuable things. That's
'That's why ...는' '…인 이유가 바로 그것이다'라는 뜻으로, 앞에서 언급한 것이 why 이하의 어떤 행위나 현상의 원인임을 말할 때 쓴다.
why this lock looks like a fish.
look like+명사: ~처럼 보이다

Peter: Now I understand.

traditional 전통의, 전통적인
symbol 상징, 기호
be full of ~으로 가득 차다
pillow 베개
remind 생각나게 하다, 상기시키다
darkness 어둠, 암흑
scary 무서운, 두려운
greet 맞이하다, 환영하다
watch over ~을 주시하다, 지키다
valuable 값비싼, 귀중한

확인문제

● 다음 문장이 본문의 내용과 일치하면 T, 일치하지 않으면 F를 쓰시오.

1 Peter is going to stay at Mina's grandfather's house for a week. ☐

2 The guest room is full of modern Korean things. ☐

3 In Korea, bats are symbols of luck and a long life. ☐

4 Recently Koreans think that fish are good guards. ☐

5 Fish don't close their eyes, even when they sleep. ☐

They go outside and walk around the garden.

Peter: What is on that piece of paper? It looks scary.
= sheet　　감각동사 look 뒤에는 형용사가 온다.

Grandfather: Do you mean this painting of a rooster?
목적격 관계를 나타내는 전치사, …을, …의

Peter: Oh, is it a rooster?

Grandfather: Yes, it is. Roosters crow every morning. Their crowing means that a new day is beginning. For many years, Koreans have believed evil spirits go away when a rooster crows.
= Roosters'　　접속사
have believed는 현재완료 시제로, 여기서는 과거의 일이 현재까지 계속됨을 나타낸다.
evil spirits go away는 목적어로 쓰인 명사절이고, evil 앞에 접속사 that이 생략되어 있다.

Mina: Really? I've never heard that before.

Peter: Actually, I'm afraid of darkness and evil spirits. Could you draw a rooster for me, Mina?
= In fact　　be afraid of: ~을 무서워하다

Mina: Sure. I'll draw a big rooster for you!

Grandfather: Put the drawing above your door. Then it will protect you.

Peter: Yes, I will.

Peter's Diary　　May 28

I'm enjoying this trip so much that I want to stay longer. I love all the traditional Korean symbols in this house. Now I understand a lot of them. I want to visit Korea again with my family.
원인과 결과를 나타내는 so ... that 구문으로, so 다음에 부사 much가 쓰였다. '너무 …해서 ~하다'라는 의미이다.

rooster 수탉
crow (닭이) 울다
evil 사악한, 악마의
spirit 정신, 영혼
go away 사라지다, 떠나가다
protect 보호하다

확인문제

● 다음 문장이 본문의 내용과 일치하면 T, 일치하지 않으면 F를 쓰시오.

1 Peter asks what is on that piece of paper. ☐
2 Roosters' crowing means that a new day is ending. ☐
3 Koreans have believed evil spirits appear when a rooster crows. ☐
4 Peter is afraid of darkness and evil spirits. ☐
5 Mina will draw a big rooster for Peter. ☐
6 Peter wants to visit Korea again with his friends. ☐

• 우리말을 참고하여 빈칸에 알맞은 말을 쓰시오.

1 _______ Korean Symbols

2 Peter is visiting Korea to meet a friend, Mina, _______ _______ _______ _______.

3 Peter is going to _______ _______ her grandfather's house _______ _______ _______.

4 When he arrives, Mina shows _______ _______ _______ _______.

5 Peter, you will _______ _______.

6 This guest room _______ _______ _______ traditional Korean things.

7 _______ _______ this pillow.

8 What are _______ _______?

9 _______ bats.

10 Bats _______ _______ _______? That's _______!

11 _______ _______. In Korea, bats are _______ _______ luck and a long life.

12 That's _______. In many Western countries, bats _______ people _______ darkness and scary things.

13 Mina _______ Peter her grandfather's room.

14 Peter and Mina's grandfather _______ and _______ _______ _______.

15 Hi, Peter! _______ _______ _______ _______ this kind of lock before?

16 No, I _______. It's _______ old _______ I can't really tell, but is it a fish?

17 Yes. _______ _______ _______ _______, Koreans have thought that fish are _______ _______.

1 전통적인 한국의 상징물

2 피터는 자매 학교 친구인 미나를 만나기 위해 한국을 방문 중이다.

3 피터는 일주일간 미나네 할아버지 댁에 머무를 것이다.

4 그가 도착하자, 미나가 그에게 손님방을 보여준다.

5 피터, 넌 여기에 머무르게 될 거야.

6 이 손님방은 한국의 전통 물건들로 가득 차 있어.

7 이 베개를 봐.

8 이것들은 뭐야?

9 그건 박쥐들이야.

10 내 베개 위에 박쥐가? 그거 겁나는데!

11 그렇지 않아. 한국에서는 박쥐가 행운과 장수의 상징이거든.

12 그거 놀라운 일인데. 서구의 많은 나라들에서 박쥐는 사람들에게 어둠과 무서운 것들을 상기시키거든.

13 미나는 피터에게 할아버지의 방을 보여준다.

14 피터와 미나의 할아버지가 만나서 서로 인사한다.

15 안녕, 피터! 너는 이런 종류의 자물쇠를 전에 본 적 있니?

16 아니요, 본 적 없어요. 그 자물쇠는 너무 오래되어서 사실 알아볼 수가 없는데, 그건 물고기인가요?

17 맞아. 오랜 세월 동안, 한국인들은 물고기가 훌륭한 파수꾼이라고 생각해 왔단다.

18 Fish don't _______ _______ _______, even when they sleep.

19 That's _______.

20 We think fish can _______ _______ valuable things. _______ _______ this lock looks _______ a fish.

21 Now I _______.

22 They go outside and _______ _______ the garden.

23 What is on _______ _______ _______ _______? It looks scary.

24 _______ _______ _______ this painting of a rooster?

25 Oh, is it _______ _______?

26 Yes, it is. Roosters _______ every morning.

27 Their crowing means that _______ _______ _______ is beginning.

28 For many years, Koreans have believed evil spirits _______ _______ when a rooster _______.

29 Really? _______ _______ _______ that before.

30 _______, I'm _______ of darkness and evil spirits.

31 Could you draw a rooster _______ _______, Mina?

32 Sure. I'll _______ _______ _______ _______ for you!

33 _______ the drawing _______ your door. Then it will _______ you.

34 Yes, I _______.

35 I'm enjoying this trip _______ _______ _______ I want to stay longer.

36 I love all the _______ _______ _______ in this house.

37 Now I understand _______ _______ _______ _______.

38 I want to visit Korea again _______ _______ _______.

18 물고기는 잘 때도 눈을 감지 않거든.

19 그거 재미있군요.

20 우리는 물고기가 귀중품을 지킬 수 있다고 생각해. 그것이 이 자물쇠가 물고기 모양으로 생긴 이유란다.

21 이제 이해가 되는군요.

22 그들은 밖에 나가서 정원을 걷는다.

23 저 종이에는 무엇이 그려져 있는 거죠? 무서워 보여요.

24 이 수탉 그림을 말하는 거니?

25 오, 그게 수탉이에요?

26 응, 그렇단다. 수탉은 매일 아침 울지.

27 수탉의 울음은 새로운 날이 시작하는 것을 의미해.

28 오랫동안 한국인들은 수탉이 울 때 악령이 물러간다고 믿어 왔단다.

29 정말요? 전 그런 말을 들어본 적이 없어요.

30 사실 전 어둠과 악령을 무서워해요.

31 미나야, 날 위해 수탉을 그려 줄 수 있니?

32 물론이지. 내가 널 위해 커다란 수탉을 그려줄게!

33 그 그림을 네 문 위에 걸어 놓으렴. 그러면 그게 널 지켜 줄 거야.

34 네, 그럴게요.

35 난 이번 여행이 매우 즐거워서 더 오래 머무르고 싶다.

36 난 이 집의 모든 전통적인 한국의 상징물들이 아주 마음에 든다.

37 나는 이제 그것들을 많이 알게 되었다.

38 난 우리 가족과 함께 한국을 다시 방문하고 싶다.

Reading 교과서 확인학습 B

• 우리말을 참고하여 본문을 영작하시오.

1 전통적인 한국의 상징물

➡ ______________________________

2 피터는 자매 학교 친구인 미나를 만나기 위해 한국을 방문 중이다.

➡ ______________________________

3 피터는 일주일간 미나네 할아버지 댁에 머무를 것이다.

➡ ______________________________

4 그가 도착하자, 미나가 그에게 손님방을 보여준다.

➡ ______________________________

5 피터, 넌 여기에 머무르게 될 거야.

➡ ______________________________

6 이 손님방은 한국의 전통 물건들로 가득 차 있어.

➡ ______________________________

7 이 베개를 봐.

➡ ______________________________

8 이것들은 뭐야?

➡ ______________________________

9 그건 박쥐들이야.

➡ ______________________________

10 내 베개 위에 박쥐가? 그거 겁나는데!

➡ ______________________________

11 그렇지 않아. 한국에서는 박쥐가 행운과 장수의 상징이거든.

➡ ______________________________

12 그거 놀라운 일인데. 서구의 많은 나라들에서 박쥐는 사람들에게 어둠과 무서운 것들을 상기시키거든.

➡ ______________________________

13 미나는 피터에게 할아버지의 방을 보여준다.

➡ ______________________________

14 피터와 미나의 할아버지가 만나서 서로 인사한다.

➡ ______________________________

15 안녕, 피터! 너는 이런 종류의 자물쇠를 전에 본 적 있니?

➡ ______________________________

16 아니요, 본 적 없어요. 그 자물쇠는 너무 오래되어서 사실 알아볼 수가 없는데, 그건 물고기인가요?

➡ ______________________________

17 맞아. 오랜 세월 동안, 한국인들은 물고기가 훌륭한 파수꾼이라고 생각해 왔단다.

➡ ______________________________

18 물고기는 잘 때도 눈을 감지 않거든.
➡ ______

19 그거 재미있군요.
➡ ______

20 우리는 물고기가 귀중품을 지킬 수 있다고 생각해. 그것이 이 자물쇠가 물고기 모양으로 생긴 이유란다.
➡ ______

21 이제 이해가 되는군요.
➡ ______

22 그들은 밖에 나가서 정원을 걷는다.
➡ ______

23 저 종이에는 무엇이 그려져 있는 거죠? 무서워 보여요.
➡ ______

24 이 수탉 그림을 말하는 거니?
➡ ______

25 오, 그게 수탉이에요?
➡ ______

26 응, 그렇단다. 수탉은 매일 아침 울지.
➡ ______

27 수탉의 울음은 새로운 날이 시작하는 것을 의미해.
➡ ______

28 오랫동안 한국인들은 수탉이 울 때 악령이 물러간다고 믿어 왔단다.
➡ ______

29 정말요? 전 그런 말을 들어본 적이 없어요.
➡ ______

30 사실 전 어둠과 악령을 무서워해요.
➡ ______

31 미나야, 날 위해 수탉을 그려 줄 수 있니?
➡ ______

32 물론이지. 내가 널 위해 커다란 수탉을 그려줄게!
➡ ______

33 그 그림을 네 문 위에 걸어 놓으렴. 그러면 그게 널 지켜 줄 거야.
➡ ______

34 네, 그럴게요.
➡ ______

35 난 이번 여행이 매우 즐거워서 더 오래 머무르고 싶다.
➡ ______

36 난 이 집의 모든 전통적인 한국의 상징물들이 아주 마음에 든다.
➡ ______

37 나는 이제 그것들을 많이 알게 되었다.
➡ ______

38 난 우리 가족과 함께 한국을 다시 방문하고 싶다.
➡ ______

Reading 시험대비 실력평가

[01~03] 다음 글을 읽고, 물음에 답하시오.

Peter is visiting Korea to meet a friend, Mina, from a sister school. Peter is going to stay at her grandfather's house for a week. When he arrives, Mina shows him the guest room.

Mina: Peter, you will stay here. This guest room is full of traditional Korean things. Look at this pillow.

Peter: What are these things?

Mina: They're bats.

Peter: Bats on my pillow? ⓐThat's scary!

Mina: ⓑNot really. In Korea, bats are symbols of luck and a long life.

Peter: That's surprising. In many Western countries, bats remind people of darkness and scary things.

서답형

01 위 글의 밑줄 친 ⓐThat이 가리키는 것을 우리말로 쓰시오.

➡ ______________________

서답형

02 미나가 밑줄 친 ⓑ처럼 말한 이유를 우리말로 쓰시오.

➡ ______________________

03 위 글의 내용과 일치하지 않는 것은?

① 피터는 자매 학교 친구인 미나를 만나기 위해 한국을 방문 중이다.
② 피터는 한 달 동안 미나네 할아버지 댁에 머무를 것이다.
③ 미나의 할아버지 댁의 손님방은 한국의 전통 물건들로 가득 차 있다.
④ 한국에서는 박쥐가 행운과 장수의 상징이다.
⑤ 서구의 많은 나라들에서, 박쥐는 사람들에게 어둠과 무서운 것들을 상기시켜 준다.

[04~06] 다음 글을 읽고, 물음에 답하시오.

Grandfather: Hi, Peter! ⓐHave you ever seen this kind of lock before?

Peter: ⓑ아니, 없어요. It's so old that I can't really tell, but is it a fish?

Grandfather: Yes. For a long time, Koreans have thought that fish are good guards. Fish don't close their eyes, even when they sleep.

Peter: That's interesting.

Grandfather: We think fish can ___(A)___ valuable things. That's why this lock looks like a fish.

Peter: Now I understand.

04 위 글의 빈칸 (A)에 들어갈 알맞은 말을 고르시오.

① show around
② wait for
③ look into
④ watch over
⑤ look forward to

중요

05 위 글의 밑줄 친 ⓐ와 현재완료의 용법이 같은 것을 모두 고르시오.

① She has lost her handbag.
② How long have you stayed here?
③ How many times have you read it?
④ I have just finished my work.
⑤ She has been to New York.

서답형

06 위 글의 밑줄 친 ⓑ의 우리말에 맞게 3단어로 영작하시오.

➡ ______________________

[07~09] 다음 글을 읽고, 물음에 답하시오.

Peter is visiting Korea to meet a friend, Mina, from a ___ⓐ___. Peter is going to stay at her grandfather's house for a week. When he arrives, Mina shows him the guest room.

Mina: Peter, you will stay here. This guest room is full of traditional Korean things. Look at this pillow.
Peter: What are these things?
Mina: They're bats.
Peter: Bats on my pillow? That's scary!
Mina: ___ⓑ___ In Korea, bats are symbols of luck and a long life.
Peter: That's surprising. In many Western countries, bats remind people of darkness and scary things.

서답형
07 주어진 영영풀이를 참고하여 빈칸 ⓐ에 철자 s로 시작하는 단어를 쓰시오.

a school which is financially, historically or socially linked to another

➡ ________________

08 위 글의 빈칸 ⓑ에 들어갈 알맞은 말을 고르시오.

① That's right.
② Why not?
③ You can say that again.
④ You said it.
⑤ Not really.

중요
09 위 글에서 베개에 있는 박쥐 디자인에 대한 'Peter'의 심경 변화로 가장 알맞은 것을 고르시오.

① surprised → excited
② disappointed → scared
③ bored → disappointed
④ scared → surprised
⑤ ashamed → depressed

[10~12] 다음 글을 읽고, 물음에 답하시오.

Grandfather: Hi, Peter! Have you ever seen this ⓐkind of lock before?
Peter: No, I haven't. ⓑIt's so old that I can't really tell, but is it a fish?
Grandfather: Yes. For a long time, Koreans have thought that fish are good guards. Fish don't close their eyes, even when they sleep.
Peter: That's interesting.
Grandfather: We think fish can watch over valuable things. ⓒ그것이 이 자물쇠가 물고기 모양으로 생긴 이유란다.
Peter: Now I understand.

10 위 글의 밑줄 친 ⓐkind와 같은 의미로 쓰인 것을 고르시오.

① You've been very kind.
② Thank you for your kind invitation.
③ What kind of house do you live in?
④ It was really kind of you to help me.
⑤ He was a very kind and helpful man.

서답형
11 위 글의 밑줄 친 ⓑIt이 가리키는 것을 다음 빈칸에 쓰시오.

➡ the ________ that Mina's grandfather showed Peter

서답형
12 위 글의 밑줄 친 ⓒ의 우리말에 맞게 한 단어를 보충하여, 주어진 어휘를 알맞게 배열하시오.

fish / lock / that's / like / this / a / looks

➡ ________________________________

[13~15] 다음 글을 읽고, 물음에 답하시오.

They go outside and walk around the garden.
Peter: What is on that piece of paper? ⓐIt looks like scary.
Grandfather: Do you mean this painting of a rooster?
Peter: Oh, is it a rooster?
Grandfather: Yes, it is. Roosters crow every morning. Their crowing means that a new day is beginning. For many years, Koreans have believed evil spirits go away when a rooster crows.
Mina: Really? I've never heard that before.
Peter: Actually, I'm afraid of darkness and evil spirits. Could you draw a rooster for me, Mina?
Mina: Sure. I'll draw a big rooster for you!
Grandfather: Put the drawing above your door. Then it will protect you.
Peter: Yes, I will.

서답형
13 위 글의 밑줄 친 ⓐ에서 어법상 틀린 부분을 찾아 고치시오.

__________ ➡ __________

중요
14 위 글의 제목으로 알맞은 것을 고르시오.

① Enjoy Walking around the Garden
② Look at the Scary Painting of a Rooster
③ What Does the Painting of a Rooster Mean?
④ The Reason Roosters Crow Every Morning
⑤ Why Is Peter Afraid of Darkness and Evil Spirits?

15 위 글을 읽고 대답할 수 없는 질문은?

① Who goes outside and walks around the garden?
② Does Peter know what is on the piece of paper?
③ What's the meaning of the roosters' crowing?
④ What will Mina draw for Peter?
⑤ Why does Grandfather tell Peter to put the drawing above his door, not below the door?

[16~17] 다음 일기를 읽고, 물음에 답하시오.

Peter's Diary

May 28

ⓐI'm enjoying this trip so much that I want to stay longer. I love all the traditional Korean symbols in this house. Now I understand a lot of them. I want to visit Korea again with my family.

서답형
16 위 일기의 밑줄 친 ⓐ를 다음과 같이 바꿔 쓸 때 빈칸 (A)와 (B)에 들어갈 알맞은 말을 〈보기〉에서 골라 쓰시오.

보기
Such/such, So/so, For/for, As/as, But/but

• (A)__________ I'm enjoying this trip very much, I want to stay longer.
• I'm enjoying this trip very much, (B)__________ I want to stay longer.

17 위 일기의 내용과 일치하지 않는 것은?

① 피터는 이번 여행이 매우 즐거워서 더 오래 머무르고 싶어 한다.
② 피터는 방문한 집의 전통적인 한국의 상징물들이 모두 마음에 든다.
③ 이제 피터는 전통적인 한국의 상징물들을 많이 알게 되었다.
④ 피터는 전통적인 한국의 상징물들에 대해 계속 공부하고 싶어 한다.
⑤ 피터는 가족들과 함께 한국을 다시 방문하고 싶어 한다.

[18~19] 다음 글을 읽고, 물음에 답하시오.

Do you know about traditional Chinese dances? There are many kinds. ___ⓐ___, there are a lion dance, a fan dance, and an umbrella dance. One of the most famous dances is the lion dance. In this dance, two dancers dress and act like lions. They usually dance on special days, such as New Year's Day. I think their dance moves are great. I hope to practice this dance someday.

18 위 글의 빈칸 ⓐ에 들어갈 알맞은 말을 고르시오.

① However ② In other words
③ Therefore ④ In addition
⑤ For example

서답형
19 다음 문장에서 위 글의 내용과 다른 부분을 찾아서 고치시오. (두 군데)

A lion dance is a traditional Chinese dance and people usually perform it at any time. In this dance, three dancers dress and act like lions.

➡ (1) ______________________
(2) ______________________

[20~21] 다음 글을 읽고, 물음에 답하시오.

My trip to Korea was great. My friend Mina and her grandfather were very kind to me. (A)[During / For] my trip, I learned (B)[a lot / a lot of] about traditional Korean symbols. That was so (C)[interesting / interested] that I want to visit Korea again with my family.

I: Peter

서답형
20 위 글의 괄호 (A)~(C)에서 어법상 알맞은 낱말을 골라 쓰시오.

➡ (A)________ (B)________ (C)________

중요
21 위 글을 읽고 피터의 여행에 대해 알 수 없는 것을 고르시오.

① 여행 장소 ② 여행 기간
③ 같이 지낸 사람들 ④ 여행에서 배운 것
⑤ 여행에 대한 느낌

[22~24] 다음 글을 읽고, 물음에 답하시오.

Peter: What is on that piece of paper? It looks scary.
Grandfather: Do you mean this painting of a rooster?
Peter: Oh, is it a rooster?
Grandfather: Yes, it is. Roosters crow every morning. Their crowing means that a new day is (A)[beginning / ending]. For many years, Koreans have believed evil spirits go away when a rooster crows.
Mina: Really? I've never heard that before.
Peter: ⓐActually, I'm afraid of darkness and evil spirits. ⓑCould you draw a rooster for me, Mina?
Mina: Sure. I'll draw a big rooster for you!
Grandfather: Put the drawing above your door. Then it will (B)[prevent / protect] you.
Peter: Yes, I (C)[do / will].

서답형
22 위 글의 괄호 (A)~(C)에서 문맥이나 어법상 알맞은 낱말을 골라 쓰시오.

➡ (A)________ (B)________ (C)________

23 위 글의 밑줄 친 ⓐActually와 바꿔 쓸 수 있는 말을 모두 고르시오.

① As a result ② In fact
③ Above all ④ In other words
⑤ As a matter of fact

서답형
24 다음 빈칸 (A)와 (B)에 들어갈 알맞은 단어를 본문에서 찾아, Peter가 밑줄 친 ⓑ처럼 말한 이유를 완성하시오.

Because Peter is (A)__________ of darkness and evil spirits and he wants them to (B)__________ __________ thanks to the painting of a rooster.

[01~03] 다음 글을 읽고, 물음에 답하시오.

Peter is visiting Korea to meet a friend, Mina, from a sister school. Peter is going to stay at her grandfather's house for a week. When he arrives, ⓐMina shows him the guest room.

Mina: Peter, you will stay here. This guest room is full of traditional Korean things. Look at this pillow.

Peter: What are these things?

Mina: They're bats.

Peter: Bats on my pillow? That's scary!

Mina: Not really. In Korea, bats are symbols of luck and a long life.

Peter: That's surprising. In many Western countries, bats remind people of darkness and scary things.

중요

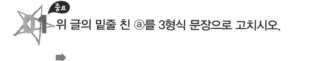

01 위 글의 밑줄 친 ⓐ를 3형식 문장으로 고치시오.

➡ ______________________

02 다음 질문에 대한 알맞은 대답을 주어진 단어로 시작하여 쓰시오. (5 단어)

Q: What do bats symbolize in Korea?
A: They symbolize ______________.

03 다음 문장에서 위 글의 내용과 다른 부분을 찾아서 고치시오.

Bats remind people of happiness and pleasant things in many Western countries.

__________ ➡ __________

[04~07] 다음 글을 읽고, 물음에 답하시오.

Mina shows Peter her grandfather's room. ⓐPeter and Mina's grandfather meet and greet to each other.

Grandfather: Hi, Peter! ⓑ너는 이런 종류의 자물쇠를 전에 본 적 있니?

Peter: No, I haven't. It's so old that I can't really tell, but is it a fish?

Grandfather: Yes. For a long time, Koreans have thought that fish are good guards. Fish don't close their eyes, even when they sleep.

Peter: That's interesting.

Grandfather: We think fish can watch over valuable things. That's why this lock looks like a fish.

Peter: Now I understand.

04 위 글의 밑줄 친 ⓐ에서 어법상 틀린 부분을 찾아 고치시오.

__________ ➡ __________

중요

05 위 글의 밑줄 친 ⓑ의 우리말에 맞게 한 단어를 보충하여, 주어진 어휘를 알맞게 배열하시오.

seen / lock / this / you / kind / ever / of / have

➡ ______________________

06 다음 질문에 대한 알맞은 대답을 주어진 단어로 시작하여 쓰시오. (9 단어)

Q: Why have Koreans thought that fish are good guards?
A: Because ______________________
______________________.

07 본문의 내용과 일치하도록 다음 빈칸에 알맞은 단어를 쓰시오.

> The lock that Mina's grandfather shows Peter looks like __________ __________.

[08~10] 다음 글을 읽고, 물음에 답하시오.

> They go outside and walk around the garden.
> **Peter:** What is on that piece of paper? It looks scary.
> **Grandfather:** Do you mean this painting of a rooster?
> **Peter:** Oh, is it a rooster?
> **Grandfather:** Yes, it is. Roosters crow every morning. Their crowing means that a new day is beginning. For many years, Koreans have believed evil spirits go away when a rooster crows.
> **Mina:** Really? ⓐ<u>전 그런 말을 들어본 적이 없어요.</u>
> **Peter:** Actually, I'm afraid of darkness and evil spirits. Could you draw a rooster for me, Mina?
> **Mina:** Sure. I'll draw a big rooster for you!
> **Grandfather:** Put the drawing above your door. Then it will protect you.
> **Peter:** Yes, I will.

08 다음 질문에 대한 알맞은 대답을 5 단어로 쓰시오.

> **Q:** What is on the piece of paper that Peter is pointing to?

➡ ______________________________

중요
09 위 글을 읽고 (1) 수탉의 울음소리의 의미와 (2) 그에 대한 한국 사람들의 믿음이 무엇인지를 우리말로 쓰시오.

➡ (1) ______________________________
(2) ______________________________

10 위 글의 밑줄 친 ⓐ의 우리말에 맞게 주어진 어휘를 이용하여 5단어로 영작하시오.

> that

➡ ______________________________

[11~13] 다음 글을 읽고, 물음에 답하시오.

> Peter is ①<u>visiting</u> Korea to meet a friend, Mina, from a sister school. Peter is going to stay at her grandfather's house for a week. When he arrives, Mina ②<u>shows</u> him the guest room.
> **Mina:** Peter, you will ③<u>stay</u> here. This guest room ⓐ<u>is full of</u> traditional Korean things. Look at this pillow.
> **Peter:** What are these things?
> **Mina:** They're bats.
> **Peter:** Bats on my pillow? That's scary!
> **Mina:** ④<u>Not really</u>. In Korea, bats are symbols of luck and a long life.
> **Peter:** That's ⑤<u>reasonable</u>. In many Western countries, bats remind people of darkness and scary things.

11 위 글의 밑줄 친 ⓐ와 바꿔 쓸 수 있는 말을 쓰시오. (3단어)

➡ ______________

중요
12 위 글의 밑줄 친 ①~⑤에서 문맥상 낱말의 쓰임이 적절하지 <u>않은</u> 것을 찾아 알맞게 고치시오.

➡ ______________

13 본문의 내용과 일치하도록 다음 빈칸 (A)와 (B)에 알맞은 단어를 쓰시오. (한 칸에 여러 단어를 쓸 수 있음.)

> In Korea, bats remind people of positive things such as (A)__________ and (B)__________. On the other hand, in many Western countries, bats are symbols of (C)__________ things such as darkness and scary things.

교과서

구석구석

Project Link

We made our own class flag. The flag is a triangle. It means we always work together. There is a tiger on the flag. It shows that we are powerful. The red represents our energy.

(own: (형) 자기 자신의, 자신이 직접 한 / triangle: 삼각형 / means: 의미하다 / always: 빈도부사로 '항상'의 의미를 가지며, 일반동사 앞에 위치한다. / It = The tiger / that we are powerful: shows의 목적어로 that절이 사용되었다. / represents: 나타내다, 상징하다)

구문해설 • work together: 함께 일하다

해석 우리는 우리 반의 깃발을 만들었다. 깃발은 삼각형이다. 그것은 우리가 항상 함께 일하는 것을 의미한다. 깃발에 호랑이가 한 마리가 있다. 그것은 우리가 강력하다는 것을 보여준다. 빨간색은 우리의 에너지를 나타낸다.

Think and Write

Do you know about traditional Chinese dances? There are many kinds. For example, there are a lion dance, a fan dance, and an umbrella dance. One of the most famous dances is the lion dance. In this dance, two dancers dress and act like lions. They usually dance on special days, such as New Year's Day. I think their dance moves are great.

I hope to practice this dance someday.

(There are: ~이 있다 / For example: 예를 들어 / there are: ~이 있다 / One of the most famous dances: one of the 복수 명사: ~ 중의 하나 / is: are(×) / like: ~처럼 / usually: be동사나, 조동사 뒤, 일반동사 앞에 쓴다. / such as = like / great: be동사의 보어 / to practice: 명사적 용법의 to부정사 (목적어))

구문해설 • traditional: 전통적인 • kind: 종류 • fan dance: 부채춤 • usually: 대개 • dance move: 춤 동작 • someday: 언젠가

당신은 전통적인 중국 춤에 대해 아는가? 많은 종류들이 있다. 예를 들면, 사자춤, 부채춤, 그리고 우산춤이 있다. 가장 유명한 춤들 중의 하나가 사자춤이다. 이 춤에서, 두 명의 댄서들이 사자처럼 옷을 입고 행동한다. 사람들은 사자춤을 대개 설날과 같은 특별한 날에 춘다. 나는 그들의 춤 동작들이 멋지다고 생각한다. 나는 언젠가 이 춤을 연습하기를 바란다.

Presentation Time

Do you want to have a good time in Korea? Then follow these steps. First, please take off your shoes when you go into people's homes. Next, bow when you greet others. Also, use two hands when you give something to older people. And do not blow your nose at the table and do not point at people. Lastly, do not call older people by their first names.

(have a good time: 즐거운 시간을 보내다 / First: (여러 가지를 나열할 때) 첫째(로) / when: 때를 나타내는 접속사 / you give something to older people = you give older people something / blow your nose: 코를 풀다 / at the table: 식탁에서(식사할 때) / call ... by their first names: ~를 이름으로 부르다)

구문해설 • follow: 따르다 • take off: 벗다 • bow: 절하다 • greet: 인사하다 • point at: ~을 가리키다, 손가락질하다

한국에서 즐거운 시간을 보내고 싶은가요? 그러면 다음 단계를 따르세요. 먼저 사람들의 집에 들어갈 때는 신발을 벗으세요. 다음에 다른 사람들에게 인사할 때 절을 하세요. 또한 나이가 많은 사람들에게 무언가를 줄 때는 두 손을 사용하세요. 그리고 식탁에서 코를 풀지 말고 사람들을 가리키지 마세요. 마지막으로 나이가 많은 사람들을 이름으로 부르지 마세요.

영역별 핵심문제

Words & Expressions

01 다음 대화의 빈칸에 들어갈 말을 고르시오.

> A: Have you ever ______ Chinese food?
> B: Yes, I have.

① got ② took ③ tried
④ served ⑤ tied

02 다음 대화에서 밑줄 친 'face'와 같은 의미로 쓰인 것을 모두 고르시오.

> G: Oh, look at that boy. That's really rude.
> B: Which boy?
> G: The boy who is making the V sign. His palm is facing toward himself.

① The palms should face the ceiling.
② His face was covered with wrinkles.
③ It's a brush used for soaping your face.
④ Be sure that the photos you want to scan are facing up.
⑤ The garden faces south.

[03~04] 다음 빈칸에 공통으로 들어갈 단어를 주어진 철자로 시작하여 쓰시오.

03

> • A pear drops when a c______ flies from the tree.
> • They c______ at the same time every morning when the sun rises.

04

> • He cupped her chin in the p______ of his hand.
> • They can climb up p______ trees easily.

Conversation

[05~06] 다음 대화를 읽고, 물음에 답하시오.

> G: ①Have you ever been to Brazil?
> B: No, I haven't. Have you?
> G: ②Yes, I have. ③I have been there last year. ④There was a big samba festival.
> B: That sounds interesting. ⑤I hope to go there someday.

05 대화의 밑줄 친 ①~⑤ 중에서 어색한 곳을 고르고 바르게 고치시오.

➡ ______________________

06 <보기>에서 대화의 내용과 일치하는 않는 것의 개수를 고르시오.

> 보기
> ⓐ The boy has never been to Brazil.
> ⓑ The girl visited Brazil last year.
> ⓒ The girl wants to go to Brazil.
> ⓓ The girl has ever been to Brazil.
> ⓔ There was a samba festival in Brazil last year.
> ⓕ The boy had a fun time in Brazil.

① 1개 ② 2개 ③ 3개 ④ 4개 ⑤ 5개

07 다음 중 어색한 대화를 고르시오.

① A: Have you ever played *gorodki*?
B: No, I haven't. What is it?
② A: What does that mean?
B: It means victory or peace.
③ A: Should I bring anything?
B: No, but please wear white clothes.
④ A: Have you ever gone to Brazil?
B: No. Have you?
⑤ A: What is that?
B: It's a traditional Indian festival.

[08~11] 다음 대화를 읽고, 물음에 답하시오.

G: Hello, Santiago! What brings you here today?
B: *Bienvenido*, Cathy. (①)
G: Me, too. But what did you just say?
B: *Bienvenido*! It (A)______ "welcome" in Spanish. (②) Look at those dancers. Their dance moves are so great. (③)
G: Yes, they are.
B: 전에 스페인 축제에 가 본 적 있니?
G: No, I haven't. Santiago, can you see the big letters on the stage? (④) What does that mean? (⑤)
B: Oh, *gracias*. That (B)______ "thank you."

08 위 대화의 ①~⑤ 중 주어진 문장이 들어갈 알맞은 곳은?

I came to see the Spanish festival.

① ② ③ ④ ⑤

09 빈칸 (A)와 (B)에 공통으로 들어갈 말을 대화의 어휘 중에서 찾아 어법에 맞게 쓰시오.

➡ ____________

10 위 대화의 밑줄 친 우리말을 영작하시오.

➡ ______________________________

11 위 대화의 내용과 일치하지 않는 것을 고르시오.

① Santiago knows the meaning of some Spanish words.
② Cathy didn't know the meaning of *gracias*.
③ Cathy has never been to Spain.
④ There are small letters, *gracias*, on the stage.
⑤ Cathy came to see the Spanish festival.

[12~13] 다음 대화를 읽고, 물음에 답하시오.

W: Welcome (A)________ the International Games Festival. You can play many different traditional games here.
B: Wow! It looks exciting! Which game should I play first?
W: Let's see. Have you ever played *gorodki*?
B: No, I haven't. What is it?
W: It's a traditional game (B)_____ Russia.
B: How do I play it?
W: Put five sticks (C)______ the ground. Then throw a bat (D)_____ them.
B: That sounds fun. I'll try that first.

12 빈칸 (A)~(D)에 알맞은 것을 〈보기〉에서 골라 쓰시오.

보기
on from at to

➡ (A)_______ (B)_______
(C)_______ (C)_______

13 주어진 영영풀이에 해당하는 단어를 대화에서 찾아 쓰시오.

being part of something that people have done for a long time

➡ ____________

Grammar

14 다음 중 밑줄 친 부분의 쓰임이 〈보기〉와 같은 것을 모두 고르면?

보기
Have you ever been to America?

① Nolan has learned English for 6 years.
② The train has just left the station.
③ I have watched *Avatar* three times.
④ I haven't met a famous movie star.
⑤ My smartphone has broken.

15 다음 우리말을 영어로 바르게 옮긴 것은?

그는 너무 천천히 걸어서 회의에 늦었다.

① He walked too slowly as he was late for the meeting.
② He walked slowly so that he was late for the meeting.
③ He walked so slowly that he was late for the meeting.
④ He walked slowly enough that he was late for the meeting.
⑤ He walked too slowly to be late for the meeting.

16 다음 중 어법상 어색한 것은?

① When have you visited London?
② Have you watched *The Wizard of Oz*?
③ Lindsay has visited Korea twice.
④ We have known her since she was a little girl.
⑤ Jake has been sick for two weeks.

17 다음 두 문장을 한 문장으로 바르게 연결한 것은?

• Mom became very angry. • Mom yelled at me.

① Mom became very angry that she yelled at me.
② Mom became enough angry to yell at me.
③ Mom became too angry to yell at me.
④ Mom became angry as that she yelled at me.
⑤ Mom became so angry that she yelled at me.

18 다음 우리말에 맞게 빈칸에 알맞은 말을 쓰시오.

Sonya는 너무 피곤해서 곧 잠이 들었다.

➡ Sonya was ________ tired ________ she fell asleep in a moment.

19 다음 우리말과 의미가 같도록 빈칸에 알맞은 말을 쓰시오.

(1) 그는 인도를 방문해 본 적이 없다.
➡ He ________ never ________ to India.
(2) Shirley는 영국에 가서 여기 없다.
➡ Shirley ________ ________ to England.

20 다음 중 어법상 어색한 것은?

① He is so smart that he can solve all these math problems without a calculator.
② Nicole was very tired that she couldn't go shopping.
③ Ms. Winslet is such a nice teacher that she gives all her students gifts.
④ The little boy was too short to reach the shelf.
⑤ Edan studied hard enough to pass the math test.

21 괄호 안에 주어진 어휘를 이용하여 다음을 영작하시오.

(1) 그 차는 너무 빨라서 경찰은 그것을 잡을 수 없었다. (the car, fast, that, the police, catch)
➡ ________________________________
(2) 그 콘서트는 너무 좋아서 많은 사람들이 그것을 다시 보러 갔다. (the concert, good, that, see, again)
➡ ________________________________

22 주어진 두 문장을 현재완료를 이용해 한 문장으로 만드시오.

(1) Lin spent all the money for shopping. So she doesn't have any money now.

➡ ____________________

(2) Jeremy started to play the piano six years ago. And he still plays the piano.

➡ ____________________

Reading

[23~24] 다음 글을 읽고, 물음에 답하시오.

Peter is visiting Korea ⓐto meet a friend, Mina, from a sister school. Peter is going to stay at her grandfather's house for a week. When he arrives, Mina shows him the guest room.

Mina: Peter, you will stay here. This guest room is full of (A)[modern / traditional] Korean things. Look at this pillow.

Peter What are these things?

Mina: They're bats.

Peter: Bats on my pillow? That's (B)[scary / terrific]!

Mina: Not really. In Korea, bats are symbols of luck and a long life.

Peter: That's surprising. In many Western countries, bats (C)[remind / remain] people of darkness and scary things.

23 위 글의 밑줄 친 ⓐto meet과 to부정사의 용법이 같은 것을 모두 고르시오.

① I went to the store to buy some eggs.
② It wasn't easy to solve the problem.
③ He wanted to get a good grade.
④ I have some questions to ask her.
⑤ He studied hard to be a scientist.

24 위 글의 괄호 (A)~(C)에서 문맥상 알맞은 낱말을 골라 쓰시오.

➡ (A)________ (B)________ (C)________

[25~27] 다음 글을 읽고, 물음에 답하시오.

Mina shows Peter her grandfather's room. Peter and Mina's grandfather meet and greet each other.

Grandfather: Hi, Peter! Have you ever seen this kind of lock before?

Peter: No, I haven't. It's ___ⓐ___ old ___ⓑ___ I can't really tell, but is it a fish?

Grandfather: Yes. For a long time, Koreans have thought that fish are good guards. Fish don't close their eyes, even when they sleep.

Peter: ⓒThat's interesting.

Grandfather: We think fish can watch over valuable things. That's why this lock looks like a fish.

Peter: Now I understand.

25 위 글의 빈칸 ⓐ와 ⓑ에 들어갈 알맞은 말을 고르시오.

① such – that
② too – as
③ enough – that
④ so – that
⑤ so – as

26 위 글의 밑줄 친 ⓒThat이 가리키는 것을 본문에서 찾아 쓰시오.

➡ ____________________

27 위 글의 주제로 알맞은 것을 고르시오.

① the reason Mina shows Peter her grandfather's room
② the most popular kind of lock in Korea
③ the reason fish don't close their eyes
④ various kinds of locks in traditional Korean houses
⑤ the reason the lock looks like a fish

[28~30] 다음 글을 읽고, 물음에 답하시오.

Peter: What is on that piece of paper? It looks scary.
Grandfather: Do you mean this painting of a rooster?
Peter: Oh, is it a rooster?
Grandfather: Yes, it is. Roosters crow every morning. Their crowing means that a new day is beginning. For many years, Koreans have believed ___ⓐ___ when a rooster crows.
Mina: Really? I've never heard that before.
Peter: Actually, I'm afraid ___ⓑ___ darkness and evil spirits. Could you draw a rooster ___ⓒ___ me, Mina?
Mina: Sure. I'll draw a big rooster ___ⓒ___ you!
Grandfather: Put the drawing above your door. Then it will protect you.
Peter: Yes, I will.

28 위 글의 빈칸 ⓐ에 들어갈 알맞은 말을 고르시오.

① evil spirits go away
② darkness follows
③ people go to sleep
④ evil spirits arrive
⑤ it gets dark

29 위 글의 빈칸 ⓑ와 ⓒ에 들어갈 전치사가 바르게 짝지어진 것은?

① in – to ② of – at
③ of – for ④ for – to
⑤ in – for

30 위 글의 내용과 일치하지 않는 것은?

① 피터는 종이 위에 있는 그림을 무서워한다.
② 피터는 종이 위에 수탉 그림이 있는 것을 알고 있었다.
③ 수탉의 울음은 새로운 날이 시작하는 것을 의미한다.
④ 피터는 어둠과 악령을 무서워한다.
⑤ 미나는 피터를 위해 커다란 수탉을 그려줄 것이다.

[31~32] 다음 일기를 읽고, 물음에 답하시오.

Peter's Diary

May 28

I'm enjoying this trip so much that I want ⓐ to stay longer. I love all the traditional Korean symbols in this house. ⓑNow I understand a lot of it. I want to visit Korea again with my family.

31 아래 〈보기〉에서 위 일기의 밑줄 친 ⓐto stay와 문법적 쓰임이 같은 것의 개수를 고르시오.

보기

① It is time to go to bed.
② She decided to meet him again.
③ I worked hard to pass the test.
④ He is the last man to tell a lie.
⑤ It is good to help the old.

① 1개 ② 2개 ③ 3개 ④ 4개 ⑤ 5개

32 위 일기의 밑줄 친 ⓑ에서 어법상 틀린 부분을 찾아 고치시오.

__________ ➡ __________

단원별 예상문제

[01~02] 주어진 문장의 뒤에 나올 대화의 순서를 알맞게 쓰시오.

출제율 90%

01

There is a Holi festival in Busan this year.

(A) That sounds exciting. Have you ever been to a Holi festival?
(B) It's a traditional Indian festival. People throw colored powder and water at each other.
(C) A Holi festival? What is that?
(D) No, I haven't. But my Indian friend told me a lot about it.

➡ ____________________

출제율 85%

02

Oh, look at that boy. That's really rude.

(A) What's wrong with that?
(B) It has a bad meaning in England. But showing your palm and making a V sign is okay.
(C) It means victory or peace.
(D) Which boy?
(E) What does that mean?
(F) The boy who is making the V sign. His palm is facing toward himself.

➡ ____________________

[03~04] 다음 대화를 읽고, 물음에 답하시오.

G: Have you ever been to Brazil?
B: No, I (A)_________. (B)_________ you?
G: Yes, I (C)_________. I went there last year. There (D)_________ a big samba festival.
B: That (E)_________ interesting. I hope (F)_________ there someday.

출제율 100%

03 빈칸 (A)~(C)에 들어갈 단어를 쓰시오. (각 1 단어)

➡ (A)________ (B)________ (C)________

출제율 90%

04 빈칸 (D)~(F)에 들어갈 말이 바르게 짝지어진 것은?

	(D)	(E)	(F)
①	is	sounds	go
②	is	sounds like	to go
③	was	sounds like	going
④	was	sounds	to go
⑤	were	sounds like	going

[05~07] 다음 대화를 읽고, 물음에 답하시오.

B: Ling's birthday is this Wednesday, isn't it?
G: Yes. I'm going to buy a book for her. (①) What about you?
B: Well, I'm thinking about buying her an umbrella. I found a cute one in a gift shop. (②)
G: Oh, that's not a good gift for (A)_________ people. (③) It means something bad.
B: Really? What does an umbrella mean in China?
G: (④) The words for *separation* and *umbrella* sound the same in (B)_________.
B: I see. (⑤) Then how about chocolate?
G: That's a good idea.

출제율 85%

05 위 대화의 ①~⑤ 중 주어진 문장이 들어갈 알맞은 곳은?

It means separation.

① ② ③ ④ ⑤

출제율 95%

06 (A)와 (B)에 공통으로 들어갈 말을 쓰시오. (대화의 단어를 이용해서 쓸 것)

➡ ____________________

출제율 90%

07 주어진 영영풀이에 해당하는 단어를 대화에서 찾아 쓰시오.

the act of moving two things or people apart

➡ ____________________

출제율 100%

08 빈칸에 공통으로 알맞은 단어를 쓰시오.

- Have you heard ________ the Flower Fair?
- I'm thinking ________ buying her an umbrella.
- People like to talk ________ the leisure time.

출제율 90%

09 다음 제시된 의미에 맞는 단어를 주어진 철자로 시작하여 빈칸에 쓰고, 알맞은 것을 골라 문장을 완성하시오. (형태 변화 가능)

- b________: to lower your head or bend your body
- c________: to make the loud sound that a rooster makes
- l________: to keep happening for a certain amount of time

(1) The meeting ________ three hours yesterday.
(2) The rooster ________ about once an hour.
(3) I always ________ to my teacher.

출제율 90%

10 다음 대화의 빈칸 (A)와 (B)를 주어진 단어를 이용해 완성하시오.

A: Have you ever (A)________(listen) to (B)________ (Spain) music?
B: Yes, I have.

출제율 90%

11 다음 대화의 밑줄 친 우리말을 주어진 단어를 써서 영작하시오.

A: What does eating 12 grapes on New Year's Day mean in Spain?
B: <u>12개월 동안 행운을 의미한다</u>. (luck, for)

➡ ____________________

출제율 95%

12 다음 중 어법상 올바른 문장을 <u>모두</u> 고르시오.

① I have met him several times.
② Mary has lived here since 10 years.
③ Have you ever gone to Malaysia?
④ Scarlet has moved to Los Angeles 5 years ago.
⑤ He has been sick for two days.

출제율 90%

13 다음 우리말과 일치하도록 괄호 안의 어구를 바르게 배열하여 문장을 완성하시오.

(1) 그는 너무 뚱뚱해서 맞는 셔츠가 거의 없다.
(hardly / so / he / him / shirt / there / is / is / fits / fat / that / that / any).
➡ ____________________

(2) 그의 목소리가 너무 작아서 나는 그가 말하는 것을 듣지 못했다.
(I / couldn't / his voice / talk / so / was / hear / small / him / that).
➡ ____________________

(3) Jenny는 Sunny를 한 시간 동안 기다려 왔다.
(Jenny / Sunny / waited / hour / has / an / for / for).
➡ ____________________

출제율 95%

14 다음 중 어법상 어색한 문장을 고르시오.

① Taylor was so hungry that he has eaten all the food on the table.
② Jonathan woke up so late that he missed the first train to London.
③ After cleaning her home, she was so tired that she couldn't take a walk.
④ The table was so heavy that I couldn't move it by myself.
⑤ The cell phone was so expensive that I couldn't buy it.

출제율 90%

15 다음 두 문장을 한 문장으로 바꾸시오.

(1) It started to rain a week ago. And it still rains.
➡ ______________________________
(2) Elvis went to Wien. And he is there now.
➡ ______________________________

[16~18] 다음 글을 읽고, 물음에 답하시오.

Mina: Peter, you will stay here. (A)이 손님방은 한국 전통 물건들로 가득 차 있어. Look at this pillow.
Peter: What are these things?
Mina: They're bats.
Peter: Bats on my pillow? That's scary!
Mina: Not really. In Korea, bats are ___ⓐ___ of luck and a long life.
Peter: That's surprising. In many Western countries, bats remind people ___ⓑ___ darkness and scary things.

출제율 90%

16 위 글의 빈칸 ⓐ에 들어갈 가장 알맞은 말을 고르시오.

① subjects ② traditions
③ opinions ④ symbols
⑤ cultures

출제율 85%

17 위 글의 빈칸 ⓑ에 들어갈 알맞은 전치사를 쓰시오.

➡ ______________________

출제율 95%

18 위 글의 밑줄 친 (A)의 우리말에 맞게 한 단어를 보충하여, 주어진 어구를 알맞게 배열하시오.

Korean / full / this / things / guest room / traditional / is

➡ ______________________________

[19~21] 다음 글을 읽고, 물음에 답하시오.

Mina shows Peter her grandfather's room. Peter and Mina's grandfather meet and greet each other.
Grandfather: Hi, Peter! Have you ever seen this kind of lock before?
Peter: No, I (A)[don't / haven't]. ⓐIt's so old that I can't really tell, but is it a fish?
Grandfather: Yes. For a long time, Koreans have thought that fish (B)[is / are] good guards. Fish don't close their eyes, even when they sleep.
Peter: That's interesting.
Grandfather: We think fish can watch over valuable things. That's (C)[because / why] this lock looks like a fish.
Peter: Now I understand.

출제율 95%

19 위 글의 괄호 (A)~(C)에서 어법상 알맞은 낱말을 골라 쓰시오.

➡ (A)________ (B)________ (C)________

출제율 90%

20 위 글의 밑줄 친 ⓐ를 우리말로 옮기시오.

➡ ____________________

출제율 85%

21 위 글의 내용과 일치하지 않는 것은?

① 피터와 미나의 할아버지가 만나서 서로 인사한다.
② 피터는 미나의 할아버지가 보여주신 종류의 자물쇠를 전에 본 적이 없다.
③ 오랜 세월 동안, 한국인들은 물고기가 훌륭한 파수꾼이라고 생각해 왔다.
④ 물고기는 잘 때 그들의 눈을 감는다.
⑤ 한국인들은 물고기가 귀중품을 지킬 수 있다고 생각한다.

[22~24] 다음 글을 읽고, 물음에 답하시오.

Peter: What is on that ⓐpiece of paper? It looks scary.
Grandfather: Do you mean this painting of a rooster?
Peter: Oh, is it a rooster?
Grandfather: Yes, it is. Roosters crow every morning. Their crowing means that a new day is beginning. For many years, Koreans have believed evil spirits go away when a rooster crows.
Mina: Really? I've never heard that before.
Peter: Actually, I'm afraid of darkness and evil spirits. Could you draw a rooster for me, Mina?
Mina: Sure. I'll draw a big rooster for you!
Grandfather: Put the drawing above your door. Then ⓑit will protect you.
Peter: Yes, I will.

출제율 95%

22 위 글의 밑줄 친 ⓐpiece와 바꿔 쓸 수 있는 말을 쓰시오.

➡ ____________________

출제율 90%

23 위 글의 밑줄 친 ⓑit이 가리키는 것을 본문에서 찾아 쓰시오.

➡ ____________________

출제율 95%

24 위 글의 요지로 알맞은 것을 고르시오.

① 종이 위에 그린 부적은 미신이다.
② 수탉이 매일 아침 울어야 새로운 날이 시작한다.
③ 오랫동안 한국인들은 수탉이 울 때 악령이 물러간다고 믿고 문 위에 수탉 그림을 걸어놓았다.
④ 미나는 피터를 위해 큰 수탉을 그려줄 것이다.
⑤ 수탉 그림은 문 위에 붙여놓아야 한다.

[25~26] 다음 일기를 읽고, 물음에 답하시오.

Peter's Diary

May 28

I'm enjoying this trip so much that I want to stay longer. I love all the traditional Korean symbols in this house. Now I understand a lot of them. ⓐI want visiting Korea again with my family.

출제율 95%

25 다음 질문에 대한 알맞은 대답을 주어진 단어로 시작하여 쓰시오. (7 단어)

Q: Why does Peter want to stay longer?
A: Because ____________________.

출제율 90%

26 위 일기의 밑줄 친 ⓐ에서 어법상 틀린 부분을 찾아 고치시오.

____________ ➡ ____________

서술형 실전문제

[01~03] 다음 대화를 읽고, 물음에 답하시오.

B: Ling's birthday is this Wednesday, isn't it?
G: Yes. I'm going (A)______ a book for her. What about you?
B: Well, I'm thinking about (B)______ her an umbrella. I found a cute (C)one in a gift shop.
G: Oh, ①that's a good gift for Chinese people. It means something bad.
B: Really? ②What does an umbrella mean in China?
G: ③It means separation. ④The words for *separation* and *umbrella* sound the same in Chinese.
B: I see. Then how about chocolate?
G: ⑤That's a good idea.

01 buy를 이용하여 빈칸 (A)와 (B)에 들어갈 말을 쓰시오.

➡ (A)____________ (B) ____________

02 중요 ①~⑤ 중 대화의 흐름상 어색한 것을 고르고 바르게 고치시오.

____________ ➡ ____________

03 밑줄 친 (C)가 가리키는 것을 본문에서 찾아 쓰시오.

➡ ____________________

04 주어진 두 문장을 현재완료를 이용해 한 문장으로 만드시오.

(1) Charlie started to study Korean six months ago. He still studies Korean.
➡ ______________________________

(2) I lost my umbrella. So I don't have it now.
➡ ______________________________

05 다음 우리말을 괄호 안에 주어진 어구를 이용하여 영작하시오.

(1) 나의 삼촌은 2007년 이래로 그 회사에서 일해오고 있다. (work for, company, since)
➡ ______________________________

(2) 나는 그렇게 아름다운 다리를 본 적이 없다. (such, never, see, beautiful)
➡ ______________________________

(3) 그 산은 너무 높아서 나는 꼭대기까지 걸어갈 수가 없다. (high, that, to the top)
➡ ______________________________

(4) 나의 부모님은 너무 현명하셔서 나는 보통 그분들의 조언을 따른다. (wise, follow, usually)
➡ ______________________________

06 중요 다음 두 문장을 접속사 that을 사용하여 한 문장으로 연결하시오.

(1) • The dogs are really cute.
• I can't take my eyes off them.
➡ ______________________________

(2) • The weather was very nice.
• They went on a picnic.
➡ ______________________________

[07~09] 다음 글을 읽고, 물음에 답하시오.

Peter is visiting Korea to meet a friend, Mina, from a sister school. Peter is going to stay at her grandfather's house (A)[during / for] a week. When he arrives, Mina shows (B)[him / to him] the guest room.

Mina: Peter, you will stay here. This guest room is full of traditional Korean things. Look at this pillow.
Peter: What are these things?
Mina: They're bats.
Peter: Bats on my pillow? That's scary!
Mina: Not really. In Korea, bats are symbols of luck and a long life.
Peter: ⓐThat's (C)[surprising / surprised]. In many Western countries, bats remind people of darkness and scary things.

07 중요 위 글의 괄호 (A)~(C)에서 어법상 알맞은 낱말을 골라 쓰시오.

➡ (A)________ (B)________ (C)________

08 위 글의 밑줄 친 ⓐThat이 가리키는 것을 본문에서 찾아 쓰시오.

➡ ______________________________

09 중요 위 글을 읽고, 한국과 서구의 많은 나라들에서 박쥐가 상징하는 것이 어떻게 다른지 우리말로 쓰시오.

➡ 한국: ____________________
서구의 많은 나라들: ____________________
____

[10~12] 다음 글을 읽고, 물음에 답하시오.

Peter: What is on that piece of paper? It looks scary.
Grandfather: ⓐ이 수탉 그림을 말하는 거니?
Peter: Oh, is it a rooster?
Grandfather: Yes, it is. Roosters crow every morning. Their crowing means that a new day is beginning. For many years, Koreans have believed evil spirits go away when a rooster crows.
Mina: Really? I've never heard ⓑthat before.
Peter: Actually, I'm afraid of darkness and evil spirits. Could you draw a rooster for me, Mina?
Mina: Sure. I'll draw a big rooster for you!
Grandfather: Put the drawing above your door. Then it will protect you.
Peter: Yes, I will.

10 위 글의 밑줄 친 ⓐ의 우리말에 맞게 한 단어를 보충하여, 주어진 어휘를 알맞게 배열하시오.

mean / painting / you / rooster / this / do / a

➡ ______________________________

11 다음 문장에서 위 글의 내용과 다른 부분을 찾아서 고치시오. (본문의 단어를 사용하시오.)

The meaning of roosters' crowing is that the sun is setting. For many years, Koreans have believed evil spirits disappear with the crowing of roosters.

____________ ➡ ____________

12 중요 위 글의 밑줄 친 ⓑthat이 가리키는 것을 본문에서 찾아 쓰시오.

➡ ______________________________
____

01 다음 주어진 단어와 그림을 참고하여 대화를 완성하시오.

A: Have you ever ____________________?
B: No, ____________________. Have you?
A: Yes, I have. I ____________________ last year. (visit) There was a La Tomatina festival.
B: What is La Tomatina festival?
A: It's ____________________ festival. People ____________________.
B: ____________________?
A: It's the last Tuesday in August.
B: I'd like to go. It sounds interesting.

02 다음 내용을 바탕으로 학급 신문에 다른 나라의 전통 문화를 소개하는 글을 쓰시오.

1. Q: What do you want to talk about?
   A: I want to talk about traditional Chinese dances.
2. Q: What are some examples?
   A: There are a lion dance, a fan dance, and an umbrella dance.
3. Q: Choose one and search for more information about it.
   A: In the lion dance, two dancers dress and act like lions. They do the dance on special days.
4. Q: What do you think of it?
   A: I think their dance moves are great.

An Amazing Traditional Chinese Dance
Do you know about (A)_______ Chinese dances? There are many kinds. For example, there are a lion dance, a fan dance, and an umbrella dance. One of the most famous dances (B)______ the lion dance. In this dance, two dancers dress and act (C)______ lions. They usually dance on (D) _________ days, such as New Year's Day. I think their dance moves are great. I hope (E) ________ this dance someday.

단원별 모의고사

[01~03] 다음 대화를 읽고, 물음에 답하시오.

G: ⓐHow a nice picture! Are these your friends?
B: Yes. (①) We took this picture at the beach. We had a lot of fun.
G: Oh, look at that boy. (②) That's really rude.
B: ⓑWho boy?
G: ⓒThe boy whose is making the V sign. ⓓHis palm is facing toward him. (③)
B: What's wrong with that?
G: (④) But ⓔshowing your palm and making a V sign is okay.
B: What does that mean?
G: (⑤) It means victory or peace.

01 위 대화의 ①~⑤ 중 주어진 문장이 들어갈 알맞은 곳은?

It has a bad meaning in England.

① ② ③ ④ ⑤

02 위 대화의 밑줄 친 ⓐ~ⓔ 중 어법상 틀린 개수를 고르시오.

① 1개 ② 2개 ③ 3개 ④ 4개 ⑤ 5개

03 주어진 영영풀이에 해당하는 단어를 위 대화에서 찾아 쓰시오.

(1)

the inside part of the hand between the wrist and the fingers

➡ ____________

(2)

to have the front part toward something

➡ ____________

[04~05] 다음 대화를 읽고, 물음에 답하시오.

G: Hello, Santiago! What ①__________ you here today?
B: *Bienvenido*, Cathy. I came ②__________ the Spanish festival.
G: Me, too. But what did you just say?
B: *Bienvenido*! It means "welcome" ③__________. Look at those dancers. Their dance ④__________ are so great.
G: Yes, they are.
B: Have you ever been to a Spanish festival before?
G: No, I ⑤__________. Santiago, can you see the big letters on the stage? 무슨 뜻이야?
B: Oh, *gracias*. That means "thank you."

04 위 대화의 빈칸 ①~⑤에 들어갈 말이나 설명으로 적절하지 않은 것은?

① brings
② to see, to부정사의 부사적 용법으로 '보기 위해서'의 의미로 사용되었다.
③ in Spain, '스페인어로'의 의미로 사용되었다.
④ moves
⑤ haven't

05 위 대화의 밑줄 친 우리말을 영작하시오.

➡ ____________

06 다음 대화에서 어색한 부분을 모두 찾아 고치시오. (2개)

G: Have you ever been to Brazil?
B: No, I haven't. Do you?
G: Yes, I do. I went there last year. There was a big samba festival.
B: That sounds interesting. I hope to go there someday.

(1) __________ ➡ __________
(2) __________ ➡ __________

[07~09] 다음 대화를 읽고, 물음에 답하시오.

W: ①Welcome to the International Games Festival. ②You can play many different traditional games here.
B: Wow! ③It looks exciting! (A)_______ game should I play first?
W: Let's see. 고로드키(*gorodki*) 게임 해 본 적 있나요?
B: No, I haven't. (B)_________ is it?
W: ④It's a traditional game from Russia.
B: (C)_________ do I play it?
W: ⑤Putting five sticks on the ground. Then throw a bat at them.
B: That sounds fun. I'll try that first.

07 (A)~(C)에 알맞은 의문사를 〈보기〉에서 골라 쓰시오.

보기				
Who	Which	What	Why	How

➡ (A)________ (B)________ (C)________

08 위 대화의 밑줄 친 우리말을 영작하시오.

➡ ____________________________________

09 ①~⑤ 중 문법상 어색한 부분을 고르고 바르게 고치시오.

______________ ➡ ______________

[10~12] 다음 대화를 읽고, 물음에 답하시오.

B: There is a Holi festival in Busan this year. (①)
G: A Holi festival? What is that?
B: (②) ⓐPeople throw colored powder and water at each other.
G: That sounds exciting. (③) ⓑHave you ever been to a Holi festival?
B: ⓒYes, I have. But my Indian friend told me a lot about it.
G: When is the festival?
B: (④) ⓓIt's on the last full moon of the Hindu calendar. This year, it's on March 21.
G: ⓔI'd like to go. Should I bring anything?
B: No, but you should wear white clothes. (⑤) Then the colored powder on your clothes will look more beautiful.
G: Okay. Thank you for the information.

10 위 대화의 ①~⑤ 중 주어진 문장이 들어갈 알맞은 곳은?

> It's a traditional Indian festival.

① ② ③ ④ ⑤

11 ⓐ~ⓔ 중 대화의 흐름상 어색한 부분을 고르시오.

① ⓐ ② ⓑ ③ ⓒ ④ ⓓ ⑤ ⓔ

12 위 대화의 내용과 일치하도록 빈칸을 채우시오.

> A Holi festival is ________________. It will be held in ________ this year. In a Holi festival, people ______________ ______________. When people wear ____________, the colored powder on the white clothes can ______________.

13 〈보기〉의 밑줄 친 'has swum'과 같은 용법으로 쓰인 것은?

> 보기
> Evan has never swum in this lake before.

① Amy has just finished her homework.
② Chuck has lived in Seoul since 2002.
③ The concert has already started.
④ Rosalind has gone to France.
⑤ I have watched the movie twice.

14 다음 문장과 같은 뜻의 문장을 to부정사를 이용하여 쓰시오.

(1) The soup smelled so bad that I couldn't have it.

➡ ______________________________

(2) Einstein was so clever that he could understand the theory.

➡ ______________________________

15 다음 문장의 틀린 곳을 고쳐 다시 쓰시오.

(1) When have you gone there?

➡ ______________________________

(2) I have studied English since 5 years.

➡ ______________________________

(3) I was so busy to help her.

➡ ______________________________

____

(4) The bunjee jump was scary so that we screamed a lot.

➡ ______________________________

16 다음 문장의 빈칸에 for나 since 중 알맞은 것을 쓰시오.

(1) Christine has stayed in Seoul ________ five years.

(2) We have known her ________ 2002.

17 다음 두 문장을 접속사 that을 사용하여 한 문장으로 연결하시오.

• Phillip has lived in China for a long time.
• He can speak Chinese very well.

➡ ______________________________

____

[18~20] 다음 글을 읽고, 물음에 답하시오.

Mina: Peter, you will stay here. This guest room is full of traditional Korean things. Look at this pillow.
Peter: What are these things?
Mina: They're bats.
Peter: ⓐBats on my pillow? That's scary!
Mina: Not really. In Korea, bats are symbols of luck and a long life.
Peter: That's surprising. In many Western countries, ⓑ박쥐는 사람들에게 어둠과 무서운 것들을 상기시키거든.

18 위 글의 밑줄 친 ⓐ에서 알 수 있는 피터의 심경으로 알맞지 않은 것을 고르시오.

① terrified ② grateful
③ frightened ④ afraid
⑤ scared

19 위 글의 밑줄 친 ⓑ의 우리말에 맞게 주어진 어휘를 이용하여 8 단어로 영작하시오.

remind, of

➡ ______________________________

20 위 글의 목적으로 알맞은 것을 고르시오.

① 자매학교 친구를 방문하는 방법을 설명하기 위한 글이다.
② 손님방을 한국 전통 물건들로 가득 채우는 방법을 설명하기 위한 글이다.
③ 베개에 있는 박쥐 디자인에 대한 피터의 반응을 소개하기 위한 글이다.
④ 전통적인 한국의 상징물들 중 박쥐의 의미를 소개하기 위한 글이다.
⑤ 서구의 많은 나라들에서 박쥐들이 상징하는 것을 소개하기 위한 글이다.

[21~23] 다음 글을 읽고, 물음에 답하시오.

Grandfather: Hi, Peter! Have you ever seen this kind of lock before?
Peter: No, I haven't. It's so old that I can't really tell, but is it a fish?
Grandfather: Yes. For a long time, Koreans have thought that fish are good ___ⓐ___. Fish don't close their eyes, even when they sleep.
Peter: That's interesting.
Grandfather: We think fish can watch over valuable things. That's why this lock looks ⓑlike a fish.
Peter: Now I understand.

21 주어진 영영풀이를 참고하여 빈칸 ⓐ에 철자 g로 시작하는 단어를 쓰시오.

people who watch over something or someone

➡ ____________________

22 위 글의 밑줄 친 ⓑlike와 같은 의미로 쓰인 것을 고르시오.

① Do you like this music?
② How did you like the movie?
③ I like my coffee strong.
④ She sounds like a serious person.
⑤ I like to hear the boy singing.

23 빈칸 (A)와 (B)에 알맞은 단어를 넣어, 위 글에서 자물쇠가 물고기처럼 생긴 이유를 완성하시오.

Fish (A)________ ________ their eyes even when they sleep, so people think fish can (B)________ ________ valuable things. For that reason, this lock looks like a fish.

(A) ____________ (B) ____________

[24~25] 다음 글을 읽고, 물음에 답하시오.

Peter: What is on that piece of paper? It looks scary.
Grandfather: Do you mean this painting of a rooster?
Peter: Oh, is it a rooster?
Grandfather: Yes, it is. Roosters crow every morning. Their crowing means that a new day is beginning. For many years, Koreans ⓐhave believed evil spirits go away when a rooster crows.
Mina: Really? I've never heard that before.
Peter: Actually, I'm afraid of darkness and evil spirits. Could you draw a rooster for me, Mina?
Mina: Sure. I'll draw a big rooster for you!
Grandfather: Put the drawing above your door. ⓑThen it will protect you.
Peter: Yes, I will.

24 아래 〈보기〉에서 위 글의 밑줄 친 ⓐ와 현재완료의 용법이 다른 것의 개수를 고르시오.

보기
① She has gone to America.
② It has been fine since last week.
③ Have you solved it yet?
④ I have visited New York three times.
⑤ They have already seen it.

① 1개 ② 2개 ③ 3개 ④ 4개 ⑤ 5개

25 다음 빈칸에 알맞은 단어를 넣어 ⓑThen에 대한 설명을 완성하시오.

____________ you put the drawing above your door,

➡ ____________________

INSIGHT on the textbook

교과서 파헤치기

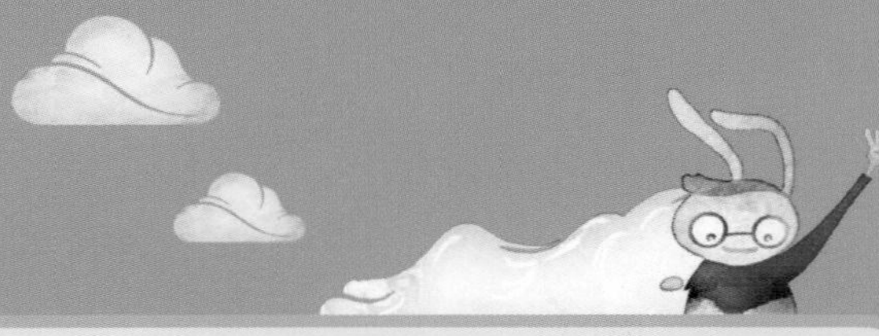

Lesson 1 Express Yourself

Lesson 2 Eat Right, Be Happy!

Lesson 3 Understand the World

단어 Test

Step1

※ 다음 영어를 우리말로 쓰시오.

01 personal ____________

02 carefully ____________

03 appropriate ____________

04 comment ____________

05 bring ____________

06 dictionary ____________

07 awesome ____________

08 filter ____________

09 understand ____________

10 finally ____________

11 impossible ____________

12 share ____________

13 borrow ____________

14 exciting ____________

15 hurt ____________

16 part ____________

17 silly ____________

18 etiquette ____________

19 bother ____________

20 restroom ____________

21 public ____________

22 subject ____________

23 solve ____________

24 incorrect ____________

25 interesting ____________

26 report ____________

27 teens ____________

28 surprisingly ____________

29 environment ____________

30 recipe ____________

31 prepare ____________

32 outdoors ____________

33 sometimes ____________

34 nervous ____________

35 from A to B ____________

36 keep in mind ____________

37 break the law ____________

38 spend 시간 -ing ____________

39 have fun ____________

40 in front of ____________

41 just like ____________

42 check out ____________

43 find out ____________

단어 Test

Step2

※ 다음 우리말을 영어로 쓰시오.

01 (법률 · 약속 등을) 어기다 ____________
02 캐리어, 운반[이동] 장치 ____________
03 사진술 ____________
04 올리다, 게시하다 ____________
05 복사하다 ____________
06 사실 ____________
07 포스터 ____________
08 주제 ____________
09 준비하다 ____________
10 건강에 좋은, 건강한 ____________
11 완벽한 ____________
12 (작품을) 전시하다, 보여주다 ____________
13 남기다 ____________
14 긴장되는, 불안해하는 ____________
15 야외에서, 옥외에서 ____________
16 환경 ____________
17 고르다 ____________
18 가끔 ____________
19 아마도 ____________
20 놀랍게도 ____________
21 결과 ____________

22 셀피 ____________
23 조리법 ____________
24 무례한 ____________
25 옷 ____________
26 조사 ____________
27 적절한 ____________
28 빌리다 ____________
29 불가능한 ____________
30 괴롭히다 ____________
31 이해하다 ____________
32 사전 ____________
33 화장실 ____________
34 ~을 보다 ____________
35 ~에 관심[흥미]이 있다 ____________
36 법을 어기다 ____________
37 무엇보다도 ____________
38 명심하다 ____________
39 ~에 동의하다 ____________
40 ~ 앞에 ____________
41 확인하다 ____________
42 발견하다, 찾아보다 ____________
43 세계 곳곳에 ____________

단어 Test

Step3

※ 다음 영영풀이에 알맞은 단어를 <보기>에서 골라 쓴 후, 우리말 뜻을 쓰시오.

1 __________: good for your body: __________

2 __________: available for anyone to use: __________

3 __________: to have or use something with other people: __________

4 __________: correct or suitable for a particular time, situation, or purpose: __________

5 __________: to find or provide a way of dealing with a problem: __________

6 __________: an opinion that you express about someone or something: __________

7 __________: a piece of information that is known to be true: __________

8 __________: a set of instructions for cooking a particular type of food: __________

9 __________: the formal rules for polite behavior in society or in a particular group: __________

10 __________: to make plans or arrangements for something that will happen in the future: __________

11 __________: the art, profession, or method of producing photographs or the scenes in films: __________

12 __________: speaking or behaving in a way that is not polite and is likely to offend or annoy people: __________

13 __________: to put a message or computer document on the Internet so that other people can see it: __________

14 __________: something that happens or exists because of something that happened before: __________

15 __________: to take something or someone with you to the place where you are now, or to the place you are talking about: ____________

16 __________: to take and use something that belongs to someone else for a period of time before returning it: __________

보기

etiquette	comment	healthy	post
solve	prepare	recipe	result
share	bring	fact	public
borrow	photography	rude	appropriate

※ 다음 우리말과 일치하도록 빈칸에 알맞은 말을 쓰시오.

해석

Listen & Talk 1 A

G: ________ ________ these club posters . What are you ________ ________?

B: I'm interested ________ ________. ________ ________ you?

G: I'm ________ ________ photography.

G: 동아리 포스터들을 봐. 너는 어떤 것에 관심이 있니?
B: 나는 요리에 관심이 있어. 너는 어때?
G: 나는 사진에 관심이 있어.

Listen & Talk 1 B

B: What ________ you ________ ________ do this weekend?

G: I'm ________ ________ ________ to a baseball game ________ my brother.

B: ________ you ________ ________ baseball?

G: Not really. I'm ________ to the baseball game ________ my brother likes baseball.

B: You're so nice! Then ________ are you ________ in?

G: I'm ________ ________ in soccer. I ________ ________ ________ to a soccer game ________ .

B: 이번 주말에 뭐 할 거야?
G: 나는 동생하고 야구 보러 갈 거야.
B: 너는 야구에 관심 있니?
G: 사실은 좋아하지 않아. 나는 내 동생이 좋아해서 야구 보러 가는 거야.
B: 너 정말 착하다! 그럼 너는 어떤 것에 관심 있니?
G: 나는 축구에 더 관심 있어. 언젠가 축구 경기를 보러 가고 싶어.

Listen & Talk 1 C

G: ________ are you ________ ________?

B: I'm looking at TV program ________. What show ________ I ________?

G: Well, what are you ________ ________?

B: ________ ________ in music.

G: Then how ________ ________ the *Friday Pop Music Show*?

B: I'm actually not ________ ________ ________ ________ pop music. I like to ________ ________ rap music.

G: Then ________ ________ you watch *Hit the Beat*?

B: Good idea.

G: 뭐 보고 있니?
B: TV 프로그램 편성표 보고 있어. 어떤 걸 봐야 할까?
G: 음, 너 어떤 분야에 관심이 있니?
B: 나는 음악에 관심이 있어.
G: 그러면 "Friday Pop Music Show"를 보는 게 어때?
B: 사실 팝 음악을 많이 좋아하지는 않아. 나는 랩 음악 듣는 걸 좋아해.
G: 그러면 "Hit the Beat"을 보는 건 어때?
B: 좋은 생각이야.

Listen & Talk 1 D

A: ________ are you ________ ________?

B: I'm interested ________ games and social media. ________ ________ you?

A: I'm ________ ________ music and ________ ________.

B: ________ are ________ interested in social media.

A: 너는 무엇에 관심이 있니?
B: 나는 게임과 소셜 미디어에 관심이 있어. 너는 어때?
A: 나는 음악과 소셜 미디어에 관심이 있어.
B: 우리는 둘 다 소셜 미디어에 관심이 있구나.

Listen & Talk 2 A

B: May I ________ my dog ________ the bus?

W: Yes, you ________. But you ________ ________ your dog in the carrier.

B: 버스에 제 개를 데리고 타도 되나요?
W: 네, 됩니다. 하지만 당신은 개를 캐리어에 넣어야 해요.

Listen & Talk 2 B

G: Hi. ________ I ________ in now?

M: Sure. ________ me ________ your ticket, please.

G: ________ it is. ________ I ________ the music in the concert hall?

M: ________, you ________ ________.

G: Okay. May I ________ ________ ________ the band?

M: No, you ________ ________. You can only ________ pictures ________ ________ ________ the concert hall. Please ________ the concert.

G: Oh, okay. Thank you.

G: 안녕하세요. 지금 안에 들어가도 되나요?
M: 그럼요. 티켓을 보여 주시겠어요?
G: 여기 있어요. 콘서트홀 안에서 노래 녹음해도 되나요?
M: 아니요, 안 됩니다.
G: 알겠습니다. 밴드 사진은 찍어도 되나요?
M: 아니요, 안 됩니다. 콘서트홀 밖에 서만 사진을 찍을 수 있어요. 즐거운 관람되세요.
G: 아, 알겠습니다. 감사합니다.

Listen & Talk 2 C

B: ________ me.

W: Hello. ________ can I do ________ you?

B: ________ I ________ this new science book?

W: No, ________ ________ ________. Students ________ ________ new books ________.

B: Then ________ I ________ some pages from the book? I need them for my science report.

W: ________, ________ ________. But please ________ ________ them online.

B: Okay, I ________. Thank you!

B: 실례합니다.
W: 안녕하세요. 무엇을 도와드릴까요?
B: 이 새로 출시된 과학책 빌려도 될까 요?
W: 아뇨, 불가능합니다. 학생들은 새로 출시된 책을 집으로 가져갈 수 없어요.
B: 그러면 책에서 몇 장 정도 복사해도 될까요? 과학 보고서 쓰는 데 필요해서요.
W: 네, 그러세요. 하지만 그걸 인터넷상에 공유하지는 마세요.
B: 네, 안 그럴게요. 감사합니다!

Let's communicate 1

A: What ________ you interested ________?

B: ________ ________ ________ music.

A: ________ ________ you go to a concert hall this weekend?

B: ________ good. ________ I ________ the music there?

A: Yes, you ________. / No, you ________ ________.

A: 너는 무엇에 관심이 있니?
B: 나는 음악에 관심이 있어.
A: 이번 주에 콘서트홀에 가는 건 어때?
B: 그거 좋겠다. 거기서 음악을 녹음해도 될까?
A: 그래, 돼. / 아니, 안 돼.

Do It Yourself A

M: Hey, Yumi. What ________ you ________?

G: Hello, Mr. King. I'm ________ for tomorrow's ________. It is about ________ ________ my interests .

M: That ________ ________! What ________ you ________ ________?

G: I'm ________ ________ photography. I will ________ ________ it tomorrow.

M: Oh, I'm ________ ________ photography, ________.

G: Really? Then ________ I ________ you for some advice for my presentation?

M: Sure.

M: 유미야, 뭐 하고 있니?
G: 안녕하세요, King씨. 저는 내일 발표를 준비하고 있어요. 제 관심사 중 하나에 대한 거예요.
M: 그거 재미있겠다! 너는 어떤 것에 관심이 있니?
G: 저는 사진에 관심이 있어요. 저는 그것에 대해 내일 이야기할 거예요.
M: 오, 나도 역시 사진에 관심이 있어.
G: 정말요? 그렇다면 제 발표에 대해 몇 가지 조언을 부탁해도 될까요?
M: 물론이지.

※ 다음 우리말에 맞도록 대화를 영어로 쓰시오.

해석

Listen & Talk 1 A

G: ______________________
B: ______________________
G: ______________________

G: 동아리 포스터들을 봐. 너는 어떤 것에 관심이 있니?
B: 나는 요리에 관심이 있어. 너는 어때?
G: 나는 사진에 관심이 있어.

Listen & Talk 1 B

B: ______________________
G: ______________________
B: ______________________
G: ______________________
B: ______________________
G: ______________________

B: 이번 주말에 뭐 할 거야?
G: 나는 동생하고 야구 보러 갈 거야.
B: 너는 야구에 관심 있니?
G: 사실은 좋아하지 않아. 나는 내 동생이 좋아해서 야구 보러 가는 거야.
B: 너 정말 착하다! 그럼 너는 어떤 것에 관심 있니?
G: 나는 축구에 더 관심 있어. 언젠가 축구 경기를 보러 가고 싶어.

Listen & Talk 1 C

G: ______________________
B: ______________________
G: ______________________
B: ______________________
G: ______________________
B: ______________________
G: ______________________
B: ______________________

G: 뭐 보고 있니?
B: TV 프로그램 편성표 보고 있어. 어떤 걸 봐야 할까?
G: 음, 너 어떤 분야에 관심이 있니?
B: 나는 음악에 관심이 있어.
G: 그러면 "Friday Pop Music Show"를 보는 게 어때?
B: 사실 팝 음악을 많이 좋아하지는 않아. 나는 랩 음악 듣는 걸 좋아해.
G: 그러면 "Hit the Beat"을 보는 건 어때?
B: 좋은 생각이야.

Listen & Talk 1 D

A: ______________________
B: ______________________
A: ______________________
B: ______________________

A: 너는 무엇에 관심이 있니?
B: 나는 게임과 소셜 미디어에 관심이 있어. 너는 어때?
A: 나는 음악과 소셜 미디어에 관심이 있어.
B: 우리는 둘 다 소셜 미디어에 관심이 있구나.

Listen & Talk 2 A

B: ______________________
W: ______________________

B: 버스에 제 개를 데리고 타도 되나요?
W: 네, 됩니다. 하지만 당신은 개를 캐리어에 넣어야 해요.

Listen & Talk 2 B

G:

M:

G:

M:

G:

M:

G:

G: 안녕하세요. 지금 안에 들어가도 되나요?
M: 그럼요. 티켓을 보여 주시겠어요?
G: 여기 있어요. 콘서트홀 안에서 노래 녹음해도 되나요?
M: 아니요, 안 됩니다.
G: 알겠습니다. 밴드 사진은 찍어도 되나요?
M: 아니요, 안 됩니다. 콘서트홀 밖에 서만 사진을 찍을 수 있어요. 즐거운 관람되세요.
G: 아, 알겠습니다. 감사합니다.

Listen & Talk 2 C

B:

W:

B:

W:

B:

W:

B:

B: 실례합니다.
W: 안녕하세요. 무엇을 도와드릴까요?
B: 이 새로 출시된 과학책 빌려도 될까 요?
W: 아뇨, 불가능합니다. 학생들은 새로 출시된 책을 집으로 가져갈 수 없어요.
B: 그러면 책에서 몇 장 정도 복사해도 될까요? 과학 보고서 쓰는 데 필요해서요.
W: 네, 그러세요. 하지만 그걸 인터넷상에 공유하지는 마세요.
B: 네, 안 그럴게요. 감사합니다!

Let's communicate 1

A:

B:

A:

B:

A:

A: 너는 무엇에 관심이 있니?
B: 나는 음악에 관심이 있어.
A: 이번 주에 콘서트홀에 가는 건 어때?
B: 그거 좋겠다. 거기서 음악을 녹음해도 될까?
A: 그래, 돼. / 아니, 안 돼.

Do It Yourself A

M:

G:

M:

G:

M:

G:

M:

M: 유미야. 뭐 하고 있니?
G: 안녕하세요, King씨. 저는 내일 발표를 준비하고 있어요. 제 관심사 중 하나에 대한 거예요.
M: 그거 재미있겠다! 너는 어떤 것에 관심이 있니?
G: 저는 사진에 관심이 있어요. 저는 그것에 대해 내일 이야기할 거예요.
M: 오, 나도 역시 사진에 관심이 있어.
G: 정말요? 그렇다면 제 발표에 대해 몇 가지 조언을 부탁해도 될까요?
M: 물론이지.

※ 다음 우리말과 일치하도록 빈칸에 알맞은 것을 골라 쓰시오.

1 ________ ________ Selfies!
A. About B. All

2 #________ ________
A. Facts B. Selfie

3 ________ you ________ ________ selfies?
A. in B. interested C. are

4 You ________ like to ________ selfies on social media, but how ________ do you know about selfies?
A. much B. post C. probably

5 ________ are some interesting ________.
A. facts B. here

6 Robert Cornelius ________ the world's ________ selfie ________ 1839.
A. in B. first C. took

7 *Selfie* ________ a new ________ in the ________ in 2013.
A. word B. became C. dictionary

8 Buzz Aldrin ________ the first ________ ________ in 1966.
A. selfie B. space C. took

9 #________ ________
A. Survey B. Selfie

10 ________ selfies is part of ________ life for many teens, but do teens really ________ it?
A. enjoy B. daily C. taking

11 ________ find ________, we did a ________.
A. survey B. out C. to

12 We asked three ________ to 300 students from ________ 14 ________ 16.
A. to B. questions C. ages

13 ________ look ________ the results.
A. at B. let's

14 ________, 90 ________ of the girls take selfies, but ________ 15 percent of the boys take selfies.
A. only B. percent C. surprisingly

15 ________, 93 percent of these students said ________ they use ________.
A. filters B. that C. also

16 The ________ also ________ that the students ________ selfies at school the most.
A. take B. showed C. survey

17 ________ ________ some of the students' ________.
A. comments B. out C. check

18 Lewis, 14, ________ Selfies are ________.
A. awesome B. England

1 셀피에 대한 모든 것!

2 셀피와 관련된 사실들

3 당신은 셀피에 관심이 있는가?

4 당신은 아마 소셜 미디어에 셀피를 게시하기를 좋아할지도 모르지만, 셀피에 대해 얼마나 많이 알고 있는가?

5 여기 몇 가지 재미있는 사실들이 있다.

6 로버트 코닐리어스가 1839년에 전 세계 최초의 셀피를 찍었다.

7 selfie는 2013년에 사전에 신조어로 등재되었다.

8 버즈 올드린이 1966년에 최초의 우주 셀피를 찍었다.

9 셀피 설문 조사

10 셀피 찍기는 많은 십대들에게 일상생활의 한 부분인데, 십대들은 정말로 그것을 즐기고 있는가?

11 알아보기 위해 우리는 설문 조사를 했다.

12 우리는 14세에서 16세 사이의 학생 300명에게 세 가지를 질문했다.

13 그 결과를 보자.

14 놀랍게도, 소녀들의 90퍼센트가 셀피를 찍지만, 소년들의 15퍼센트만이 셀피를 찍는다.

15 또한 이 학생들의 93퍼센트는 필터를 사용한다고 대답했다.

16 설문은 또한 학생들이 학교에서 가장 많이 셀피를 찍는다는 것을 보여 주었다.

17 학생들의 의견 몇 가지를 확인해 보라.

18 루이스, 14세, 영국: 셀피는 굉장하다.

19 Making ________ faces is ________ fun!
A. really B. silly

20 Minwoo, 16, Korea I enjoy ________ selfies, but some students ________ too much time ________ it.
A. doing B. taking C. spend

21 Kate, 15, Denmark My pictures ________ ________ when I ________ filters.
A. use B. good C. look

22 But ________ my selfies don't ________ ________ me.
A. like B. sometimes C. look

23 #________ ________
A. Etiquette B. Selfie

24 You should follow ________ for ________.
A. selfies B. etiquette

25 Ask ________ these questions ________ you take, ________, or look at selfies.
A. post B. before C. yourself

26 1. ________ ________ I?
A. am B. where

27 Choose ________ places to take ________.
A. selfies B. appropriate

28 ________ take selfies in ________ or public ________.
A. hospitals B. don't C. restrooms

29 It may ________ ________ people.
A. other B. bother

30 2. ________ can see ________?
A. this B. who

31 ________ in mind that ________ can ________ your selfies.
A. see B. anyone C. keep

32 ________ carefully ________ you ________ them.
A. post B. choose C. when

33 3. What ________ of ________ should I ________?
A. leave B. comments C. kinds

34 ________ nice ________ on ________ people's selfies.
A. other B. leave C. comments

35 ________ be rude. That ________ easy, ________ it?
A. doesn't B. sounds C. don't

36 ________ these ________ and have ________ with your selfies.
A. tips B. follow C. fun

19 우스꽝스러운 표정을 짓는 것은 정말로 재미있다!

20 민우, 16세, 한국: 나는 셀피 찍는 것을 즐기지만 몇몇 학생들은 그것을 하는 데 너무 많은 시간을 쓴다.

21 케이트, 15세, 덴마크: 내 사진은 필터를 사용할 때 멋져 보인다.

22 하지만 가끔 나의 셀피가 나처럼 보이지 않는다.

23 셀피 예절

24 당신은 셀피 예절을 따라야 한다.

25 셀피를 찍고, 게시하거나 보기 전에 스스로 이 질문들을 물어보라.

26 1. 내가 어디에 있는가?

27 셀피를 찍기에 적합한 장소를 선택하라.

28 병원이나 공중화장실에서 셀피를 찍지 마라.

29 그것은 다른 사람들을 신경 쓰이게 할 수 있다.

30 2. 누가 이것을 볼 수 있는가?

31 누구나 당신의 셀피를 볼 수 있다는 것을 명심하라.

32 그것들을 게시할 때 신중하게 골라라.

33 3. 어떤 코멘트를 남겨야 하는가?

34 다른 사람들의 셀피에 상냥한 코멘트를 남겨라.

35 무례하게 굴지 마라. 쉬운 것처럼 들린다, 그렇지 않은가?

36 이러한 조언들을 따라서 당신의 셀피와 즐거운 시간을 보내라!

본문 Test

Step2

※ 다음 우리말과 일치하도록 빈칸에 알맞은 말을 쓰시오.

1 All _______ Selfies!

2 #Selfie _______

3 Are you _______ _______ selfies?

4 You probably _______ _______ _______ selfies on social media, but _______ _______ do you know _______ selfies?

5 _______ _______ some interesting _______.

6 Robert Cornelius _______ the world's _______ _______ in 1839.

7 *Selfie* _______ a new word _______ _______ _______ in 2013.

8 Buzz Aldrin _______ the _______ _______ selfie in 1966.

9 #Selfie _______

10 _______ _______ is part of _______ _______ for many teens, _______ do teens really enjoy it?

11 _______ _______ _______, we did a _______.

12 We _______ three questions to 300 students _______ _______ 14 _______ 16.

13 _______ _______ _______ the results.

14 _______, 90 percent of the girls _______ _______, but only _______ _______ _______ _______ _______ take selfies .

15 Also, 93 percent of these students said _______ they _______ _______.

16 The _______ also _______ that the students _______ _______ at school the most.

17 _______ _______ some of the students' _______.

18 Lewis, 14, England _______ are _______.

1 셀피에 대한 모든 것!

2 셀피와 관련된 사실들

3 당신은 셀피에 관심이 있는가?

4 당신은 아마 소셜 미디어에 셀피를 게시하기를 좋아할지도 모르지만, 셀피에 대해 얼마나 많이 알고 있는가?

5 여기 몇 가지 재미있는 사실들이 있다.

6 로버트 코닐리어스가 1839년에 전 세계 최초의 셀피를 찍었다.

7 selfie는 2013년에 사전에 신조어로 등재되었다.

8 버즈 올드린이 1966년에 최초의 우주 셀피를 찍었다.

9 셀피 설문 조사

10 셀피 찍기는 많은 십대들에게 일상생활의 한 부분인데, 십대들은 정말로 그것을 즐기고 있는가?

11 알아보기 위해 우리는 설문 조사를 했다.

12 우리는 14세에서 16세 사이의 학생 300명에게 세 가지를 질문했다.

13 그 결과를 보자.

14 놀랍게도, 소녀들의 90퍼센트가 셀피를 찍지만, 소년들의 15퍼센트만이 셀피를 찍는다.

15 또한 이 학생들의 93퍼센트는 필터를 사용한다고 대답했다.

16 설문은 또한 학생들이 학교에서 가장 많이 셀피를 찍는다는 것을 보여 주었다.

17 학생들의 의견 몇 가지를 확인해 보라.

18 루이스, 14세, 영국: 셀피는 굉장하다.

19 ________ silly ________ is really fun!

20 Minwoo, 16, Korea I ________ ________ ________, but some students ________ too much time ________ it .

21 Kate, 15, Denmark My pictures ________ ________ when I ________ ________.

22 But ________ my selfies ________ ________ ________ me.

23 #Selfie ________.

24 You ________ ________ ________ for selfies.

25 ________ ________ these questions before you ________, ________, or ________ ________ selfies.

26 1. ________ ________ I?

27 Choose ________ places ________ ________ ________.

28 ________ ________ selfies in hospitals or ________ ________.

29 It may ________ ________ people.

30 2. Who ________ ________ this ?

31 ________ ________ ________ that anyone can see your selfies.

32 ________ carefully ________ you ________ them.

33 3. ________ ________ ________ comments should I ________?

34 ________ nice comments on ________ ________ ________.

35 Don't ________ ________. That sounds easy, ________ ________?

36 ________ these tips and ________ ________ with your selfies.

19 우스꽝스러운 표정을 짓는 것은 정말로 재미있다!

20 민우, 16세, 한국: 나는 셀피 찍는 것을 즐기지만 몇몇 학생들은 그것을 하는 데 너무 많은 시간을 쓴다.

21 케이트, 15세, 덴마크: 내 사진은 필터를 사용할 때 멋져 보인다.

22 하지만 가끔 나의 셀피가 나처럼 보이지 않는다.

23 셀피 예절

24 당신은 셀피 예절을 따라야 한다.

25 셀피를 찍고, 게시하거나 보기 전에 스스로 이 질문들을 물어보라.

26 1. 내가 어디에 있는가?

27 셀피를 찍기에 적합한 장소를 선택하라.

28 병원이나 공중화장실에서 셀피를 찍지 마라.

29 그것은 다른 사람들을 신경 쓰이게 할 수 있다.

30 2. 누가 이것을 볼 수 있는가?

31 누구나 당신의 셀피를 볼 수 있다는 것을 명심하라.

32 그것들을 게시할 때 신중하게 골라라.

33 3. 어떤 코멘트를 남겨야 하는가?

34 다른 사람들의 셀피에 상냥한 코멘트를 남겨라.

35 무례하게 굴지 마라. 쉬운 것처럼 들린다, 그렇지 않은가?

36 이러한 조언들을 따라서 당신의 셀피와 즐거운 시간을 보내라!

본문 Test

Step3

※ 다음 문장을 우리말로 쓰시오.

1 All About Selfies!

➡ ______________________________

2 Selfie Facts

➡ ______________________________

3 Are you interested in selfies?

➡ ______________________________

4 You probably like to post selfies on social media, but how much do you know about selfies?

➡ ______________________________

5 Here are some interesting facts.

➡ ______________________________

6 Robert Cornelius took the world's first selfie in 1839.

➡ ______________________________

7 *Selfie* became a new word in the dictionary in 2013.

➡ ______________________________

8 Buzz Aldrin took the first space selfie in 1966.

➡ ______________________________

9 Selfie Survey

➡ ______________________________

10 Taking selfies is part of daily life for many teens, but do teens really enjoy it?

➡ ______________________________

11 To find out, we did a survey.

➡ ______________________________

12 We asked three questions to 300 students from ages 14 to 16.

➡ ______________________________

13 Let's look at the results.

➡ ______________________________

14 Surprisingly, 90 percent of the girls take selfies, but only 15 percent of the boys take selfies.

➡ ______________________________

15 Also, 93 percent of these students said that they use filters.

➡ ______________________________

16 The survey also showed that the students take selfies at school the most.

➡ ______________________________

17 Check out some of the students' comments.

➡ ______________________________

18 Lewis, 14, England Selfies are awesome.

➡ ______________________________

19 Making silly faces is really fun!

➡ ______________________________

20 Minwoo, 16, Korea I enjoy taking selfies, but some students spend too much time doing it.

➡ ______________________________

21 Kate, 15, Denmark My pictures look good when I use filters.

➡ ______________________________

22 But sometimes my selfies don’t look like me.

➡ ______________________________

23 Selfie Etiquette

➡ ______________________________

24 You should follow etiquette for selfies.

➡ ______________________________

25 Ask yourself these questions before you take, post, or look at selfies.

➡ ______________________________

26 Where am I?

➡ ______________________________

27 Choose appropriate places to take selfies.

➡ ______________________________

28 Don’t take selfies in hospitals or public restrooms.

➡ ______________________________

29 It may bother other people.

➡ ______________________________

30 Who can see this?

➡ ______________________________

31 Keep in mind that anyone can see your selfies.

➡ ______________________________

32 Choose carefully when you post them.

➡ ______________________________

33 What kinds of comments should I leave?

➡ ______________________________

34 Leave nice comments on other people’s selfies.

➡ ______________________________

35 Don’t be rude. That sounds easy, doesn’t it?

➡ ______________________________

36 Follow these tips and have fun with your selfies.

➡ ______________________________

본문 Test

Step4

※ 다음 괄호 안의 단어들을 우리말에 맞도록 바르게 배열하시오.

1 (Selfies! / About / All)
➡ ________________

2 (Facts / #Selfie)
➡ ________________

3 (you / are / in / selfies? / interested)
➡ ________________

4 (you / like / post / probably / selfies / to / media, / on / social / but / much / how / know / you / do / selfies? / about)
➡ ________________

5 (are / some / here / facts. / interesting)
➡ ________________

6 (Cornelius / Robert / the / took / selfie / first / 1839. / world's / in)
➡ ________________

7 (selfie / new / became / word / a / in / 2013. / dictionary / the / in)
➡ ________________

8 (Aldrin / Buzz / first / took / the / selfie / 1966. / in / space)
➡ ________________

9 (Survey / #Selfie)
➡ ________________

10 (selfies / taking / part / is / life / daily / of / teens, / many / for / but / teens / do / it? / enjoy / really)
➡ ________________

11 (out, / find / to / did / we / survey. / a)
➡ ________________

12 (we / three / asked / questions / 300 / to / ages / from / students / 16. / to / 14)
➡ ________________

13 (look / at / let's / results. / the)
➡ ________________

14 (surprisingly, / percent / of / 90 / girls / the / selfies, / take / but / 15 / only / percent / the / of / boys / selfies. / take)
➡ ________________

15 (percent / also, / of / 93 / students / these / said / they / filters. / use / that)
➡ ________________

16 (showed / survey / the / also / that / students / the / selfies / take / at / most. / the / school)
➡ ________________

17 (out / check / of / some / the / comments. / students')
➡ ________________

18 (England / 14, / Lewis, // awesome. / are / selfies)
➡ ________________

1 셀피에 대한 모든 것!
2 셀피와 관련된 사실들
3 당신은 셀피에 관심이 있는가?
4 당신은 아마 소셜 미디어에 셀피를 게시하기를 좋아할지도 모르지만, 셀피에 대해 얼마나 많이 알고 있는가?
5 여기 몇 가지 재미있는 사실들이 있다.
6 로버트 코닐리어스가 1839년에 전 세계 최초의 셀피를 찍었다.
7 selfie는 2013년에 사전에 신조어로 등재되었다.
8 버즈 올드린이 1966년에 최초의 우주 셀피를 찍었다.
9 셀피 설문 조사
10 셀피 찍기는 많은 십대들에게 일상생활의 한 부분인데, 십대들은 정말로 그것을 즐기고 있는가?
11 알아보기 위해 우리는 설문 조사를 했다.
12 우리는 14세에서 16세 사이의 학생 300명에게 세 가지를 질문했다.
13 그 결과를 보자.
14 놀랍게도, 소녀들의 90퍼센트가 셀피를 찍지만, 소년들의 15퍼센트만이 셀피를 찍는다.
15 또한 이 학생들의 93퍼센트는 필터를 사용한다고 대답했다.
16 설문은 또한 학생들이 학교에서 가장 많이 셀피를 찍는다는 것을 보여 주었다.
17 학생들의 의견 몇 가지를 확인해 보라.
18 루이스, 14세, 영국: 셀피는 굉장하다.

19 (faces / silly / making / fun! / really / is)

➡ ______________________________

20 (Korea / 16, / Minwoo, // I / selfies, / taking / enjoy / but / too / spend / students / some / time / it. / doing / much)

➡ ______________________________

____

21 (Denmark / 15, / Kate, // my / look / pictures / good / I / when / filters. / use)

➡ ______________________________

22 (sometimes / but / selfies / my / look / me. / don't / like)

➡ ______________________________

23 (Etiquette / #Selfie)

➡ ______________________________

24 (you / follow / etiquette / should / selfies. / for)

➡ ______________________________

25 (ask / these / yourself / questions / you / before / post, / take, / or / selfies. / at / look)

➡ ______________________________

26 (I? / am / where)

➡ ______________________________

27 (choose / places / to / appropriate / selfies. / take)

➡ ______________________________

28 (selfies / don't / take / hospitals / in / restrooms. / or / public)

➡ ______________________________

29 (it / bother / people. / may / other)

➡ ______________________________

30 (see / this? / can / who)

➡ ______________________________

31 (mind / in / keep / that / can / anyone / see / selfies. / your)

➡ ______________________________

32 (carefully / choose / you / when / them. / post)

➡ ______________________________

33 (kinds / what / comments / of / leave? / I / should)

➡ ______________________________

34 (nice / leave / comments / other / on / selfies. / people's)

➡ ______________________________

35 (be / don't / rude. // that / easy, / it? / doesn't / sounds)

➡ ______________________________

36 (these / follow / tips / and / fun / have / selfies. / your / with)

➡ ______________________________

19 우스꽝스러운 표정을 짓는 것은 정말로 재미있다!

20 민우, 16세, 한국: 나는 셀피 찍는 것을 즐기지만 몇몇 학생들은 그것을 하는 데 너무 많은 시간을 쓴다.

21 케이트, 15세, 덴마크: 내 사진은 필터를 사용할 때 멋져 보인다.

22 하지만 가끔 나의 셀피가 나처럼 보이지 않는다.

23 셀피 예절

24 당신은 셀피 예절을 따라야 한다.

25 셀피를 찍고, 게시하거나 보기 전에 스스로 이 질문들을 물어보라.

26 1. 내가 어디에 있는가?

27 셀피를 찍기에 적합한 장소를 선택하라.

28 병원이나 공중화장실에서 셀피를 찍지 마라.

29 그것은 다른 사람들을 신경 쓰이게 할 수 있다.

30 2. 누가 이것을 볼 수 있는가?

31 누구나 당신의 셀피를 볼 수 있다는 것을 명심하라.

32 그것들을 게시할 때 신중하게 골라라.

33 3. 어떤 코멘트를 남겨야 하는가?

34 다른 사람들의 셀피에 상냥한 코멘트를 남겨라.

35 무례하게 굴지 마라. 쉬운 것처럼 들린다, 그렇지 않은가?

36 이러한 조언들을 따라서 당신의 셀피와 즐거운 시간을 보내라!

※ 다음 우리말을 영어로 쓰시오.

1 셀피에 대한 모든 것!
➡ ______

2 셀피와 관련된 사실들
➡ ______

3 당신은 셀피에 관심이 있는가?
➡ ______

4 당신은 아마 소셜 미디어에 셀피를 게시하기를 좋아할지도 모르지만, 셀피에 대해 얼마나 많이 알고 있는가?
➡ ______

5 여기 몇 가지 재미있는 사실들이 있다.
➡ ______

6 로버트 코닐리어스가 1839년에 전 세계 최초의 셀피를 찍었다.
➡ ______

7 *selfie*는 2013년에 사전에 신조어로 등재되었다.
➡ ______

8 버즈 올드린이 1966년에 최초의 우주 셀피를 찍었다.
➡ ______

9 셀피 설문 조사
➡ ______

10 셀피 찍기는 많은 십대들에게 일상생활의 한 부분인데, 십대들은 정말로 그것을 즐기고 있는가?
➡ ______

11 알아보기 위해 우리는 설문 조사를 했다.
➡ ______

12 우리는 14세에서 16세 사이의 학생 300명에게 세 가지를 질문했다.
➡ ______

13 그 결과를 보자.
➡ ______

14 놀랍게도, 소녀들의 90퍼센트가 셀피를 찍지만, 소년들의 15퍼센트만이 셀피를 찍는다.
➡ ______

15 또한 이 학생들의 93퍼센트는 필터를 사용한다고 대답했다.
➡ ______

16 설문은 또한 학생들이 학교에서 가장 많이 셀피를 찍는다는 것을 보여 주었다.
➡ ______

17 학생들의 의견 몇 가지를 확인해 보라.
➡ ______

18 루이스, 14세, 영국: 셀피는 굉장하다.
➡ ______

19 우스꽝스러운 표정을 짓는 것은 정말로 재미있다!

➡ ______

20 민우, 16세, 한국: 나는 셀피 찍는 것을 즐기지만 몇몇 학생들은 그것을 하는 데 너무 많은 시간을 쓴다.

➡ ______

21 케이트, 15세, 덴마크: 내 사진은 필터를 사용할 때 멋져 보인다.

➡ ______

22 하지만 가끔 나의 셀피가 나처럼 보이지 않는다.

➡ ______

23 셀피 예절

➡ ______

24 당신은 셀피 예절을 따라야 한다.

➡ ______

25 셀피를 찍고, 게시하거나 보기 전에 스스로 이 질문들을 물어보라.

➡ ______

26 내가 어디에 있는가?

➡ ______

27 셀피를 찍기에 적합한 장소를 선택하라.

➡ ______

28 병원이나 공중화장실에서 셀피를 찍지 마라.

➡ ______

29 그것은 다른 사람들을 신경 쓰이게 할 수 있다.

➡ ______

30 누가 이것을 볼 수 있는가?

➡ ______

31 누구나 당신의 셀피를 볼 수 있다는 것을 명심하라.

➡ ______

32 그것들을 게시할 때 신중하게 골라라.

➡ ______

33 어떤 코멘트를 남겨야 하는가?

➡ ______

34 다른 사람들의 셀피에 상냥한 코멘트를 남겨라.

➡ ______

35 무례하게 굴지 마라. 쉬운 것처럼 들린다, 그렇지 않은가?

➡ ______

36 이러한 조언들을 따라서 당신의 셀피와 즐거운 시간을 보내라.

➡ ______

※ 다음 우리말과 일치하도록 빈칸에 알맞은 말을 쓰시오.

Project Link

1. Our group ________ ________ ________ dance.
2. We ________ a dance.
3. We ________ a dance video and ________ it online.
4. You ________ see it ________ www.yutu.com.

1. 우리 그룹은 춤에 관심이 있다.
2. 우리는 춤을 만들었다.
3. 우리는 춤 비디오를 녹화하고 그것을 온라인에 올렸다.
4. 너는 그것을 www.yutu.com.에서 볼 수 있다.

Think and Write

1. ________ a Great Internet ________!
2. ________ we use the internet, we ________ ________ some ________.
3. Then we ________ ________ the internet ________.
4. ________ of all, we ________ follow language rules ________ people ________ not understand us.
5. ________, we should ________ only ________ information.
6. People ________ believe our ________ information.
7. ________, we ________ ________ ________ rude comments.
8. We ________ hurt ________ feelings.
9. ________ these rules ________ ________.
10. Then you ________ ________ a great internet user!

1. 멋진 인터넷 사용자가 되어라!
2. 우리가 인터넷을 사용할 때, 우리는 몇 가지 규칙을 따라야 한다.
3. 그러면 우리는 인터넷을 더 즐길 수 있다.
4. 무엇보다, 사람들이 우리를 이해하지 못할 수도 있기 때문에 우리는 언어 규칙들을 따라야 한다.
5. 또한, 우리는 오직 사실인 정보만을 게시해야 한다.
6. 사람들은 우리의 부정확한 정보를 믿을지도 모른다.
7. 마지막으로, 무례한 코멘트를 남기지 말아야 한다.
8. 우리는 다른 사람들의 감정을 다치게 할 수 있다.
9. 이런 규칙들을 명심해라.
10. 그러면 너는 멋진 인터넷 사용자가 될 것이다!

Culture Link

1. A student ________ the United States is ________ in the ________.
2. He ________ a cartoon ________, *GoGreenMan*, and ________ it online.
3. He ________ helps the environment ________ ________ his character, *GoGreenMan*.

1. 미국 출신의 한 학생은 환경에 관심이 있다.
2. 그는 GoGreenMan이라는 만화의 수퍼 영웅을 만들어 인터넷에 게시했다.
3. 그는 또한 그의 캐릭터인 GoGreenMan과 꼭 같이 환경을 돕는다.

구석구석 지문 Test

※ 다음 우리말을 영어로 쓰시오.

Project Link

1. 우리 그룹은 춤에 관심이 있다.
➡ ______________________________
2. 우리는 춤을 만들었다.
➡ ______________________________
3. 우리는 춤 비디오를 녹화하고 그것을 온라인에 올렸다.
➡ ______________________________
4. 너는 그것을 www.yutu.com.에서 볼 수 있다.
➡ ______________________________

Think and Write

1. 멋진 인터넷 사용자가 되어라!
➡ ______________________________
2. 우리가 인터넷을 사용할 때, 우리는 몇 가지 규칙을 따라야 한다.
➡ ______________________________
3. 그러면 우리는 인터넷을 더 즐길 수 있다.
➡ ______________________________
4. 무엇보다, 사람들이 우리를 이해하지 못할 수도 있기 때문에 우리는 언어 규칙들을 따라야 한다.
➡ ______________________________
5. 또한, 우리는 오직 사실인 정보만을 게시해야 한다.
➡ ______________________________
6. 사람들은 우리의 부정확한 정보를 믿을지도 모른다.
➡ ______________________________
7. 마지막으로, 무례한 코멘트를 남기지 말아야 한다.
➡ ______________________________
8. 우리는 다른 사람들의 감정을 다치게 할 수 있다.
➡ ______________________________
9. 이런 규칙들을 명심해라.
➡ ______________________________
10. 그러면 너는 멋진 인터넷 사용자가 될 것이다!
➡ ______________________________

Culture Link

1. 미국 출신의 한 학생은 환경에 관심이 있다.
➡ ______________________________
2. 그는 GoGreenMan이라는 만화의 수퍼 영웅을 만들어 인터넷에 게시했다.
➡ ______________________________
3. 그는 또한 그의 캐릭터인 GoGreenMan과 꼭 같이 환경을 돕는다.
➡ ______________________________

단어 Test

Step1

※ 다음 영어를 우리말로 쓰시오.

01 common ____________
02 vegetable ____________
03 meat ____________
04 more ____________
05 British ____________
06 drop ____________
07 else ____________
08 mixed ____________
09 fresh ____________
10 slowly ____________
11 sweet ____________
12 other ____________
13 traditional ____________
14 sweets ____________
15 as ____________
16 fry ____________
17 have ____________
18 part ____________
19 choice ____________
20 contest ____________
21 carrot ____________
22 include ____________
23 Indian ____________
24 instead ____________
25 always ____________
26 Western ____________
27 less ____________
28 local ____________
29 often ____________
30 usually ____________
31 onion ____________
32 rule ____________
33 side dish ____________
34 celebrate ____________
35 at least ____________
36 be ready to+동사원형 ____________
37 check out ____________
38 come with ____________
39 for a long time ____________
40 had better+동사원형 ____________
41 have ~ in common ____________
42 heat ~ up ____________
43 such as ____________

단어 Test

Step2

※ 다음 우리말을 영어로 쓰시오.

01 식료품 ____________

02 특별한 ____________

03 아침 식사 ____________

04 동양의 ____________

05 더하다 ____________

06 운동하다 ____________

07 문화 ____________

08 콩 ____________

09 피곤한 ____________

10 음식물을 제공하다[권하다] ____________

11 튀겨진 ____________

12 카레 ____________

13 맛있는 ____________

14 스페인의 ____________

15 식전 음식 ____________

16 건강에 좋은 ____________

17 칠면조 ____________

18 제안 ____________

19 균형이 잡힌 ____________

20 가끔, 때때로 ____________

21 건강 ____________

22 과일 ____________

23 주문하다 ____________

24 국수 ____________

25 추천하다 ____________

26 베트남의 ____________

27 또한 ____________

28 주요리 ____________

29 충분한 ____________

30 특히 ____________

31 전통적인 ____________

32 섞인, 복합된 ____________

33 대신에 ____________

34 흔한 ____________

35 ~의 끝에 ____________

36 A와 B 둘 다 ____________

37 할인받다 ____________

38 A를 B에 넣다 ____________

39 머무르다 ____________

40 ~을 돌보다 ____________

41 요즘, 최근 ____________

42 버리다 ____________

43 상을 받다 ____________

※ 다음 영영풀이에 알맞은 단어를 <보기>에서 골라 쓴 후, 우리말 뜻을 쓰시오.

1 __________: having been cooked in hot oil: __________

2 __________: feeling that you want to sleep or rest: __________

3 __________: the meal you have in the morning: __________

4 __________: a small dish that you eat before a meal: __________

5 __________: happening often and to many people or in many places: __________

6 __________: consisting of several different types of things or people: __________

7 __________: to ask for food or a drink in a restaurant, bar etc.: __________

8 __________: food and other goods that are sold by a grocer or a supermarket: __________

9 __________: a small piece of sweet food made of sugar or chocolate: __________

10 __________: relating to the particular area you live in, or the area you are talking about: __________

11 __________: an idea, plan, or possibility that someone mentions, or the act of mentioning it: __________

12 __________: a plant that is eaten raw or cooked, such as a cabbage, a carrot, or peas: __________

13 __________: a competition or a situation in which two or more people or groups are competing with each other: __________

14 __________: to give someone food or drink, especially as part of a meal or in a restaurant, bar etc: ____________

15 __________: to advise someone to do something, especially because you have special knowledge of a situation or subject: __________

16 __________: a long thin piece of food made from a mixture of flour, water, and eggs, usually cooked in soup or boiling water: __________

보기

recommend	vegetable	noodle	sweets
breakfast	grocery	order	tired
serve	local	contest	common
fried	mixed	suggestion	appetizer

대화문 Test

※ 다음 우리말과 일치하도록 빈칸에 알맞은 말을 쓰시오.

Listen & Talk 1 A

G: I ________ I ________ too many sweets ________ ________.

B: That's ________ ________ ________ your health. ________ ________ ________ fruit instead.

Listen & Talk 1 B

G: You ________ very ________ today. ________ you ________ well?

B: Yes, I did. But I ________ ________ ________ these days, ________ in the morning.

G: Do you ________ ________ breakfast?

B: No, I ________.

G: ________ ________ ________ breakfast. Breakfast ________ you ________.

B: I ________ know that. Do you ________ any ________ ________?

G: Well, you ________ ________ ________ every day. That ________ ________ you.

B: Okay. I ________.

Listen & Talk 1 C

G: Justin, our school ________ ________ is tomorrow. What ________ you ________ ________ make?

B: I'm ________ ________ ________ sandwiches.

G: What do you ________ ________ ________ in them?

B: ________, cheese, and ________.

G: You'd ________ ________ vegetables ________ your sandwiches. ________ ________ onions and carrots?

B: No, I'm ________ ________ ________ add them. I ________ ________ those vegetables.

G: That's not a good ________. Mr. Kim said we ________ ________ ________ food for the contest.

B: You're ________. I ________ ________ grocery shopping and ________ onions and carrots.

Listen and Talk 2 A

G: It's my ________ ________ here. ________ do you ________?

M: I ________ the pizza and salad.

해석

G: 나 요즘 단 걸 너무 많이 먹는 것 같아.

B: 그건 건강에 좋지 않아. 대신에 과일을 먹는 게 좋아.

G: 너 오늘 매우 피곤해 보인다. 잠을 잘 못 잤니?

B: 아니, 잘 잤어. 그런데, 나 요즘 자주, 특히 아침에 쉽게 피곤해져.

G: 너 아침밥을 주로 먹니?

B: 아니, 먹지 않아.

G: 아침밥을 먹는 게 좋아. 아침밥은 너한테 힘을 주거든.

B: 나 그건 몰랐어. 또 다른 제안해 줄 것 있니?

G: 음, 너는 또한 매일 운동해야 해. 그게 도움이 될 거야.

B: 알겠어. 그럴게.

G: Justin, 우리 학교 요리 대회가 내일이야. 뭐 만들 거니?

B: 샌드위치 만들 거야.

G: 뭐 넣을 거니?

B: 치킨이랑 치즈랑 계란.

G: 너 샌드위치에 채소 넣는 게 좋을 거야. 양파랑 당근은 어때?

B: 싫어. 안 넣을 거야. 나 그 채소들 싫어해.

G: 그건 좋은 생각이 아니야. 김 선생님은 요리 대회에서 건강에 좋은 음식을 만들어야 한다고 했어.

B: 네 말이 맞아. 나 식료품 쇼핑 가서 양파와 당근을 사야겠다.

G: 저 여기 처음 왔어요. 추천해 주시겠어요?

M: 저는 피자와 샐러드를 추천해요.

Listen and Talk 2 B

B: Good morning, Jiwoo. ________ are you doing ________ ________?

G: I'm ________ ________ a restaurant ________ my class party.

B: Wow! ________ is the party?

G: It's next Friday. We ________ ________ ________ to Bella's Restaurant, ________ it is ________ ________.

B: ________ ________ you ________ ________ Chang's Restaurant? I went there ________. The food and ________ were ________.

G: ________ great. What do you ________ there?

B: I recommend the ________ ________.

G: I ________ we ________ ________ there. Thank you.

B: 안녕, Jiwoo. 너 지금 뭐 하고 있니?
G: 학급 파티 때 갈 식당을 찾고 있어.
B: 와! 파티가 언제야?
G: 다음 주 금요일이야. 우리는 Bella 식당에 가고 싶은데, 너무 비싸.
B: Chang 식당을 찾아보는 건 어때? 나 거기 한번 간 적 있어. 음식이랑 가격 다 괜찮았어.
G: 좋을 것 같아. 거기서 어떤 것을 추천하니?
B: 나는 국수를 추천해.
G: 내 생각에 우리 거기 가야겠다. 고마워.

Listen and Talk 2 C

W: Hello. ________ you ________ ________ order?

B: It's my ________ ________ here. What ________ you ________?

W: I ________ the chicken sandwich. It is the ________ ________ ________ at our restaurant.

B: Well, I ________ ________ chicken very much. ________ you ________ ________ ________?

W: ________ ________ the turkey sandwich?

B: Oh, I ________ turkey. I'll ________ that.

W: ________ ________ you ________ a drink with the sandwich? You can ________ ________ 500-won ________.

B: That's great. Then I'll ________ an orange juice, ________.

W: 안녕하세요. 주문하시겠어요?
B: 저 여기 처음 왔어요. 추천해주시겠어요?
W: 치킨 샌드위치 추천합니다. 그게 우리 식당에서 가장 인기 있는 메뉴에요.
B: 음, 제가 치킨을 별로 안 좋아해요. 다른 거 추천해주시겠어요?
W: 칠면조 샌드위치는 어떠세요?
B: 아, 저 칠면조 좋아해요. 그걸로 주세요.
W: 음료랑 샌드위치를 같이 주문하는 게 어떠세요? 500원 할인받을 수 있어요.
B: 좋네요. 그럼 오렌지 주스도 주세요.

Do It Yourself A

G: ________ ________ lunch today?

B: We ________ four ________. ________ ________ do you want?

G: Well, I want ________ ________. What do you ________?

B: I recommend the ________ ________.

G: That ________ ________. I will ________ that. ________ ________ you?

B: I ________ know. I'm ________ ________.

G: ________ ________ your health, ________ ________ have some food. ________ ________ you ________ some tomato soup?

B: All ________. I will.

G: 오늘 점심은 어떤 거야?
B: 우리에겐 네 개의 선택들이 있어. 너는 어떤 것을 원하니?
G: 글쎄, 나는 면을 원해. 너는 어떤 것을 추천하니?
B: 나는 볶음면을 추천해.
G: 그거 맛있겠다. 나는 그걸 먹을래. 너는 어때?
B: 나는 잘 모르겠어. 배가 고프지 않아.
G: 하지만, 너의 건강을 위해서는 음식을 좀 먹는 게 좋아. 토마토 수프를 먹어 보는 게 어떻겠니?
B: 그래. 그렇게 할게.

대화문 Test

※ 다음 우리말에 맞도록 대화를 영어로 쓰시오.

해석

Listen & Talk 1 A

G: ____________________

B: ____________________

G: 나 요즘 단 걸 너무 많이 먹는 것 같아.
B: 그건 건강에 좋지 않아. 대신에 과일을 먹는 게 좋아.

Listen & Talk 1 B

G: ____________________

B: ____________________

G: ____________________

B: ____________________

G: ____________________

B: ____________________

G: ____________________

B: ____________________

G: 너 오늘 매우 피곤해 보인다. 잠을 잘 못 잤니?
B: 아니, 잘 잤어. 그런데, 나 요즘 자주, 특히 아침에 쉽게 피곤해져.
G: 너 아침밥을 주로 먹니?
B: 아니, 먹지 않아.
G: 아침밥을 먹는 게 좋아. 아침밥은 너한테 힘을 주거든.
B: 나 그건 몰랐어. 또 다른 제안해 줄 것 있니?
G: 음, 너는 또한 매일 운동해야 해. 그게 도움이 될 거야.
B: 알겠어. 그럴게.

Listen & Talk 1 C

G: ____________________

B: ____________________

G: ____________________

B: ____________________

G: ____________________

B: ____________________

G: ____________________

B: ____________________

G: Justin, 우리 학교 요리 대회가 내일이야. 뭐 만들 거니?
B: 샌드위치 만들 거야.
G: 뭐 넣을 거니?
B: 치킨이랑 치즈랑 계란.
G: 너 샌드위치에 채소 넣는 게 좋을 거야. 양파랑 당근은 어때?
B: 싫어. 안 넣을 거야. 나 그 채소들 싫어해.
G: 그건 좋은 생각이 아니야. 김 선생님은 요리 대회에서 건강에 좋은 음식을 만들어야 한다고 했어.
B: 네 말이 맞아. 나 식료품 쇼핑 가서 양파와 당근을 사야겠다.

Listen and Talk 2 A

G: ____________________

M: ____________________

G: 저 여기 처음 왔어요. 추천해 주시겠어요?
M: 저는 피자와 샐러드를 추천해요.

Listen & Talk 2 B

B: ______________________________

G: ______________________________

B: ______________________________

G: ______________________________

B: ______________________________

____

G: ______________________________

B: ______________________________

G: ______________________________

B: 안녕, Jiwoo. 너 지금 뭐 하고 있니?
G: 학급 파티 때 갈 식당을 찾고 있어.
B: 와! 파티가 언제야?
G: 다음 주 금요일이야. 우리는 Bella 식당에 가고 싶은데, 너무 비싸.
B: Chang 식당을 찾아보는 건 어때? 나 거기 한번 간 적 있어. 음식이랑 가격 다 괜찮았어.
G: 좋을 것 같아. 거기서 어떤 것을 추천하니?
B: 나는 국수를 추천해.
G: 내 생각에 우리 거기 가야겠다. 고마워.

Listen and Talk 2 C

W: ______________________________

B: ______________________________

W: ______________________________

B: ______________________________

W: ______________________________

B: ______________________________

W: ______________________________

B: ______________________________

W: 안녕하세요. 주문하시겠어요?
B: 저 여기 처음 왔어요. 추천해주시겠어요?
W: 치킨 샌드위치 추천합니다. 그게 우리 식당에서 가장 인기 있는 메뉴에요.
B: 음, 제가 치킨을 별로 안 좋아해요. 다른 거 추천해주시겠어요?
W: 칠면조 샌드위치는 어떠세요?
B: 아, 저 칠면조 좋아해요. 그걸로 주세요.
W: 음료랑 샌드위치를 같이 주문하는 게 어떠세요? 500원 할인받을 수 있어요.
B: 좋네요. 그럼 오렌지 주스도 주세요.

Do It Yourself A

G: ______________________________

B: ______________________________

G: ______________________________

B: ______________________________

G: ______________________________

B: ______________________________

G: ______________________________

____

B: ______________________________

G: 오늘 점심은 어떤 거야?
B: 우리에겐 네 개의 선택들이 있어. 너는 어떤 것을 원하니?
G: 글쎄, 나는 면을 원해. 너는 어떤 것을 추천하니?
B: 나는 볶음면을 추천해.
G: 그거 맛있겠다. 나는 그걸 먹을래. 너는 어때?
B: 나는 잘 모르겠어. 배가 고프지 않아.
G: 하지만, 너의 건강을 위해서는 음식을 좀 먹는 게 좋아. 토마토 수프를 먹어 보는 게 어떻겠니?
B: 그래. 그렇게 할게.

본문 Test

※ 다음 우리말과 일치하도록 빈칸에 알맞은 것을 골라 쓰시오.

1 School Lunches ________ the ________

A. World B. Around

1 세계 각국의 학교 급식

2 Hello, ________ ________ food reporter Minjun ________ Korea.

A. from B. is C. this

2 안녕하세요, 저는 한국에서 온 음식 취재 기자 민준입니다.

3 For ________ students, lunch is the ________ ________ of the school day.

A. part B. best C. many

3 많은 학생들에게 점심시간은 학교 일과 중 가장 좋은 부분입니다.

4 ________ Korea, we ________ eat rice and soup ________ lunch.

A. for B. often C. in

4 한국에서는 점심으로 자주 밥과 국을 먹습니다.

5 We also have ________ ________, such ________ *Bulgogi* or *Gimchi*.

A. as B. dishes C. side

5 우리는 불고기나 김치 같은 반찬도 먹습니다.

6 ________ our school ________ special dish, ________ as pizza, *Bibimbap*, or pasta.

A. such B. serves C. sometimes

6 때때로 우리 학교는 피자, 비빔밥 또는 파스타 같은 특식을 제공합니다.

7 ________ do students ________ live in in ________ countries eat for lunch?

A. other B. who C. what

7 다른 나라에서 사는 학생들은 점심으로 무엇을 먹을까요?

8 ________ hear ________ our food reporters!

A. from B. let's

8 우리 음식 취재 기자들에게서 들어보겠습니다!

9 ________, ________

A. France B. Belle

9 벨, 프랑스

10 Our school ________ healthy and ________ ________.

A. meals B. balanced C. serves

10 우리 학교는 건강하고 균형 잡힌 식사를 제공합니다.

11 We ________ eat a salad ________ an ________.

A. appetizer B. as C. usually

11 우리는 보통 식전 음식으로 샐러드를 먹습니다.

12 ________ dishes often ________ meat or ________.

A. fish B. include C. main

12 주요리는 보통 고기나 생선을 포함합니다.

13 We also eat ________ fruit ________ the ________ of the lunch.

A. at B. fresh C. end

13 우리는 점심의 끝에 신선한 과일도 먹습니다.

14 Oh, I ________ ________ forget about baguettes!

A. never B. can

14 오, 절대 바게트를 빠뜨릴 수는 없죠!

15 They're ________ ________ cheese.

A. with B. great

15 바게트는 치즈와 잘 어울립니다.

16 ________ school ________ has a special ________.

A. rule B. also C. our

16 우리 학교에는 또한 특별한 규칙이 있습니다.

17 We must ________ ________ the lunch table ________ at ________ 30 minutes.

A. least B. at C. for D. stay

17 우리는 적어도 30분간 점심 식탁에 반드시 머물러야 합니다.

18 ________, ________

A. Brazil B. Bruno

19 ________, we have ________ and rice for lunch.

A. beans B. usually

20 ________ and vegetables are ________ in our ________ dishes.

A. side B. common C. meat

21 My ________ lunch ________ ________ plantains.

A. with B. comes C. favorite

22 A ________ is a fruit ________ looks ________ a banana.

A. plantain B. like C. which

23 We ________ ________ plantains.

A. fry B. usually

24 Our school lunches are ________ ________ the vegetables and fruit ________ from ________ farms.

A. local B. because C. come D. fresh

25 ________, ________

A. Singapore B. Nicole

26 People who live in Singapore come from many ________ cultures, so we ________ both ________ and ________ dishes at lunch.

A. Western B. have C. different D. Eastern

27 Students can ________ ________ many dishes, ________ ________ curry, noodle soup, or pasta, each day.

A. as B. from C. such D. choose

28 My school won an ________ for ________ school food ________ year.

A. last B. healthy C. award

29 Our lunches are always ________, and they ________ good, ________!

A. too B. taste C. healthy

30 ________ school lunch do you ________ to ________?

A. try B. which C. want

31 Does it ________ anything ________ ________ with your school lunch?

A. have B. common C. in

32 Please ________ your comments ________ www.chopchoplunch.com.

A. at B. leave

18 브루노, 브라질

19 보통, 우리는 점심으로 콩과 밥을 먹습니다.

20 우리의 곁들임 음식에는 고기와 채소가 흔히 나옵니다.

21 내가 가장 좋아하는 점심에는 플랜테인이 나옵니다.

22 플랜테인은 바나나처럼 생긴 과일입니다.

23 우리는 보통 플랜테인을 튀깁니다.

24 채소와 과일이 현지 농장에서 오기 때문에 우리 학교 급식은 신선합니다.

25 니콜, 싱가포르

26 싱가포르에 사는 사람들은 매우 다양한 문화권에서 오기 때문에, 우리는 점심에 동양식과 서양식을 모두 먹습니다.

27 학생들은 매일 카레, 국수 또는 파스타와 같이 많은 요리 중에서 선택할 수 있습니다.

28 우리 학교는 작년에 건강한 학교 음식 상을 받았습니다.

29 우리의 점심은 항상 건강에 좋고, 맛 또한 좋습니다!

30 여러분은 어떤 학교 급식을 먹어 보고 싶나요?

31 그것이 여러분의 학교 급식과 공통되는 것이 있습니까?

32 여러분의 의견을 www.chopchoplunch.com에 남겨 주세요.

본문 Test

※ 다음 우리말과 일치하도록 빈칸에 알맞은 말을 쓰시오.

1 School Lunches _______ the _______

2 Hello, _______ _______ food _______ Minjun _______ Korea.

3 _______ many students, lunch is _______ _______ _______ _______ the school day.

4 In Korea, we _______ _______ rice and soup _______ _______.

5 We also have _______ _______, such _______ *Bulgogi* or *Gimchi*.

6 Sometimes our school _______ special _______, _______ _______ pizza, *Bibimbap*, or pasta.

7 What do _______ _______ _______ in _______ _______ eat for lunch?

8 _______ _______ _______ our food reporters!

9 Belle, _______

10 Our school serves _______ and _______ _______.

11 We _______ _______ a salad _______ an appetizer.

12 Main dishes _______ _______ meat or _______.

13 We _______ _______ fresh fruit _______ _______ _______ _______ the lunch.

14 Oh, I _______ _______ _______ about baguettes!

15 They're _______ _______ cheese.

16 Our school _______ _______ a _______ _______.

17 We _______ _______ _______ the lunch table for _______ _______ 30 minutes.

1 세계 각국의 학교 급식

2 안녕하세요. 저는 한국에서 온 음식 취재 기자 민준입니다.

3 많은 학생들에게 점심시간은 학교 일과 중 가장 좋은 부분입니다.

4 한국에서는 점심으로 자주 밥과 국을 먹습니다.

5 우리는 불고기나 김치 같은 반찬도 먹습니다.

6 때때로 우리 학교는 피자, 비빔밥 또는 파스타 같은 특식을 제공합니다.

7 다른 나라에서 사는 학생들은 점심으로 무엇을 먹을까요?

8 우리 음식 취재 기자들에게서 들어보겠습니다!

9 벨, 프랑스

10 우리 학교는 건강하고 균형 잡힌 식사를 제공합니다.

11 우리는 보통 식전 음식으로 샐러드를 먹습니다.

12 주요리는 보통 고기나 생선을 포함합니다.

13 우리는 점심의 끝에 신선한 과일도 먹습니다.

14 오, 절대 바게트를 빠뜨릴 수는 없죠!

15 바게트는 치즈와 잘 어울립니다.

16 우리 학교에는 또한 특별한 규칙이 있습니다.

17 우리는 적어도 30분간 점심 식탁에 반드시 머물러야 합니다.

18 Bruno, ________

19 Usually, we ________ ________ and ________ for lunch.

20 Meat and vegetables are ________ ________ our ________ ________.

21 My ________ lunch ________ ________ plantains.

22 A plantain is a ________ which ________ ________ a banana.

23 We ________ ________ plantains.

24 Our school lunches are ________ ________ the vegetables and fruit ________ ________ ________ ________.

25 Nicole, ________

26 People ________ ________ ________ Singapore ________ ________ many different cultures, so we have ________ Eastern ________ Western dishes at lunch.

27 Students ________ ________ ________ many dishes, ________ ________ curry, noodle soup, or pasta, ________ ________.

28 My school ________ ________ ________ for healthy school food ________ ________.

29 Our lunches are ________ ________, and they ________ ________, too!

30 ________ school lunch do you ________ ________ ________?

31 Does it ________ anything ________ ________ ________ your school lunch?

32 Please ________ ________ ________ at www.chopchoplunch.com.

18 브루노, 브라질

19 보통, 우리는 점심으로 콩과 밥을 먹습니다.

20 우리의 곁들임 음식에는 고기와 채소가 흔히 나옵니다.

21 내가 가장 좋아하는 점심에는 플랜테인이 나옵니다.

22 플랜테인은 바나나처럼 생긴 과일입니다.

23 우리는 보통 플랜테인을 튀깁니다.

24 채소와 과일이 현지 농장에서 오기 때문에 우리 학교 급식은 신선합니다.

25 니콜, 싱가포르

26 싱가포르에 사는 사람들은 매우 다양한 문화권에서 오기 때문에, 우리는 점심에 동양식과 서양식을 모두 먹습니다.

27 학생들은 매일 카레, 국수 또는 파스타와 같이 많은 요리 중에서 선택할 수 있습니다.

28 우리 학교는 작년에 건강한 학교 음식 상을 받았습니다.

29 우리의 점심은 항상 건강에 좋고, 맛 또한 좋습니다!

30 여러분은 어떤 학교 급식을 먹어 보고 싶나요?

31 그것이 여러분의 학교 급식과 공통되는 것이 있습니까?

32 여러분의 의견을 www.chopchoplunch.com에 남겨 주세요.

본문 Test

※ 다음 문장을 우리말로 쓰시오.

1 School Lunches Around the World

➡ ______________________

2 Hello, this is food reporter Minjun from Korea.

➡ ______________________

3 For many students, lunch is the best part of the school day.

➡ ______________________

4 In Korea, we often eat rice and soup for lunch.

➡ ______________________

5 We also have side dishes, such as *Bulgogi* or *Gimchi* .

➡ ______________________

6 Sometimes our school serves special dishes, such as pizza, *Bibimbap* , or pasta.

➡ ______________________

7 What do students who live in other countries eat for lunch?

➡ ______________________

8 Let's hear from our food reporters!

➡ ______________________

9 Belle, France

➡ ______________________

10 Our school serves healthy and balanced meals.

➡ ______________________

11 We usually eat a salad as an appetizer.

➡ ______________________

12 Main dishes often include meat or fish.

➡ ______________________

13 We also eat fresh fruit at the end of the lunch.

➡ ______________________

14 Oh, I can never forget about baguettes!

➡ ______________________

15 They're great with cheese.

➡ ______________________

16 Our school also has a special rule.

➡ ______________________

17 We must stay at the lunch table for at least 30 minutes.

➡ ______________________

18 Bruno, Brazil

➡ ____________________

19 Usually, we have beans and rice for lunch.

➡ ____________________

20 Meat and vegetables are common in our side dishes.

➡ ____________________

21 My favorite lunch comes with plantains.

➡ ____________________

22 A plantain is a fruit which looks like a banana.

➡ ____________________

23 We usually fry plantains.

➡ ____________________

24 Our school lunches are fresh because the vegetables and fruit come from local farms.

➡ ____________________

25 Nicole, Singapore

➡ ____________________

26 People who live in Singapore come from many different cultures, so we have both Eastern and Western dishes at lunch.

➡ ____________________

27 Students can choose from many dishes, such as curry, noodle soup, or pasta, each day.

➡ ____________________

28 My school won an award for healthy school food last year.

➡ ____________________

29 Our lunches are always healthy, and they taste good, too!

➡ ____________________

30 Which school lunch do you want to try?

➡ ____________________

31 Does it have anything in common with your school lunch?

➡ ____________________

32 Please leave your comments at www.chopchoplunch.com.

➡ ____________________

본문 Test

※ 다음 괄호 안의 단어들을 우리말에 맞도록 바르게 배열하시오.

1 (Around / Lunches / the / School / World)
➡ ______________________________

2 (hello, / is / this / reporter / food / Korea. / from / Minjun)
➡ ______________________________

3 (students, / many / for / lunch / is / best / part / the / of / day. / school / the)
➡ ______________________________

4 (Korea, / in / we / eat / often / soup / and / rice / lunch. / for)
➡ ______________________________

5 (also / we / side / have / dishes, / or / such / *Gimchi*. / as / *Bulgogi*)
➡ ______________________________

6 (our / sometimes / school / serves / dishes, / special / as / pizza, / such / or / pasta. / *Bibimbap*,)
➡ ______________________________

7 (students / do / what / live / who / countries / in / other / lunch? / for / eat)
➡ ______________________________

8 (hear / let's / from / reporters! / food / our)
➡ ______________________________

9 (France / Belle,)
➡ ______________________________

10 (school / serves / our / healthy / meals. / balanced / and)
➡ ______________________________

11 (we / eat / usually / salad / as / a / appetizer. / an)
➡ ______________________________

12 (dishes / main / include / often / fish. / or / meat)
➡ ______________________________

13 (also / we / eat / fruit / fresh / at / end / the / of / lunch. / the)
➡ ______________________________

14 (oh, / can / I / forget / never / baguettes! / about)
➡ ______________________________

15 (great / with / they're / cheese.)
➡ ______________________________

16 (school / our / has / a / rule. / also / special)
➡ ______________________________

17 (must / we / at / stay / the / table / lunch / for / least / minutes. / at / 30)
➡ ______________________________

1 세계 각국의 학교 급식

2 안녕하세요. 저는 한국에서 온 음식 취재 기자 민준입니다.

3 많은 학생들에게 점심시간은 학교 일과 중 가장 좋은 부분입니다.

4 한국에서는 점심으로 자주 밥과 국을 먹습니다.

5 우리는 불고기나 김치 같은 반찬도 먹습니다.

6 때때로 우리 학교는 피자, 비빔밥 또는 파스타 같은 특식을 제공합니다.

7 다른 나라에서 사는 학생들은 점심으로 무엇을 먹을까요?

8 우리 음식 취재 기자들에게서 들어보겠습니다!

9 벨, 프랑스

10 우리 학교는 건강하고 균형 잡힌 식사를 제공합니다.

11 우리는 보통 식전 음식으로 샐러드를 먹습니다.

12 주요리는 보통 고기나 생선을 포함합니다.

13 우리는 점심의 끝에 신선한 과일도 먹습니다.

14 오, 절대 바게트를 빠뜨릴 수는 없죠!

15 바게트는 치즈와 잘 어울립니다.

16 우리 학교에는 또한 특별한 규칙이 있습니다.

17 우리는 적어도 30분간 점심 식탁에 반드시 머물러야 합니다.

18 (Brazil / Bruno,)
➡ ______________________________

19 (we / usually, / beans / have / rice / and / lunch. / for)
➡ ______________________________

20 (vegetables / and / meat / are / in / common / our / dishes. / side)
➡ ______________________________

21 (favorite / my / lunch / plantains. / with / comes)
➡ ______________________________

22 (plantain / a / fruit / is / a / which / a / banana. / like / looks)
➡ ______________________________

23 (usually / plantains. / we / fry)
➡ ______________________________

24 (school / are / our / lunches / fresh / because / vegetables / the / fruit / and / from / farms. / local / come)
➡ ______________________________
____

25 (Singapore / Nicole,)
➡ ______________________________

26 (live / who / people / Singapore / in / from / come / different / many / cultures, / so / have / we / and / Eastern / both / dishes / Western / lunch. / at)
➡ ______________________________
____

27 (can / students / from / choose / dishes, / many / as / such / noodle soup, / or / curry, / day. / pasta, / each)
➡ ______________________________
____

28 (school / my / won / award / an / healthy / for / food / year. / school / last)
➡ ______________________________

29 (lunches / are / our / healthy, / always / and / taste / too! / they / good,)
➡ ______________________________

30 (school / which / lunch / you / do / try? / to / want)
➡ ______________________________

31 (it / does / have / anything / with / common / in / lunch? / school / your)
➡ ______________________________

32 (your / leave / please / at / comments / www.chopchoplunch.com.)
➡ ______________________________

18 브루노, 브라질

19 보통, 우리는 점심으로 콩과 밥을 먹습니다.

20 우리의 곁들임 음식에는 고기와 채소가 흔히 나옵니다.

21 내가 가장 좋아하는 점심에는 플랜테인이 나옵니다.

22 플랜테인은 바나나처럼 생긴 과일입니다.

23 우리는 보통 플랜테인을 튀깁니다.

24 채소와 과일이 현지 농장에서 오기 때문에 우리 학교 급식은 신선합니다.

25 니콜, 싱가포르

26 싱가포르에 사는 사람들은 매우 다양한 문화권에서 오기 때문에, 우리는 점심에 동양식과 서양식을 모두 먹습니다.

27 학생들은 매일 카레, 국수 또는 파스타와 같이 많은 요리 중에서 선택할 수 있습니다.

28 우리 학교는 작년에 건강한 학교 음식 상을 받았습니다.

29 우리의 점심은 항상 건강에 좋고, 맛 또한 좋습니다!

30 여러분은 어떤 학교 급식을 먹어 보고 싶나요?

31 그것이 여러분의 학교 급식과 공통되는 것이 있습니까?

32 여러분의 의견을 www.chopchoplunch.com에 남겨 주세요.

본문 Test

※ 다음 우리말을 영어로 쓰시오.

1 세계 각국의 학교 급식

➡ ______________________________

2 안녕하세요, 저는 한국에서 온 음식 취재 기자 민준입니다.

➡ ______________________________

3 많은 학생들에게 점심시간은 학교 일과 중 가장 좋은 부분입니다.

➡ ______________________________

4 한국에서는 점심으로 자주 밥과 국을 먹습니다.

➡ ______________________________

5 우리는 불고기나 김치 같은 반찬도 먹습니다.

➡ ______________________________

6 때때로 우리 학교는 피자, 비빔밥 또는 파스타 같은 특식을 제공합니다.

➡ ______________________________

7 다른 나라에서 사는 학생들은 점심으로 무엇을 먹을까요?

➡ ______________________________

8 우리 음식 취재 기자들에게서 들어보겠습니다!

➡ ______________________________

9 벨, 프랑스

➡ ______________________________

10 우리 학교는 건강하고 균형 잡힌 식사를 제공합니다.

➡ ______________________________

11 우리는 보통 식전 음식으로 샐러드를 먹습니다.

➡ ______________________________

12 주요리는 보통 고기나 생선을 포함합니다.

➡ ______________________________

13 우리는 점심의 끝에 신선한 과일도 먹습니다.

➡ ______________________________

14 오, 절대 바게트를 빠뜨릴 수는 없죠!

➡ ______________________________

15 바게트는 치즈와 잘 어울립니다.

➡ ______________________________

16 우리 학교에는 또한 특별한 규칙이 있습니다.

➡ ______________________________

17 우리는 적어도 30분간 점심 식탁에 반드시 머물러야 합니다.

➡ ______________________________

18 브루노, 브라질

➡ ______________________________

19 보통, 우리는 점심으로 콩과 밥을 먹습니다.

➡ ______________________________

20 우리의 곁들임 음식에는 고기와 채소가 흔히 나옵니다.

➡ ______________________________

21 내가 가장 좋아하는 점심에는 플랜테인이 나옵니다.

➡ ______________________________

22 플랜테인은 바나나처럼 생긴 과일입니다.

➡ ______________________________

23 우리는 보통 플랜테인을 튀깁니다.

➡ ______________________________

24 채소와 과일이 현지 농장에서 오기 때문에 우리 학교 급식은 신선합니다.

➡ ______________________________

25 니콜, 싱가포르

➡ ______________________________

26 싱가포르에 사는 사람들은 매우 다양한 문화권에서 오기 때문에, 우리는 점심에 동양식과 서양식을 모두 먹습니다.

➡ ______________________________

27 학생들은 매일 카레, 국수 또는 파스타와 같이 많은 요리 중에서 선택할 수 있습니다.

➡ ______________________________

28 우리 학교는 작년에 건강한 학교 음식 상을 받았습니다.

➡ ______________________________

29 우리의 점심은 항상 건강에 좋고, 맛 또한 좋습니다!

➡ ______________________________

30 여러분은 어떤 학교 급식을 먹어 보고 싶나요?

➡ ______________________________

31 그것이 여러분의 학교 급식과 공통되는 것이 있습니까?

➡ ______________________________

32 여러분의 의견을 www.chopchoplunch.com에 남겨 주세요.

➡ ______________________________

※ 다음 우리말과 일치하도록 빈칸에 알맞은 말을 쓰시오.

Think and Write

1. ________ of My ________ Restaurant
2. ________ favorite ________ is Antonio's Restaurant.
3. It is a ________ restaurant.
4. It is ________ my home.
5. Mixed paella is the ________ ________ ________ at this restaurant.
6. ________ of the food ________ really fresh and ________, and the prices are ________.
7. I ________ this restaurant!

1. 내가 가장 좋아하는 음식점 방문 후기
2. 내가 가장 좋아하는 음식점은 Antonio's Restaurant이야.
3. 그곳은 스페인 음식점이야.
4. 그곳은 나의 집에서 가까워.
5. 이 음식점에서 가장 인기 있는 음식은 혼합 파엘라야.
6. 모든 음식이 정말 신선하고 맛있으며 가격도 싸.
7. 나는 이 음식점을 추천해.

Culture Link

1. ________ China, people eat noodles ________ their birthday.
2. Chinese people don't want ________ ________ the noodles ________ ________ a long life.
3. Doro wat is a chicken ________ ________ Ethiopia.
4. There are ________ ________ ________ vegetables in it.
5. People eat this ________ for New Year's ________.
6. Bánh xu xê is a ________ ________ cake.
7. People eat this cake ________ ________.
8. ________ the cake ________ the husbands and wife will ________ ________ ________ ________ together.
9. In the United States, people ________ ________ ________ ________ Thanksgiving.
10. They ________ ________ ________ the food and their health.

1. 중국에서 사람들은 그들의 생일에 국수를 먹는다.
2. 중국 사람들은 장수하려고 국수를 자르려 하지 않는다.
3. Doro wat은 에티오피아의 치킨카레 요리이다.
4. 그 안에 많은 야채가 들어 있다.
5. 사람들은 이 음식을 새해 만찬으로 먹는다.
6. Bánh xu xê는 전통적인 베트남 케이크이다.
7. 사람들은 이 케이크를 결혼식에서 먹는다.
8. 이 케이크를 먹는 것은 남편과 아내가 함께 행복한 삶을 살 것을 의미한다.
9. 미국에서 사람들은 추수감사절을 기념하기 위해 칠면조 요리를 먹는다.
10. 그들은 음식과 그들의 건강에 대해 감사한다.

구석구석 지문 Test

Step2

※ 다음 우리말을 영어로 쓰시오.

Think and Write

1. 내가 가장 좋아하는 음식점 방문 후기
➡ ______________________________
2. 내가 가장 좋아하는 음식점은 Antonio's Restaurant이야.
➡ ______________________________
3. 그곳은 스페인 음식점이야.
➡ ______________________________
4. 그곳은 나의 집에서 가까워.
➡ ______________________________
5. 이 음식점에서 가장 인기 있는 음식은 혼합 파엘라야.
➡ ______________________________
6. 모든 음식이 정말 신선하고 맛있으며 가격도 싸.
➡ ______________________________
7. 나는 이 음식점을 추천해.
➡ ______________________________

Culture Link

1. 중국에서 사람들은 그들의 생일에 국수를 먹는다.
➡ ______________________________
2. 중국 사람들은 장수하려고 국수를 자르려 하지 않는다.
➡ ______________________________
3. Doro wat은 에티오피아의 치킨카레 요리이다.
➡ ______________________________
4. 그 안에 많은 야채가 들어 있다.
➡ ______________________________
5. 사람들은 이 음식을 새해 만찬으로 먹는다.
➡ ______________________________
6. Bánh xu xê는 전통적인 베트남 케이크이다.
➡ ______________________________
7. 사람들은 이 케이크를 결혼식에서 먹는다.
➡ ______________________________
8. 이 케이크를 먹는 것은 남편과 아내가 함께 행복한 삶을 살 것을 의미한다.
➡ ______________________________
9. 미국에서 사람들은 추수감사절을 기념하기 위해 칠면조 요리를 먹는다.
➡ ______________________________
10. 그들은 음식과 그들의 건강에 대해 감사한다.
➡ ______________________________

단어 Test

Step1

※ 다음 영어를 우리말로 쓰시오.

01 rude ______
02 last ______
03 Chinese ______
04 calendar ______
05 evil ______
06 lock ______
07 face ______
08 colored ______
09 full moon ______
10 try ______
11 bow ______
12 separation ______
13 represent ______
14 guard ______
15 international ______
16 last year ______
17 Vietnamese ______
18 guest ______
19 greet ______
20 palm ______
21 spirit ______
22 sister school ______
23 scary ______
24 shake ______
25 protect ______
26 symbol ______
27 valuable ______
28 good luck ______
29 crow ______
30 pillow ______
31 remind ______
32 traditional ______
33 peace ______
34 darkness ______
35 talk about ______
36 blow one's nose ______
37 watch over ______
38 take off ______
39 be afraid of ______
40 have been to 장소 ______
41 be full of ______
42 go away ______
43 remind A of B ______

단어 Test

Step2

※ 다음 우리말을 영어로 쓰시오.

01 해변, 바닷가 ______________

02 가루, 분말 ______________

03 옷, 의복 ______________

04 (닭이) 울다 ______________

05 경험 ______________

06 축제 ______________

07 박쥐 ______________

08 우산 ______________

09 선물 가게 ______________

10 어둠, 암흑 ______________

11 베개 ______________

12 인도의, 인도 사람의 ______________

13 자물쇠; 잠그다 ______________

14 반달 ______________

15 도착하다 ______________

16 뮤지컬 ______________

17 운 ______________

18 전통의, 전통적인 ______________

19 지불하다 ______________

20 의미하다 ______________

21 평화, 화해 ______________

22 수탉 ______________

23 생각나게 하다 ______________

24 말하다, (정확히) 알다 ______________

25 승리 ______________

26 ~쪽으로 ______________

27 영혼, 정신 ______________

28 손바닥 ______________

29 나타내다, 상징하다 ______________

30 무례한 ______________

31 보호하다 ______________

32 채색된 ______________

33 사악한, 악마의 ______________

34 흔들다, 흔들리다 ______________

35 사라지다, 떠나가다 ______________

36 (옷 등을) 벗다 ______________

37 A에게 B를 생각나게 하다 ______________

38 ~을 가리키다 ______________

39 ~에 대해 이야기하다 ______________

40 ~으로 가득 차다 ______________

41 ~을 듣다 ______________

42 ~을 주시하다, 지키다 ______________

43 ~을 두려워하다 ______________

단어 Test

Step3

※ 다음 영영풀이에 알맞은 단어를 <보기>에서 골라 쓴 후, 우리말 뜻을 쓰시오.

1 __________: a male chicken: __________

2 __________: no light: __________

3 __________: morally bad or wicked: __________

4 __________: a soft thing to put your head on while you sleep: __________

5 __________: to say hello or welcome: __________

6 __________: to have the front part toward something: __________

7 __________: to stand for something else: __________

8 __________: to make the loud sound that a rooster makes: __________

9 __________: success in defeating an opponent: __________

10 __________: very important or expensive: __________

11 __________: the inside part of the hand between the wrist and the fingers: __________

12 __________: to keep something or someone safe from danger: __________

13 __________: to make someone remember something: __________

14 __________: making people feel afraid, frightening: __________

15 __________: to lower your head or bend your body: __________

16 __________: an object that represents something: __________

보기

scary	greet	protect	bow
face	palm	evil	symbol
darkness	crow	represent	valuable
remind	victory	rooster	pillow

대화문 Test

Step1

※ 다음 우리말과 일치하도록 빈칸에 알맞은 말을 쓰시오.

해석

Listen & Talk 1 A

G: ________ you ever ________ ________ Brazil?
B: No, I ________. ________ you?
G: Yes, I ________. I went there ________ year. There ________ a big samba festival.
B: That ________ interesting. I hope ________ ________ there ________.

G: 너는 브라질 가 봤니?
B: 아니, 못 가 봤어. 너는 가 봤니?
G: 응. 가 봤어. 작년에 거기 갔었어. 큰 삼바 축제가 있었어.
B: 재미있게 들린다. 나도 언젠가 거기 가고 싶어.

Listen & Talk 1 B

W: ________ ________ the International Games Festival. You can play many ________ ________ games here.
B: Wow! It ________ ________! ________ game ________ I play first?
W: ________ see. ________ you ever ________ *gorodki*?
B: No, I ________. What is it?
W: It's a ________ game ________ Russia.
B: ________ do I ________ it?
W: ________ five sticks ________ the ground. Then ________ a bat ________ them.
B: That ________ ________. I'll ________ that first.

W: 국제 게임 축제에 오신 걸 환영합니다. 당신은 여기서 많은 종류의 전통 게임을 할 수 있습니다.
B: 와! 재미있을 것 같아요! 어떤 게임 먼저 해야 하나요?
W: 어디 봅시다. 고로드키 게임 해 본 적 있나요?
B: 아니요. 그게 무엇인가요?
W: 러시아의 전통 게임이에요.
B: 어떻게 하나요?
W: 바닥에 다섯 개의 막대기를 놓으세요. 그리고 그것들을 향해 배트를 던지세요.
B: 재미있겠네요. 그거 먼저 할게요.

Listen & Talk 1 C

B: There ________ a Holi festival in Busan ________ ________.
G: A Holi ________? ________ is that?
B: It's a ________ ________ festival. People ________ colored powder and water ________ ________ ________.
G: That ________ ________. ________ you ever ________ ________ a Holi festival?
B: No, I ________. But my Indian friend ________ me ________ ________ about it.
G: ________ is the festival?
B: It's ________ the last ________ ________ of the Hindu calendar. This year, it's ________ ________ ________.
G: I'd like to go. ________ I ________ anything?
B: No, but you ________ ________ white clothes. Then the ________ powder on your clothes will ________ more ________.
G: Okay. ________ ________ ________ the information.

B: 올해에는 부산에서 Holi Festival이 있어.
G: Holi Festival? 그게 뭐야?
B: 인도의 전통 축제야. 사람들은 서로에게 색 파우더와 물을 던지지.
G: 재미있겠다. Holi festival에 가 본 적 있니?
B: 아니, 없어. 근데 인도 친구가 그것에 대해 많이 이야기해 줬어.
G: 축제가 언제야?
B: 힌두교 달력으로 마지막 보름달이 뜨는 날이야. 올해는 3월 21일이네.
G: 가고 싶다. 나 뭐 가져가야 하니?
B: 아니, 하지만 하얀 옷을 입어야 돼. 그러면 네 옷에 묻은 색 파우더가 더 예쁘게 보일 거야.
G: 알겠어. 정보 알려줘서 고마워.

Listen and Talk 2 A

G: Jinwoo, my Korean friend, ________ me *Yeot* ________ a gift. ________ does that ________ in Korea ?
B: It ________ good luck ________ ________ ________.

G: 내 한국인 친구인 진우가 선물로 엿을 줬어. 한국에서는 이게 어떤 의미니?
B: 시험 잘 보라는 뜻이야.

Listen and Talk 2 B

B: Ling's birthday is ________ Wednesday, ________ ________?
G: Yes. I'm ________ ________ ________ a book ________ her. What ________ you?
B: Well, I'm ________ ________ buying her an umbrella. I found a ________ ________ in a gift shop.
G: Oh, that's not a ________ ________ ________ Chinese people. It means ________ ________.
B: Really? What ________ an umbrella ________ in ________?
G: It ________ ________. The words for separation and *umbrella* sound the same ________ ________.
B: I see. Then ________ ________ chocolate?
G: That's a good ________.

B: Ling의 생일이 이번 수요일이야, 그렇지 않니?
G: 응. 나는 그녀에게 책을 사 줄 거야. 너는?
B: 음, 나는 우산을 사려고 생각하고 있어. 선물 가게에서 귀여운 걸 찾았거든.
G: 어, 그건 중국 사람들에게 좋은 선물이 아니야. 뭔가 나쁜 걸 뜻하거든.
B: 진짜? 중국에서 우산이 뭘 의미하는데?
G: 이별을 뜻해. 중국에서는 이별을 뜻하는 단어와 우산을 뜻하는 단어의 발음이 같거든.
B: 알겠어. 그러면 초콜릿 어때?
G: 좋은 생각이야.

Listen and Talk 2 C

G: ________ ________ ________ picture! Are these your friends?
B: Yes. We ________ this picture at the beach. We had ________ ________ ________ fun.
G: Oh, ________ ________ that boy. That's really ________.
B: ________ boy?
G: The boy who ________ ________ the V sign. His palm is ________ ________ himself.
B: What's ________ ________ that?
G: It has a ________ ________ in England. But ________ your palm and ________ a V sign is okay.
B: What ________ that ________?
G: It ________ victory or ________.

G: 이 사진 정말 멋지다! 네 친구들이니?
B: 응. 우리는 해변에서 이 사진을 찍었어. 정말 재미있었어.
G: 어, 저 남자애 봐. 정말 무례하다.
B: 누구?
G: V사인을 하고 있는 애. 손바닥이 자기 쪽을 향하고 있어.
B: 그게 뭐 잘못됐어?
G: 영국에서는 나쁜 뜻을 갖고 있어. 하지만 손바닥을 보여 주면서 V사인을 만드는 건 괜찮아.
B: 그건 무슨 뜻인데?
G: 승리나 평화를 뜻해.

Do It Yourself A

G: Hello, Santiago! What ________ you here today?
B: *Bienvenido*, Cathy. I came ________ ________ the ________ festival.
G: Me, ________. But what ________ you just ________?
B: *Bienvenido*! It ________ "welcome" in Spanish. ________ ________ those dancers. Their dance ________ are so great.
G: Yes, ________ are.
B: ________ you ever ________ ________ a Spanish festival ________?
G: No, I ________. Santiago, can you see the big letters ________ the stage? ________ does that ________?
B: Oh, gracias. That ________ "thank you."

G: 안녕, Santiago! 오늘 여기 어쩐 일이야?
B: Bienvenido, Cathy. 나는 스페인 축제를 보러 왔어.
G: 나도. 그런데 방금 뭐라고 말했니?
B: Bienvenido! 스페인어로 "환영합니다."라는 뜻이야. 저 무용수들을 봐. 그들의 춤 움직임은 정말 멋지다.
G: 응, 그렇네.
B: 전에 스페인 축제에 가 본 적 있니?
G: 아니, 가 본 적 없어. Santiago, 무대에 있는 큰 글씨들 볼 수 있니? 무슨 뜻이야?
B: 아, gracias. 저건 "감사합니다."라는 뜻이야.

※ 다음 우리말에 맞도록 대화를 영어로 쓰시오.

해석

Listen & Talk 1 A

G: ______________________________

B: ______________________________

G: ______________________________

B: ______________________________

G: 너는 브라질 가 봤니?
B: 아니, 못 가 봤어. 너는 가 봤니?
G: 응. 가 봤어. 작년에 거기 갔었어. 큰 삼바 축제가 있었어.
B: 재미있게 들린다. 나도 언젠가 거기 가고 싶어.

Listen & Talk 1 B

W: ______________________________
____

B: ______________________________

W: ______________________________

B: ______________________________

W: ______________________________

B: ______________________________

W: ______________________________

B: ______________________________

W: 국제 게임 축제에 오신 걸 환영합니다. 당신은 여기서 많은 종류의 전통 게임을 할 수 있습니다.
B: 와! 재미있을 것 같아요! 어떤 게임 먼저 해야 하나요?
W: 어디 봅시다. 고로드키 게임 해 본 적 있나요?
B: 아니요. 그게 무엇인가요?
W: 러시아의 전통 게임이에요.
B: 어떻게 하나요?
W: 바닥에 다섯 개의 막대기를 놓으세요. 그리고 그것들을 향해 배트를 던지세요.
B: 재미있겠네요. 그거 먼저 할게요.

Listen & Talk 1 C

B: ______________________________

G: ______________________________

B: ______________________________
____

G: ______________________________

B: ______________________________

G: ______________________________

B: ______________________________

G: ______________________________

B: ______________________________
____

G: ______________________________

B: 올해에는 부산에서 Holi Festival이 있어.
G: Holi Festival? 그게 뭐야?
B: 인도의 전통 축제야. 사람들은 서로에게 색 파우더와 물을 던지지.
G: 재미있겠다. Holi festival에 가 본 적 있니?
B: 아니, 없어. 근데 인도 친구가 그것에 대해 많이 이야기해 줬어.
G: 축제가 언제야?
B: 힌두교 달력으로 마지막 보름달이 뜨는 날이야. 올해는 3월 21일이네.
G: 가고 싶다. 나 뭐 가져가야 하니?
B: 아니, 하지만 하얀 옷을 입어야 돼. 그러면 네 옷에 묻은 색 파우더가 더 예쁘게 보일 거야.
G: 알겠어. 정보 알려줘서 고마워.

Listen and Talk 2 A

G: ______________________________

B: ______________________________

G: 내 한국인 친구인 진우가 선물로 엿을 줬어. 한국에서는 이게 어떤 의미니?
B: 시험 잘 보라는 뜻이야.

Listen and Talk 2 B

B: ______________________________
G: ______________________________
B: ______________________________
G: ______________________________
B: ______________________________
G: ______________________________
____
B: ______________________________
G: ______________________________

B: Ling의 생일이 이번 수요일이야, 그렇지 않니?
G: 응. 나는 그녀에게 책을 사 줄 거야. 너는?
B: 음, 나는 우산을 사려고 생각하고 있어. 선물 가게에서 귀여운 걸 찾았거든.
G: 어, 그건 중국 사람들에게 좋은 선물이 아니야. 뭔가 나쁜 걸 뜻하거든.
B: 진짜? 중국에서 우산이 뭘 의미하는데?
G: 이별을 뜻해. 중국에서는 이별을 뜻하는 단어와 우산을 뜻하는 단어의 발음이 같거든.
B: 알겠어. 그러면 초콜릿 어때?
G: 좋은 생각이야.

Listen and Talk 2 C

G: ______________________________
B: ______________________________
G: ______________________________
B: ______________________________
G: ______________________________
B: ______________________________
G: ______________________________
____
B: ______________________________
G: ______________________________

G: 이 사진 정말 멋지다! 네 친구들이니?
B: 응. 우리는 해변에서 이 사진을 찍었어. 정말 재미있었어.
G: 어, 저 남자애 봐. 정말 무례하다.
B: 누구?
G: V사인을 하고 있는 애. 손바닥이 자기 쪽을 향하고 있어.
B: 그게 뭐 잘못됐어?
G: 영국에서는 나쁜 뜻을 갖고 있어. 하지만 손바닥을 보여 주면서 V사인을 만드는 건 괜찮아.
B: 그건 무슨 뜻인데?
G: 승리나 평화를 뜻해.

Do It Yourself A

G: ______________________________
B: ______________________________
G: ______________________________
B: ______________________________
____
G: ______________________________
B: ______________________________
G: ______________________________
____
B: ______________________________

G: 안녕, Santiago! 오늘 여기 어쩐 일이야?
B: Bienvenido, Cathy. 나는 스페인 축제를 보러 왔어.
G: 나도. 그런데 방금 뭐라고 말했니?
B: Bienvenido! 스페인어로 "환영합니다."라는 뜻이야. 저 무용수들을 봐. 그들의 춤 움직임은 정말 멋지다.
G: 응, 그렇네.
B: 전에 스페인 축제에 가 본 적 있니?
G: 아니, 가 본 적 없어. Santiago, 무대에 있는 큰 글씨들 볼 수 있니? 무슨 뜻이야?
B: 아, gracias. 저건 "감사합니다."라는 뜻이야.

※ 다음 우리말과 일치하도록 빈칸에 알맞은 것을 골라 쓰시오.

1 ________ Korean ________
A. symbols B. traditional

2 Peter is ________ Korea ________ meet a friend, Mina, ________ a sister school.
A. from B. to C. visiting

3 Peter is going to ________ ________ her grandfather's house ________ a week.
A. at B. stay C. for

4 When he ________, Mina ________ him the ________ room.
A. guest B. shows C. arrives

5 Peter, you will ________ ________.
A. here B. stay

6 This ________ room is ________ of ________ Korean things.
A. traditional B. full C. guest

7 Look ________ this ________.
A. pillow B. at

8 What ________ these ________?
A. things B. are

9 ________ ________.
A. bats B. they're

10 Bats ________ my ________? That's ________!
A. scary B. pillow C. on

11 Not really. In Korea, bats are ________ of ________ and a long ________.
A. life B. symbols C. luck

12 That's ________. In many Western countries, bats ________ people of ________ and scary things.
A. darkness B. surprising C. remind

13 Mina ________ Peter ________ ________ room.
A. grandfather's B. her C. shows

14 Peter and Mina's grandfather ________ and ________ each ________.
A. other B. greet C. meet

15 Hi, Peter! ________ you ever ________ this ________ of lock before?
A. kind B. seen C. have

16 No, I ________. It's ________ old ________ I can't really tell, but is it a fish?
A. that B. haven't C. so

17 Yes. ________ a long time, Koreans have ________ that fish are good ________.
A. guards B. thought C. for

1 전통적인 한국의 상징물

2 피터는 자매 학교 친구인 미나를 만나기 위해 한국을 방문 중이다.

3 피터는 일주일간 미나네 할아버지 댁에 머무를 것이다.

4 그가 도착하자, 미나가 그에게 손님방을 보여준다.

5 피터, 넌 여기에 머무르게 될 거야.

6 이 손님방은 한국의 전통 물건들로 가득 차 있어.

7 이 베개를 봐.

8 이것들은 뭐야?

9 그건 박쥐들이야.

10 내 베개 위에 박쥐가? 그거 겁나는데!

11 그렇지 않아. 한국에서는 박쥐가 행운과 장수의 상징이거든.

12 그거 놀라운 일인데. 서구의 많은 나라들에서 박쥐는 사람들에게 어둠과 무서운 것들을 상기시키거든.

13 미나는 피터에게 할아버지의 방을 보여준다.

14 피터와 미나의 할아버지가 만나서 서로 인사한다.

15 안녕, 피터! 너는 이런 종류의 자물쇠를 전에 본 적 있니?

16 아니요, 본 적 없어요. 그 자물쇠는 너무 오래되어서 사실 알아볼 수가 없는데, 그건 물고기인가요?

17 맞아. 오랜 세월 동안, 한국인들은 물고기가 훌륭한 파수꾼이라고 생각해 왔단다.

18 Fish don't _______ their eyes, _______ when they _______.
A. sleep B. even C. close

19 _______ _______.
A. interesting B. that's

20 We think fish can watch _______ valuable things. That's _______ this lock looks _______ a fish.
A. like B. why C. over

21 _______ I _______.
A. understand B. now

22 They go _______ and _______ _______ the garden.
A. around B. walk C. outside

23 What is _______ that _______ of paper ? It looks _______.
A. piece B. scary C. on

24 Do you _______ this _______ of a rooster?
A. painting B. mean

25 Oh, is _______ a _______?
A. rooster B. it

26 Yes, it is. Roosters _______ _______ morning.
A. every B. crow

27 Their _______ means _______ a new day is _______.
A. beginning B. that C. crowing

28 For many years, Koreans have believed _______ spirits go _______ when a rooster _______.
A. away B. crows C. evil

29 Really? I've _______ _______ that _______.
A. before B. heard C. never

30 _______, I'm _______ of darkness and evil _______.
A. spirits B. actually C. afraid

31 Could you _______ a rooster _______ me, Mina?
A. for B. draw

32 Sure. I'll _______ a big _______ for you!
A. rooster B. draw

33 _______ the drawing _______ your door. Then it will _______ you.
A. protect B. above C. put

34 _______, I _______.
A. will B. yes

35 I'm enjoying this trip _______ much _______ I want to stay _______.
A. longer B. that C. so

36 I love _______ the _______ Korean symbols _______ this house.
A. in B. traditional C. all

37 Now I _______ a _______ of them.
A. lot B. understand

38 I _______ to _______ Korea again _______ my family.
A. with B. visit C. want

18 물고기는 잘 때도 눈을 감지 않거든.
19 그거 재미있군요.
20 우리는 물고기가 귀중품을 지킬 수 있다고 생각해. 그것이 이 자물쇠가 물고기 모양으로 생긴 이유란다.
21 이제 이해가 되는군요.
22 그들은 밖에 나가서 정원을 걷는다.
23 저 종이에는 무엇이 그려져 있는 거죠? 무서워 보여요.
24 이 수탉 그림을 말하는 거니?
25 오, 그게 수탉이에요?
26 응, 그렇단다. 수탉은 매일 아침 울지.
27 수탉의 울음은 새로운 날이 시작하는 것을 의미해.
28 오랫동안 한국인들은 수탉이 울 때 악령이 물러간다고 믿어 왔단다.
29 정말요? 전 그런 말을 들어본 적이 없어요.
30 사실 전 어둠과 악령을 무서워해요.
31 미나야, 날 위해 수탉을 그려 줄 수 있니?
32 물론이지. 내가 널 위해 커다란 수탉을 그려줄게!
33 그 그림을 네 문 위에 걸어 놓으렴. 그러면 그게 널 지켜 줄 거야.
34 네, 그럴게요.
35 난 이번 여행이 매우 즐거워서 더 오래 머무르고 싶다.
36 난 이 집의 모든 전통적인 한국의 상징물들이 아주 마음에 든다.
37 나는 이제 그것들을 많이 알게 되었다.
38 난 우리 가족과 함께 한국을 다시 방문하고 싶다.

※ 다음 우리말과 일치하도록 빈칸에 알맞은 말을 쓰시오.

1 _______ Korean _______

2 Peter is _______ Korea _______ _______ a friend, Mina, _______ a sister school.

3 Peter is _______ _______ _______ _______ her grandfather's house _______ a week .

4 _______ he _______, Mina shows him the _______ _______.

5 Peter, you _______ _______ _______.

6 This guest room _______ _______ _______ _______ Korean things.

7 _______ _______ this pillow.

8 What are _______ _______?

9 They're _______.

10 _______ _______ my _______? That's _______!

11 Not really. In Korea, bats are _______ _______ _______ and a _______ _______.

12 That's surprising. In many _______ _______, bats _______ people _______ _______ and _______ things.

13 Mina _______ Peter her _______ _______.

14 Peter and Mina's grandfather _______ and _______ _______ _______.

15 Hi, Peter! _______ you ever _______ this _______ _______ _______ before?

16 No, I _______. It's _______ old _______ I _______ really tell, but is it a fish?

17 Yes. _______ _______ _______ _______., Koreans _______ _______ that fish are good guards .

1 전통적인 한국의 상징물

2 피터는 자매 학교 친구인 미나를 만나기 위해 한국을 방문 중이다.

3 피터는 일주일간 미나네 할아버지 댁에 머무를 것이다.

4 그가 도착하자, 미나가 그에게 손님방을 보여준다.

5 피터, 넌 여기에 머무르게 될 거야.

6 이 손님방은 한국의 전통 물건들로 가득 차 있어.

7 이 베개를 봐.

8 이것들은 뭐야?

9 그건 박쥐들이야.

10 내 베개 위에 박쥐가? 그거 겁나는데!

11 그렇지 않아. 한국에서는 박쥐가 행운과 장수의 상징이거든.

12 그거 놀라운 일인데. 서구의 많은 나라들에서 박쥐는 사람들에게 어둠과 무서운 것들을 상기시키거든.

13 미나는 피터에게 할아버지의 방을 보여준다.

14 피터와 미나의 할아버지가 만나서 서로 인사한다.

15 안녕, 피터! 너는 이런 종류의 자물쇠를 전에 본 적 있니?

16 아니요, 본 적 없어요. 그 자물쇠는 너무 오래되어서 사실 알아볼 수가 없는데, 그건 물고기인가요?

17 맞아. 오랜 세월 동안, 한국인들은 물고기가 훌륭한 파수꾼이라고 생각해 왔단다.

18 Fish _______ _______ their eyes , even _______ they _______.

19 That's _______.

20 We think fish can _______ _______ valuable things. That's _______ this lock _______ _______ a fish.

21 _______ I _______.

22 They _______ _______ and _______ _______ the garden.

23 What is _______ _______ _______ of paper? It _______ _______.

24 Do you _______ this painting of a _______?

25 Oh, _______ _______ a rooster?

26 Yes, it is. Roosters _______ _______ _______.

27 Their crowing _______ that a new day is _______.

28 For many years, Koreans _______ _______ evil spirits _______ _______ _______ a rooster _______.

29 Really? I've _______ _______ that _______.

30 _______, I'm _______ _______ darkness and _______ _______.

31 _______ you _______ a rooster _______ me, Mina?

32 Sure. I'll _______ a big rooster _______ you!

33 _______ the drawing _______ your door. Then it _______ _______ you.

34 Yes, I _______.

35 I'm enjoying this trip _______ much _______ I want _______ _______ _______.

36 I love all the _______ _______ _______ in this house.

37 Now I understand _______ _______ _______ them.

38 I _______ _______ _______ Korea again _______ my family.

18 물고기는 잘 때도 눈을 감지 않거든.

19 그거 재미있군요.

20 우리는 물고기가 귀중품을 지킬 수 있다고 생각해. 그것이 이 자물쇠가 물고기 모양으로 생긴 이유란다.

21 이제 이해가 되는군요.

22 그들은 밖에 나가서 정원을 걷는다.

23 저 종이에는 무엇이 그려져 있는 거죠? 무서워 보여요.

24 이 수탉 그림을 말하는 거니?

25 오, 그게 수탉이에요?

26 응, 그렇단다. 수탉은 매일 아침 울지.

27 수탉의 울음은 새로운 날이 시작하는 것을 의미해.

28 오랫동안 한국인들은 수탉이 울 때 악령이 물러간다고 믿어 왔단다.

29 정말요? 전 그런 말을 들어본 적이 없어요.

30 사실 전 어둠과 악령을 무서워해요.

31 미나야, 날 위해 수탉을 그려 줄 수 있니?

32 물론이지. 내가 널 위해 커다란 수탉을 그려줄게!

33 그 그림을 네 문 위에 걸어 놓으렴. 그러면 그게 널 지켜 줄 거야.

34 네, 그럴게요.

35 난 이번 여행이 매우 즐거워서 더 오래 머무르고 싶다.

36 난 이 집의 모든 전통적인 한국의 상징물들이 아주 마음에 든다.

37 나는 이제 그것들을 많이 알게 되었다.

38 난 우리 가족과 함께 한국을 다시 방문하고 싶다.

본문 Test

Step3

※ 다음 문장을 우리말로 쓰시오.

1 Traditional Korean Symbols

➡ ______________________________

2 Peter is visiting Korea to meet a friend, Mina, from a sister school.

➡ ______________________________

3 Peter is going to stay at her grandfather's house for a week.

➡ ______________________________

4 When he arrives, Mina shows him the guest room.

➡ ______________________________

5 Peter, you will stay here.

➡ ______________________________

6 This guest room is full of traditional Korean things.

➡ ______________________________

7 Look at this pillow.

➡ ______________________________

8 What are these things?

➡ ______________________________

9 They're bats.

➡ ______________________________

10 Bats on my pillow? That's scary!

➡ ______________________________

11 Not really. In Korea, bats are symbols of luck and a long life.

➡ ______________________________

12 That's surprising. In many Western countries, bats remind people of darkness and scary things.

➡ ______________________________

13 Mina shows Peter her grandfather's room.

➡ ______________________________

14 Peter and Mina's grandfather meet and greet each other.

➡ ______________________________

15 Hi, Peter! Have you ever seen this kind of lock before?

➡ ______________________________

16 No, I haven't. It's so old that I can't really tell, but is it a fish?

➡ ______________________________

17 Yes. For a long time, Koreans have thought that fish are good guards.

➡ ______________________________

18 Fish don't close their eyes, even when they sleep.
➡ ______

19 That's interesting.
➡ ______

20 We think fish can watch over valuable things. That's why this lock looks like a fish.
➡ ______

21 Now I understand
➡ ______

22 They go outside and walk around the garden.
➡ ______

23 What is on that piece of paper? It looks scary.
➡ ______

24 Do you mean this painting of a rooster?
➡ ______

25 Oh, is it a rooster?
➡ ______

26 Yes, it is. Roosters crow every morning.
➡ ______

27 Their crowing means that a new day is beginning.
➡ ______

28 For many years, Koreans have believed evil spirits go away when a rooster crows.
➡ ______

29 Really? I've never heard that before.
➡ ______

30 Actually, I'm afraid of darkness and evil spirits.
➡ ______

31 Could you draw a rooster for me, Mina?
➡ ______

32 Sure. I'll draw a big rooster for you!
➡ ______

33 Put the drawing above your door. Then it will protect you.
➡ ______

34 Yes, I will.
➡ ______

35 I'm enjoying this trip so much that I want to stay longer.
➡ ______

36 I love all the traditional Korean symbols in this house.
➡ ______

37 Now I understand a lot of them.
➡ ______

38 I want to visit Korea again with my family.
➡ ______

본문 Test

Step4

※ 다음 괄호 안의 단어들을 우리말에 맞도록 바르게 배열하시오.

1 (Symbols / Korean / Traditional)
➡ ____________________

2 (is / Peter / Korea / visiting / meet / to / friend, / a / Mina, / school. / a / from / sister)
➡ ____________________

3 (is / to / going / at / Peter / stay / grandfather's / her / house / week. / a / for)
➡ ____________________

4 (arrives, / he / when / Mina / the / shows / room. / him / guest)
➡ ____________________

5 (you / Peter, / here / will / stay)
➡ ____________________

6 (is / guest / this / room / of / full / things. / Korean / traditional)
➡ ____________________

7 (look / this / at / pillow.)
➡ ____________________

8 (are / things? / these / what)
➡ ____________________

9 (bats. / they're)
➡ ____________________

10 (my / bats / pillow? / on // scary! / that's)
➡ ____________________

11 (really. / not // Korea, / in / are / bats / of / symbols / luck / and / life. / long / a)
➡ ____________________

12 (surprising. / that's // many / countries, / in / Western / remind / bats / of / darkness / people / things. / and / scary)
➡ ____________________
____

13 (Peter / shows / Mina / room. / grandfather's / her)
➡ ____________________

14 (Mina's / and / Peter / grandfather / greet / and / other. / meet / each)
➡ ____________________

15 (Peter! / Hi, // you / have / seen / ever / this / lock / before? / of / kind)
➡ ____________________

16 (haven't. / no, / I // it's / that / old / so / I / really / can't / tell, / but / fish? / a / it / is)
➡ ____________________

17 (yes. // a / time, / for / long / Koreans / thought / have / that / are / guards. / good / fish)
➡ ____________________

1 전통적인 한국의 상징물

2 피터는 자매 학교 친구인 미나를 만나기 위해 한국을 방문 중이다.

3 피터는 일주일간 미나네 할아버지 댁에 머무를 것이다.

4 그가 도착하자, 미나가 그에게 손님방을 보여준다.

5 피터, 넌 여기에 머무르게 될 거야.

6 이 손님방은 한국의 전통 물건들로 가득 차 있어.

7 이 베개를 봐.

8 이것들은 뭐야?

9 그건 박쥐들이야.

10 내 베개 위에 박쥐가? 그거 겁나는데!

11 그렇지 않아. 한국에서는 박쥐가 행운과 장수의 상징이거든.

12 그거 놀라운 일인데. 서구의 많은 나라들에서 박쥐는 사람들에게 어둠과 무서운 것들을 상기시키거든.

13 미나는 피터에게 할아버지의 방을 보여준다.

14 피터와 미나의 할아버지가 만나서 서로 인사한다.

15 안녕, 피터! 너는 이런 종류의 자물쇠를 전에 본 적 있니?

16 아니요, 본 적 없어요. 그 자물쇠는 너무 오래되어서 사실 알아볼 수가 없는데, 그건 물고기인가요?

17 맞아. 오랜 세월 동안, 한국인들은 물고기가 훌륭한 파수꾼이라고 생각해 왔단다.

18 (don't / fish / eyes, / their / close / even / sleep. / they / when)
➡ ______________________________

19 (interesting. / that's)
➡ ______________________________

20 (we / fish / can / think / over / watch / things. / valuable // that's / this / why / lock / a / fish. / like / looks)
➡ ______________________________
____

21 (understand. / I / now)
➡ ______________________________

22 (outside / go / they / and / around / garden. / the / walk)
➡ ______________________________

23 (is / what / that / on / paper? / of / piece // scary. / looks / it)
➡ ______________________________

24 (mean / you / do / painting / this / rooster? / a / of)
➡ ______________________________

25 (it / is / oh, / rooster? / a)
➡ ______________________________

26 (is. / it / yes, / roosters / morning. / every / crow)
➡ ______________________________

27 (crowing / their / means / that / a / beginning. / is / day / new)
➡ ______________________________

28 (years, / many / for / Koreans / believed / have / spirits / evil / away / when / go / crows. / rooster / a)
➡ ______________________________
____

29 (really? / never / I've / heard / before. / that)
➡ ______________________________

30 (actually, / I'm / darkness / of / afraid / and / spirits. / evil)
➡ ______________________________

31 (you / rooster / could / a / draw / Mina? / me, / for)
➡ ______________________________

32 (sure. // draw / I'll / big / for / a / rooster / you!)
➡ ______________________________

33 (the / put / above / drawing / door. / your // then / will / you. / it / protect)
➡ ______________________________

34 (will. / I / yes,)
➡ ______________________________

35 (I'm / this / enjoying / trip / much / so / that / longer. / I / stay / to / want)
➡ ______________________________

36 (all / love / I / the / Korean / traditional / symbols / house. / in / this)
➡ ______________________________

37 (I / now / understand / a / them. / of / lot)
➡ ______________________________

38 (I / visit / to / want / again / Korea / family. / my / with)
➡ ______________________________

18 물고기는 잘 때도 눈을 감지 않거든.
19 그거 재미있군요.
20 우리는 물고기가 귀중품을 지킬 수 있다고 생각해. 그것이 이 자물쇠가 물고기 모양으로 생긴 이유란다.
21 이제 이해가 되는군요.
22 그들은 밖에 나가서 정원을 걷는다.
23 저 종이에는 무엇이 그려져 있는 거죠? 무서워 보여요.
24 이 수탉 그림을 말하는 거니?
25 오, 그게 수탉이에요?
26 응, 그렇단다. 수탉은 매일 아침 울지.
27 수탉의 울음은 새로운 날이 시작하는 것을 의미해.
28 오랫동안 한국인들은 수탉이 울 때 악령이 물러간다고 믿어 왔단다.
29 정말요? 전 그런 말을 들어본 적이 없어요.
30 사실 전 어둠과 악령을 무서워해요.
31 미나야, 날 위해 수탉을 그려 줄 수 있니?
32 물론이지. 내가 널 위해 커다란 수탉을 그려줄게!
33 그 그림을 네 문 위에 걸어 놓으렴. 그러면 그게 널 지켜 줄 거야.
34 네, 그럴게요.
35 난 이번 여행이 매우 즐거워서 더 오래 머무르고 싶다.
36 난 이 집의 모든 전통적인 한국의 상징물들이 아주 마음에 든다.
37 나는 이제 그것들을 많이 알게 되었다.
38 난 우리 가족과 함께 한국을 다시 방문하고 싶다.

※ 다음 우리말을 영어로 쓰시오.

1 전통적인 한국의 상징물
➡ ______

2 피터는 자매 학교 친구인 미나를 만나기 위해 한국을 방문 중이다.
➡ ______

3 피터는 일주일간 미나네 할아버지 댁에 머무를 것이다.
➡ ______

4 그가 도착하자, 미나가 그에게 손님방을 보여준다.
➡ ______

5 피터, 넌 여기에 머무르게 될 거야.
➡ ______

6 이 손님방은 한국의 전통 물건들로 가득 차 있어.
➡ ______

7 이 베개를 봐.
➡ ______

8 이것들은 뭐야?
➡ ______

9 그건 박쥐들이야.
➡ ______

10 내 베개 위에 박쥐가? 그거 겁나는데!
➡ ______

11 그렇지 않아. 한국에서는 박쥐가 행운과 장수의 상징이거든.
➡ ______

12 그거 놀라운 일인데. 서구의 많은 나라들에서 박쥐는 사람들에게 어둠과 무서운 것들을 상기시키거든.
➡ ______

13 미나는 피터에게 할아버지의 방을 보여준다.
➡ ______

14 피터와 미나의 할아버지가 만나서 서로 인사한다.
➡ ______

15 안녕, 피터! 너는 이런 종류의 자물쇠를 전에 본 적 있니?
➡ ______

16 아니요, 본 적 없어요. 그 자물쇠는 너무 오래되어서 사실 알아볼 수가 없는데, 그건 물고기인가요?
➡ ______

17 맞아. 오랜 세월 동안, 한국인들은 물고기가 훌륭한 파수꾼이라고 생각해 왔단다.
➡ ______

18 물고기는 잘 때도 눈을 감지 않거든.
➡ ____________________

19 그거 재미있군요.
➡ ____________________

20 우리는 물고기가 귀중품을 지킬 수 있다고 생각해. 그것이 이 자물쇠가 물고기 모양으로 생긴 이유란다.
➡ ____________________

21 이제 이해가 되는군요.
➡ ____________________

22 그들은 밖에 나가서 정원을 걷는다.
➡ ____________________

23 저 종이에는 무엇이 그려져 있는 거죠? 무서워 보여요.
➡ ____________________

24 이 수탉 그림을 말하는 거니?
➡ ____________________

25 오, 그게 수탉이에요?
➡ ____________________

26 응, 그렇단다. 수탉은 매일 아침 울지.
➡ ____________________

27 수탉의 울음은 새로운 날이 시작하는 것을 의미해.
➡ ____________________

28 오랫동안 한국인들은 수탉이 울 때 악령이 물러간다고 믿어 왔단다.
➡ ____________________

29 정말요? 전 그런 말을 들어본 적이 없어요.
➡ ____________________

30 사실 전 어둠과 악령을 무서워해요.
➡ ____________________

31 미나야, 날 위해 수탉을 그려 줄 수 있니?
➡ ____________________

32 물론이지. 내가 널 위해 커다란 수탉을 그려줄게!
➡ ____________________

33 그 그림을 네 문 위에 걸어 놓으렴. 그러면 그게 널 지켜 줄 거야.
➡ ____________________

34 네, 그럴게요.
➡ ____________________

35 난 이번 여행이 매우 즐거워서 더 오래 머무르고 싶다.
➡ ____________________

36 난 이 집의 모든 전통적인 한국의 상징물들이 아주 마음에 든다.
➡ ____________________

37 나는 이제 그것들을 많이 알게 되었다.
➡ ____________________

38 난 우리 가족과 함께 한국을 다시 방문하고 싶다.
➡ ____________________

※ 다음 우리말과 일치하도록 빈칸에 알맞은 말을 쓰시오.

Think and Write

1. Do you know about ________ ________ ________?
2. ________ ________ many kinds.
3. ________ ________, there ________ a lion dance, a ________ dance, and an umbrella dance.
4. ________ ________ the most famous ________ ________ the lion dance.
5. In this dance, two dancers ________ and ________ ________ lions.
6. They ________ dance ________ special days, ________ ________ New Year's Day.
7. I think their ________ ________ are ________.
8. I hope ________ ________ this dance ________.

1. 당신은 전통적인 중국 춤에 대해 아는가?
2. 많은 종류들이 있다.
3. 예를 들면, 사자춤, 부채춤, 그리고 우산 춤이 있다.
4. 가장 유명한 춤들 중의 하나가 사자춤이다.
5. 이 춤에서, 두 명의 댄서들이 사자처럼 옷을 입고 행동한다.
6. 사람들은 사자춤을 대개 설날과 같은 특별한 날에 춘다.
7. 나는 그들의 춤 동작들이 멋지다고 생각한다.
8. 나는 언젠가 이 춤을 연습하기를 바란다.

Presentation Time

1. Do you want to ________ ________ ________ ________ in Korea?
2. Then ________ these steps.
3. First, please ________ ________ your shoes ________ you ________ ________ people's homes.
4. Next, ________ when you greet ________.
5. Also, use two hands when you ________ ________ ________ ________ ________.
6. And do not ________ ________ ________ at the table and do not ________ ________ people.
7. ________, do not ________ older people ________ their ________ ________.

1. 한국에서 즐거운 시간을 보내고 싶은가요?
2. 그러면 다음 단계를 따르세요.
3. 먼저 사람들의 집에 들어갈 때는 신발을 벗으세요.
4. 다음에 다른 사람들에게 인사할 때 절을 하세요.
5. 또한 나이가 많은 사람들에게 무언가를 줄 때는 두 손을 사용하세요.
6. 그리고 식탁에서 코를 풀지 말고 사람들을 가리키지 마세요.
7. 마지막으로 나이가 많은 사람들을 이름으로 부르지 마세요.

구석구석 지문 Test

Step2

※ 다음 우리말을 영어로 쓰시오.

Think and Write

1. 당신은 전통적인 중국 춤에 대해 아는가?
➡ ______
2. 많은 종류들이 있다.
➡ ______
3. 예를 들면, 사자춤, 부채춤, 그리고 우산 춤이 있다.
➡ ______
4. 가장 유명한 춤들 중의 하나가 사자춤이다.
➡ ______
5. 이 춤에서, 두 명의 댄서들이 사자처럼 옷을 입고 행동한다.
➡ ______
6. 사람들은 사자춤을 대개 설날과 같은 특별한 날에 춘다.
➡ ______
7. 나는 그들의 춤 동작들이 멋지다고 생각한다.
➡ ______
8. 나는 언젠가 이 춤을 연습하기를 바란다.
➡ ______

Presentation Time

1. 한국에서 즐거운 시간을 보내고 싶은가요?
➡ ______
2. 그러면 다음 단계를 따르세요.
➡ ______
3. 먼저 사람들의 집에 들어갈 때는 신발을 벗으세요.
➡ ______
4. 다음에 다른 사람들에게 인사할 때 절을 하세요.
➡ ______
5. 또한 나이가 많은 사람들에게 무언가를 줄 때는 두 손을 사용하세요.
➡ ______
6. 그리고 식탁에서 코를 풀지 말고 사람들을 가리키지 마세요.
➡ ______
7. 마지막으로 나이가 많은 사람들을 이름으로 부르지 마세요.
➡ ______

MEMO

MEMO

영어 기출 문제집

적중100

1학기

정답 및 해설

능률 | 김성곤

중2

적중100

영어 기출 문제집

적중100

1학기

정답 및 해설

능률 | 김성곤

중2

적중100

Lesson 1

Express Yourself

시험대비 실력평가 p.08

01 impossible 02 ⑤ 03 ① 04 ③
05 ② 06 ③ 07 ② 08 ②
09 (1) displayed (2) hurt (3) share (4) understand

01 주어진 단어는 반의어 관계이다. perfect: 완벽한 imperfect: 불완전한 possible: 가능한 impossible: 불가능한
02 break: (법률·약속 등을) 어기다 / 그들은 어린 아이들을 고용함으로써 법률을 어기고 있다.
03 impossible: 불가능한 / 시끄러운 소음이 잠을 불가능하게 만들었다.
04 like: ~을 좋아하다 just like: 꼭 ~와 같이
05 incorrect: 틀린, 정확하지 않은 / 당신이 우리에게 준 정보는 사실이 아니었다.
06 ③ borrow: 빌리다
07 post: 올리다, 게시하다 / 다른 사람들이 볼 수 있도록 인터넷에 컴퓨터 기록이나 메시지를 올리다
08 healthy: 건강에 좋은 / 너의 몸에 좋은
09 (1) display: (작품을) 전시하다, 보여주다 (2) hurt: 다치다, 해치다 (3) share: 공유하다 (4) understand: 이해하다

서술형 시험대비 p.09

01 (1) (r)ude (2) public (3) result
02 out
03 (1) interesting (2) carefully (3) perfect (4) impossible
04 (1) always, (n)ervous
(2) probably, best
05 (1) Is it OK if I bring some friends to the party?
(2) Could you copy this letter and send it out?
(3) Their last concert was really awesome.
06 (c)omment / (e)tiquette / (r)esult
(1) result (2) etiquette (3) comments

01 (1) 반의어 관계, polite: 공손한 rude: 무례한 (2) 반의어 관계, stupid: 멍청한 smart: 똑똑한 private: 사적인 public: 공공의 (3) 동의어 관계, reason: 이유 cause: 원인 consequence: 결과 result: 결과
02 check out: 확인하다 find out: 발견하다, 찾아보다
03 (1) interesting: 흥미로운, 재미있는 (2) carefully: 신중하게, 조심스럽게 (3) perfect: 완벽한 (4) impossible: 불가능한
04 (1) always: 항상 nervous: 긴장되는, 불안해 하는 (2) probably: 아마도 best: 최고의
06 (1) result: 결과 (2) etiquette: 에티켓, 예절 (3) comment: 의견, 논평

교과서

Conversation

핵심 Check p.10~11

1 What, interested / I'm, interested
2 (1) Are you interested in animals / I'm interested in plants (2) What subject are you interested in
3 (1) Is it, if, borrow (2) I, on / afraid
4 I'm wondering if I can share your umbrella

교과서 대화문 익히기

Check(√) True or False p.12

(1) T (2) F (3) T (4) T

교과서 확인학습 p.14~15

Listen & Talk 1 A
posters, What / in cooking / in photography
Listen & Talk 1 B
What, going to do / I'm going, with / Are, in / because / what are you / more interested, go to / someday
Listen & Talk 1 C
What show / what are you interested in / I'm interested in / about watching / a big fan of / don't you
Listen & Talk 1 D
What, in / I'm / interested in, social media / We, both
Listen & Talk 2 A
bring / Yes, you may / in the carrier
Listen & Talk 2 B
go / Let, see / record / may not / take / No, you may not, in front of

Listen & Talk 2 C

can I / borrow / may not, take / copy / may, share / won't

Let's communicate 1

What are / I'm interested / Why / May I

Do It Yourself A

doing / presentation, interests / are you interested / I'm interested in / I'm interested in / ask, for some advice

시험대비 기본평가 p.16

01 ④ 02 ③ 03 ③

01 ④ '당신은 여기서 사진을 찍어 줄 수 있습니까?'라는 질문이므로 주어진 문장과 다른 의미이다.

02 새로운 과학책을 빌려도 되느냐는 물음에 새 책은 집으로 가져갈 수 없다는 대답을 했으므로, 빈칸에는 허락 요청에 대한 거절의 대답이 나와야 한다.

03 무엇에 관심이 있는지 묻는 질문에, 축구에 관심이 있다고 대답한다. 축구장에 가는 것을 권유하자, 애완동물을 축구장에 데려갈 수 있는지 허락 여부를 묻고, 된다고 상대방이 대답을 한다. be interested in: ~에 관심[흥미]이 있다 Why don't you ~?: ~하는 게 어때?(권유)

시험대비 실력평가 p.17~18

01 ④ 02 ⑤ 03 ③ 04 ①
05 ② 06 some pages from the new book
07 ⑤ will → won't/will not 08 ③ 09 May I feed the birds there? 10 ② 11 ①
12 ⓐ interest → interests 13 are interested, photography, will, presentation, tomorrow, for advice, her presentation

01 대중음악 방송을 볼 것을 권유하는 말에, 대중음악이 아닌 랩을 좋아한다는 대답을 하는 것이 적절하다.

02 (A) 이후에 언급된 음악 방송이나 남자아이가 랩을 좋아한다는 말을 볼 때, 음악에 흥미있다는 말이 어울린다. science: 과학 art: 미술, 예술 movie: 영화 music: 음악

03 ③ The Friday Pop Music Show는 랩이 아니라 pop 음악(대중음악)과 관련이 있다.

04 책을 빌릴 수 있는지와 복사를 할 수 있는지 묻고 있으므로, 도서관에서 이루어지는 대화이다. ① library: 도서관 ② theater: 극장 ③ hospital: 병원 ④ classroom: 교실 ⑤ concert hall: 콘서트 홀, 연주회장

05 학생들이 새 책을 집에 가져갈 수 없다고 했으므로, 책을 빌려갈 수 있는지 허락을 묻는 질문에 부정의 대답이 나와야 한다.

06 them이 가리키는 것은 새로운 책의 몇 페이지를 의미한다.

07 공유하지 말라는 말에, 공유할 거라고 대답하는 것은 어색하다.

08 동물에 관심이 있는 상대방에게 가라고 권유할 수 있는 장소이자, 새에게 먹이를 줄 수 있는 장소는 동물원이다. (an art museum→ a zoo) animal: 동물 museum: 박물관

09 May I 동사원형 ~?: 제가 ~해도 될까요? feed: 먹이를 주다

10 앉아도 좋다는 승낙의 대답을 한 후 임자가 있다는 말이 이어지는 것은 어색하다.

11 주어진 문장은 무엇을 하고 있는지에 대한 대답이 될 수 있다. 또한 다음 문장의 'It is about one of my interests.'에서 It이 주어진 문장의 tomorrow's presentation을 지칭하므로 ①의 자리에 들어가야 알맞다.

12 one of 복수명사: ~ 중의 하나 interest: 관심사, 흥미

13 both: 둘 다 be interested in: ~에 관심[흥미]이 있다 photography: 사진 ask for advice: 충고를 구하다

서술형 시험대비 p.19

01 (A) What (B) what
02 Are you interested in baseball?
03 ⑤ less → more 04 bring 05 Yes, you may. 06 (D) – (B) – (A) – (C) 07 ④ talk → will talk, ⑤ advise → advice

01 be going to 동사원형: ~할 예정이다 this weekend: 이번 주말에 What are you going to do?: 너는 무엇을 할 예정[계획]이니? be interested in: ~에 관심[흥미]이 있다 What are you interested in?: 너는 무엇에 관심이 있니?

02 be동사가 있는 의문문은 주어와 be동사의 위치를 바꾸어 만들 수 있다.

03 무엇에 관심이 있는지 묻는 질문에, 언젠가 축구 경기를 보러 가고 싶다는 말이 나왔으므로, 축구에 관심이 있다는 것을 유추할 수 있다. 그러므로 축구에 덜 관심 있다는 말보다 더 관심이 있다는 말이 어울린다.

04 어떤 것이나 사람을 지금 있는 장소나 말하는 장소로 가져오거나 데려오다 / bring: 데려오다

05 접속사 But 이후에 캐리어 안에 넣어야 한다는 내용이 나오는 것으로 보아, 버스에 데리고 탈 수는 있지만, 캐리어에 넣어야 하는 것을 알 수 있다.

06 (D) 무엇에 관심을 가지는지 묻자, (B) 음악에 관심이 있다고 대답한다. (A) 팝음악방송을 보는 것을 권유하자 (C) 팝보다 랩

을 좋아한다고 대답한다.

07 ④ 내일 말하는 것이므로 미래시제나 'be going to/be planning to+동사원형'을 사용해야 한다. ⑤ advise: 충고하다 advice: 충고

교과서

Grammar

핵심 Check

p.20~21

1 (1) Taking (2) reading
2 Make → Making
3 (1) nervous (2) sad (3) interesting
4 look → look like

시험대비 기본평가

p.22

01 (1) Walk → Walking[To walk] (2) are → is (3) sweetly → sweet (4) a star → like a star
02 ③ 03 ④ 04 ②

01 (1) 주어가 없으므로 동명사나 to부정사가 주어가 되도록 해야 한다. (2) 동명사 주어는 단수 취급한다. (3) 감각동사는 형용사를 보어로 취한다. 부사를 쓰지 않으므로 주의해야 한다. (4) 감각동사 뒤에 보어로 명사가 올 때는 명사 앞에 like를 쓴다.

02 동명사가 문장의 주어가 되도록 해야 한다.

03 동명사 주어는 단수 취급한다.

04 감각동사는 형용사를 보어로 취한다. rough는 형용사이다.

시험대비 실력평가

p.23~25

01 ④ 02 ⑤ 03 (1) excited (2) like a princess (3) Growing (4) exercising 04 ②
05 ① 06 ③, ④ 07 (1) How about watching the Olympic Games on TV? (2) Her song sounds beautiful. 08 ② 09 Playing soccer
10 ② 11 ① 12 like 13 ④
14 ③ 15 (1) playing (2) Smiling (3) writing (4) going 16 ⑤ 17 ④ 18 ①
19 (1) playing (2) Having[To have] (3) seeing[to see] (4) swinging 20 ③ 21 (1) Solving math problems is interesting. (2) Lisa is good at solving difficult math problems. (3) Strawberry candy tastes sweet. (4) You look like a totally new person in that suit.

01 ④번은 과거진행형을 만드는 현재분사이고, 나머지는 모두 동명사이다.

02 감각동사는 형용사를 보어로 취한다.

03 (1) 감각동사 다음에는 형용사가 나와야 한다. (2) 감각동사 뒤에 보어로 명사가 올 때는 명사 앞에 like를 쓴다. (3) 동명사가 주어가 되도록 해야 한다. (4) 전치사의 목적어로 동명사가 적절하다. 목적어 Teakwondo가 뒤에 있으므로 exercise를 명사로 생각하면 안 된다.

04 형용사를 보어로 취할 수 있는 감각동사 looked가 적절하다.

05 ① is의 보어로 동명사 practicing이나 to practice가 적절하다. practice에 명사도 있으므로 보어로 적절하다고 생각할 수 있으나 뒤에 drawing이 목적어로 나와 있으므로 단순히 명사 보어로 생각하면 안 된다.

06 동명사 swimming을 목적어로 가질 수 있는 동사로 enjoy와 practice가 적절하다.

07 (1) 전치사의 목적어로 동명사가 적절하다. (2) 감각동사의 보어로 형용사가 적절하다.

08 감각동사 다음에 보어가 형용사로 와야 한다.

09 동명사가 문장의 주어가 되도록 해야 한다.

10 Kenneth agreed to practice playing the piano every day. ③ Erica couldn't finish doing the dishes. ④ Do you mind coming here? ⑤ Harry gave up going to the concert on account of a bad cold.

11 감각동사 다음에는 형용사가 나와야 한다.

12 감각동사 다음에 명사가 나올 때는 "감각동사+like+명사'로 쓴다.

13 stop의 목적어로 동명사가 적절하다. to부정사가 오면 '~하기 위해서 멈추다'라는 뜻이 된다.

14 감각동사 다음에 보어로 형용사가 나와야 한다.

15 (1) give up의 목적어로 동명사, (2) 동명사 또는 to부정사로 문장의 주어, (3) finish의 목적보어로 동명사, (4) 전치사의 목적어로 동명사가 적절하다.

16 ⑤ 감각동사 다음에는 형용사가 나와야 한다.

17 <보기>와 ④번은 동사의 목적어로 쓰였다. ① 주어로 쓰인 동명사, ② 보어로 쓰인 동명사, ③ 진행형을 만드는 현재분사, ⑤ 전치사의 목적어로 쓰인 동명사

18 문장의 의미에 맞는 감각동사를 선택한다.

19 (1) practice는 동명사를 목적어로 취한다. (2) 동명사나 to부정사가 주어가 되도록 해야 한다. (3) 동명사나 to부정사가 보어가 되도록 해야 한다. (4) 동명사가 전치사의 목적어가 되도록 해야 한다.

20 ③ The cake was very cold and hard, so it felt like a rock. '감각 동사+like+명사'

21 (1) 동명사 주어는 단수 취급한다. (2) 전치사의 목적어로 동명사가 적절하다. (3) 감각동사는 형용사를 보어로 취한다. (4) 감각동사 뒤에 보어로 명사가 올 때는 명사 앞에 like를 쓴다.

서술형 시험대비 p.19

01 (1) doing (2) Having[To have] (3) reading (4) inviting
02 (1) Playing, fun
(2) Being, difficult
(3) Sleeping, happy
(4) Not eating, healthy
(5) Working, tired
03 (1) tasted delicious
(2) felt tired
(3) looked happy
(4) smelled nice
(5) sounded upset
04 tasted delicious
05 (1) I am interested in studying art history.
(2) I enjoy bike riding when I have free time.
06 cooking, famous
07 looked like a good
08 (1) Learning
(2) Swimming, is not easy.
(3) playing
(4) cooking
(5) taking care of
09 (1) Grandmother's story sounded really interesting.
(2) Judy didn't like the food. She said the food tasted very bitter.
(3) The meat we had at the restaurant didn't taste like beef.
(4) Watching[To watch] action movies is exciting.
(5) Keeping[To keep] early hours is good for the health.
10 (1) nervous
(2) beautiful
(3) listening, Listening
(4) eating, Eating
11 Cooking looks interesting.

01 (1) suggest의 목적어로 동명사, (2) Having 또는 To have로 문장의 주어, (3) 전치사의 목적어로 동명사, (4) 전치사의 목적어로 동명사가 적절하다.
02 동명사가 주어가 되도록 하고 동명사의 부정은 'not+동명사'로 나타낸다. make의 목적격보어로 부사가 아닌 형용사가 쓰인다.
03 감각동사 다음에는 형용사가 와야 한다. 시제에 주의하여 작성한다.
04 smelled great, looked tasty 등 어법에 맞게 '감각동사+형용사'로 쓰면 정답.
05 전치사와 동사 enjoy의 목적어로 동명사를 써서 어법에 맞게 작성하면 정답.
06 동명사가 loves의 목적어가 되도록 해야 하고, looks의 보어로 형용사가 적절하다.
07 감각동사 뒤에 보어로 명사가 올 때는 명사 앞에 like를 써야 한다.
08 동명사가 문장의 주어, 보어, 목적어 또는 전치사의 목적어가 되도록 해야 한다.
09 (1), (2) 감각동사의 보어로 형용사가 적절하다. (3) 감각동사 뒤에 보어로 명사가 올 때는 명사 앞에 like를 쓴다. (4), (5) 주어가 없으므로 동명사나 to부정사가 주어가 되도록 해야 하며 동명사나 to부정사 주어는 단수 취급한다.
10 (1), (2) 감각동사는 형용사를 보어로 취한다. (3), (4) 동명사가 주어나 목적어가 되도록 한다. nerve(명): 신경, nervous(형): 불안해[초조해/두려워] 하는
11 동명사가 주어가 되도록 하고 감각동사의 보어로 형용사를 쓴다.

교과서

Reading

확인문제 p.28

1 F 2 T 3 T 4 F 5 F

확인문제 p.29

1 T 2 T 3 F 4 T

교과서 확인학습 A p.30~31

01 About 02 Facts 03 Are, interested in 04 to post selfies, how much 05 Here are 06 took the world's first selfie 07 became a new word 08 took the first space selfie 09 Survey 10 Taking selfies, of daily life 11 To find out 12 from ages 14 to 16 13 Let's look at 14 90 percent of the girls, take selfies 15 Also, they use filters. 16 take selfies at school 17 some of the students' comments 18 awesome 19 Making silly faces 20 taking selfies, doing it 21 look good 22 don't look like me 23 Etiquette 24 follow etiquette for 25 Ask yourself, before 26 am I 27 appropriate places 28 Don't take selfies

29 bother 30 see this 31 Keep in mind 32 Choose carefully 33 What kinds of, leave 34 Leave, comments on 35 be rude, sounds easy, doesn't it 36 have fun with

교과서 p.32~33

1 All About Selfies!
2 Selfie Facts
3 Are you interested in selfies?
4 You probably like to post selfies on social media, but how much do you know about selfies?
5 Here are some interesting facts.
6 Robert Cornelius took the world's first selfie in 1839.
7 Selfie became a new word in the dictionary in 2013.
8 Buzz Aldrin took the first space selfie in 1966.
9 Selfie Survey
10 Taking selfies is part of daily life for many teens, but do teens really enjoy it?
11 To find out, we did a survey.
12 We asked three questions to 300 students from ages 14 to 16.
13 Let's look at the results.
14 Surprisingly, 90 percent of the girls take selfies, but only 15 percent of the boys take selfies.
15 Also, 93 percent of these students said that they use filters.
16 The survey also showed that the students take selfies at school the most.
17 Check out some of the students' comments.
18 Lewis, 14, England Selfies are awesome.
19 Making silly faces is really fun!
20 Minwoo, 16, Korea I enjoy taking selfies, but some students spend too much time doing it.
21 Kate, 15, Denmark My pictures look good when I use filters.
22 But sometimes my selfies don't look like me.
23 Selfie Etiquette
24 You should follow etiquette for selfies.
25 Ask yourself these questions before you take, post, or look at selfies.
26 Where am I?
27 Choose appropriate places to take selfies.
28 Don't take selfies in hospitals or public restrooms.
29 It may bother other people.
30 Who can see this?
31 Keep in mind that anyone can see your selfies.
32 Choose carefully when you post them.
33 What kinds of comments should I leave?
34 Leave nice comments on other people's selfies.
35 Don't be rude. That sounds easy, doesn't it?
36 Follow these tips and have fun with your selfies.

시험대비 실력평가 p.34~39

01 (A) interested (B) are (C) interesting 02 ④ 03 ② 04 ③ 05 **우리는 14세부터 16세 사이의 300명의 학생들에게 세 가지 질문을 물어보았다.** 06 ④ 07 (1) Where am I? (2) Who can see this? (3) What kinds of comments should I leave? 08 ③ 09 no one → anyone 10 ①, ④ 11 how much do you know about selfies? 12 Buzz Aldrin 13 ④ 14 ② 15 ⑤ 16 she uses filters 17 (A) Where am I? (B) them (C) easy 18 ②, ⑤ 19 ⑤ 20 the results of the selfie survey 21 ④ 22 ③

01 (A) 감정을 나타내는 동사는 사람을 수식할 때는 과거분사로 써야 하므로 interested가 적절하다. (B) 주어가 복수(facts)이므로 are가 적절하다. (C) 감정을 나타내는 동사는 사물을 수식할 때는 현재분사로 써야 하므로 interesting이 적절하다.
02 위 글은 셀피에 관한 몇 가지 재미있는 사실들을 소개하는 글이므로, 제목으로는 ④번 'Selfie Facts'가 적절하다.
03 ② 너는 아마 소셜 미디어에 셀피를 게시하는 것을 좋아할지도 모른다고 쓰여 있지만, '소셜 미디어에 셀피를 게시하려고 셀피를 찍는다.'고는 언급되어 있지 않다.
04 ⓐ와 ③은 동명사, 나머지는 모두 현재분사이다.
05 from ages 14 to 16: '14세부터 16세 사이'
06 ④ 학생들이 두 번째로 셀피를 많이 찍는 장소는 '집'이다.
07 뒤에 나오는 질문들을 쓰면 된다.
08 ⓑ와 ③은 형용사적 용법, ① 부사적 용법(원인), ② 부사적 용법(이유), ④ 명사적 용법, ⑤ 부사적 용법(결과)
09 셀피를 찍거나 게시하거나 보기 전에 '누구나' 너의 셀피를 볼 수 있다는 것을 명심해야 한다고 해야 하므로, no one을 anyone으로 고치는 것이 적절하다.
10 ⓐ와 ①, ④ 아마, ② 실제로, ③ 정확히, ⑤ 완전히
11 how를 보충하면 된다.
12 최초의 우주 셀피를 찍은 사람은 '버즈 올드린'이다.
13 ④ 학생들이 왜 학교에서 셀피를 찍는 것을 좋아하는지는 대답할 수 없다. ① 90 percent. ② 279 students. (300명 중에서

93퍼센트가 필터를 사용한다.) ③ 35 percent. ⑤ At home.

14 ②는 형용사적 용법이고 ⓐ와 나머지는 모두 부사적 용법이다. ⓐ 부사적 용법(목적), ① 부사적 용법(목적), ③ 부사적 용법(목적), ④ 부사적 용법(형용사 수식), ⑤ 부사적 용법(이유)

15 ⑤ awesome: 경탄할 만한, 어마어마한, 엄청난, ① 끔찍한, ② 어색한, ③ 재미없는, 지루한, ④ 실망스러운, '우스꽝스러운 표정을 짓는 것은 정말 재미있다!'는 말이 이어지므로, 셀피는 '굉장하다.'고 하는 것이 적절하다.

16 케이트는 '필터를 사용하기 때문에' 가끔 그녀의 셀피가 그녀처럼 보이지 않는다고 말한다.

17 (A) '내가 어디에 있는가?'는 Where am I?(혼자일 때)나 Where are we?(나를 포함하여 여럿이 물을 때)라고 해야 한다. here는 부사라서 주어 자리에 쓸 수 없다. (B) 'your selfies'를 가리키므로 them이 적절하다. (C) 감각동사 sounds 다음에 '형용사 보어'를 써야 하므로 easy가 적절하다.

18 appropriate = proper = suitable: 적절한, ① 인기 있는, ③ 흔한, ④ 매우 좋아하는

19 ⓑ on: ~에 대해서,~에 관한, ⓒ have fun with: ~와 재미있게 놀다

20 셀피 설문조사의 결과를 가리킨다.

21 ④번 다음 문장이 주어진 문장의 답에 해당하므로 ④번이 적절하다.

22 Bonny는 셀피를 가장 많이 찍는 장소를 모른다.

서술형 시험대비

p.40~41

01 interest
02 Here are some interesting facts.
03 possible → impossible
04 Choose appropriate places to take selfies.
05 it may bother other people
06 comments
07 interested
08 post
09 in 1839
10 taking selfies
11 60 또는 Sixty
12 at school

01 have의 목적어로 명사 interest를 쓰면 된다.

02 주어가 some interesting facts이므로 동사를 are로 쓰는 것이 적절하다.

03 selfie는 2013년에 사전에 새로운 단어로 실렸기 때문에, 2013년 전에는 사전에서 찾을 수 없는 단어였다.

04 appropriate: 적합한, 적절한

05 그것은 '다른 사람들을 신경 쓰이게 할 수 있기' 때문이다.

06 '어떤 코멘트를 남겨야 하는가?'라는 질문에 대한 답으로 다른 사람들의 셀피에 상냥한 '코멘트'를 남기라고 하는 것이 적절하다.

07 be interested in: ~에 관심[흥미]이 있다 / interesting을 변형하여 쓰면 된다.

08 post: 게시하다 / 웹사이트나 소셜 미디어를 사용하여 메시지나 사진과 같은 것을 게재하다

09 세계 최초로 Robert Cornelius가 셀피를 찍은 것은 1839년이었다.

10 '셀피 찍기'를 가리킨다.

11 300명 중에서 20%가 카페나 식당에서 셀피를 찍는다고 말했기 때문에, '60명'이 적절하다.

12 학생들은 '학교에서' 셀피를 가장 많이 찍는다.

영역별 핵심문제

p.43~47

01 ③
02 (1) sometimes, to (2) silly (3) there, public
(4) warm, outdoors
03 (1) sound (2) spends (3) did (4) having 04 ②
05 ③ 06 ④ 07 going 08 ①
09 interesting → interested 10 ④
11 What are you interested in?
12 We are both interested in social media.
13 (1) inviting (2) Playing 14 ② 15 ③
16 ⑤
17 (1) Watching a movie is an adventure.
(2) Reading this book was like having a coffee with a friend.
(3) I want to stop talking about my personal life.
(4) Circles feel soft because they have no angles.
(5) My computer sounds strange.
18 (1) greatly → great (2) fish → like fish 19 ④
20 (1) to spend → spending
(2) Break, are → Breaking[To break], is
21 ⓐ in ⓒ on 22 ②
23 (A) much (B) interesting (C) new 24 To take
25 ⓐ 90 ⓑ 15 ⓒ 93 26 ③ 27 ②
28 ④ 29 ⓐ Facts ⓑ Survey ⓒ Etiquette
30 ②

01 ① displayed, display: (작품을) 전시하다, 보여주다 ② Prepare, prepare: 준비하다 ③ bother, bother: 괴롭히다 ④ left, leave: 남기다 ⑤ understand, understand: 이해하다

02 (1) sometimes: 가끔 have to 동사원형: ~해야 한다 (2)

silly: 바보 같은, 어리석은 (3) there is 단수명사: ~가 있다 public: 공공의 (4) warm: 따뜻한 outdoors: 야외에서

03 (1) sound+형용사: ~하게 들리다 (2) spend 시간 -ing: ~하는 데 시간을 보내다 (3) do a survey: 조사를 하다 (4) have fun: 즐거운 시간을 보내다

04 ②는 반의어 관계이고 나머지 보기는 동의어 관계이다. ① display: 전시하다 exhibit: 전시하다 ② exciting: 신나는 boring: 지루한 ③ fact: 사실 truth: 진실 ④ hurt: 해치다 injure: 다치게 하다 ⑤ nervous: 불안한 anxious: 불안한

05 from A to B: A에서 B까지 awesome: 멋진, 굉장한 keep in mind: 명심하다 in front of: ~ 앞에서

06 ④ Of course.라고 허락하는 대답을 하고 바로 뒤에 미안하다는 말은 어울리지 않는다.

07 be going to 동사원형: ~할 것(예정)이다

08 나의 남동생이 야구를 좋아하기 때문에 내가 야구 경기를 보러 간다는 의미이므로, 이유를 나타내는 접속사 because가 어울린다.

09 be interested in: ~에 관심[흥미]이 있다 Are you interested in~?: 너는 ~에 관심이 있니?

10 ① 여자아이는 이번 주에 야구 경기를 보러 간다. ② 여자아이의 남동생은 야구를 좋아한다. ③ 여자아이는 사실 야구를 좋아하지 않는다. ④ 남자아이가 무엇에 관심을 가졌는지는 나와 있지 않다. ⑤ 여자아이는 언젠가 축구 경기를 보러 가기를 원한다.

11 be interested in: ~에 관심[흥미]이 있다 What are you interested in?: 너는 무엇에 관심이 있니?

12 both: 둘 다

13 (1) 전치사의 목적어로 동명사 (2) 주어로 동명사가 적절하다.

14 ② 감각동사는 형용사를 보어로 취한다. friendly는 'friend(명사)+ly'로 형용사이다.

15 ③번은 some birds를 수식하는 현재분사이고 나머지는 모두 동명사이다. ① 주어 ② 동사의 목적어 ④ 보어 ⑤ 전치사의 목적어

16 감각동사 다음에는 보어로 형용사가 나와야 한다. 보어로 명사가 올 때는 명사 앞에 like를 쓴다.

17 (1), (2), (3) 동명사가 주어, 동사와 전치사의 목적어가 되도록 한다. (4), (5) 감각동사의 보어로 형용사를 쓴다.

18 감각동사 다음에는 보어로 형용사가 와야 한다. 보어로 명사가 올 때는 명사 앞에 like를 쓴다.

19 ④ Stop reading that book, and go out and play.

20 (1) deny는 동명사를 목적어로 갖는다. (2) 주어가 없으므로 동명사나 to부정사가 주어가 되도록 해야 하며 동명사나 to부정사 주어는 단수 취급한다.

21 ⓐ be interested in: ~에 관심[흥미]이 있다, ⓒ post on: ~에 올리다, 게시하다

22 ⓑ와 ②는 명사적 용법(목적어), ① 형용사적 용법, ③ 부사적 용법(형용사 수식), ④ 형용사적 용법, ⑤ 부사적 용법(조건)

23 (A) 양을 나타내므로 much가 적절하다. (B) 몇 가지 '재미있는' 사실들이 있다고 해야 하므로 interesting이 적절하다. boring: 지루한, (C) 사전에 '신조어'로 등재되었다고 해야 하므로 new가 적절하다.

24 주어로 쓰인 동명사이므로 to부정사로 바꿔 쓸 수 있다.

25 ⓐ 소녀들의 '90' 퍼센트가 셀피를 찍는다. ⓑ 소년들의 '15' 퍼센트만이 셀피를 찍는다. ⓒ 학생들의 '93' 퍼센트는 필터를 사용한다고 말했다.

26 ① awesome: 경탄할 만한, 어마어마한, 엄청난, amazing: 놀랄 만한, 굉장한, ③ 민우는 셀피 찍는 것을 즐기지만 '몇몇 학생들은' 그것을 하는 데 너무 많은 시간을 보낸다고 말했다.

27 위 글은 셀피 예절에 관한 글이므로, 제목으로는 ②번 'Selfie Etiquette'가 적절하다.

28 ④ 어디에 셀피를 게시해야 하는지는 대답할 수 없다. ① 1. Choose appropriate places to take selfies. 2. Keep in mind that anyone can see your selfies. 3. Leave nice comments on other people's selfies. ② Before we take, post, or look at selfies. ③ Anyone can see them. ⑤ We should leave nice comments on other people's selfies.

29 ⓐ 셀피에 관한 '사실들', ⓑ 셀피 '설문조사' ⓒ 셀피 '예절'

30 ⓑ Do you use filters on your selfies to look good? ⓒ Where do you usually take selfies?

단원별 예상문제 p.48~51

01 (1) carefully (2) incorrect
02 (a)ppropriate / (p)ublic / (r)ude
(1) Public (2) rude (3) appropriate 03 ③
04 ② 05 ④ 06 (E) – (A) – (C) – (B) – (D)
07 ① 08 ③ 09 No, you may not.
10 ② 11 ③ 12 ④, ⑤ 13 looks lovely 14 ② 15 (1) Read → Reading[To read] (2) say → saying (3) sweetly → sweet (4) sound → sound like
16 (1) Robert Cornelius는 1839년에 세계 최초의 셀피를 찍었다.
(2) selfie는 2013년에 사전에 신조어로 실렸다.
(3) Buzz Aldrin은 1966년에 최초의 우주 셀피를 찍었다.
17 ② 18 were many space selfies → was no space selfie 19 (A) etiquette (B) questions 20 ②
21 isn't that → doesn't it 22 (1) 몇몇 학생들은 자신들의 셀피에 필터를 너무 많이 사용한다. (2) 몇몇 학생들이 똑같은 셀피를 반복해서 게시하는 것은 시간 낭비이다. 23 ④

01 주어진 보기는 반의어의 관계이다. (1) carelessly: 부주의하게 carefully: 신중하게 (2) correct: 맞는 incorrect: 틀린

02 (1) public: 공공의 / 누구든지 사용 가능한 / 공공 도서관은 정보를 찾기 좋다. (2) rude: 무례한 / 공손하지 않거나, 사람들의 기분을 상하게 하거나, 짜증나게 하기 쉬운 방식의 말과 행동을 하는 / 나는 무례하게 굴려고 하는 것은 아니었지만, 일찍 떠나야만 했어. (3) appropriate: 적절한 / 특정한 시간, 장소, 목적에 맞거나 적합한 / 나는 청바지가 파티에 적합하다고 생각하지 않는다.

03 unexpectedly: 뜻밖에, 예상 외로 surprisingly: 놀랍게도, 의외로

04 deal with: (문제·과제 등을) 처리하다 solve: 해결하다

05 ④번은 내용을 확인하기 위해 물어보는 것이며, 나머지는 허락을 요청하기 위해 묻는 문장들이다.

06 무엇을 하고 있는지 묻는 질문에, (E) 내일 발표를 준비한다고 대답하며. 발표 내용이 자신의 관심사 중 하나라고 얘기한다. (A) 무엇에 관심을 가졌는지 질문하자 (C) 사진에 관심이 있다고 대답한다. (B) 그러자 상대방도 사진에 역시 관심이 있다고 말하자 (D) 상대방에게 내일 발표에 대해 도움을 요청한다.

07 주어진 문장은 표를 보여 달라는 말이므로, 이 다음에는 표를 보여주는 Here it is. (여기 있어요.)가 나와야 적절하다.

08 허락을 요청하는 표현에는 May I ~?, Can I ~?, Is it OK if I ~?, I'm wondering if I ~., Would it be all right if I ~?, Do you mind if I ~? 등이 있다.

09 오직 콘서트홀 앞에서만 사진을 찍을 수 있다.

10 ① 콘서트홀 입구에서 대화하고 있다. ② 밴드가 무슨 종류의 음악을 연주하는지는 알 수 없다. ③ 밴드의 사진을 찍는 것은 불가능하다. ④ 콘서트홀 앞에서만 사진 촬영이 가능하다. ⑤ 여자아이는 콘서트홀 안에서 녹음할 수 없다.

11 학생들이 새 책을 집에 못 가져가는 것이 새로운 과학책을 빌리는 것을 허락하지 않는 구체적 이유이므로 No, you may not. 다음에 나와야 적절하다.

12 ④ 모든 책이 아니라 새 책만 가져갈 수 없다. ⑤ 대화에 없는 내용이다. 과학 보고서를 위해 책이 필요하다는 내용만 언급되어 있다.

13 감각동사는 형용사를 보어로 취한다.

14 ①, ③, ⑤ give up, practice, mind 등은 동명사를 목적어로 받는다. ④ 동명사나 to부정사가 주어가 되도록 해야 한다.

15 (1) 동명사나 부정사가 주어가 되도록 해야 한다. (2) 전치사의 목적어로 동명사를 써야 한다. (3) 감각동사는 형용사를 보어로 취한다. (4) 감각동사 뒤에 보어로 명사가 올 때는 명사 앞에 like를 쓴다.

16 뒤에 이어지는 내용을 쓰면 된다.

17 take a selfie: 셀피를 찍다

18 1966년에 첫 번째 우주 셀피를 찍었다고 했기 때문에 1966년 전에는 '우주 셀피가 없었다.'고 하는 것이 적절하다.

19 셀피를 찍을 때, 따라야 하는 '예절'이 있다. 스스로에게 '여기가 어디인가?' '누가 그것을 볼 수 있는가?' '어떤 종류의 댓글을 남겨야 할까?'와 같은 '질문들'을 한 다음에 셀피를 찍거나 게시하거나 보아야 한다.

20 '누구나 당신의 셀피를 볼 수 없도록 해야 한다는 것'은 셀피 예절에 속하지 않는다.

21 문장의 동사가 일반동사이므로 'doesn't'를 쓰고 That을 'it'으로 바꾸는 것이 적절하다

22 Why? 다음의 내용을 쓰면 된다.

23 ⓐ와 ④ 낭비, ① 낭비하다(동사), ② 쓰레기, ③ 낭비하다, 막 쓰다(동사), ⑤ 쓸모가 없어진, 폐물이 된(형용사)

서술형 실전문제

p.52~53

01 ⓐ for ⓑ of ⓒ in ⓓ about

02 in photography

03 may I ask you for some advice for my presentation?

04 (1) Watch → Watching[To watch]
(2) to do → doing
(3) become → becoming[to become]
(4) arrive → arriving
(5) nicely → nice
(6) smell → smell like

05 (1) Learning English is interesting.
(2) Students spend too much time doing computer games.
(3) She turned pale at hearing the news.
(4) The fruit didn't taste like strawberries.
(5) They felt so soft and warm.

06 playing the computer game

07 taking selfies

08 My pictures look good when I use filters.

09 (A) appropriate (B) bother (C) rude

10 To take[Taking] selfies in hospitals or public restrooms

11 enjoy yourself **또는** have a good time

01 ⓐ prepare for: ~을 준비하다 ⓑ one of 복수명사: ~ 중의 하나 ⓒ be interested in: ~에 관심[흥미]이 있다 ⓓ talk about: ~에 대해서 말하다

02 문장 맨 끝의 too가 있는 것으로 보아, 똑같이 사진에 관심을 가진 것을 알 수 있다. photography: 사진

03 May I 동사원형 ~?: 제가 ~해도 될까요? ask for advice: 충고를 구하다

04 (1) 동명사나 부정사가 주어가 되도록 해야 한다. (2) keep은 동명사를 목적어로 가지는 동사이다. (3) 동명사나 부정사가 보

어가 되도록 해야 한다. (4) 전치사의 목적어로 동명사가 적절하다. (5) 감각동사는 형용사를 보어로 취한다. (6) 감각동사 뒤에 보어로 명사가 올 때는 명사 앞에 like를 쓴다.

05 (1) 주어로 동명사, (2) spend+시간+동명사: ~하는 데 시간을 보내다, (3) 전치사의 목적어로 동명사, (4) 감각동사 뒤에 보어로 명사가 올 때는 명사 앞에 like를 쓴다. (5) 감각동사는 형용사를 보어로 취한다.

06 stop이 있고 컴퓨터를 끄겠다고 했으므로 동명사를 목적어로 하여 게임을 그만둘 것이다'라고 하는 것이 적절하다.

07 '셀피를 찍는 것'을 가리킨다.

08 good을 보충하면 된다.

09 (A) 셀피를 찍기에 '적합한' 장소를 선택하라고 해야 하므로 appropriate가 적절하다. appropriate: 적합한, 적절한, unsuitable: 적합하지[알맞지] 않은, (B) 공중 화장실에서 셀피를 찍는 것은 다른 사람들을 '신경 쓰이게 할 수 있다'고 해야 하므로 bother가 적절하다. bother: 신경 쓰이게 하다, 괴롭히다, encourage: 격려하다, 용기를 북돋우다, (C) 다른 사람들의 셀피에 상냥한 코멘트를 남기고 '무례하게' 굴지 마라고 해야 하므로 rude가 적절하다. polite: 예의 바른, 공손한, rude: 무례한

10 병원이나 공중 화장실에서 셀피를 찍는 것'을 가리킨다. It이 주어이므로 to부정사나 동명사를 사용하여 쓰는 것이 적절하다.

11 have fun = enjoy oneself = have a good time: 즐기다, 즐겁게 보내다

창의사고력 서술형 문제 p.52

|모범답안|

01 A: What are you interested in?
A: Why don't you go to a museum?/How[What] about going to a museum?
B: May I take pictures[photos]
A: No, you may not. / I'm afraid not.

02 (1) You look nervous.
(2) She feels happy.
(3) The soup smells sweet.
(4) The food tasted terrible.
(5) The news sounded good.

03 (A) language rules (B) incorrect (C) Finally (D) in mind

단원별 모의고사 p.53~56

01 ④ 02 ① 03 (1) will, able / (e)tiquette (2) an interesting question (3) enjoy shopping , clothes (4) lot, choose
04 (1) looked (2) sounds (3) agree (4) spend
05 (A) movies (B) Why (C) eat snacks
06 (A) borrow (B) copy 07 share 08 ②
09 (A) I'm interested in games and social media.
(B) I'm interested in music and social media.
10 We are both interested in social media.
11 May I take pictures of the band? 12 in
13 ③ 14 ④ 15 ⑤
16 like an orange 17 (1) My pictures look beautiful when I use filters. (2) Stop playing games and be sincere. 18 posting 19 ②
20 ② 21 (A) awesome (B) good (C) like
22 ③ 23 after → before
24 remember 25 ②

01 'awesome: 멋진, 굉장한 ① 놀라운, 멋진 ② 굉장한, 훌륭한 ③ 환상적인, 멋진 ④ 끔찍한 ⑤ 훌륭한, 좋은

02 ①은 반의어 관계이고 나머지 보기는 동의어 관계이다. ① rude: 무례한 polite: 공손한 ② finally: 마지막으로 lastly: 마지막으로 ③ bother: 괴롭히다 annoy: 귀찮게 하다 ④ comment: 의견 remark: 견해 ⑤ advice: 충고 tip: 충고

03 (1) etiquette: 에티켓, 예절 (2) interesting: 흥미로운, 재미있는 question: 질문 (3) clothes: 옷 enjoy 동사ing: ~하는 것을 즐기다 (4) a lot of: 많은 choose: 고르다

04 (1) twin: 쌍둥이 (2) sound+형용사: ~하게 들리다 (3) agree with: ~에 동의하다 (4) spend 시간 동사ing: ~하는 데 시간을 보내다

05 (A) 극장에 가는 것을 권유하고 있으므로 영화에 관심이 있는 것을 유추할 수 있다. (B) Why don't you ~?: ~하는 게 어때?(권유하기) (C) take photos of the paintings: 그림 사진을 찍다 eat snacks: 과자를 먹다 feed the birds: 새에게 먹이를 주다 record the music: 음악을 녹음하다

06 borrow: 빌리다 copy: 복사하다

07 다른 사람과 함께 무언가를 갖거나 사용하다 share: 공유하다

08 새로운 과학책을 빌려줄 수 있는지 허락을 요청하는 말에 거절했으므로, 학생들이 집에 새 책을 가져갈 수 있다는 말은 어색하다. can을 can't로 고쳐야 적절하다.

09 be interested in: ~에 관심[흥미]이 있다 social media: 소셜 미디어

10 both: 둘 다 social media: 소셜 미디어

11 May I 동사원형 ~?: 제가 ~해도 될까요? take a picture[photo] (of): (~의) 사진을 찍다

12 in: ~ 안에서 in front of: ~ 앞에서

13 ③ I'm proud of winning the prize.

14 want는 형용사를 보어로 쓰지 않는다.

15 ⑤번은 목적격 보어로 쓰인 현재분사이고 나머지는 모두 동명사이다.

16 '감각동사+like+명사'

17 (1) 감각동사는 형용사를 보어로 취한다. (2) 동명사가 Stop의 목적어로 쓰여야 한다.

18 like는 목적어로 to부정사와 동명시를 둘 다 쓸 수 있다.

19 여기에 몇 가지 재미있는 사실들이 있다고 했으므로 '셀피에 관한 몇 가지 재미있는 사실들'이 이어질 것이다.

20 학생들의 '댓글'들이 이어지고 있으므로 comments가 적절하다. ① 보고서, ③ (신문 • 잡지의) 글, 기사, ④ 수필, ⑤ 요약, 개요

21 (A) 셀피는 '경탄할 만하다'고 해야 하므로 awesome이 적절하다. awful: 끔찍한, 지독한, awesome: 경탄할 만한, 어마어마한, 엄청난, (B) 내 사진들은 필터를 사용할 때 '좋아' 보인다고 해야 하므로 good이 적절하다. 감각동사 look 다음에 형용사를 써야 하는데, well은 형용사일 때 '건강한'이라는 뜻이다. (C) 가끔 나의 셀피들은 나 '같이 보이지' 않는다고 해야 하므로 like가 적절하다. look like: ~인 것처럼 보이다

22 ③ 7 percent of the 'students로 고쳐야 한다.

23 네가 셀피를 찍거나 게시하거나 보기 '전에' 이런 질문들을 스스로에게 물으라고 하는 것이 적절하다.

24 keep in mind = be sure to remember: ~을 명심하다

25 ②번은 '팁, 봉사료'이고, ⓒ와 나머지는 다 '조언들'이라는 뜻이다.

Lesson 2

Eat Right, Be Happy!

시험대비 실력평가 p.60

01 (1) traditional (2) Vietnamese
02 (1) choice (2) arrival 03 healthy 04 ④
05 ① 06 ① 07 ③
08 (1) more (2) often (3) slowly

01 주어진 보기는 명사와 형용사의 관계이다. Korea: 한국 Korean: 한국의 (1) tradition: 전통 traditional: 전통적인 (2) Vietnam: 베트남 Vietnamese: 베트남의

02 주어진 보기는 동사와 명사의 관계이다. suggest: 제안하다 suggestion: 제안 (1) choose: 고르다 choice: 선택 (2) arrive: 도착하다 arrival: 도착

03 health: 건강 healthy: 건강에 좋은

04 ① fry: 튀기다 ② recommend: 추천하다 ③ other: 다른 ④ usually: 보통, 대개 ⑤ breakfast: 아침 식사

05 ① vegetables: 야채 / 비타민 A는 간과 푸른색 야채에서 발견된다. ② meat: 고기, 육류 ③ flower: 꽃 ④ carrot: 당근 ⑤ meal: 식사

06 ① contest: 대회, 콘테스트 / 나는 내일 웅변 대회에 나가요. ② concert: 연주회, 콘서트 ③ content: 내용 ④ compete: 경쟁하다 ⑤ prize: 상

07 try + 음식: 음식을 먹어 보다, 맛을 보다 / 새로운 음식을 맛보는 것은 흥미로운 경험이다.

08 (1) more: 더 큰, 더 많은 (2) often: 종종, 자주 (3) slowly: 천천히

서술형 시험대비 p.61

01 common
02 get
03 (1) going, (c)elebrate (2) enough money
(3) Fresh fruit, vegetables
04 (1) common (2) enough
05 (1) contest (2) sweets
06 (1) side dish (2) suggestion (3) onion (4) grocery
07 (1) Do you want me to cut the cake?
(2) I've always wanted to go to Paris.

01 common: 흔한 have ~ in common: 공통으로 ~을 가지다
02 get a cold: 감기에 걸리다 get a discount: 할인받다
03 (1) be going out: 외출할 것이다 celebrate: 축하하다, 기념하다 (2) enough: 충분한 money: 돈 (3) fresh: 신선한 fruit: 과일 vegetables: 야채
04 (1) high: 높은 low: 낮은 (반의어 관계) rare: 희귀한, 드문 common: 흔한 (2) awesome: 엄청난 wonderful: 훌륭한 (동의어 관계) sufficient: 충분한 enough: 충분한
05 (1) contest: 대회, 콘테스트 / 둘 또는 그 이상의 사람이나 그룹이 서로 겨루는 경쟁이나 상황 (2) sweets: 단 음식, 단것 / 설탕이나 초콜릿으로 만들어진 작은 조각의 단 음식
06 (1) side dish: 반찬 (2) suggestion: 제안 (3) onion: 양파 (4) grocery: 식료품
07 (1) cut: 자르다 (2) always: 항상

교과서

Conversation

핵심 Check

p.62~63

1 You'd better, before / I'll
2 (B) → (D) → (A) → (C)
3 you recommend / There
4 What sport do you recommend?
I strongly recommend
5 What book do you recommend?
I'd like to recommend this book.

교과서 대화문 익히기

Check(√) True or False

p.64

(1) F (2) F (3) T (4) T

교과서 확인학습

p.66~67

Listen & Talk 1 A

I think I eat, sweets these days / good for, health. You'd bette, instead

Listen & Talk 1 B

look / often feel tired / usually eat / You'd better eat, gives you energy / any other suggestions / should also exercise

Listen & Talk 1 C

contest, going to / What, put in them / You'd better, in, about / I'm not going to / we should, healthy / I should

Listen and Talk 2 A

It's, first time, What, recommend / I recommend

Listen and Talk 2 B

What are you doing / searching for / When / too expensive / don't you check, went / Sounds, What do, recommend / recommend the noodle soup / think we should

Listen and Talk C

Are you ready / What do you recommend / recommend, sandwich, the most popular / recommend something else / about / don't you, with, get, discount

Do It Yourself A

What's / one / What do you recommend / fried / sounds delicious / health, better, don't you try / will

시험대비 기본평가

p.68

01 ⑤ 02 ② 03 ④
04 (C) → (B) → (A)

01 상대방에게 매일 아침을 먹으라고 충고하는 표현으로 매일 아침을 먹으라고 권유하는 문장인 Why don't you eat breakfast every day?로 바꿔 쓸 수 있다.
02 단것을 너무 많이 먹는다는 상대에게 과일을 대신 먹으라는 충고를 할 수 있다. fruit: 과일 instead: 대신에
03 처음 와서 어떻게 주문할지 모르는 상황에서 추천을 요청하고 있다. 이에 대한 대답으로 피자와 샐러드를 추천해 준다. recommend: 추천하다
04 have a cold: 감기에 걸리다 recommend: 추천하다 You'd better 동사원형 ~: 너는 ~하는 편이 좋겠다 green tea: 녹차

시험대비 실력평가

p.69~70

01 ④ 02 ② 03 ⑤
04 exercising every day 05 ③ 06 ①
07 ① 08 vegetable(s) 09 ④
10 you had better drink milk 11 ④
12 ③ 13 ③ 14 ④

01 남자아이가 아침 식사를 안 한다는 말에, 아침 식사를 하는 게 좋겠다고 얘기하는 것이 어울리므로 ④가 적절하다.

02 ① 행복한 ② 피곤한 ③ 화난 ④ 흥미로운 ⑤ 신난 / 다음 문장에서 잠을 잘 못 잤느냐고 질문하는 것으로 보아, 피곤해 보인다고 말하는 것이 어울린다.

03 ① 그래서 ② ~ 때문에 ③ 그리고 ④ ~ 때문에, ~한 이후로 ⑤ 하지만 / 잠을 잘 잤다는 내용과 나는 아침에 자주 피곤하다는 것을 연결하기 위해서는 But(하지만)이 어울린다.

04 (C)의 that은 앞 문장의 매일 운동하는 것을 가리킨다. exercise: 운동하다 every day: 매일

05 남자아이의 대답인 '나는 샌드위치를 만들 것이다.'로 미래의 계획에 대해 이야기하고 있으므로 be going to 동사원형을 이용한 질문을 할 수 있다. be going to 동사원형: ~할 것이다. ~할 예정이다

06 put A in B: A를 B 안에 넣다

07 ⓐ, ⓑ, ⓒ는 샌드위치 ⓓ, ⓔ는 양파와 당근을 가리킨다.

08 vegetable: 야채 / 예를 들어 양배추, 당근 또는 완두콩 같은 날것으로 먹거나 요리해 먹는 식물

09 ④ 집에 일찍 가서 쉬라고 충고해 주는 말에 너는 괜찮을 거라는 말은 어색하다. ① You'd better+동사원형 ~: ~하는 게 좋겠다 go to bed early: 일찍 잠자리에 들다 ② I think you should ~: 나는 네가 ~해야 한다고 생각한다. ③ What kind of ~: 무슨 종류의 ~ ④ Why don't you ~?: 네가 ~하는 건 어때? ⑤ recommendation: 추천

10 You'd better + 동사원형 ~: ~하는 게 좋겠다 drink: 마시다

11 한 번도 Chang's 식당을 가 본 적이 없는데 음식과 가격이 좋았다고 말하는 것은 어색하다.

12 right now: 바로 지금 ① (형) 정확한 ② (명) 권리 ③ (부) 바로 ④ (형) 올바른, 옳은 ⑤ (명) 오른쪽

13 Why don't you ~?(~하는 게 어때?)는 충고하는 표현이다.

14 ④ Chang's 식당에 대한 위치는 언급되어 있지 않다.

서술형시험대비 p.71

01 (C) → (B) → (A) → (D)
02 (B) → (C) → (A)
03 ③ Yes, I do → No, I don't.
04 suggestions
05 you should also exercise every day
06 (A) What (B) When (C) Why
07 for
08 ⓒ Bella's Restaurant ⓓ to Chang's Restaurant

02 무엇을 만들지 묻는 질문에 (B) 샌드위치를 만들 것이라고 대답한다. (C) 이어서, 샌드위치 안에 무엇을 넣을지 묻는 질문에 (A) 닭고기, 치즈, 달걀을 넣을 거라고 대답한다.

03 여자아이가 아침 식사를 하는 편이 좋겠다고 충고하고 있으므로, 남자아이는 아침식사를 하지 않는 것을 알 수 있다.

04 suggestion: 제안

05 should + 동사원형: ~해야 한다 also: 또한 exercise: 운동하다 every day: 매일

06 (A) 지금 무엇을 하는지 질문하고 있다. (B) 다음 주 금요일이 대답이므로, 시간의 정보에 관해서 묻고 있다. (C) Why don't you ~?: ~하는 건 어때?

07 search for: ~을 찾다 for: ~를 위해

08 ⓒ는 Bella 식당을 의미하고, ⓓ는 Chang 식당을 의미한다.

교과서

Grammar

핵심 Check p.72~73

1 (1) who[that] (2) which[that]
2 (1) always (2) often (3) never

시험대비 기본평가 p.74

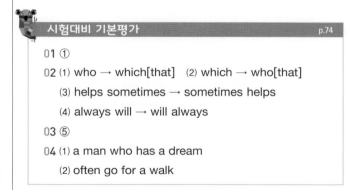

01 ①
02 (1) who → which[that] (2) which → who[that]
(3) helps sometimes → sometimes helps
(4) always will → will always
03 ⑤
04 (1) a man who has a dream
(2) often go for a walk

01 선행사가 the person으로 사람이며 came의 주어 역할을 할 수 있는 주격 관계대명사 who나 that이 적절하다.

02 (1) 선행사가 사물이므로 who를 which나 that으로 고쳐야 한다. (2) 선행사가 사람이므로 which를 who나 that으로 고쳐야 한다. (3) 빈도부사는 일반동사 앞에 위치한다. (4) 빈도부사는 조동사나 be동사 뒤에 위치한다.

03 좋아하지 않는다고 했으므로 seldom이 적절하다. seldom: 거의 ~ 않다

04 (1) 선행사가 사람이므로 who를 쓴다. (2) 빈도부사는 일반동사 앞에 위치한다.

시험대비 실력평가 p.75~77

01 ④ 02 ③ 03 ① 04 ②

05 (1) rarely goes (2) is often (3) who (4) which (5) that 06 ⑤

07 My mom always gets up early in the morning.

08 ④

09 How often do you help him after school

10 (1) If you hurry up, you can always go to school on time.
(2) Parents often make great sacrifices for their children.
(3) This is hardly the place to talk about the problem.

11 ③ 12 (1) that (2) who is

13 (1) Americans usually fly the nest
(2) It is always so hard to
(3) I will never do anything

14 (1) A baguette is a type of bread which is popular in France.
(2) I met the woman who came from England.
(3) I have a dog that has brown hair.
(4) There is a house whose windows are broken.
(5) I like the book that Mom bought for me.

15 ② 16 ⑤ 17 ① 18 ③

19 ④

20 (1) Are you the person who dropped this?
(2) We have to break the bad habits which can cause serious problems.
(3) She always uses my phone without asking.

01 선행사가 사물이므로 which나 that이 적절하다.

02 ③ 빈도부사는 일반동사 앞에, 조동사 뒤에 위치한다.

03 모두 주격이나 목적격으로 사용된 관계대명사 that이 들어갈 수 있지만 ①번은 소유격 관계대명사 whose가 들어가야 한다.

04 빈도부사는 조동사나 be동사 다음에 위치한다.

05 (1), (2) 빈도부사는 일반동사 앞에, be동사나 조동사 뒤에 위치한다. (3), (4), (5) 선행사가 사람이면 who나 that을 쓰고 선행사가 사물이나 동물이면 which나 that을 쓴다.

06 관계대명사의 선행사가 사람이면 who, whom이나 that을 쓰고, 사물이면 which나 that을 쓴다.

07 빈도부사는 일반동사 앞에 위치한다.

08 선행사가 사람이므로 who나 that을 이용하고 주격이므로 관계대명사 뒤에 주어로 쓰인 she는 쓰지 말아야 한다.

09 가끔 도와준다고 했으므로 often을 이용하면 얼마나 자주 돕는지 물어야 한다.

10 빈도부사는 일반동사 앞, 조동사나 be동사 뒤에 위치한다.

11 ③번은 접속사이지만 나머지는 모두 관계대명사이다.

12 목적격 관계대명사와 '주격 관계대명사+be동사'는 생략할 수 있다.

13 빈도부사는 일반동사 앞에, 조동사나 be동사 다음에 위치한다.

14 관계대명사는 공통으로 쓰이는 (대)명사와 접속사의 역할을 한다. 선행사인 (대)명사가 주어이면 주격, 목적어이면 목적격, 소유격이면 소유격 관계대명사를 쓴다.

15 빈도부사는 일반동사 앞에, 조동사나 be동사 다음에 위치한다. 조동사 used to의 경우, 보통 빈도부사가 그 앞에 위치한다.

16 선행사가 사물이므로 which나 that을 쓰고, 관계대명사는 접속사와 대명사 역할을 하므로 주어나 목적어로 쓰인 it이 없어야 한다.

17 책 읽는 것을 좋아한다고 했으므로 ①번이 어울린다.

18 선행사가 사람이면 who나 that을 쓰고 선행사가 사물이나 동물이면 which나 that을 쓴다.

19 frequent는 형용사이며, 빈도를 나타내는 부사는 frequently이다.

20 (1), (2) 선행사가 사람이면 who나 that을 쓰고 선행사가 사물이나 동물이면 which나 that을 쓴다. (3) 빈도부사는 일반동사 앞에 위치한다.

서술형 시험대비 p.80~81

01 (1) The girl is eating rice noodle soup.
(2) It is made in Korea.
(3) Emily bought a new computer.
(4) They were dancing.

02 (1) Amy never studied math last week.
(2) Don often studied math last week.
(3) Ann sometimes studied math last week.

03 (1) The girl who is wearing a red skirt is my daughter.
(2) Jenny has a brother who plays the violin well.
(3) A cheetah is an animal that can run fast.
(4) Bill always gets up late on Sundays.
(5) Cindy is often busy at the end of the month.

04 (1) reading / who[that] is reading (2) sleeping / which[that] is sleeping

05 is never late / always sends text messages / usually uses the Internet

06 (1) whom[who] (2) that (3) with whom (4) I spent my vacation with

07 I can hardly wait to see you.

08 has two sons who became doctors

09 (1) On a hot day, sunlight is usually enough to melt chocolate.
(2) He always wears very clean clothes.

(3) I can never find a parking space downtown.
10 which[that] mean long life
11 (1) It is a TV show which[that] is always popular.
(2) The painting shows a couple who[that] are dancing.
(3) I took the train that had a restaurant.
(4) I am never late for school.

01 주격 관계대명사는 선행사가 사람이면 who나 that, 사물이나 동물이면 which나 that을 쓰고 관계대명사절에서 주어 역할을 하며 다음에 동사가 나온다.
02 빈도부사(frequency adverb)를 사용하여 답한다.
03 빈도부사는 일반동사 앞에, 조동사나 be동사 다음에 위치한다.
04 '주격 관계대명사+ be동사'는 생략 가능하다.
05 빈도부사는 조동사나 be동사 다음에, 일반동사 앞에 위치한다.
06 선행사가 사람이므로 whom[who]이나 that을 쓴다. 관계대명사가 전치사의 목적격일 경우 전치사를 관계대명사 앞으로 옮길 수 있으나 관계대명사 that은 전치사 다음에 쓸 수 없다. 목적격 관계대명사는 생략 가능하다.
07 빈도부사는 조동사 다음에 위치한다. hard: 열심히, 몹시 hardly: 거의 ~ 않는
08 선행사가 사람이고 주어로 쓰여야 하므로 주격 관계대명사 who를 써서 문장을 완성한다.
09 빈도부사는 일반동사 앞에, 조동사나 be동사 다음에 위치한다.
10 선행사가 사물이므로 which나 that을 쓴다..
11 (1), (2), (3) 선행사가 사람이면 who나 that이 적절하고 선행사가 사물이면 which나 that이 적절하다. (4) 빈도부사는 be동사 다음에 위치한다.

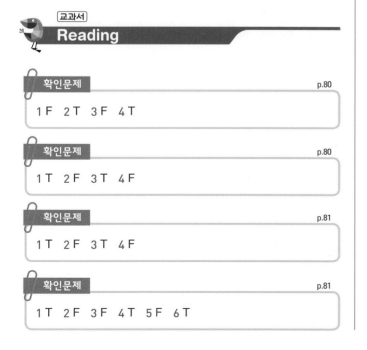

교과서

Reading

확인문제 p.80

1 F 2 T 3 F 4 T

확인문제 p.80

1 T 2 F 3 T 4 F

확인문제 p.81

1 T 2 F 3 T 4 F

확인문제 p.81

1 T 2 F 3 F 4 T 5 F 6 T

교과서 확인학습 A p.82~83

01 Around the World 02 this is, from 03 the best part 04 often, for lunch 05 have side dishes 06 serves special dishes 07 who live in other 08 hear from 09 France 10 healthy and balanced 11 usually, as an appetizer 12 often include 13 at the end of the lunch 14 can never forget 15 with cheese 16 has a special rule 17 for at least, minutes 18 Brazil 19 beans and rice 20 common in 21 comes with plantains 22 which looks like 23 usually fry 24 come from local farms 25 Singapore 26 who, from many different cultures, both Eastern and Western dishes 27 choose from, such as 28 won an award for 29 healthy, taste good 30 Which school lunch 31 have, in common with 32 leave, at

교과서 확인학습 B p.84~85

1 School Lunches Around the World
2 Hello, this is food reporter Minjun from Korea.
3 For many students, lunch is the best part of the school day.
4 In Korea, we often eat rice and soup for lunch.
5 We also have side dishes, such as *Bulgogi* or *Gimchi*.
6 Sometimes our school serves special dishes, such as pizza, *Bibimbap*, or pasta.
7 What do students who live in other countries eat for lunch?
8 Let's hear from our food reporters!
9 Belle, France
10 Our school serves healthy and balanced meals.
11 We usually eat a salad as an appetizer.
12 Main dishes often include meat or fish.
13 We also eat fresh fruit at the end of the lunch.
14 Oh, I can never forget about baguettes!
15 They're great with cheese.
16 Our school also has a special rule.
17 We must stay at the lunch table for at least 30 minutes.
18 Bruno, Brazil
19 Usually, we have beans and rice for lunch.

20 Meat and vegetables are common in our side dishes.
21 My favorite lunch comes with plantains.
22 A plantain is a fruit which looks like a banana.
23 We usually fry plantains.
24 Our school lunches are fresh because the vegetables and fruit come from local farms.
25 Nicole, Singapore
26 People who live in Singapore come from many different cultures, so we have both Eastern and Western dishes at lunch.
27 Students can choose from many dishes, such as curry, noodle soup, or pasta, each day.
28 My school won an award for healthy school food last year.
29 Our lunches are always healthy, and they taste good, too!
30 Which school lunch do you want to try?
31 Does it have anything in common with your school lunch?
32 Please leave your comments at www.chopchoplunch.com.

시험대비 실력평가

p.86~91

01 ②, ④ 02 ② 03 ⑤ 04 ①
05 ⑤ 06 They usually have beans and rice.
07 ④ 08 학생들은 적어도 30분간 점심 식탁에 반드시 머물러야 한다. 09 ④
10 1. 점심에 동양식과 서양식을 모두 먹는다.
2. 점심이 항상 건강에 좋고 맛 또한 좋다.
11 like 12 ④ 13 ③ 14 ①, ④
15 (A) balanced (B) include (C) at least
16 baguettes 17 ②
18 (A) beans and rice (B) meat and vegetables
19 (A) a banana (B) fry 20 ②, ⑤
21 여러분이 먹어 보고 싶은 학교 급식
22 in common 23 ④ 24 that
25 The girl who is wearing glasses is eating rice noodle soup. 26 happily → happy
27 A: 한국, 이유: 김치를 아주 좋아하기 때문에.
B: 프랑스, 이유: 바게트와 치즈를 좋아하고, 적어도 30분간 점심 식탁에 머물러야 하는 것이 재미있기 때문에.
C: 싱가포르, 이유: 급식으로 동양식과 서양식을 모두 선택하는 것이 재미있게 들리기 때문에.
28 ②

01 선행사가 사람(students)이고 주어 자리이므로, 주격 관계대명사 who나 that이 적절하다.
02 위 글은 한국의 학교 급식에 대해 소개하는 글이므로, 제목으로는 ② '한국의 학교 급식'이 가장 적절하다.
03 '가끔' 제공해 준다.
04 ⓐ come with: ~와 함께 나오다, ⓒ come from: ~에서 나오다[비롯되다/생산되다]
05 ⓑ와 ⑤ '~와 같이', 나머지는 모두 '좋아하다'
06 그들은 보통 '콩과 밥'을 먹는다.
07 주어진 문장의 They에 주목한다. ④번 앞 문장의 baguettes를 받고 있으므로 ④번이 적절하다.
08 뒤에 이어지는 내용을 쓰면 된다.
09 싱가포르에 사는 사람들은 매우 다양한 '문화권'에서 오기 때문에, 점심에 동양식과 서양식을 모두 먹는다. ① 의견, ② 목적, ③ 관심사, ④ 문화, ⑤ 믿음
10 1. 싱가포르에 사는 사람들은 매우 다양한 문화권에서 오기 때문에, 점심에 동양식과 서양식을 모두 먹는다. 2. 니콜의 학교는 작년에 건강한 학교 음식 상을 받았다.
11 such as = like: ~와 같은
12 (C)에서 한국에서는 점심으로 자주 밥과 국을 먹는다고 한 다음 (A)에서 also를 사용하여 반찬과 특식을 소개하므로 (C) 다음에 (A)가 이어지고 그 다음에 (B)에서 다른 나라에 사는 학생들은 점심으로 무엇을 먹는지에 대해 음식 취재 기자들에게서 들어보겠다고 하는 것이 적절하므로 (A) 다음에 (B)가 와야 한다. 그러므로 (C)-(A)-(B)의 순서가 적절하다.
13 ⓐ와 ③ 요리, ①과 ⑤ 설거지감[그릇들], ② (요리를 접시에) 담아 주다, ④ 접시들
14 ② 특식, ③ 주요리, ⑤ 특식
15 (A) '균형 잡힌' 식사라고 해야 하므로 balanced가 적절하다. (B) 고기나 생선을 '포함한다'고 해야 하므로 include가 적절하다. exclude: 제외[배제]하다, (C) '적어도' 30분간이라고 해야 하므로 at least가 적절하다. at least: 적어도, at last: 마침내, 드디어
16 '바게트'를 가리킨다.
17 ②는 의문형용사이고, ⓐ와 나머지는 모두 관계대명사이다.
18 (A) 주요리: 콩과 밥, (B) 흔한 곁들임 음식: 고기와 채소
19 플랜테인은 '바나나'처럼 생긴 과일이다. 브라질에서는 보통 플랜테인을 '튀긴다.'
20 ⓐ와 ①, ③, ④는 명사적 용법, ② 형용사적 용법, ⑤ 부사적 용법(목적)
21 앞 문장에서 물어보고 있는 내용을 가리킨다.
22 have something in common with somebody: (특징 등을) 공통적으로 지니다
23 ⓓ have something in common with somebody: (특징 등을) 공통적으로 지니다, ⓔ 전화번호나 이메일 주소를 알려 줄 때

at을 사용한다.

24 ⓐ 주격 관계대명사 which나 that을 쓸 수 있다. ⓑ 주격 관계대명사 who나 that을 쓸 수 있다.

25 'is'를 보충하면 된다.

26 감각동사 look의 보어로 형용사를 쓰는 것이 적절하다.

27 본문을 참조할 것.

28 ⓑ와 ②는 동명사이고, 나머지는 모두 현재분사이다.

서술형 시험대비 p.90~91

01 rice and soup
02 such as 또는 like
03 lives → live
04 dessert
05 during → for
06 must stay at the lunch table for at least 30 minutes
07 (A) like (B) fry (C) local
08 (A) meat, (B) vegetables
09 fried potatoes → plantains
10 people who live in Singapore come from many different cultures
11 good
12 prize
13 Review
14 high → low
15 (A) fresh (B) delicious

01 한국에서는 점심으로 자주 '밥과 국'을 먹는다.

02 such as = like: ~와 같은

03 선행사가 복수(students)이므로, 'live'로 고쳐야 한다.

04 디저트: 식사 끝에 먹는 과일이나 푸딩과 같은 달콤한 것

05 뒤에 숫자가 나오므로 for로 고치는 것이 적절하다. during+기간을 나타내는 명사

06 학생들이 적어도 30분간 점심 식탁에 반드시 머물러야 하는 것이 벨의 학교의 특별한 규칙이다.

07 (A) 바나나'처럼' 생겼다고 해야 하므로 like가 적절하다. look like: ~인 것처럼 보이다, look at: ~을 보다, (B) '튀긴다'라고 해야 하므로 fry가 적절하다. fry: 튀기다, fly: 날다, (C) 채소와 과일이 '현지의' 농장에서 오기 때문에 신선하다고 해야 하므로 local이 적절하다. local: 현지의, global: 세계적인

08 곁들임 음식에 '고기와 채소'가 흔하다고 했다.

09 브루노가 가장 좋아하는 점심에는 '플랜테인'이 나온다.

10 '싱가포르에 사는 사람들은 매우 다양한 문화권에서 오기' 때문에, 점심에 동양식과 서양식을 모두 먹는다.

11 니콜의 학교 급식은 건강에 '좋고' 맛 또한 '좋다'.

12 award = prize: 상

13 위 글은 '음식점 방문 후기'이다. review (책·연극·영화 등에 대한) 논평[비평], 감상문

14 가격이 '싸기' 때문에 추천한다고 해야 하므로, high를 low로 고쳐야 한다. price가 비싸거나 싼 것을 표현할 때는 보통 high나 low를 사용한다.

15 정말 '신선하고' '맛있는' 음식 때문에, 글쓴이는 Antonio's Restaurant를 추천한다.

영역별 핵심문제 p.97~101

01 ② 02 ④ 03 ③ 04 ④
05 ①
06 you'd better drink milk / for your advice
07 It's my first time here / I recommend the pizza
08 ① much → many ② eating → eat 09 ④
10 Do you usually eat breakfast?
11 (B) eat (C) gives 12 ③ 13 ④
14 (A) to (B) about (C) with 15 ④
16 ②, ⑤ 17 ③ 18 ④ 19 ①
20 (1) which(또는 that) sells noodles
(2) which(또는 that) sells sushi
(3) which(또는 that) sells pizza
21 (1) are always (2) rarely knew (3) should always
22 ⑤
23 (1) I am looking for the girl who left her cell phone on the bus.
(2) An elephant is an animal which has a long nose.
(3) The box which has many books is very heavy.
(4) Dad always drives his car very carefully.
(5) You should never leave a baby alone.
24 ⑤ 25 ④ 26 ② 27 ②
28 ④ 29 ② 30 ③ 31 ①, ④
32 ② 33 Our lunches

01 ② sweets: 단 음식, 단것

02 traditional: 전통적인

03 ① choice: 선택, 종류 ② culture: 문화 ③ health: 건강 ④ contest: 대회 ⑤ appetizer: 전채, 식욕을 돋우는 것

04 주어진 대화의 have는 '먹다'의 의미이다. ① have to 동사원형: ~해야 한다 ②, ⑤ 가지다 ③ 당하다 ④ 먹다

05 come from: ~에서 나오다, ~ 출신이다 come with: ~와 함께 나오다, ~이 딸려 있다

06 had better+동사원형: ~하는 게 좋겠다 thank you for ~: ~에 대해 감사하다 advice: 충고

07 first: 처음의 recommend: 추천하다.

08 ① snack은 셀 수 있는 명사로 many의 수식을 받는다.

② had better+동사원형: ~하는 게 좋겠다

09 아침을 먹으라는 조언을 한 이유를 듣고 또 다른 조언이 있는지 질문하고 있다.

10 빈도부사는 일반동사의 앞에, be동사나 조동사의 뒤에 위치한다.

11 (B) had better+동사원형: ~하는 게 좋겠다 (C) Breakfast는 3인칭 단수이고 일반적인 사실을 말하므로, 현재형을 써야 하며 동사에 's'를 붙인다.

12 should: ~해야 한다

13 the more popular → the most popular

14 (A) be ready to 동사원형: ~할 준비가 되다 (B) How about ~?: ~은 어때? (C) with: ~와 함께

15 ④ 닭고기 샌드위치가 가장 인기 있는 샌드위치이다.

16 주어진 문장과 ②, ⑤번의 who는 주격 관계대명사이다. ①, ③번은 목적격 관계대명사, ④번은 의문대명사

17 ③ 빈도부사는 조동사 다음에 위치한다.

18 ④ 선행사가 사물이므로 which나 that을 써야 한다.

19 빈도부사는 조동사나 be동사 뒤에, 일반동사 앞에 위치한다.

20 선행사가 restaurant로 사물이므로 which나 that을 쓴다.

21 빈도부사는 일반동사 앞에, 조동사나 be동사 뒤에 위치한다.

22 빈도부사는 일반동사 앞에, 조동사나 be동사 뒤에 위치한다.

23 (1), (2), (3) 선행사가 사람이면 who를 쓰고 선행사가 사물이나 동물이면 which를 쓴다. (4), (5) 빈도부사는 일반동사 앞에, 조동사 다음에 위치한다.

24 주어진 문장은 ⑤번 다음 문장에서 들어보려고 하는 내용에 해당하므로 ⑤번이 적절하다.

25 ⓐ food reporter Minjun from Korea: 한국에서 온 음식 취재 기자 민준, hear from: ~로부터 듣다, ⓑ For many students: 많은 학생들에게, for lunch: 점심으로

26 왜 많은 학생들에게 점심시간이 학교 일과 중 가장 좋은 부분인지는 대답할 수 없다. ① From Korea. ③ Rice and soup. ④ *Bulgogi* or *Gimchi*. ⑤ Pizza, *Bibimbap*, or pasta.

27 ⓐ와 ② [역할·자격·기능·성질 따위를 나타내어] ~으로서(의), ① ~와 같이, ~하는 대로, ③ ~이므로, ~이기 때문에, ④ [보통 as ~ as ~로 형용사·부사 앞에서] ~와 같은 정도로, ⑤ ~일 때

28 벨의 학교에서 '카레'를 먹는다는 말은 없다.

29 주어진 글에서 주요리에 관해 말했고 이어서 (B)에서 곁들임 음식에 대해 계속 말하고 있으므로 (B)가 제일 먼저 오고, (A)에서 (B)의 마지막에 나오는 플랜테인을 설명하고 있으므로 (B) 다음에 (A)가 이어지고, (C)에서는 앞에서 말한 음식들이 신선한 이유를 설명하고 있으므로 (A) 다음에 (C)가 와야 한다. 그러므로 (B)-(A)-(C)의 순서가 적절하다.

30 ③ 플랜테인은 바나나처럼 생겼고 보통 튀긴다고 했을 뿐이다.

31 선행사가 사물(a fruit)이고 주어 자리이므로, 주격 관계대명사 that이나 which가 적절하다.

32 ⓒ 'each+단수 명사'이므로 → each day, ⓔ 긍정문에서 '역시'는 'too'로 써야 한다. 부정문에서 '역시'라는 뜻일 때는 'either'를 사용한다.

33 '우리의 점심'을 가리킨다.

단원별 예상문제

p.98~101

01 That's good for your health. → That's not good for your health.

02 You'd better eat fruit instead.

03 up 04 at 05 ④ 06 ④

07 (1) (f)resh (2) (d)ifferent (3) (c)ommon (4) (i)nclude 08 ② 09 ③

10 ⑤ 11 ③ 12 ④ 13 ①, ④

14 ⑤

15 (1) I want to buy a vest which has many pockets.
(2) I met Eva who was listening to music on the bus.
(3) She has a parrot which can speak 100 words.
(4) Math problems are always difficult for me.

16 (1) Dad usually goes to work by bike.
(2) Dorothy is always busy every day.
(3) I can never forget about baguettes.

17 (A) this (B) What (C) eat 18 ③

19 (A) lunch (B) such as 20 ⑤

21 appetizer 22 ③ 23 ⑤

24 the vegetables and fruit come from local farms

25 which → who 또는 that 26 ⓑ Eastern, ⓒ Western

27 ④

01 be good for: ~에 좋다 health: 건강

02 had better + 동사원형: ~하는 게 좋겠다 fruit: 과일 instead: 대신에

03 get up: 일어나다 heat ~ up: ~을 덥히다

04 at least: 적어도, 최소한 at the end of ~: ~의 끝에

05 파엘라(쌀, 닭고기, 생선, 채소를 넣은 스페인 요리)

06 public transportation: 공공 운송[교통] 기관

07 주어진 보기는 반의어의 관계이다. Eastern: 동양의 Western: 서양의 (1) rotten: 상한, 부패한 fresh: 신선한 (2) same: 같은 different: 다른 (3) rare: 희귀한, 드문 common: 흔한 (4) exclude: 배제하다 include: 포함하다

08 엄마의 생일이 다가오는데 돈이 없어서 직접 선물을 만들라고 추천하는 것이 어울리므로, enough를 no로 바꿔야 적절하다.

09 점심 먹고 대개 복통이 있다는 말에, 천천히 먹으라는 충고를 할 수 있다.

10 여자아이가 샌드위치에 채소(양파와 당근)를 넣으라고 충고하고, 그 의견을 받아들이는 것이 마지막 문장(You're right.)이므로, 그 뒤에 주어진 문장이 나와야 적절하다 go shopping: 쇼핑하러 가다 grocery: 식료품

11 여기서 them은 샌드위치이며, 질문은 샌드위치에 무엇을 넣는지 질문하고 있으므로 put in them이 적절하다. put A in B: A를 B에 넣다

12 ④ 양파와 당근을 첨가하지 않을 것이라는 말 뒤에 그 야채를 좋아한다는 말이 나오는 것은 어색하다. I don't like those vegetables.로 바꿔야 적절하다.

13 선행사가 사람이고 주격이므로 who나 that을 써야 한다.

14 빈도부사는 일반동사 앞에, 조동사나 be동사 다음에 위치한다.

15 (1)~(3) 선행사가 사람이면 who를, 사물이나 동물이면 which를 쓴다. (4) 빈도부사는 일반동사 앞에, 조동사나 be동사 다음에 위치한다.

16 빈도부사는 일반동사 앞에, 조동사나 be동사 다음에 위치한다.

17 (A) 자신을 소개할 때 this is가 적절하다. (B) eat의 목적어를 써야 하므로 What이 적절하다. (C) 조동사 do 다음에 본동사 eat이 적절하다.

18 ⓐ와 ③은 관계대명사이고, 나머지는 모두 의문대명사이다.

19 민준이는 주요리, 반찬 그리고 특식과 '같은' 한국의 학교 '점심'에 대해 소개한다.

20 (C)에서 식전 음식에 대해 설명하고 있으므로 제일 먼저 오고 (B)에서 후식에 대한 설명이 이어지므로 (C) 다음에 (B)가 이어지고 (A)의 They가 (B)의 마지막에 나오는 바게트를 가리키므로 (B) 다음에 (A)가 와야 한다. 그러므로 (C)-(B)-(A)의 순서가 적절하다.

21 appetizer: 식전 음식, 적은 양의 음식으로 된 식사의 첫 번째 코스

22 'ⓑ with cheese: 치즈와 함께 먹으면, ⓒ for+숫자: ~ 동안

23 왜 사람들이 대개 플랜테인을 튀기는지는 알 수 없다. ① Beans and rice. ② Meat and vegetables. ③ With plantains. ④ A fruit which looks like a banana.

24 '채소와 과일이 현지 농장에서 오기 때문에' 브루노의 학교 점심이 신선하다.

25 선행사가 사람(People)이고 주어 자리이므로, which를 주격 관계대명사 who나 that으로 고쳐야 한다.

26 각각 형용사로 고치면 된다.

27 ④ '작년에' 수상했다.

서술형 실전문제 p.102~103

01 ① No, I didn't. → Yes, I did.

02 breakfast

03 often feels tired, the boy should, also exercise every day

04 (1) I think Minhee is a girl who[that] is always kind.
(2) Teresa who[that] is singing on the stage has a beautiful voice.
(3) Cloe lives in a house which[that] has a nice swimming pool.
(4) I like the dog which[that] belongs to Kelly.
(5) There were a man and his horse that were crossing the river.

05 (1) The man who[that] works at this restaurant is serving food.
(2) These are the poems which[that] were written by Robert Frost.
(3) The girl who[that] wears a white dress is very pretty.

06 Lunch

07 We also have side dishes, such as *Bulgogi* or *Gimchi*. 또는 We have side dishes, such as *Bulgogi* or *Gimchi*, too.

08 another → other

09 (A) special rule (B) for at least 30 minutes

10 (A) a salad (B) meat or fish (C) fresh fruit

11 with cheese

01 But이 있으므로, 잠을 잘 잤음에도 피곤하다는 의미가 들어가야 어울리므로, 'Yes, I did.'로 고치는 게 적절하다.

02 아침에 먹는 식사 / breakfast: 아침식사

03 often: 종종, 자주 tired: 피곤한 should 동사원형: ~해야 한다 exercise: 운동하다 every day: 매일

04 (1), (2) 선행사가 사람이므로 관계대명사 who나 that을 써야 한다. (3), (4) 선행사가 사물이나 동물이므로 관계대명사 which나 that을 써야 한다. (5) 선행사가 '사람+동물'이므로 관계대명사 that을 써야 한다.

05 (1) 선행사가 사람이므로 that이나 who가 적절하다. (2) 선행사가 사물이므로 that이나 which를 쓴다. 또한 관계대명사절에서 그 수는 선행사에 일치시키므로 poems에 맞추어 were가 되어야 한다. (3) who를 목적격 whom 대신 쓸 수 있지만 whom을 who 대신 쓰지는 않는다.

06 많은 학생들에게 '점심시간'이 학교 일과 중 가장 좋은 부분이다.

07 also를 동사 앞에 또는 too를 문장 끝에 보충하면 된다.

08 '다른 나라들'에서 사는 학생들이라고 해야 하므로 other countries라고 하는 것이 적절하다. another+단수 명사

09 벨의 학교의 '특별한 규칙'은 학생들이 '적어도 30분간' 점심 식탁에 있어야 한다는 것이다.

10 식전 음식: 샐러드, 주요리: 고기나 생선, 후식: 신선한 과일

11 바게트는 '치즈와 함께 먹으면' 맛이 아주 좋다.

창의사고력 서술형 문제

p.104

|모범답안|

01 B: You had better write her a letter.
B: I think you also should give a little present to your friend with words of apology.

02 (1) a smart phone which my dad bought for me
(2) a computer which is very nice
(3) some pictures which were taken when I visited my grandmother's
(4) some comic books which are very interesting

03 (A) Spanish (B) Mixed paella
(C) fresh, delicious (D) low

단원별 모의고사

p.105~108

01 in 02 for
03 (l)ocal / (r)ecommend / (m)ixed
(1) mixed (2) local (3) recommend
04 (1) check (2) such (3) take (4) tasted
05 (1) I get often colds these days. → I often get colds these days.
(2) a lot → a lot of/lots of/much
(3) washed → wash
06 (1) Which food do you recommend?
(2) Do you have any recommendations?
07 (A) What are you doing right now?
(B) When is the party?
(C) Why don't you check out Chang's Restaurant?
(D) What do you recommend there?
08 ⑤ 09 I think we should go there.
10 ② 11 ⑤ 12 order
13 Could you recommend something else?
14 ④ 15 ⑤ 16 ③ 17 ②, ④
18 (1) Mom usually gets up at 7 in the morning.
(2) Abigail is always kind and frequently smiles.
(3) Richard seldom went swimming in the river.
19 (1) who → which[that]
(2) which he → who[that]
(3) helps never → never helps 20 ③
21 ④ 22 ② 23 ②
24 because of → because 25 fry
26 curry, noodle soup, or pasta 27 ①

01 live in: ~에서 살다 put A in B: A를 B에 넣다

02 for+기간: ~ 동안 for a long time: 오랫동안 be good for: ~에 좋다 thanks for ~: ~에 대해 감사하다

03 (1) mixed: 섞인, 복합된 / 식초가 섞인 와인이 좋았다. (2) local: 현지의, 지역의 / 우리는 지역 시장을 방문했고, 예쁜 귀걸이를 보았다. (3) recommend: 추천하다 / 그 여자를 위해 무엇을 추천합니까?

04 (1) check out: 확인하다, 조사하다 (2) such as: ~와 같은 (3) take care of: ~을 돌보다 (4) taste+형용사: ~한 맛이 나다

05 (1) 빈도부사는 일반동사의 앞에, be동사와 조동사의 뒤에 위치한다. (2) a lot of: 많은 (3) drink와 wash는 and로 연결된 병렬구조이다.

06 추천하는 표현으로 What do you recommend?, Which 명사 do you recommend?, Do you have any recommendations? 등이 있다.

07 (A) be동사의 현재형+동사ing: ~하고 있다 What are you doing right now?: 너 지금 뭐 하고 있니? (B) when: 언제 (C) check out: 확인하다, 조사하다 (D) recommend: 추천하다

08 The food and prices가 주어로 복수형이기 때문에 was를 were로 바꾸어야 한다.

09 I think 주어 should 동사원형: 나는 ~가 …해야 한다고 생각한다.

10 추천을 요청하는 말에, 닭고기 샌드위치가 가장 인기 있다고 대답했다. ② 뒤의 문장 It이 the chicken sandwich를 받는 대명사이다.

11 ① 병원 ② 학교 ③ 집 ④ 빵집 ⑤ 식당

12 order: 주문하다

13 Could you recommend something else? = What else do you recommend?: 다른 제안해 줄 것 있니? -thing으로 끝나는 말(something, anything, nothing 등)은 보통의 다른 명사들과 달리 형용사가 뒤에서 수식한다.

14 get a discount: 할인받다

15 선행사가 사물일 경우 주격 관계대명사는 that이나 which를 쓴다.

16 ③ 빈도부사는 일반동사 앞에, be동사나 조동사 다음에 위치한다.

17 ①, ③, ⑤는 접속사로 쓰인 that이고, ②와 ④는 관계대명사이다.

18 빈도부사는 일반동사 앞에, be동사나 조동사 다음에 위치한다.

19 (1) 선행사가 사물이므로 who를 which나 that으로 고쳐야 한다. (2) 선행사가 사람이므로 which를 who나 that으로 고쳐야 하며 관계대명사가 접속사와 대명사의 역할을 하므로 주어로 쓰인 he를 삭제해야 한다. (3) 빈도부사는 일반동사 앞에 위치한다.

20 위 글은 한국의 급식에 대해 소개하는 글인데, '전 세계에 많은

맛있는 반찬들이 있다'는 ③번 문장은 전체 글의 흐름에서 벗어난다.

21 특식을 '제공한다'고 해야 하므로 'serves'가 적절하다. serve: (음식을) 제공하다, (음식을 상에) 차려 주다

22 다른 나라에서 사는 학생들은 점심으로 무엇을 먹는지 음식 취재 기자들에게서 들어보겠다고 했기 때문에, 뒤에 올 내용으로는 ②번이 적절하다.

23 주어진 문장의 plantains에 주목한다. ②번 다음 문장에서 플랜테인에 대한 설명을 하고 있으므로 ②번이 적절하다.

24 because of 뒤에는 '주어+동사'가 올 수 없고, because 뒤에 '주어+동사'가 올 수 있다.

25 플랜테인을 보통 '튀긴다'고 했다.

26 카레, 국수, 혹은 파스타가 ⓐ에 해당한다.

27 ⓑ choose from: ~로부터 선택하다, ⓒ an award for: ~에 대한 상

Lesson 3

Understand the World

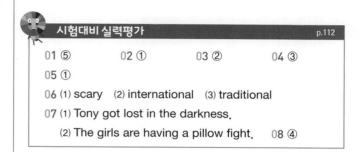

시험대비 실력평가 p.112

01 ⑤ 02 ① 03 ② 04 ③
05 ①
06 (1) scary (2) international (3) traditional
07 (1) Tony got lost in the darkness.
(2) The girls are having a pillow fight. 08 ④

01 last: 계속되다, 지속되다

02 greet: 맞이하다, 환영하다 welcome: 환영하다

03 represent: 나타내다, 상징하다 wreath: 화환, 화관

04 ③ try -ing: (시험삼아) ~해 보다 pray: 기도하다 ease: 편안하게 하다 ④ meditation: 명상

05 lock: 자물쇠; 잠그다

06 (1) scary: 무서운, 두려운, 겁나는/그녀는 내게 무서운 이야기들을 해 주었다. (2) international: 국제적인, 세계적인/수출 법규가 국제 통상에서 중요한 요인이 되었다. (3) traditional: 전통의, 전통적인/그녀는 한국 전통 의상을 입고 있다.

07 (1) darkness: 어둠, 암흑 (2) pillow: 베개

08 toward: ~ 쪽으로

서술형 시험대비 p.113

01 (1) (r)ude (2) (t)ry (3) (e)vil (4) (v)ictory
02 (1) experience (2) mean (3) arrive (4) celebrate
03 (1) face (2) separation, able
04 colored
05 (1) at (2) of
06 (1) She greeted us with a kind smile.
(2) The meeting lasted three hours.
(3) I put the coin in her palm.
(4) A red flag represents danger.

01 보기는 동의어 관계이다. good: 좋은 nice: 좋은 (1) impolite: 버릇없는, 무례한 rude: 무례한 (2) attempt: 시도하다 try: 한 번 해 보다 (3) wicked: 못된, 사악한 evil: 사악한, 악마의 (4) success: 성공, 성과 victory: 승리, 성공

02 (1) experience: 경험하다/호기심을 지키는 것은 내가 지속적

으로 새로운 것을 배우는 즐거움을 경험하도록 할 것이다. (2) mean: 의미하다/그것이 내가 게으르다는 것을 의미하는 것은 아니다. (3) arrive: 도착하다/다음 기차는 언제 도착하나요? (4) celebrate: 축하하다/그들은 크리스마스와 새해를 같이 축하한다.

03 (1) face: ~을 향하다 (2) separation: 분리, 이별 be able to 동사원형: ~할 수 있다

04 color: ~에 색칠하다 colored: 채색된, 색깔이 있는

05 (1) stay at: ~에서 머무르다 point at: ~을 가리키다 (2) be afraid of: ~을 두려워하다 remind A of B: A에게 B를 생각나게 하다

06 (1) greet: 맞이하다, 환영하다 (2) last: 계속되다, 지속되다 (3) palm: 손바닥 (4) represent: 나타내다, 상징하다

교과서

Conversation

핵심 Check p.114~115

1 (C) → (A) → (B) 2 explain what, means
3 I'd like to know what that means.
It means you should think carefully
4 Have you watched / have, Have
5 (C) → (A) → (D) → (B)
6 Have you had *gimchi* before?

교과서 대화문 익히기

Check(√) True or False p.116

(1) T (2) T (3) F (4) T

교과서 확인학습 p.118~119

Listen & Talk 1 A

Have you, been / haven't, Have / have, last year, was / sounds, to go, someday

Listen & Talk 1 B

to, Festival, many different traditional games / looks, Which, should / Have you ever / No, I haven't / from / How / on, throw, at / sounds fun

Listen & Talk 1 C

There is, in, this / a traditional Indian festival, colored powder, each / sounds exciting. Have you ever been / told me / When / on, on / like, Should / clothes, the colored powder, clothes / for

Listen and Talk 2 A

gave me, What does that mean in Korea / means

Listen and Talk 2 B

this, isn't it / about buying, one / something bad / What does, mean in China / means separation, separation / about

Listen and Talk 2 C

What a, Are / took / look at, rude / who is making, palm is facing toward / meaning in / What does that mean / victory or peace

Do It Yourself

brings / to / means / Have you ever been to / I haven't, What does / means

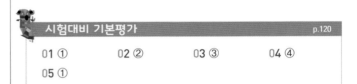

시험대비 기본평가 p.120

01 ① 02 ② 03 ③ 04 ④
05 ①

01 경험 유무를 물을 때 "Have you (ever) 과거분사 ~?"로 말한다.

02 mean: 의미하다 in Korea: 한국에서

03 'Have you 과거분사 ~?'는 경험을 묻는 표현이다.

04 (C) 고로드키 게임을 해 봤는지 묻자, (A) 안 해봤다고 대답하고 무엇인지 질문한다. (B) 상대방은 고로드키 게임이 러시아 전통 게임이라고 설명해 준다.

05 'have been to 장소'는 '~에 가 본 경험이 있다'의 의미이고, 'have gone to 장소'는 '~에 갔다(그래서 지금 없다)'는 의미이므로 gone을 been으로 바꿔야 적절하다.

시험대비 실력평가 p.121~122

01 ③ 02 ② 03 ② 04 What does an umbrella mean in China? 05 ②
06 ②, ④ 07 (A) What is that? (B) Have you ever been to a Holi festival? (C) When is the festival? (D) Should I bring anything? 08 ④ 09 ③
10 exciting 11 ① 12 a traditional game from, play, putting five sticks, throwing a bat

01 (A) give+me(간접목적어)+Yeot(직접목적어): 나에게 엿을 주다 (B) What does that mean (in Korea)?: (한국에서는) 이게 어떤 의미니? mean: 의미하다

02 브라질에 가 본 경험을 묻는 질문에, (B) 없다고 대답하며 상대방의 경험을 묻고 (A) 작년에 갔었는데 삼바 축제가 있었다고 답하자 (C) 삼바 축제에 흥미를 가지며 가고 싶다고 말한다.

03 'What about you?'는 상대방의 생각이나 의견을 묻는 표현이다. 여자아이는 상대방의 질문에 답하면서 상대방은 무엇을 살지 'What about you?'로 물어보고 있다.

04 What does ~ mean?: ~이 어떤 의미니?

05 ⓓ bad something → something bad, -thing으로 끝나는 부정대명사(something, anything, nothing 등)는 형용사가 뒤에서 수식한다. ⓔ sounds → sound, 주어가 the words로 복수 명사이므로 동사에 s를 붙이지 않는다.

06 ① 여자아이는 책을 Ling의 선물로 살 것이다. ② 중국에서 책의 의미는 대화에서 나와 있지 않다. ③ 이번 주 수요일이 Ling의 생일이다. ④ 초콜릿을 사러 갈 장소는 나와 있지 않다. ⑤ 중국인에게 우산은 이별을 의미하므로, 좋은 선물이 아니다.

07 (A) 다음에 Holi festival에 대해 설명하고 있다. (B) 다음에 'No, I haven't.'라고 답하고 있다. (C) 다음에 언제인지 답하고 있다. (D) 다음에 하얀 옷을 입어야 한다고 답하고 있다.

08 ④ 색깔이 있는 옷이 아니라 하얀 옷을 입어야 한다.

09 상대방의 경험에 대해 물어볼 때는, 현재완료 시제를 사용하여 'Have you 과거분사 ~?'라고 묻는다. 경험을 묻는 말에 'Yes, I have.'나 'No, I haven't.'로 대답할 수 있다.

10 exciting: 흥미로운

11 ⓑ~ⓔ는 gorodki를 가리키지만 ⓐ는 여러 가지 전통적인 게임을 하는 것을 가리킨다.

12 traditional: 전통적인 from: (출처·기원) … 출신의[에서 온] the way to 동사원형: ~하는 방법 throw: ~을 던지다 at: (방향) ~으로

서술형 시험대비 p.123

01 His palm is facing toward himself.
02 meaning
03 ③ which → who
04 showing your palm and making a V sign
05 What
06 getting her hair cut on a Tuesday
07 It means bad luck.
08 Have you ever been to Brazil?

01 palm: 손바닥 face: ~을 향하다 toward: ~쪽으로

02 mean: 의미하다 meaning: 의미

03 사람(The boy)이 선행사이므로 주격 관계대명사 who를 사용해야 한다. The boy who is making the V sign: V사인을 하고 있는 소년

04 (C)가 가리키는 것은 여자아이가 말한 손바닥을 보여 주면서 V 사인을 만드는 것을 의미한다..

05 What do you see in this picture?: 이 그림에서 무엇이 보이니? What does that mean?: 이게 어떤 의미니?

06 get+목적어+목적격보어(p.p): 목적어가 ~되도록 시키다 on+요일: ~요일에

07 mean: 의미하다 bad luck: 불운

08 Have you ever been to 장소?: ~에 가 본 적 있니? Brazil: 브라질

교과서

Grammar

핵심 Check p.124~125

1 (1) have gone (2) have, visited (3) Have, read
2 (1) so busy that (2) so big that

시험대비 기본평가 p.126

01 (1) visit → visited (2) has finished → finished
(3) Do you have → Have you (4) what → that
(5) very → so (6) for → since (7) have → has
02 ③ 03 ①

01 (1) 현재완료는 'have[has]+과거분사'의 형태이다. (2) 현재완료는 과거를 나타내는 어구와 함께 쓸 수 없다. (3) 현재완료의 의문문은 have 동사를 주어 앞으로 보낸다. (4), (5) 'so+형용사[부사]+that+주어+동사'의 형태로 '매우 …해서 ~하다'는 의미를 나타낸다. (6) 현재완료에서 'since+시간 명사', 'for+기간 명사'를 쓴다. (7) 주어가 3인칭 단수이므로 has를 써야 한다.

02 ③ Joel has worked for 6 hours straight.

03 so ... that ~: 너무 …해서 ~하다

시험대비 실력평가 p.131~133

01 ④ 02 ① 03 ⑤ 04 ③
05 (1) visited (2) has (3) gone (4) before (5) hasn't
06 ① 07 ⑤ 08 (1) so (2) that

(3) such (4) couldn't 09 ④ 10 ②

11 ②

12 (1) Julia got too angry to speak.
(2) Sean is rich enough to buy the expensive car.
(3) The panda is too cute for me to take my eyes off him.
(4) The house was nice enough for Melanie to want to live there.

13 ④ 14 ④

15 (1) Suyeon has just arrived at Busan Station. 또는 Suyeon arrived at Busan Station an hour ago.
(2) Ron and his sisters have gone to England.
(3) Grace was too fat to wear the beautiful dress. Grace was so fat that she couldn't wear the beautiful dress.
(4) The drama was so boring that I turned off the TV.
(5) He has lived in Busan since 2010.

16 ⓐ visited ⓑ been

17 (1) for → since (2) gone → been (3) too → so
(4) poor enough → so poor (5) has lost → lost

18 ②

01 현재완료 의문문은 'Have+주어+과거분사~?'이다. 'have gone to ~'는 '~에 가버리고 없다'는 뜻이므로 1인칭 주어를 쓸 수 없다.

02 '…해서 ~하다'의 의미인 'so ... that ~' 구문이다.

03 현재완료형의 질문에 대한 답은 have[has] 동사를 이용해 답한다.

04 so ... that ~'은 '너무[매우] ~해서 …하다'의 의미로 원인과 결과를 나타낸다.

05 (1) 현재완료는 'have[has]+과거분사'의 형태이다. (2) 주어가 3인칭 단수이므로 has가 적절하다. (3) have[has] gone to는 '~에 가고 없다'는 결과를 나타낸다. (4) ago는 단독으로 쓸 수 없다. (5) 현재완료의 부정형은 'have[has] not+과거분사'이다.

06 ① Dad's explanation was so clear that we could understand it easily.

07 현재완료의 부정은 have 다음에 not이나 never를 붙인다.

08 (1), (2) '매우 …해서 ~하다'의 의미인 'so ... that ~' 구문이다. (3) 'so ... that' 구문에서 that 앞에 형용사나 부사 대신 명사가 오면 so 대신 such를 쓴다. (4) so+형용사/부사+that+주어+couldn't+동사원형: 너무 ~하여 …할 수 없었다

09 현재완료에서 'since+시간 명사', 'for+기간 명사'

10 'so ... that ~'은 so 뒤의 형용사나 부사가 원인을 나타내며, 접속사 that 뒤에는 그에 따른 결과를 나타낸다.

11 ②번은 경험 용법으로 쓰였고 나머지는 다 완료 용법으로 쓰였다.

12 (1) so ... that 주어 can't ~ = too ... to ~ (2) so ... that 주어 can ~ = ... enough to ~ (3), (4) 'so ... that ~' 구문에서 주어가 서로 다를 경우 'too ... to ~'나 '... enough to ~'로 바꿔 쓸 때 'for+목적격'으로 주어를 나타낸다.

13 현재완료의 결과적 용법(…해서 (그 결과) 지금 ~하다)을 이용하여 과거에 러시아로 가서 아직도 그곳에 머무르고 있다는 현재의 결과를 나타내도록 한다.

14 so ... that ~: 너무 …해서 ~하다

15 (1) 현재완료는 과거를 나타내는 어구와 함께 쓸 수 없다. (2) have[has] been to는 '~에 가 본적이 있다'는 경험을 나타내고, have[has] gone to는 '~에 가고 없다'는 결과를 나타내므로 have gone to로 고쳐야 한다. (3), (4) 'so ... that ~'이나 'too ... to ~'로 나타내는 것이 적절하다. (5) 현재완료에서 'since+시간 명사', 'for+기간 명사'

16 ⓐ last week이라는 과거를 나타내는 부사구가 있으므로 과거형으로 써야 한다. ⓑ 'have gone to'는 결과를 나타내는 말로 1인칭을 주어로 쓸 수 없다. 여기서 there는 to Vietnam을 대신하고 있다.

17 (1) 현재완료에서 'since+시간 명사', 'for+기간 명사' (2) have[has] been to는 '~에 가 본 적이 있다'는 경험을 나타내고, have[has] gone to는 '~에 가고 없다'는 결과를 나타낸다. (3), (4) so ... that ~: 너무 …해서 ~하다 (5) 현재완료는 과거를 나타내는 어구와 함께 쓸 수 없다.

18 too ... to ~ = so ... that 주어 can't ~, ... enough to ~ = so ... that 주어 can

서술형 시험대비

p.130~131

01 (1) Laura has lived in Chicago since 1998.
(2) Dan has lost his cell phone.

02 (1) Kate is so young that she can't drive a car.
(2) Stefanie is so wise that she can give advice to her friends.

03 (1) James has played soccer since he was a child.
(2) It rains so heavily that we can't go outside.
(3) Charlie has studied Korean for six months.

04 (1) Mr. Brown has lived in New York since 2015.
(2) We have been to Sydney.
(3) Elle didn't take a walk yesterday.
(4) My long padding coat is warm enough for me to endure the winter.
(5) Lylian was so afraid that she couldn't open her eyes.

05 (1) Mike was too sick to go to work yesterday.
(2) The *samgyetang* was so hot that Amy could not eat it.
(3) His essay was nice enough for his teacher to be satisfied.
(4) Tom ran so fast that he could catch the last bus.

06 (1) His neighbor's party was so noisy that he couldn't sleep at all.
(2) Rose has not arrived at the library yet.
(3) The man was so kind that he helped me right away.
(4) I have been to Paris once.
(5) Andrew has left his smartphone in the train.

07 (1) Bella has never(not) driven a car before.
(2) Bella has visited Angkor Wat before.
(3) Bella has never[not] tasted Vietnamese food before.
(4) Bella has practiced yoga before.

08 (1) The flowers are so beautiful that many people come to see them.
(2) The house was so expensive that we decided not to buy it.
(3) This dish is so spicy that I need to drink a lot of milk.
(4) The movie was so sad that I cried a lot.
(5) You are so smart that you always get A's.

09 has gone

01 (1) 1998년에 살기 시작해서 지금도 살고 있는 것이므로 현재완료의 '계속'을 이용한다. (2) cell phone을 잃어버려서 지금 없는 것이므로 현재완료의 '결과'를 이용한다.

02 too ... to ~ = so ... that 주어 can't ~, ... enough to ~ = so ... that 주어 can

03 (1), (3) 현재완료의 계속적 용법을 이용한다. (2) so ... that 주어 can't ~: 너무 …해서 ~할 수 없다

04 (1) 현재완료에서 'since+시간 명사', 'for+기간 명사' (2) have gone to는 3인칭만 주어가 될 수 있다. (3) 현재완료는 과거를 나타내는 부사와 함께 쓸 수 없다. (4) enough 는 형용사 다음에 와서 '... enough to ~'의 형식으로 쓰인다. (5) so ... that 주어 can't ~ = too ... to ~: 너무 …해서 ~할 수 없다

05 too ... to ~ = so ... that 주어 can't ~, ... enough to부정사 = so ... that 주어 can ~ / 이때 to부정사 앞에 for 목적격으로 쓰인 것은 to부정사의 의미상의 주어로 that 이하의 절로 바꿀 때는 주격으로 바꿔야 하며, to부정사로 썼을 때 생략된 동사의 목적어는 써 주어야 한다.

06 (1), (3) so+형용사[부사]+that+주어+동사: 매우 …해서 ~하다 (2) 현재완료의 '완료' 용법 (4) 현재완료의 '경험' 용법 (5) 현재완료의 '결과' 용법

07 현재완료의 '경험' 용법을 이용한다.

08 'so+형용사[부사]+that+주어+동사'의 형태로 '매우 …해서 ~하다'라는 의미이다. so 뒤의 형용사나 부사는 원인을 나타내며, 접속사 that 뒤에 나오는 내용은 그에 따른 결과를 나타낸다.

09 현재완료의 '결과' 용법을 이용한다.

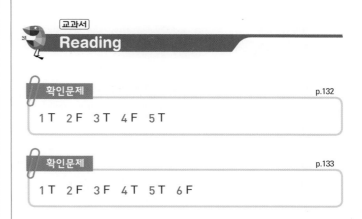

교과서

Reading

확인문제 p.132

1 T 2 F 3 T 4 F 5 T

확인문제 p.133

1 T 2 F 3 F 4 T 5 T 6 F

교과서 확인학습 A p.134~135

01 Traditional 02 from a sister school
03 stay at, for a week 04 him the guest room 05 stay here 06 is full of
07 Look at 08 these things 09 They're
10 on my pillow, scary 11 Not really, symbols of 12 surprising, remind, of
13 shows 14 meet, greet each other
15 Have you ever seen
16 haven't, so, that 17 For a long time, good guards 18 close their eyes 19 interesting 20 watch over, That's why, like 21 understand 22 walk around
23 that piece of paper 24 Do you mean
25 a rooster 26 crow 27 a new day
28 go away, crows 29 I've never heard 30 Actually, afraid
31 for me 32 draw a big rooster
33 Put, above, protect 34 will
35 so much that 36 traditional Korean symbols
37 a lot of them 38 with my family

교과서 확인학습 B p.136~137

1 Traditional Korean Symbols
2 Peter is visiting Korea to meet a friend, Mina, from a sister school.
3 Peter is going to stay at her grandfather's house for a week.
4 When he arrives, Mina shows him the guest room.
5 Peter, you will stay here.
6 This guest room is full of traditional Korean things.
7 Look at this pillow.
8 What are these things?
9 They're bats.
10 Bats on my pillow? That's scary!
11 Not really. In Korea, bats are symbols of luck and a long life.
12 That's surprising. In many Western countries, bats remind people of darkness and scary things.
13 Mina shows Peter her grandfather's room.
14 Peter and Mina's grandfather meet and greet each other.
15 Hi, Peter! Have you ever seen this kind of lock before?
16 No, I haven't. It's so old that I can't really tell, but is it a fish?
17 Yes. For a long time, Koreans have thought that fish are good guards.
18 Fish don't close their eyes, even when they sleep.
19 That's interesting.
20 We think fish can watch over valuable things. That's why this lock looks like a fish.
21 Now I understand.
22 They go outside and walk around the garden.
23 What is on that piece of paper? It looks scary.
24 Do you mean this painting of a rooster?
25 Oh, is it a rooster?
26 Yes, it is. Roosters crow every morning.
27 Their crowing means that a new day is beginning.
28 For many years, Koreans have believed evil spirits go away when a rooster crows.
29 Really? I've never heard that before.
30 Actually, I'm afraid of darkness and evil spirits.
31 Could you draw a rooster for me, Mina?
32 Sure. I'll draw a big rooster for you!
33 Put the drawing above your door. Then it will protect you.
34 Yes, I will.
35 I'm enjoying this trip so much that I want to stay longer.
36 I love all the traditional Korean symbols in this house.
37 Now I understand a lot of them.
38 I want to visit Korea again with my family.

시험대비 실력평가 p.138~141

01 내 베개 위에 박쥐가 있는 것
02 한국에서는 박쥐가 행운과 장수의 상징이기 때문이다.
03 ② 04 ④ 05 ③, ⑤
06 No, I haven't. 07 sister school 08 ⑤
09 ④ 10 ③ 11 lock
12 That's why this lock looks like a fish.
13 looks like → looks 14 ③ 15 ⑤
16 (A) As (B) so 17 ④ 18 ⑤
19 (1) at any time → on special days, such as New Year's Day
(2) three → two
20 (A) During (B) a lot (C) interesting
21 ② 22 (A) beginning (B) protect (C) will
23 ②, ⑤ 24 (A) afraid (B) go away

01 that은 지시대명사로 앞 문장의 내용을 받는다.
02 바로 뒤에 그 이유를 설명하고 있다.
03 ② 피터는 '일주일'간 미나네 할아버지 댁에 머무를 것이다.
04 ④ watch over: ~을 보살피다[보호하다/지켜보다], ~을 지키다, ① ~에게 (~을) 둘러보도록 안내하다[구경시켜 주다], ② ~을 기다리다, ③ ~을 조사하다, ⑤ ~을 기대하다, 즐거운 마음으로 기다리다
05 ⓐ와 ③과 ⑤는 경험 용법, ① 결과 용법, ② 계속 용법, ④ 완료 용법
06 현재완료로 물었기 때문에 No, I haven't.로 답하는 것이 적절하다.
07 sister school: 자매학교, 재정적으로, 역사적으로 혹은 사회적으로 다른 학교에 연결되어 있는 학교
08 베개에 박쥐 디자인이 있다는 것에 대해 Peter가 '무섭다'고 하니까 미나는 한국에서 박쥐는 행운과 장수의 상징이라고 말하고 있으므로 빈칸에는 동의하지 않는 말이 들어가야 한다. 그러므로 ⑤번의 '사실은 그렇지 않아.'가 적절하다. 나머지는 다 동의를 나타낼 때 쓰는 말이다. ② Why not?: (동의를 나타내어) 왜 아니겠어?
09 베개에 박쥐가 있는 것에 '무서워'하다가 한국에서 박쥐는 행운과 장수의 상징이라는 말에 '놀라워'했다. disappointed: 실망한, scared: 무서워하는, ashamed: 부끄러운, ⑤ depressed: 우울한

10 ⓐ와 ③은 '종류(명사)', 나머지는 다 '친절한(형용사)'
11 미나의 할아버지가 Peter에게 보여주신 '자물쇠'를 가리킨다.
12 'why'를 보충하면 된다.
13 look + 형용사, look like + 명사: ~처럼 보이다
14 위 글은 수탉 그림의 의미를 설명하는 글이므로, 제목으로는 ③번 '수탉 그림이 무엇을 의미하는가?'가 적절하다.
15 ⑤ 할아버지가 피터에게 그 그림을 그의 문 아래가 아닌 문 위에 걸어 놓으라고 한 이유는 대답할 수 없다. ① Peter, Mina's grandfather, and Mina. ② No, he doesn't. ③ It means that a new day is beginning. ④ A big rooster.
16 문장 앞에 As를 쓰거나 문장 중간에 so를 써서 고치는 것이 적절하다. For는 부가적인 이유를 나타낼 때 쓸 수 있으므로 (A)에 들어가기에는 적절하지 않다.
17 ④ '피터가 전통적인 한국의 상징물들에 대해 계속 공부하고 싶어 한다'는 내용은 본문에 없다.
18 앞의 내용의 예가 나오고 있으므로 For example이 가장 적절하다. ① 그러나, ② 다시 말해, ③ 그러므로, ④ 게다가
19 (1) 사람들은 사자춤을 '설날과 같은 특별한 날에' 춘다. (2) '두 명'의 댄서들이 사자처럼 옷을 입고 행동한다.
20 (A) 'during+특정 기간을 나타내는 명사', 'for+숫자가 붙은 기간'이므로 During이 적절하다. (B) 뒤에 명사가 없으므로 a lot이 적절하다. a lot of+명사 (C) 감정을 나타내는 말은 사람을 수식할 때는 보통 과거분사로, 사물을 수식할 때는 보통 현재분사로 쓰기 때문에 interesting이 적절하다.
21 ② 여행 기간은 알 수 없다. ① 한국, ③ 미나와 미나의 할아버지, ④ 전통적인 한국의 상징물들, ⑤ 재미있었다.
22 (A) 수탉이 매일 아침 운다고 했으므로, 수탉의 울음은 새로운 날이 '시작하는(beginning)' 것을 의미한다고 하는 것이 적절하다. (B) 그것이 너를 '지켜줄' 거라고 해야 하므로 protect가 적절하다. prevent: 막다[예방/방지하다], (C) '네, 그럴게요.'라고 해야 하므로 will이 적절하다.
23 Actually = In fact = As a matter of fact: 사실, ① 그 결과, ③ 무엇보다도, 특히, ④ 다시 말해서
24 피터는 어둠과 악령들을 '무서워하고,' 수탉 그림 덕분에 그것들이 '물러가기를' 원하기 때문이다.

서술형 시험대비 p.142~143

01 Mina shows the guest room to him.
02 luck and a long life
03 happiness and pleasant → darkness and scary
04 greet to → greet
05 Have you ever seen this kind of lock before?
06 fish don't close their eyes, even when they sleep
07 a fish
08 The painting of a rooster.
09 (1) **새로운 날이 시작하는 것을 의미한다.**
(2) **수탉이 울 때 악령이 물러간다.**
10 I've never heard that before.
11 is filled with
12 **⑤번,** → surprising
13 (A) luck (B) a long life (C) negative

01 show는 to를 사용하여 3형식으로 고친다.
02 한국에서 박쥐는 '행운과 장수'를 상징한다.
03 서구의 많은 나라들에서, 박쥐는 사람들에게 '어둠과 무서운 것들'을 상기시켜 준다.
04 greet: ~에게 인사하다(타동사)
05 'before'를 보충하면 된다.
06 물고기는 잘 때도 눈을 감지 않기 때문이다.
07 미나의 할아버지가 피터에게 보여주는 자물쇠는 '물고기'처럼 생겼다.
08 피터가 가리키고 있는 종이 위에는 '수탉 그림'이 있다.
09 수탉의 울음은 '새로운 날이 시작하는 것을 의미'하고, 여러 해 동안, 한국 사람들은 '수탉이 울 때 악령이 물러간다.'고 믿어 왔다.
10 5단어로 영작하기 위하여 I have를 I've로 축약하면 된다.
11 be full of = be filled with: ~로 가득 차 있다
12 피터는 서구의 많은 나라들에서 박쥐는 사람들에게 어둠과 무서운 것들을 상기시켜 준다고 말하고 있기 때문에, 한국에서 박쥐가 행운과 장수의 상징이라는 미나의 말에 대한 응답으로는 'reasonable'이 아니라 'surprising'과 같이 '놀랍다'는 뜻의 단어로 고치는 것이 적절하다. reasonable: 타당한, 사리에 맞는, 합리적인
13 한국에서 박쥐는 사람들에게 '행운'과 '장수'와 같은 긍정적인 것들을 상기시켜 준다. 반면에, 서구의 많은 나라들에서, 박쥐는 어둠과 무서운 것들과 같은 '부정적인' 것들의 상징이다.

영역별 핵심문제 p.145~149

01 ③ 02 ①, ④, ⑤ 03 (c)row 04 (p)alm
05 ③ have been → went, 또는 last year → before
06 ② 07 ④ 08 ① 09 means
10 Have you ever been to a Spanish festival before?
11 ④ 12 (A) to (B) from (C) on (C) at
13 traditional 14 ③, ④ 15 ③ 16 ①
17 ⑤ 18 so, that
19 (1) has, been (2) has gone
20 ②
21 (1) The car was so fast that the police couldn't catch it.

(2) The concert was so good that many people went to see it again.
22 (1) Lin has spent all the money for shopping.
(2) Jeremy has played the piano for six years.
23 ①, ⑤ 24 (A) traditional (B) scary (C) remind
25 ④ 26 Fish don't close their eyes, even when they sleep. 27 ⑤ 28 ①
29 ③ 30 ② 31 ②
32 it → them

01 ③ try는 '한번 해 보다'의 뜻으로 여기서는 '한번 먹어 보다'의 의미로 사용되었다.

02 face: ~을 향하다 ① 손바닥은 천장을 향해 있어야 됩니다. ④ 스캔할 사진 면이 위를 향하도록 해야 합니다. ⑤ 정원은 남쪽을 향해 있습니다. ②, ③ face: 얼굴 wrinkle: 주름

03 crow: 까마귀; (닭이) 울다/까마귀 날자 배 떨어진다./ 그들은 해가 뜨는 매일 아침 같은 시간에 웁니다.

04 palm: 손바닥; 야자나무 / 그가 손바닥으로 그녀의 턱을 괴었다. / 그들은 야자나무에 쉽게 올라갈 수 있다.

05 완료 시제를 사용할 때는 ~ ago, yesterday, when 등과 같이 명백한 과거를 나타내는 말과 함께 사용하지 않는다.

06 ⓒ와 ⓕ를 제외한 나머지 보기는 대화의 내용과 일치한다.

07 ④ have been to: ~에 가 본 적이 있다.

08 'What brings you here today?'가 어떤 일로 여기 왔는지 질문을 하는 것이므로, 주어진 문장이 이에 대한 대답이 될 수 있다.

09 mean: 의미하다

10 Have you ever been to~?: ~에 가 본 적 있니? Spanish: 스페인의 festival: 축제

11 ④ 무대에 큰 글씨 gracias가 있다.

12 (A) welcome to ~: ~에 오신 걸 환영합니다 (B) from: (출처·기원) ~ 출신의[에서 온] (C) on: ~ 위에 on the ground: 바닥에 (D) throw: ~을 던지다 at: (방향) ~으로

13 traditional: 전통적인

14 <보기>의 문장과 ③, ④번은 현재완료의 '경험'이다. ① 계속 ② 완료 ⑤ 결과

15 'so ... that ~'은 '너무[매우] ~해서 …하다'의 의미로 원인과 결과를 나타낸다.

16 현재완료는 특정한 과거를 나타내는 when과 함께 쓸 수 없다. When did you visit London?으로 써야 한다.

17 'so ... that ~'은 '너무[매우] ~해서 …하다'의 의미로 원인과 결과를 나타낸다.

18 so ... that ~: 너무[매우] ~해서 …하다

19 have[has] been to는 '~에 가 본 적이 있다'는 경험을, have[has] gone to는 '~에 가고 없다'는 결과를 나타낸다.

20 ② Nicole was so tired that she couldn't go shopping.

21 'so ... that ~'은 '너무[매우] ~해서 …하다'의 의미로 원인과 결과를 나타낸다.

22 현재완료의 '결과' 용법과 '계속' 용법을 이용한다.

23 ⓐ와 ①, ⑤ 부사적 용법, ②, ③ 명사적 용법, ④ 형용사적 용법

24 (A) 이 손님방은 한국의 '전통' 물건들로 가득 차 있다고 해야 하므로 traditional이 적절하다. modern: 현대의, (B) 뒷부분에 서구의 많은 나라들에서 박쥐는 사람들에게 어둠과 무서운 것들을 상기시켜 준다는 말이 나오기 때문에, 베개에 박쥐 디자인이 있다는 것에 대해 피터는 '겁난다'고 해야 하므로 scary가 적절하다. terrific 아주 좋은, 멋진, 훌륭한, (C) 어둠과 무서운 것들을 '상기시켜 준다'고 해야 하므로 remind가 적절하다. remain: 계속[여전히] …이다

25 so ~ that ...: 너무 ~해서 …하다

26 물고기는 잘 때도 눈을 감지 않는다는 것을 가리킨다.

27 이 글은 자물쇠가 물고기처럼 생긴 이유를 설명하는 글이므로, 주제로는 ⑤ '자물쇠가 물고기처럼 생긴 이유'가 가장 적절하다.

28 수탉의 울음은 새로운 날이 시작하는 것을 의미한다고 했기 때문에, 수탉이 울 때 '악령이 물러간다.'고 믿어왔다고 하는 것이 적절하다.

29 ⓑ be afraid of: ~을 두려워하다, ⓒ draw A for B: B를 위해 A를 그려 주다

30 피터는 '저 종이에는 무엇이 그려져 있는 거죠?' '오, 그게 수탉이에요?'라고 물어보고 있으므로, 종이 위에 수탉 그림이 있는 것을 모르고 있었다.

31 ⓐ, ②, ⑤ 명사적 용법, ① 형용사적 용법(It은 비인칭주어), ③ 부사적 용법(목적), ④ 형용사적 용법

32 이 집의 모든 전통적인 한국의 상징물들을 가리키므로 'them'이 적절하다.

단원별 예상문제

p.150~153

01 (C) → (B) → (A) → (D) 02 (D) → (F) → (A) → (B) → (E) → (C) 03 (A) haven't (B) Have (C) have
04 ④ 05 ④ 06 Chinese
07 separation 08 about
09 (b)ow, (c)row, (l)ast, (1) lasted (2) crows (3) bow
10 (A) listened (B) Spanish
11 It means good luck for 12 months 12 ①, ⑤
13 (1) He is so fat that there is hardly any shirt that fits him.
(2) His voice was so small that I couldn't hear him talk.
(3) Jenny has waited for Sunny for an hour.
14 ①

15 (1) It has rained for a week.
(2) Elvis has gone to Wien.
16 ④ 17 of
18 This guest room is full of traditional Korean things.
19 (A) haven't (B) are (C) why
20 그것은 너무 오래되어서 사실 알아볼 수가 없어요.
21 ④ 22 sheet 23 the drawing above your door 24 ③
25 he is enjoying this trip so much
26 visiting → to visit

01 Holi Festival이 있다는 말에 (C)에서 Holi가 무엇인지 질문하고 (B)에서 대답한다. (A)에서 축제에 흥미를 보이며, Holi Festival에 가 본 경험을 묻고 (D)에서 대답한다.

02 주어진 글의 무례하다는 말에, (D) 누가 무례한지 묻고 (F) 남자애가 하는 행동을 설명하며 언급하고 (A) 무엇이 잘못 되었는지 묻자 (B) 손바닥이 자기 쪽을 향하는 것은 나쁜 뜻을 가지고 있고, 손바닥을 보여 주면서 브이 사인을 만드는 것은 괜찮다고 대답한다. (E) 마지막으로, 손바닥을 보여주면서 브이 사인을 만드는 것의 의미를 묻고 (C) 대답한다.

03 상대방의 경험에 대해 물어볼 때는, 현재완료 시제를 사용하여 'Have you 과거분사 ~?'라고 묻는다. 경험을 묻는 말에 긍정으로 대답할 경우에는 'Yes, I have.', 부정으로 대답할 때는 'No, I haven't.'로 대답한다. (B)의 Have you? 다음에는 'ever been to Brazil'이 생략되어 있다.

04 (D) 작년에 있었다는 내용이므로 과거형을 사용해야 한다. 또한 a big samba festival이 단수명사이므로 was가 적절하다. (E) sound+형용사: ~하게 들리다 sound like + 명사: ~하게 들리다 (F) hope+to 동사: ~하기를 희망하다

05 It이 가리키는 것이 an umbrella이므로, What does an umbrella mean in China?(중국에서 우산이 뭘 의미하는데?)의 대답으로 나와야 적절하다.

06 Chinese: 중국의; 중국어

07 separation: 분리, 이별

08 hear about: ~에 대해서 듣다 / 넌 꽃박람회에 대해 들어 본 적이 있니? think about: ~에 대해 생각[고려]하다 / 나는 그녀에게 우산을 사주려고 생각하고 있어. talk about: ~에 대해 말하다 / 사람들은 여가 시간에 관해서 말하기를 좋아한다.

09 (1) last: 계속되다, 지속되다 / 그 회의는 어제 세 시간 동안 계속되었다. (2) crow: (닭이) 울다 / 수탉은 약 한 시간에 한 번씩 운다. (3) bow: (인사를 위해) 머리를 숙이다, 절하다 / 나는 항상 선생님께 고개 숙여 인사한다.

10 Have you 과거분사 ~?: ~해 본 경험이 있니? Spanish: 스페인의

11 mean: 의미하다 good luck: 행운 for+기간: ~ 동안

12 ② Mary has lived here for 10 years. ③ Have you ever been to Malaysia? ④ Scarlet moved to Los Angeles 5 years ago.

13 (1), (2) 'so ... that ~' 구문과 (3) 현재완료의 '계속' 용법을 이용한다.

14 'so ... that ~' 구문은 맞지만 현재완료가 아니라 과거시제이므로 ate이 알맞다.

15 (1) 현재완료의 '계속', (2) '결과' 용법을 이용한다.

16 ④ 한국에서 박쥐는 행운과 장수의 '상징'이라고 하는 것이 적절하다. ① (논의 등의) 주제[대상/화제], 과목 ② 전통, ③ 의견, ⑤ 문화

17 remind A of B: A에게 B를 상기시켜 주다, A에게 B가 생각나게 하다

18 'of'를 보충하면 된다.

19 (A) 현재완료로 물었기 때문에 대답에도 haven't가 적절하다. (B) fish는 단수와 복수의 형태가 같은데 물고기 한 마리는 a fish라고 하므로, fish 다음에는 are가 적절하다. (C) That's why = For that reason으로 why 다음에는 앞의 내용의 결과에 해당하는 말이 나온다. because 다음에는 이유를 나타내는 말이 나온다.

20 so ~ that 주어 can't ... : 너무나 ~해서 …할 수 없다

21 ④ 물고기는 잘 때도 눈을 감지 않는다.

22 종이는 'piece'나 'sheet'를 사용하여 셀 수 있다.

23 '문 위에 붙여 놓은 그림'을 가리킨다.

24 ③ 이 글은 '한국인들이 문 위에 수탉 그림을 걸어놓은 이유'를 설명하는 글이다.

25 '이번 여행이 매우 즐거워서' 더 오래 머무르고 싶어 한다.

26 want는 목적어로 to부정사를 써야 한다.

서술형 실전문제 p.154~155

01 (A) to buy (B) buying
02 ① that's a good → that's not a good
03 umbrella
04 (1) Charlie has studied Korean for six months.
(2) I have lost my umbrella.
05 (1) My uncle has worked for the company since 2007.
(2) I have never seen such a beautiful bridge.
(3) The mountain is so high that I can't walk to the top.
(4) My parents are so wise that I usually follow their advice.
06 (1) The dogs are so cute that I can't take my eyes off them.

(2) The weather was so nice that they went on a picnic.
07 (A) for (B) him (C) surprising
08 In Korea, bats are symbols of luck and a long life.
09 행운과 장수의 상징이다. / 사람들에게 어둠과 무서운 것들을 상기시켜 준다.
10 Do you mean this painting of a rooster?
11 the sun is setting → a new day is beginning
12 For many years, Koreans have believed evil spirits go away when a rooster crows.

01 (A) be going to 동사원형: ~할 것이다, ~할 예정이다 (B) 전치사 다음에는 명사나 동명사가 나올 수 있다.
02 우산이 중국에서 나쁜 것을 뜻한다고 말했기 때문에, 우산이 중국 사람들에게 좋은 선물이라고 말하는 것은 어색하므로 not을 붙여서 부정문으로 바꿔야 적절하다.
03 one은 앞에 이미 언급했거나 상대방이 알고 있는 사물을 가리킬 때 명사의 반복을 피하기 위해 사용하는데, 여기서는 umbrella를 가리킨다.
04 (1) 현재완료의 '계속', (2) '결과' 용법을 이용한다.
05 (1) 현재완료의 '계속' (2) 현재완료의 '경험' (3), (4) so ... that ~: 너무[매우] ~해서 …하다
06 'so+형용사[부사]+that+주어+동사'의 형태로 '매우 …해서 ~하다'라는 의미이다.
07 (A) 'for+숫자가 붙은 기간', 'during+특정 기간을 나타내는 명사'이므로 for가 적절하다. (B) 4형식 문장이므로 간접목적어로 him을 쓰는 것이 적절하다. show는 3형식으로 고칠 때 to를 사용한다. (C) 감정을 나타내는 말은 사람을 수식할 때는 보통 과거분사로, 사물을 수식할 때는 보통 현재분사로 쓰기 때문에 surprising이 적절하다.
08 한국에서 박쥐가 행운과 장수의 상징이라는 것을 가리킨다.
09 한국에서 박쥐는 행운과 장수의 상징이지만, 서구의 많은 나라들에서, 박쥐는 사람들에게 어둠과 무서운 것들을 상기시켜 준다.
10 'of'를 보충하면 된다.
11 수탉이 매일 아침 우는 울음은 '새로운 날이 시작하는 것'을 의미한다.
12 '오랫동안 한국인들은 수탉이 울 때 악령이 물러간다고 믿어 왔다.'는 것을 가리킨다.

창의사고력 서술형 문제 p.156

|모범답안|

01 A: been to Spain
B: I haven't.
A: visited Spain
A: a traditional Spanish, throw tomatoes at each other
B: When is the festival?
02 (A) traditional (B) is (C) like (D) special (E) to practice

단원별 모의고사 p.157~160

01 ④ 02 ④ 03 (1) palm (2) face
04 ③ 05 What does that mean?
06 (1) Do you? → Have you?
(2) Yes, I do. → Yes, I have.
07 (A) Which (B) What (C) How
08 Have you ever played *gorodki*?
09 ⑤ Putting → Put 10 ② 11 ③
12 a traditional Indian festival, Busan, throw colored powder and water at each other, white clothes, look more beautiful
13 ⑤
14 (1) The soup smelled too bad for me to have.
(2) Einstein was clever enough to understand the theory.
15 (1) When did you go there?
(2) I have studied English for 5 years.
(3) I was so busy that I couldn't help her. 또는 I was too busy to help her.
(4) The bunjee jump was so scary that we screamed a lot.
16 (1) for (2) since
17 Phillip has lived in China for such a long time that he can speak Chinese very well.
18 ②
19 bats remind people of darkness and scary things
20 ④ 21 guards 22 ④
23 (A) don't close (B) watch over 24 ④
25 If 또는 When

01 접속사 But 앞에서 잘못된 이유를 이야기하고 손바닥을 보여 주면서 브이 사인을 만드는 것이 괜찮다고 말하는 것이 적절하다.
02 ⓐ What a nice picture! ⓑ Which boy? ⓒ The boy who is making the V sign. ⓓ His palm is facing toward himself.

03 (1) palm: 손바닥 (2) face: ~을 향하다

04 ③ in Spanish: 스페인어로

05 mean: 의미하다

06 브라질에 다녀온 경험에 대해 계속 이야기하고 있으므로 do동사가 아니라 have를 이용해서 질문과 대답을 해야 한다.

07 (A) 많은 다른 전통적인 게임들 중에서 하나를 선택하는 것이므로 Which가 어울린다. (B) 고로드키 게임이 무엇인지 질문하고 있다. (C) 게임을 하는 방법에 대해 설명하고 있으므로, 게임을 어떻게 하는지 질문해야 한다.

08 상대방의 경험에 대해 물어볼 때는, 현재완료 시제를 사용하여 'Have you ever 과거분사 ~?'라고 묻는다.

09 게임 방법을 명령문으로 설명하고 있다.

10 주어진 문장은 Holi festival이 무엇인지에 대한 대답이므로 ②가 어울린다.

11 ⓒ '가본 적이 있어 하지만 인도 친구가 그것에 대해 내게 많이 이야기해 줬어.'는 어색하므로, 'No, I haven't.'가 어울린다.

12 traditional: 전통적인 Indian: 인도의 festival: 축제 be held: 개최되다 in+장소: ~에서 throw: ~을 던지다 at: (방향) ~으로 colored: 채색된, 색깔이 있는 clothes: 옷, 의복

13 <보기>와 ⑤번은 경험 용법 ①, ③ 완료 용법 ② 계속 용법 ④ 결과 용법

14 (1) so ... that 주어 can't ~ = too ... (의미상의 주어: for+목적격) to ~ (2) so ... that 주어 can ~ = ... enough to ~

15 (1) 현재완료는 과거의 특정 시점을 나타내는 when과는 함께 쓰이지 않는다. (2) 현재완료에서 'since+시간 명사', 'for+기간 명사' (3) so ... that 주어 can't ~ = too ... to ~ (4) 'so+형용사[부사]+that+주어+동사'의 형태로 '매우 …해서 ~하다' 'so that ~'은 '~하도록'의 의미로 쓰인다.

16 현재완료에서 'since+시간 명사', 'for+ 기간 명사'

17 'so+형용사[부사]+that+주어+동사' 구문에서 that 앞에 형용사나 부사 대신 명사가 오면 so 대신 such를 쓴다.

18 '내 베개 위에 박쥐가? 그거 겁나는데!'라고 했기 때문에 ②번의 'grateful'은 알맞지 않다. grateful: 고마워하는, 감사하는, 나머지는 다 '무서워[두려워]하는', '겁이 난'이라는 뜻이다.

19 remind A of B: A에게 B를 상기시켜 주다, A에게 B가 생각나게 하다

20 이 글은 '전통적인 한국의 상징물들 중 박쥐의 의미를 소개'하기 위한 글이다.

21 guard: 경비[감시/수비] 요원, 파수꾼, 어떤 것이나 사람을 지키는 사람들

22 ⓑ와 ④는 '~처럼', '~와 비슷한', 나머지는 다 '좋아하다'는 뜻이다.

23 물고기는 잘 때도 눈을 '감지 않기' 때문에, 사람들은 물고기가 귀중품을 '지킬 수' 있다고 생각한다. 그런 이유로 이 자물쇠가 물고기처럼 생겼다.

24 ⓐ와 ②번은 계속 용법, ① 결과 용법, ③ 완료 용법, ④ 경험용법, ⑤ 완료 용법

25 '그러면'은 '그 그림을 네 문 위에 걸어놓으면[놓을 때]'이라는 뜻이다.

교과서 다시보기

Lesson 1

단어 TEST Step 1 p.02

01 개인의, 사적인 02 신중하게, 조심스럽게
03 적절한 04 의견, 논평
05 가져오다, 데려오다 06 사전
07 멋진, 굉장한 08 필터, 여과기 09 이해하다
10 마지막으로, 마침내 11 불가능한
12 공유하다 13 빌리다
14 신나는, 흥미진진한 15 다치다, 해치다
16 부분 17 바보 같은, 어리석은
18 에티켓, 예절 19 괴롭히다 20 화장실
21 공공의 22 과목 23 해결하다
24 틀린, 정확하지 않은
25 흥미로운, 재미있는 26 보고서
27 십대 28 놀랍게도 29 환경
30 조리법 31 준비하다
32 야외에서, 옥외에서 33 가끔
34 긴장되는, 불안해 하는 35 A에서 B로
36 명심하다 37 법을 어기다
38 ~하는 데 시간을 보내다
39 즐거운 시간을 보내다 40 ~ 앞에
41 꼭 ~와 같이 42 확인하다
43 발견하다, 찾아보다

단어 TEST Step 2 p.03

01 break	02 carrier	03 photography
04 post	05 copy	06 fact
07 poster	08 topic	09 prepare
10 healthy	11 perfect	12 display
13 leave	14 nervous	15 outdoors
16 environment	17 choose	18 sometimes
19 probably	20 surprisingly	21 result
22 selfie	23 recipe	24 rude
25 clothes	26 survey	27 appropriate
28 borrow	29 impossible	30 bother
31 understand	32 dictionary	33 restroom
34 look at	35 be interested in	
36 break the law	37 first of all	38 keep in mind
39 agree with	40 in front of	41 check out
42 find out	43 around the world	

단어 TEST Step 3 p.04

1 healthy, 건강에 좋은 2 public, 공공의
3 share, 공유하다 4 appropriate, 적절한 5 solve, 해결하다
6 comment, 의견, 논평 7 fact, 사실 8 recipe, 조리법
9 etiquette, 에티켓, 예절 10 prepare, 준비하다
11 photography, 사진술 12 rude, 무례한
13 post, 올리다, 게시하다 14 result, 결과
15 bring, 가져오다, 데려오다 16 borrow, 빌리다

대화문 TEST Step 1 p.05~06

Listen & Talk 1 A
Look at, interested in / in cooking, What about / interested in

Listen & Talk 1 B
are going to / going to do, with / Are, interested in / going, because / what, interested / most interested, want to go, someday

Listen & Talk 1 C
What, looking at / listings, should , watch, interested in / I'm interested / about watching / a big fan of, listen to / why don't

Listen & Talk 1 D
What, interested in / in, What about / interested in, social media / We both

Listen & Talk 2 A
bring, on / may, should put

Listen & Talk 2 B
Can, go / Let, see / Here, May, record / No, may not / take pictures of / may not, take, in front of, enjoy

Listen & Talk 2 C
Excuse / What, for / May, borrow, you may not, can't take, home / may, copy / Yes, you may / don't share / won't

Let's communicate 1
are, in / I'm interested in / Why don't / Sounds, May, record / may, may not

Do It Yourself A
are, doing / preparing, presentation, one of / sounds fun, are, interested in / interested in, talk about / interested in, too / may, ask

대화문 TEST Step 2 p.07~08

Listen & Talk 1 A

G: Look at these club posters. What are you interested in?

B: I'm interested in cooking. What about you?

G: I'm interested in photography.

Listen & Talk 1 B

B: What are you going to do this weekend?

G: I'm going to go to a baseball game with my brother.

B: Are you interested in baseball?

G: Not really. I'm going to the baseball game because my brother likes baseball.

B: You're so nice! Then what are you interested in?

G: I'm more interested in soccer. I want to go to a soccer game someday.

Listen & Talk 1 C

G: What are you looking at?

B: I'm looking at TV program listings. What show should I watch?

G: Well, what are you interested in?

B: I'm interested in music.

G: Then how about watching the Friday Pop Music Show?

B: I'm actually not a big fan of pop music. I like to listen to rap music.

G: Then why don't you watch Hit the Beat?

B: Good idea.

Listen & Talk 1 D

A: What are you interested in?

B: I'm interested in games and social media. What about you?

A: I'm interested in music and social media.

B: We are both interested in social media.

Listen & Talk 2 A

B: May I bring my dog on the bus?

W: Yes, you may. But you should put your dog in the carrier.

Listen & Talk 2 B

G: Hi. Can I go in now?

M: Sure. Let me see your ticket, please.

G: Here it is. May I record the music in the concert hall?

M: No, you may not.

G: Okay. May I take pictures of the band?

M: No, you may not. You can only take pictures in front of the concert hall. Please enjoy the concert.

G: Oh, okay. Thank you.

Listen & Talk 2 C

B: Excuse me.

W: Hello. What can I do for you?

B: May I borrow this new science book?

W: No, you may not. Students can't take new books home.

B: Then may I copy some pages from the book? I need them for my science report.

W: Yes, you may. But please don't share them online.

B: Okay, I won't. Thank you!

Let's communicate 1

A: What are you interested in?

B: I'm interested in music.

A: Why don't you go to a concert hall this weekend?

B: Sounds good. May I record the music there?

A: Yes, you may. / No, you may not.

Do It Yourself A

M: Hey, Yumi. What are you doing?

G: Hello, Mr. King. I'm preparing for tomorrow's presentation. It is about one of my interests.

M: That sounds fun! What are you interested in?

G: I'm interested in photography. I will talk about it tomorrow.

M: Oh, I'm interested in photography, too.

G: Really? Then may I ask you for some advice for my presentation?

M: Sure.

본문 TEST Step 1 p.09~10

01 All About
02 Selfie Facts
03 Are, interested in
04 probably, post, much
05 Here, facts
06 took, first, in
07 became, word, dictionary
08 took space selfie
09 Selfie Survey
10 Taking, daily, enjoy
11 To, out, survey
12 questions, ages, to
13 Let's, at
14 Surprisingly, percent, only
15 Also, that, filters
16 survey, showed, take
17 Check out, comments
18 England, awesome
19 silly, really
20 taking, spend, doing
21 look good, use
22 sometimes, look like
23 Selfie Etiquette
24 etiquette, selfies

25 yourself, before, post
26 Where am
27 appropriate, selfies
28 Don't, hospitals, restrooms
29 bother other
30 Who, this
31 Keep, anyone, see
32 Choose, when, post
33 kinds, comments, leave
34 Leave, comments, other
35 Don't, sounds, doesn't
36 Follow, tips, fun

본문 TEST Step 2 p.11~12

01 About
02 Facts
03 interested in
04 like to post, how much, about
05 Here are, facts
06 took, first selfie
07 became, in the dictionary
08 took, first space
09 Survey
10 Taking selfies, daily life, but
11 To find out, survey
12 asked, from ages, to
13 Let's look at
14 Surprisingly, take selfies, 15 percent of the boys
15 that, use filters
16 survey, showed, take selfies
17 Check out, comments
18 Selfies, awesome
19 Making, faces
20 enjoy taking selfies, spend, doing
21 look good, use filters
22 sometimes, don't look like
23 Etiquette
24 should follow etiquette
25 Ask yourself, take, post, look at
26 Where am
27 appropriate, to take selfies
28 Don't take, public restrooms
29 bother other
30 can see
31 Keep in mind
32 Choose, when, post
33 What kinds of, leave
34 Leave, other people's selfies
35 be rude, doesn't it
36 Follow, have fun

본문 TEST Step 3 p.13~14

1 셀피에 대한 모든 것!
2 셀피에 관련된 사실들
3 당신은 셀피에 관심이 있는가?
4 당신은 아마 소셜 미디어에 셀피를 게시하기를 좋아할지도 모르지만, 셀피에 대해 얼마나 많이 알고 있는가?
5 여기 몇 가지 재미있는 사실들이 있다.
6 로버트 코닐리어스가 1839년에 전 세계 최초의 셀피를 찍었다.
7 selfie는 2013년에 사전에 신조어로 등재되었다.
8 버즈 올드린이 1966년에 최초의 우주 셀피를 찍었다.
9 셀피 설문 조사
10 셀피 찍기는 많은 십대들에게 일상생활의 한 부분인데, 십대들은 정말로 그것을 즐기고 있는가?
11 알아보기 위해 우리는 설문 조사를 했다.
12 우리는 14세에서 16세 사이의 학생 300명에게 세 가지를 질문했다.
13 그 결과를 보자.
14 놀랍게도, 소녀들의 90퍼센트가 셀피를 찍지만, 소년들의 15퍼센트만이 셀피를 찍는다.
15 또한 이 학생들의 93퍼센트는 필터를 사용한다고 대답했다.
16 설문은 또한 학생들이 학교에서 가장 많이 셀피를 찍는다는 것을 보여 주었다.
17 학생들의 의견 몇 가지를 확인해 보라.
18 루이스, 14세, 영국: 셀피는 굉장하다.
19 우스꽝스러운 표정을 짓는 것은 정말로 재미있다!
20 민우, 16세, 한국: 나는 셀피 찍는 것을 즐기지만 몇몇 학생들은 그것을 하는 데 너무 많은 시간을 쓴다.
21 케이트, 15세, 덴마크: 내 사진은 필터를 사용할 때 멋져 보인다.
22 하지만 가끔 나의 셀피가 나처럼 보이지 않는다.
23 셀피 예절
24 당신은 셀피 예절을 따라야 한다.
25 셀피를 찍고, 게시하거나 보기 전에 스스로 이 질문들을 물어보라.
26 내가 어디에 있는가?
27 셀피를 찍기에 적합한 장소를 선택하라.
28 병원이나 공중화장실에서 셀피를 찍지 마라.
29 그것은 다른 사람들을 신경 쓰이게 할 수 있다.
30 누가 이것을 볼 수 있는가?
31 누구나 당신의 셀피를 볼 수 있다는 것을 명심하라.
32 그것들을 게시할 때 신중하게 골라라.
33 어떤 코멘트를 남겨야 하는가?
34 다른 사람들의 셀피에 상냥한 코멘트를 남겨라.
35 무례하게 굴지 마라. 쉬운 것처럼 들린다, 그렇지 않은가?
36 이러한 조언들을 따라서 당신의 셀피와 즐거운 시간을 보내라.

본문 TEST Step 4-Step 5 p.15~18

1 All About Selfies!
2 Selfie Facts
3 Are you interested in selfies?
4 You probably like to post selfies on social media, but how much do you know about selfies?
5 Here are some interesting facts.
6 Robert Cornelius took the world's first selfie in 1839.

7 *Selfie* became a new word in the dictionary in 2013.
8 Buzz Aldrin took the first space selfie in 1966.
9 Selfie Survey
10 Taking selfies is part of daily life for many teens, but do teens really enjoy it?
11 To find out, we did a survey.
12 We asked three questions to 300 students from ages 14 to 16.
13 Let's look at the results.
14 Surprisingly, 90 percent of the girls take selfies, but only 15 percent of the boys take selfies.
15 Also, 93 percent of these students said that they use filters.
16 The survey also showed that the students take selfies at school the most.
17 Check out some of the students' comments.
18 Lewis, 14, England Selfies are awesome.
19 Making silly faces is really fun!v
20 Minwoo, 16, Korea I enjoy taking selfies, but some students spend too much time doing it.
21 Kate, 15, Denmark My pictures look good when I use filters.
22 But sometimes my selfies don't look like me.
23 Selfie Etiquette
24 You should follow etiquette for selfies.
25 Ask yourself these questions before you take, post, or look at selfies.
26 Where am I?
27 Choose appropriate places to take selfies.
28 Don't take selfies in hospitals or public restrooms.
29 It may bother other people.
30 Who can see this?
31 Keep in mind that anyone can see your selfies.
32 Choose carefully when you post them.
33 What kinds of comments should I leave?
34 Leave nice comments on other people's selfies.
35 Don't be rude. That sounds easy, doesn't it?
36 Follow these tips and have fun with your selfies.

구석구석지문 TEST Step 1 p.19

Project Link

1. is interested in
2. made
3. recorded, posted
4. can, at

Think and Write

1. Be, user
2. When, should follow, rules
3. can enjoy, more
4. First, should, because, may
5. Also, post, true
6. may, incorrect
7. Fianlly, should not leave
8. can, others'
9. Keep, in mind
10. will be

Culture Link

1. from, interested, environment
2. created, superhero, posted
3. also, just like

구석구석지문 TEST Step 2 p.20

Project Link

1. Our group is interested in dance.
2. We made a dance.
3. We recorded a dance video and posted it online.
4. You can see it at www.yutu.com.

Think and Write

1. Be a Great Internet User!
2. When we use the internet, we should follow some rules.
3. Then we can enjoy the internet more.
4. First of all, we should follow language rules because people may not understand us.
5. Also, we should post only true information.
6. People may believe our incorrect information.
7. Finally, we should not leave rude comments.
8. We can hurt others' feelings.
9. Keep these rules in mind.
10. Then you will be a great internet user!

Culture Link

1. A student from the United States is interested in the environment.
2. He created a cartoon superhero, *GoGreenMan*, and posted it online.
3. He also helps the environment just like his character, *GoGreenMan*.

Lesson 2

단어 TEST Step 1
p.21

01 흔한	02 야채	03 고기, 육류
04 더 큰, 더 많은	05 영국의	06 떨어뜨리다
07 그 밖의, 다른	08 섞인, 복합된	09 신선한
10 천천히	11 달콤한, 단	12 다른
13 전통적인	14 단 음식, 단것	15 ~로서
16 튀기다	17 먹다	18 부분
19 선택, 종류	20 대회, 콘테스트	21 당근
22 포함하다	23 인도의	24 대신에
25 항상	26 서양의	
27 (양 정도가) 더 적은		28 현지의, 지역의
29 종종, 자주	30 보통, 대개	31 양파
32 규칙	33 반찬	
34 축하하다, 기념하다		35 적어도, 최소한
36 ~할 준비가 되다	37 확인하다, 조사하다	
38 ~와 함께 나오다, ~이 딸려 있다		39 오랫동안
40 ~하는 것이 좋다[낫다]		
41 공통으로 ~을 가지다		42 ~을 덮히다
43 ~와 같은		

단어 TEST Step 2
p.22

01 grocery	02 special	03 breakfast
04 Eastern	05 add	06 exercise
07 culture	08 bean	09 tired
10 serve	11 fried	12 curry
13 delicious	14 Spanish	15 appetizer
16 healthy	17 turkey	18 suggestion
19 balanced	20 sometimes	21 health
22 fruit	23 order	24 noodle
25 recommend	26 Vietnamese	27 also
28 main dish	29 enough	30 especially
31 traditional	32 mixed	33 instead
34 common	35 at the end of ~	
36 both A and B	37 get a discount	38 put A in B
39 stay at	40 take care of	41 these days
42 throw away	43 win an award	

단어 TEST Step 3
p.23

1 fried, 튀겨진 2 tired, 피곤한 3 breakfast, 아침 식사
4 appetizer, 식전 음식 5 common, 흔한
6 mixed, 섞인, 복합된 7 order, 주문하다
8 grocery, 식료품 9 sweets, 단 음식, 단것
10 local, 현지의 11 suggestion, 제안
12 vegetable, 야채 13 contest, 대회. 콘테스트
14 serve, 음식물을 제공하다 15 recommend, 추천하다
16 noodle, 국수

대화문 TEST Step 1
p.24~25

Listen & Talk 1 A

think, eat, these days / not good for, You'd better eat

Listen & Talk 1 B

look, tired, Didn't, sleep / often feel tired / especially / usually eat / don't / You'd better eat, gives, energy / didn't, have, other suggestions / should also exercise, will, help / will

Listen & Talk 1 C

cooking contest, are, going to / going to make / want to put / Chicken, eggs / better put, in, How about / not going to, don't like / idea, should make healthy / right, should go, buy

Listen & Talk 2 A

first time, What, recommend / recommend

Listen & Talk 2 B

What, right now / searching for, for / When / want to go, but, too expensive / Why don't, check out, once, prices, good / Sounds, recommend / noodle soup / think, should go

Listen & Talk 2 C

Are, ready to / first time, do, recommend / recommend, most popular item / don't like, Could, recommend something else, How about / love, have / Why don't, order / get a, discount / have, too

Do It Yourself A

What's for / have, choices which one / some noodles, recommend / fried nooldes, sounds delicious, have, What about / don't, not hungry / But for, you'd better, Why don't, try / right

대화문 TEST Step 2
p.26~27

Listen & Talk 1 A

G: I think I eat too many sweets these days.
B: That's not good for your health. You'd better eat fruit instead.

Listen & Talk 1 B

G: You look very tired today. Didn't you sleep well?

B: Yes, I did. But I often feel tired these days, especially in the morning.

G: Do you usually eat breakfast?

B: No, I don't.

G: You'd better eat breakfast. Breakfast gives you energy.

B: I didn't know that. Do you have any other suggestions?

G: Well, you should also exercise every day. That will help you.

B: Okay. I will.

Listen & Talk 1 C

G: Justin, our school cooking contest is tomorrow. What are you going to make?

B: I'm going to make sandwiches.

G: What do you want to put in them?

B: Chicken, cheese, and eggs.

G: You'd better put vegetables in your sandwiches. How about onions and carrots?

B: No, I'm not going to add them. I don't like those vegetables.

G: That's not a good idea. Mr. Kim said we should make healthy food for the contest.

B: You're right. I should go grocery shopping and buy onions and carrots.

Listen & Talk 2 A

G: It's my first time here. What do you recommend?

M: I recommend the pizza and salad.

Listen & Talk 2 B

B: Good morning, Jiwoo. What are you doing right now?

G: I'm searching for a restaurant for my class party.

B: Wow! When is the party?

G: It's next Friday. We want to go to Bella's Restaurant, but it is too expensive.

B: Why don't you check out Chang's Restaurant? I went there once. The food and prices were good.

G: Sounds great. What do you recommend there?

B: I recommend the noodle soup.

G: I think we should go there. Thank you.

Listen & Talk 2 C

W: Hello. Are you ready to order?

B: It's my first time here. What do you recommend?

W: I recommend the chicken sandwich. It is the most popular item at our restaurant.

B: Well, I don't like chicken very much. Could you recommend something else?

W: How about the turkey sandwich?

B: Oh, I love turkey. I'll have that.

W: Why don't you order a drink with the sandwich? You can get a 500-won discount.

B: That's great. Then I'll have an orange juice, too.

Do It Yourself A

G: What's for lunch today?

B: We have four choices. Which one do you want?

G: Well, I want some noodles. What do you recommend?

B: I recommend the fried noodles.

G: That sounds delicious. I will have that. What about you?

B: I don't know. I'm not hungry.

G: But for your health, you'd better have some food. Why don't you try some tomato soup?

B: All right. I will.

본문 TEST Step 1 p.28~29

01 Around, World
02 this is, from
03 many, best part
04 In, often, for
05 side dishes, as
06 Sometimes, serves, such
07 What, who, other
08 Let's, from
09 Belle, France
10 serves, balanced meals
11 usually, as, appetizer
12 Main, include, fish
13 fresh, at, end
14 can never
15 great with
16 Our, also, rule
17 stay at, for, least
18 Bruno, Brazil
19 Usually, beans
20 Meat, common, side
21 favorite, comes with
22 plantain, which, like
23 usually fry
24 fresh because, come, local
25 Nicole, Singapore
26 different, have, Eastern, Western
27 choose from, such as
28 award, healthy, last
29 healthy, tast, too
30 Which, want, try
31 have, in common
32 leave, at

본문 TEST Step 2 p.30~31

01 Around, World
02 this is, reporter, from
03 For, the best part of
04 often eat, for lunch
05 side dishes, as
06 serves, dishes, such as
07 students who live, other countries
08 Let's hear from
09 France
10 healthy, balanced meals
11 usually eat, as
12 often include, fish
13 also eat, at the end of
14 can never forget
15 great with
16 also has, special rule
17 must stay at, at least
18 Brazil
19 have beans, rice
20 common in, side dishes
21 favorite, comes with
22 fruit, look like
23 usually fry
24 fresh because, come from local farms
25 Singapore
26 who live in, come from, both, and
27 can choose from, such as, each day
28 won an award, last year
29 always healthy, taste good,
30 Which, want to try
31 have, in common with
32 leave yours comments

본문 TEST Step 3 p.32~33

1 세계 각국의 학교 급식
2 안녕하세요, 저는 한국에서 온 음식 취재 기자 민준입니다.
3 많은 학생들에게 점심시간은 학교 일과 중 가장 좋은 부분입니다.
4 한국에서는 점심으로 자주 밥과 국을 먹습니다.
5 우리는 불고기나 김치 같은 반찬도 먹습니다.
6 때때로 우리 학교는 피자, 비빔밥 또는 파스타 같은 특식을 제공합니다.
7 다른 나라에서 사는 학생들은 점심으로 무엇을 먹을까요?
8 우리 음식 취재 기자들에게서 들어보겠습니다!
9 벨, 프랑스
10 우리 학교는 건강하고 균형 잡힌 식사를 제공합니다.
11 우리는 보통 식전 음식으로 샐러드를 먹습니다.
12 주요리는 보통 고기나 생선을 포함합니다.
13 우리는 점심의 끝에 신선한 과일도 먹습니다.
14 오, 절대 바게트를 빠뜨릴 수는 없죠!
15 바게트는 치즈와 잘 어울립니다.
16 우리 학교에서 또한 특별한 규칙이 있습니다.
17 우리는 적어도 30분간 점심 식탁에서 반드시 머물러야 합니다.
18 브루노, 브라질
19 보통, 우리는 점심으로 콩과 밥을 먹습니다.
20 우리는 곁들임 음식에는 고기와 채소가 흔히 나옵니다.
21 내가 가장 좋아하는 점심에는 플랜테인이 나옵니다.
22 플랜테인은 바나나처럼 생긴 과일입니다.
23 우리는 보통 플랜테인을 튀깁니다.
24 채소와 과일이 현지 농장에서 오기 때문에 우리 학교 급식은 신선합니다.
25 니콜, 싱가포르
26 싱가포르에 사는 사람들은 매우 다양한 문화권에서 오기 때문에, 우리는 점심에 동양식과 서양식을 모두 먹습니다.
27 학생들은 매일 카레, 국수 또는 파스타와 같이 많은 요리 중에서 선택할 수 있습니다
28 우리 학교는 작년에 건강한 학교 음식 상을 받았습니다.
29 우리의 점심은 항상 건강에 좋고, 맛 또한 좋습니다!
30 여러분은 어떤 학교 급식을 먹어 보고 싶나요?
31 그것이 여러분의 학교 급식과 공통되는 것이 있습니까?
32 여러분의 의견을 www.chopchoplunch.com에 남겨 주세요.

본문 TEST Step 4-Step 5 p.34~37

1 School Lunches Around the World
2 Hello, this is food reporter Minjun from Korea.
3 For many students, lunch is the best part of the school day.
4 In Korea, we often eat rice and soup for lunch.
5 We also have side dishes, such as Bulgogi or Gimchi.
6 Sometimes our school serves special dishes, such as pizza, Bibimbap, or pasta.
7 What do students who live in other countries eat for lunch?
8 Let's hear from our food reporters!
9 Belle, France
10 Our school serves healthy and balanced meals.
11 We usually eat a salad as an appetizer.
12 Main dishes often include meat or fish.
13 We also eat fresh fruit at the end of the lunch.
14 Oh, I can never forget about baguettes!
15 They're great with cheese.
16 Our school also has a special rule.

17 We must stay at the lunch table for at least 30 minutes.
18 Bruno, Brazil
19 Usually, we have beans and rice for lunch.
20 Meat and vegetables are common in our side dishes.
21 My favorite lunch comes with plantains.
22 A plantain is a fruit which looks like a banana.
23 We usually fry plantains
24 Our school lunches are fresh because the vegetables and fruit come from local farms.
25 Nicole, Singapore
26 People who live in Singapore come from many different cultures, so we have both Eastern and Western dishes at lunch.
27 Students can choose from many dishes, such as curry, noodle soup, or pasta, each day.
28 My school won an award for healthy school food last year.
29 Our lunches are always healthy, and they taste good, too!
30 Which school lunch do you want to try?
31 Does it have anything in common with your school lunch?
32 Please leave your comments at www.chopchoplunch.com.

구석구석지문 TEST Step 1 p.38

Think and Write

1. Review, Favorite
2. My, restaurant
3. Spanish
4. near
5. most popular dish
6. All, is, delicious, low
7. recommend

Culture Link

1. In, on
2. to break, to live
3. curry from
4. a lot of
5. dish, dinner
6. traditional Vietnamese
7. at weddings
8. Eating, means, have a happy life
9. eat turkey to celebrate
10. give thanks for

구석구석지문 TEST Step 2 p.39

Think and Write

1. Review of My Favorite Restaurant
2. My favorite restaurant is Antonio's Restaurant.
3. It is a Spanish restaurant.
4. It is near my home.
5. Mixed paella is the most popular dish at this restaurant.
6. All of the food is really fresh and delicious, and the prices are low.
7. I recommend this restaurant!

Culture Link

1. In China, people eat noodles on their birthday.
2. Chinese people don't want to break the noodles to live a long life.
3. Doro wat is a chicken curry from Ethiopia.
4. There are a lot of vegetables in it.
5. People eat this dish for New Year's dinner.
6. Bánh xu xê is a traditional Vietnamese cake.
7. People eat this cake at weddings.
8. Eating the cake means the husbands and wife will have a happy life together.
9. In the United States, people eat turkey to celebrate Thanksgiving.
10. They give thanks for the food and their health.

Lesson 3

단어 TEST Step 1

p.40

01 무례한 02 계속되다, 지속되다
03 중국의; 중국어 04 달력 05 사악한, 악마의
06 자물쇠; 잠그다 07 ~을 향하다 08 채색된, 색깔이 있는
09 보름달 10 한번 해 보다
11 (인사를 위해) 머리를 숙이다, 절하다 12 분리, 이별
13 나타내다, 상징하다 14 보초, 경비병
15 국제적인, 세계적인 16 작년에
17 베트남의; 베트남어 18 손님
19 맞이하다, 환영하다 20 손바닥; 야자나무
21 영혼, 정신 22 자매 학교
23 무서운, 두려운, 겁나는 24 흔들다, 흔들리다
25 보호하다 26 상징(물), 기호
27 값비싼, 귀중한, 가치 있는 28 행운
29 (닭이) 울다; 까마귀 30 베개
31 생각나게 하다, 상기시키다 32 전통의, 전통적인
33 평화, 화해 34 어둠, 암흑
35 ~에 대해 이야기하다 36 코를 풀다
37 ~을 주시하다, 지키다 38 (옷 등을) 벗다
39 ~을 두려워하다 40 ~에 가 본 적이 있다
41 ~으로 가득 차다 42 사라지다, 떠나가다
43 A에게 B를 생각나게 하다

단어 TEST Step 2

p.41

01 beach	02 powder	03 clothes
04 crow	05 experience	06 festival
07 bat	08 umbrella	09 gift shop
10 darkness	11 pillow	12 Indian
13 lock	14 half moon	15 arrive
16 musical	17 luck	18 traditional
19 pay	20 mean	21 peace
22 rooster	23 remind	24 tell
25 victory	26 toward	27 spirit
28 palm	29 represent	30 rude
31 protect	32 colored	33 evil
34 shake	35 go away	36 take off
37 remind A of B	38 point at	39 talk about
40 be full of	41 listen to	42 watch over
43 be afraid of		

단어 TEST Step 3

p.42

1 rooster, 수탉 2 darkness, 어둠, 암흑
3 evil, 사악한, 악마의 4 pillow, 베개
5 greet, 맞이하다, 환영하다 6 face, ~을 향하다
7 represent, 나타내다, 상징하다 8 crow, (닭이) 울다
9 victory, 승리, 성공 10 valuable, 값비싼, 귀중한, 가치 있는
11 palm, 손바닥 12 protect, 보호하다
13 remind, 생각나게 하다, 상기시키다
14 scary, 무서운, 두려운, 겁나는
15 bow, (인사를 위해) 머리를 숙이다, 절하다
16 symbol, 상징(물), 기호

대화문 TEST Step 1

p.43~44

Listen & Talk 1 A

Have, been to / haven't, Have / have, last, was / sounds, to go, someday

Listen & Talk 1 B

Welcome to, different traditional / looks exciting, Which, should / Let's, Have, played / haven't / traditional, from / How, play / Put, on, throw, at / sounds fun, try

Listen & Talk 1 C

is, this year / festival, What / traditional Indian, throw, at each other / sounds exciting, Have, been to / haven't, told, a lot / When / on, full moon, on March 21 / Should, bring / should wear, colored, look, beautiful / Thank you for

Listen & Talk 2 A

gave, as, What, mean / means, on a test

Listen & Talk 2 B

this, isn't it / going to buy, for, about / thinking about, cute one / good gift for, something bad / does, mean / mean separation, in Chinese / how about / idea

Listen & Talk 2 C

What a nice / took, a lot of / look at, rude / Which / is making, facing toward / wrong with / bad meaning, showing, making / does mean / means peace

Do It Yourself A

brings / to see, Spanish / too, did, say / means, Look at, moves / they / Have, been to, before / haven't, on, What, mean / means

대화문 TEST Step 2

p.45~46

Listen & Talk 1 A

G: Have you ever been to Brazil?

B: No, I haven't. Have you?

G: Yes, I have. I went there last year. There was a big samba festival.

B: That sounds interesting. I hope to go there someday.

Listen & Talk 1 B

W: Welcome to the International Games Festival. You can play many different traditional games here.

B: Wow! It looks exciting! Which game should I play first?

W: Let's see. Have you ever played gorodki?

B: No, I haven't. What is it?

W: It's a traditional game from Russia.

B: How do I play it?

W: Put five sticks on the ground. Then throw a bat at them.

B: That sounds fun. I'll try that first.

Listen & Talk 1 C

B: There is a Holi festival in Busan this year.

G: A Holi festival? What is that?

B: It's a traditional Indian festival. People throw colored powder and water at each other.

G: That sounds exciting. Have you everbeen to a Holi festival?

B: No, I haven't. But my Indian friend told me a lot about it.

G: When is the festival?

B: It's on the last full moon of the Hindu calendar. This year, it's on March 21.

G: I'd like to go. Should I bring anything?

B: No, but you should wear white clothes. Then the colored powder on your clothes will look more beautiful.

G: Okay. Thank you for the information.

Listen & Talk 2 A

G: Jinwoo, my Korean friend, gave me Yeot as a gift. What does that mean in Korea?

B: It means good luck on a test.

Listen & Talk 2 B

B: Ling's birthday is this Wednesday, isn't it?

G: Yes. I'm going to buy a book for her. What about you?

B: Well, I'm thinking about buying her an umbrella. I found a cute one in a gift shop.

G: Oh, that's not a good gift for Chinese people. It means something bad.

B: Really? What does an umbrella mean in China?

G: It means separation. The words for separation and umbrella sound the same in Chinese.

B: I see. Then how about chocolate?

G: That's a good idea.

Listen & Talk 2 C

G: What a nice picture! Are these your friends?

B: Yes. We took this picture at the beach. We had a lot of fun.

G: Oh, look at that boy. That's really rude.

B: Which boy?

G: The boy who is making the V sign. His palm is facing toward himself.

B: What's wrong with that?

G: It has a bad meaning in England. But showing your palm and making a V sign is okay.

B: What does that mean?

G: It means victory or peace.

Do It Yourself A

G: Hello, Santiago! What brings you here today?

B: Bienvenido, Cathy. I came to see the Spanish festival.

G: Me, too. But what did you just say?

B: Bienvenido! It means "welcome" in Spanish. Look at those dancers. Their dance moves are so great.

G: Yes, they are.

B: Have you ever been to a Spanish festival before?

G: No, I haven't. Santiago, can you see the big letters on the stage? What does that mean?

B: Oh, gracias. That means "thank you."

본문 TEST Step 1 p.47~48

01 Traditional, Symbols
02 visiting, to, from 03 stay at, for
04 arrives, shows guest 05 stay here
06 guest, full, traditional 07 at, pillow
08 are, things 09 They're bats
10 on, pillow, scary
11 symbols, luck, life
12 surprising, remind, darkness
13 shows, her grandfather's
14 meet, greet, other
15 Have, seen, kind
16 haven't, so, that
17 For, thought, guards
18 close, even, sleep
19 That's interesting 20 over, why, like
21 Now understand

22 outside, walk around
23 on, piece, scary
24 mean, painting
25 it, rooster
26 crow every
27 crowing, that, beginning
28 evil, away, crows
29 never heard, before
30 Actually, afraid, spirits
31 draw, for
32 draw, rooster
33 Put, above, protect
34 Yes, will
35 so, that, longer
36 all, traditional, in
37 understand, lot
38 want, visit, with

본문 TEST Step 2 p.49~50

01 Traditional, Symbols
02 visiting, to meet, from
03 going to stay at, for
04 When, arrives, guest room
05 will stay here
06 is full of traditional
07 Look at
08 three things
09 bats
10 Bats on, pillow, scary
11 symbols of luck, long life
12 Western countries, remind, of darkness, scary
13 shows, grandfather's room
14 meet, greet each other
15 Have, seen, kind of look
16 haven't, so, that, can't
17 For a long time, have thought
18 don't close, when, sleep
19 interesting
20 watch over, why, looks like
21 Now understand
22 go outside, walk around
23 on the piece, looks scary
24 mean, rooster
25 is it
26 crow every morning
27 means, beginning
28 have believed, go away when, crows
29 never heard, before
30 Actually, afraid of, evil spirits
31 Could, draw, for
32 draw, for
33 Put, above, will protect
34 will
35 so, that, to stay longer
36 traditional Korean symbols
37 a lot of
38 want to visit, with

본문 TEST Step 3 p.51~52

1 전통적인 한국의 상징물
2 피터는 자매 학교 친구인 미나를 만나기 위해 한국을 방문 중이다.
3 피터는 일주일간 미나네 할아버지 댁에 머무를 것이다.
4 그가 도착하자, 미나가 그에게 손님방을 보여준다.
5 피터, 넌 여기에 머무르게 될 거야.
6 이 손님방은 한국의 전통 물건들로 가득 차 있어.
7 이 베개를 봐.
8 이것들은 뭐야?
9 그건 박쥐들이야.
10 내 베개 위에 박쥐가? 그거 겁나는데!
11 그렇지 않아. 한국에서는 박쥐가 행운과 장수의 상징이거든.
12 그거 놀라운 일인데. 서구의 많은 나라들에서 박쥐는 사람들에게 어둠과 무서운 것들을 상기시키거든.
13 미나는 피터에게 할아버지의 방을 보여준다.
14 피터와 미나의 할아버지가 만나서 서로 인사한다.
15 안녕, 피터! 너는 이런 종류의 자물쇠를 전에 본 적 있니?
16 아니요, 본 적 없어요. 그 자물쇠는 너무 오래되어서 사실 알아볼 수가 없는데, 그건 물고기인가요?
17 맞아. 오랜 세월 동안, 한국인들은 물고기가 훌륭한 파수꾼이라고 생각해 왔단다.
18 물고기는 잘 때도 눈을 감지 않거든.
19 그거 재미있군요.
20 우리는 물고기가 귀중품을 지킬 수 있다고 생각해. 그것이 이 자물쇠가 물고기 모양으로 생긴 이유란다.
21 이제 이해가 되는군요.
22 그들은 밖에 나가서 정원을 걷는다.
23 저 종이에는 무엇이 그려져 있는 거죠? 무서워 보여요
24 이 수탉 그림을 말하는 거니?
25 오, 그게 수탉이에요?
26 응, 그렇단다. 수탉은 매일 아침 울지.
27 수탉의 울음은 새로운 날이 시작하는 것을 의미해.
28 오랫동안 한국인들은 수탉이 울 때 악령이 물러간다고 믿어 왔단다.
29 우리의 점심은 항상 건강에 좋고, 맛 또한 좋습니다!
30 정말요? 전 그런 말을 들어본 적이 없어요.
31 미나야, 날 위해 수탉을 그려 줄 수 있니?
32 물론이지. 내가 널 위해 커다란 수탉을 그려줄게!
33 그 그림을 네 문 위에 걸어 놓으렴. 그러면 그게 널 지켜 줄 거야.
34 네, 그럴게요.
35 난 이번 여행이 매우 즐거워서 더 오래 머무르고 싶다.
36 난 이 집의 모든 전통적인 한국의 상징물들이 아주 마음에 든다.
37 나는 이제 그것들을 많이 알게 되었다.
38 난 우리 가족과 함께 한국을 다시 방문하고 싶다.

본문 TEST Step 4-Step 5 p.53~56

1 Traditional Korean Symbols
2 Peter is visiting Korea to meet a friend, Mina, from a sister school.
3 Peter is going to stay at her grandfather's house for a week.
4 When he arrives, Mina shows him the guest room.
5 Peter, you will stay here.
6 This guest room is full of traditional Korean things.
7 Look at this pillow.
8 What are these things?
9 They're bats.
10 Bats on my pillow? That's scary!
11 Not really. In Korea, bats are symbols of luck and a long life.
12 That's surprising. In many Western countries, bats remind people of darkness and scary things.
13 Mina shows Peter her grandfather's room.
14 Peter and Mina's grandfather meet and greet each other.
15 Hi, Peter! Have you ever seen this kind of lock before?
16 No, I haven't. It's so old that I can't really tell, but is it a fish?
17 Yes. For a long time, Koreans have thought that fish are good guards.
18 Fish don't close their eyes, even when they sleep.
19 That's interesting.
20 We think fish can watch over valuable things. That's why this lock looks like a fish.
21 Now I understand.
22 They go outside and walk around the garden.
23 What is on that piece of paper? It looks scary.
24 Do you mean this painting of a rooster?
25 Oh, is it a rooster?
26 Yes, it is. Roosters crow every morning.
27 Their crowing means that a new day is beginning.
28 For many years, Koreans have believed evil spirits go away when a rooster crows.
29 Really? I've never heard that before.
30 Actually, I'm afraid of darkness and evil spirits.
31 Could you draw a rooster for me, Mina?
32 Sure. I'll draw a big rooster for you!
33 Put the drawing above your door. Then it will protect you.
34 Yes, I will.
35 I'm enjoying this trip so much that I want to stay longer.
36 I love all the traditional Korean symbols in this house.
37 Now I understand a lot of them.
38 I want to visit Korea again with my family.

구석구석지문 TEST Step 1 p.57

Think and Write

1. traditional Chinese dances
2. There are
3. For example, are, fan
4. One of, dances is
5. dress, act like
6. usually, on, such as
7. dance moves, great
8. to practice, someday

Presentation Time

1. have a good time
2. follow
3. take off, when, go into
4. bow, others
5. give something to older people
6. blow your nose, point at
7. Lastly, call, by, first names

구석구석지문 TEST Step 2 p.58

Think and Write

1. Do you know about traditional Chinese dances?
2. There are many kinds.
3. For example, there are a lion dance, a fan dance, and an umbrella dance.
4. One of the most famous dances is the lion dance.
5. In this dance, two dancers dress and act like lions.
6. They usually dance on special days, such as New Year's Day.
7. I think their dance moves are great.
8. I hope to practice this dance someday.

Presentation Time

1. Do you want to have a good time in Korea?
2. Then follow these steps.
3. First, please take off your shoes when you go into people's homes.
4. Next, bow when you greet others.
5. Also, use two hands when you give something to older people.
6. And do not blow your nose at the table and do not point at people.
7. Lastly, do not call older people by their first names.

MEMO

적중100

영어 기출 문제집

정답 및 해설

능률 | 김성곤